Holy Things

Holy Things

The Genealogy of the Sacred in Thai Religion

NATHAN McGOVERN

OXFORD
UNIVERSITY PRESS

OXFORD
UNIVERSITY PRESS

Oxford University Press is a department of the University of Oxford. It furthers the University's objective of excellence in research, scholarship, and education by publishing worldwide. Oxford is a registered trade mark of Oxford University Press in the UK and in certain other countries.

Published in the United States of America by Oxford University Press
198 Madison Avenue, New York, NY 10016, United States of America.

Library of Congress Cataloging-in-Publication Data
Names: McGovern, Nathan, 1981– author.
Title: Holy things : the genealogy of the sacred in thai religion/ Nathan McGovern.
Description: 1. | New York : Oxford University Press, 2024. |
Includes bibliographical references and index.
Identifiers: LCCN 2024012952 (print) | LCCN 2024012953 (ebook) |
ISBN 9780197759882 (hardback) | ISBN 9780197759899 |
ISBN 9780197759912 | ISBN 9780197759905 (epub)
Subjects: LCSH: Buddhism—Social aspects—Thailand | Thailand—Social life and customs. | Buddhism—Thailand—History. | Thailand—Religion. |
Syncretism (Religion)
Classification: LCC BQ554 .M39 2024 (print) | LCC BQ554 (ebook) |
DDC 306.6/94309593—dc23/eng/20240402
LC record available at https://lccn.loc.gov/2024012952
LC ebook record available at https://lccn.loc.gov/2024012953

DOI: 10.1093/9780197759912.001.0001

Printed by Integrated Books International, United States of America

MIX
Paper
FSC FSC® C183721

In memory of Michael Jerryson (1974–2021)

Contents

Acknowledgments ix
Abbreviations xiii
Transliteration, Transcription, and Translation xv

1. Introduction 1

PART I: CONTEXTUALIZING HOLY THINGS

2. Buddhism as Implicit Theology 29
3. Situating Siam in History 51
4. The Genealogy of the Sacred 81

PART II: DECONSTRUCTING THE SYNCRETISM OF HOLY THINGS

5. Spirits 107
6. Gods 142
7. Buddha Images 173
8. Conclusion 201

Appendix A: Explicit Theology from Plato to the Abrahamic Traditions 209
Appendix B: Corpus of Siamese Literary Works Consulted 215
Notes 223
Bibliography 253
Index 265

Acknowledgments

This book is the product of a nearly twenty-year journey that began with my first experiences in Thailand and the writing of my master's thesis about the Ērāwan Shrine and the popular Thai worship of Brahmā. Out of that thesis, I published an article, "A Buddhist Cult of Brahmā: Thick Description and Micro-Histories in the Study of Religion," in *History of Religions* in 2016, parts of which have been adapted for use in this book with permission from the University of Chicago.[1] I would like to reiterate my thanks to Prapod Assavavirulhakarn, Vesna Wallace, David White, Helen Collins, David McMahan, Panuakdet Suwannatat, Trungchit Runmarang, and others for various forms of advice and support they provided as I wrote my thesis and adapted it into the article. *Holy Things* is an expansion of the study found in that article but also my attempt to grapple with the issue of syncretism that I feel was only partially addressed therein.

This book is part of what I expect will be a whole genre of "pandemic publications." I began work on it during the summer of 2020, just after the world went into COVID lockdown, and I completed the first draft of the manuscript during the summer of 2021, when we were still in the thick of the pandemic, albeit finally vaccinated. Writing *Holy Things* was in part a way for me to cope with the stress of the pandemic, but I could not have done it without the support of many family, friends, and colleagues. In particular, I want to thank my union sisters and brothers at AFT-Wisconsin and our local, UWW United, especially Chris Ramaekers, Brandon Thomas, and Dan Suarez. We formed our union local during the summer of 2020 in response to our chancellor at the time at UW-Whitewater, who was using the pandemic as a pretext to force an odious neoliberal program of "program prioritization" that could have led to our losing our jobs. The academic year during which I wrote the manuscript was also the year that I was going up for tenure, so it was one of the most stressful years of my life. Luckily, we managed to defeat the chancellor's agenda, and I received tenure at the end of the year. I would also like to thank my departmental colleagues, especially David Simmons, Crista Lebens, and Derek Lam, for their support, both through the union and through the department. Tracy Hawkins was awe-inspiring as a departmental colleague, Faculty Senate chair, fellow union member, and friend. I owe my survival of that year to her. Finally, I am incredibly grateful to my graduate school friends Aaron Ullrey and Alyson Prude, as well as my parents, my Aunt Helen and Uncle Frank, and my brother Eric for their support during that year, which was difficult in so many ways.

Working as a serious researcher at a teaching-oriented regional comprehensive poses certain difficulties, but I am lucky to live in Madison, Wisconsin, and enjoy many of the benefits of UW-Madison even though I do not work there. I am thankful to the Center for Southeast Asian Studies and Center for South Asia for welcoming me as an affiliate faculty member, and in particular to Anne Hansen, Ian Baird, Katherine Bowie, Mary McCoy, Anthony Cerulli, Sarah Beckham, and Andrea Fowler for various forms of support. Larry Ashmun's expertise as the Southeast Asian Studies librarian at UW-Madison has been invaluable to me as it has been to so many others in the field.

Many scholarly friends have been invaluable in making this book a better version of what it started out as. Many thanks to Chris Baker, Justin McDaniel, and Erick White for reading the full manuscript and giving copious critical comments. I am also grateful to Katherine Bowie, Angela Chiu, Arthid Sheravanichkul, Anya Foxen, and Alyson Prude for their feedback on individual chapters. Thanks are due as well to Ruth Streicher, Alicia Turner, Amanda Lucia, Kanjana Thepboriruk, Sinae Hyun, and Tari Shulman for help with particular questions I had in the course of my research. All errors, of course, remain my own.

I am grateful to many Thai friends and family who have helped me gain access and insight into Thai culture over the past twenty years. These are too numerous to name exhaustively, but they include my students at Mahidol; my mother-in-law, Rosakorn Uthai; my sisters-in-law, Nik, Name, and Nokweed; my UCSB friends Gift, Ta, Mock, Nok, Toei, P'Tik, P'Pam, Oat, Kaew, Pum; and many others. By far, the person to whom I am most indebted in writing this book is my wife, Nanda Raksakhom, who has supported me in every way imaginable. We have been together since the beginning of this project, and her love and support has given me the stability and courage to complete my graduate studies and become a successful scholar and writer. She also was the first to clue me in to the significance of "holy things" in Thai religion, and she has provided assistance and insightful advice at various times during my research. It is no overstatement to say that this book could not possibly exist without her.

Finally, I would like to thank one special friend whose support has been invaluable, Michael Jerryson, to whom this book is dedicated in memoriam. Michael was my "big brother" in graduate school, and he was the first person to encourage me to write this book. His example, both as a more senior graduate student at UC Santa Barbara and as a prolific scholar of Thai Buddhism afterward, blazed a clear trail for me to follow academically and professionally. But most of all, it was his passion, friendliness, and generosity that those of us who were lucky enough to know him benefited from and were inspired by. Michael passed away from complications due to ALS in the summer of 2021, just as I was finishing the initial manuscript of this book. I drove to Ohio to attend his funeral and was overwhelmed by the number of family, friends, and students whose lives he had touched. I continue to notice on a regular basis the various ways in which Michael, through his example, has made me a better teacher, a better scholar, and I dare say a better man. May this book be a testament to the many ways in which his memory is a blessing to those of us who knew him.

Abbreviations

AN	*Aṅguttara Nikāya*
BĀU	*Bṛhadāraṇyaka Upaniṣad*
ChU	*Chāndogya Upaniṣad*
DN	*Dīgha Nikāya*
GaruḍaP	*Garuḍa Purāṇa*
KūrmaP	*Kūrma Purāṇa*
MBh	*Mahābhārata*
MN	*Majjhima Nikāya*
Mp.	*Milindapañha*
RV	*Ṛg Veda*
ŚivaP	*Śiva Purāṇa*
SN	*Saṃyutta Nikāya*
Tim.	*Timaeus*
ViṣṇuP	*Viṣṇu Purāṇa*

Transliteration, Transcription, and Translation

Aside from words and names that have entered into common English usage under a specific spelling, foreign words with non-Roman writing systems are transliterated or transcribed according to a standardized system. Chinese words are transcribed in *pinyin* (including tone marks), and Sanskrit and Pali words are transliterated with diacritics using the common scholarly standard. (The only exceptions are Greek words, which I do not transliterate.)

There is unfortunately no universally accepted standard system of transliteration or phonetic transcription of Thai into the Roman alphabet. The Thai writing system poses several difficulties for such a system, including the fact that it has many phonetically redundant consonants whose sole purpose is to reproduce the spellings of Sanskrit and Pali words, the fact that vowel signs and consonants are not written linearly, and the fact that Thai has an unusually large number of distinct vowels. Exact transliteration would, for the first two reasons, be hardly readable to a person who does not speak Thai and is thus rarely attempted. Phonetic transcription is possible, and the closest to a standard that exists is that of the Royal Institute, which is used by the Thai government. That system, however, is imprecise and not used consistently. I have therefore used a system of my own devising in this book, which is similar to the Royal Institute's system but is precise in conveying every aspect of correct pronunciation other than tone and is applied consistently throughout the book. Since many of the readers of this book will not be specialists in the study of Thailand but may be specialists in the study of Buddhism and/or South(ern) Asia, I endeavored to make the system as intuitive as possible to someone who does not know Thai but *is* familiar with the standard system of transliteration for Sanskrit and Pali. All symbols that are found in the Sanskrit/Pali transliteration scheme have the same or similar value in this one, with additional symbols added to account for sounds found in Thai that have no equivalent in Sanskrit or Pali. (Note that Thai has only alveolar stops, like English, and does not distinguish between dentals and retroflexes as in Sanskrit/Pali. These alveolar stops are represented by the corresponding signs for dentals in Sanskrit/Pali—i.e., *t*, *th*, and *d*.)

Note that while in general I use the system that follows for *transcribing* Thai words phonetically, I do occasionally use Sanskrit/Pali *transliteration* when the word in question is best considered a Thai rendering of a Sanskrit/Pali word (e.g., the literary work *Dvādaśamāsa*), rather than a Sanskrit/Pali loan word that has entered into common Thai usage.

Vowels and Diphthongs

Transcription	Corresponding Thai Sound	Pronunciation
a	อะ	Like English *uh*
ā	อา	Like *a* in *father*
i	อิ	Like *i* in *lit*
ī	อี	Like *ea* in *leak*
u	อุ	Like *u* in *put*
ū	อู	Like *oo* in *choose*
o	โอะ	Like French *o*, but short
ō	โอ	Like French *o*, long
ü	อึ	The *u* sound pronounced through lips shaped for *i* (which is the converse of German *ü*), short
ǖ	อื	Same as previous, but long
e	เอะ	Like *e* in *bet*
ē	เอ	Like *e* in French *et*
ä	แอะ	Like *a* in *pat*, short
ǟ	แอ	Like *a* in *pat*, long
ǫ	เอาะ	Like the British pronunciation of *or*, but short
ǭ	ออ	Like the British pronunciation of *or*
ö	เออะ	Somewhere between English *er* and German *ö*, pronounced short
ȫ	เออ	Same as previous, but long
ia	เอีย	Diphthong of components as written
üa	เอือ	Diphthong of components as written
ua	อัว	Diphthong of components as written
ai	ไอ	Like *i* in *ice*
āi	อาย	Like English *I*
ao	เอา	Like *ou* in *house*
āo	อาว	Like *ou* in *house*, but drawn out long

Consonants

Transcription	Corresponding Thai Sound	Pronunciation
k	ก	Like *k* in *skate*
kh	ค	Like *k* in *kite*
ng	ง	Like *ng* in *sing*
c	จ	Like *ci* in Italian *ciao*
ch	ช	Like English *ch* or *sh* (which are allophones in Thai)
d	ด	Like *d* in *dog*
t	ต	Like *t* in *stop*
th	ท	Like *th* in *Thomas*
n	น	Like *n* in *naked*
b	บ	Like *b* in *boy*
p	ป	Like *p* in *spot*
ph	พ	Like *p* in *pants*
f	ฟ	Like *f* in *family*
m	ม	Like *m* in *monkey*
y	ย	Like *y* in *yes*
r	ร	Like *r* in Spanish and Italian (but often pronounced like *l*)
l	ล	Like *l* in *like*
w	ว	Like *w* in *wake*
s	ซ	Like *s* in *sand*
h	ฮ	Like *h* in *hot*

All translations from foreign languages, including Sanskrit, Pali, Thai, Koine Greek, and Spanish, are my own, unless otherwise noted (the major exception being the Classical Greek texts in Appendix A, for which I use the translations of others). The sources for primary texts in Thai are discussed in Appendix B. Quotations from the Greek New Testament are from the edition of Aland et al. Texts in Sanskrit are taken from the editions of Olivelle for the Upaniṣads and Manu and from the edition of Pargiter for the *Mārkaṇḍeya Purāṇa*; all others are taken from the Göttigen Register of Electronic Texts in Indian Languages. Texts in Pali are taken from the Digital Pali Reader, which is based on the Burmese edition. Although the translations of these texts are my own, I have consulted the translations of Jameson and Brereton for the *Ṛg Veda*, Olivelle for the Upaniṣads and Manu, Pargiter for the *Mārkaṇḍeya Purāṇa*, and Walsh, Ñāṇamoli, and Bodhi for the Pali canonical texts, which are listed in the bibliography.

1

Introduction

This is a book about syncretism, a phenomenon that does not exist and yet is seen everywhere. If one goes to a Buddhist country like Thailand, as I did for the first time twenty years ago, and understands Buddhism as it is naïvely portrayed in the West, one will be surprised by the forms of religiosity that predominate. By far the most common religious edifice and site of worship in Thailand is not the Buddhist temple but rather spirit shrines (see Figure 1.1) found outside nearly every building in the country, from simple private homes to large hotels and government buildings. Keeping these spirits happy is important for ensuring the safety, security, and prosperity of the building and people or enterprise found on the premises. As such, those who live or work in the building provide these spirits with daily offerings. Moreover, since these spirits are "holy" (*saksit*) and powerful, their human worshipers may, if they are in need of help, ask these spirits for mundane boons (a better job, more money, good grades, help in their love life, etc.). The mechanism by which they do so is *do ut des*: the worshiper asks the spirit for a boon and promises a certain offering in return. The system is also cash-on-delivery: if and only if the boon is received must the worshiper make the offering.

But these ordinary spirit shrines are not the only sort of shrine found ubiquitously around Thailand. Outside of larger buildings, such as hotels, hospitals, schools, police stations, and other government offices, one usually finds an even larger shrine to the god Brahmā (see Figure 1.2)—and, increasingly, one may also find shrines to other Hindu gods, such as Gaṇeśa, Śiva, and Indra. These shrines are the manifestation of a modern trend that began with the building of a shrine to Brahmā outside of the Ērāwan Hotel in the 1950s. This shrine, which is renowned throughout the country and throughout much of East and Southeast Asia, draws thousands of visitors every day. The Ērāwan Brahmā is, like a spirit shrine, a "holy thing" (*sing saksit*) with the ability to grant boons. Worshipers ask for the boon and promise to give a certain offering in return. If they receive the boon, they must return to the shrine to give Brahmā the offering they promised.

Holy Things. Nathan McGovern, Oxford University Press. © Oxford University Press 2024.
DOI: 10.1093/9780197759912.003.0001

Figure 1.1 Spirit shrines in Phūket. Photo by Nathan McGovern.

Because of these shrines to spirits and gods, it may appear to some observers that Buddhism is not the only religion practiced by Thai Buddhists. Buddhism has become "mixed" both with local spirit worship and with Hinduism. This model of religion, pertinent not only to Thailand but to many Buddhist and other religious societies around the world, is known as *syncretism*.[1] Syncretism has come under criticism in recent decades from scholars of religion, however, as reflecting a Christian theological strategy—which posits a "pure" religious essence that is then adulterated with "accretions"—rather than a meaningful explanation of actual religious practice.[2] Indeed,

Figure 1.2 A shrine to Brahmā, flanked by ordinary spirit shrines, outside of a condominium complex in Bangkok. Photo by Nathan McGovern.

in the case of the Thai Buddhist practices I have just described, the model of syncretism is easily dispensed with. Traditional forms of Buddhism, unlike the recently developed Buddhist Modernism more familiar in the West, include gods and spirits within their worldview as possible types of rebirth according to one's karma. It is thus completely understandable that Buddhists would worship them for mundane boons, for gods and spirits have powers that go beyond the human; they simply lack the power to bring one to *nirvāṇa* because they have not attained it themselves. Indeed, as the episode on Buddhism in *The Long Search*, long a staple of undergraduate pedagogy in Buddhist Studies, puts it, "Gods inhabit this universe as surely as a man and his ox. They can't bring you to *nirvāṇa* because they don't know the way."[3]

Armed with this knowledge about the important role gods and spirits play in Buddhism, one might think that all trace of syncretism will disappear. Here, however, the acute observer is challenged by the reality of many of the most popular Buddhist temples in Thailand, which serve as sites for a practice that looks suspiciously similar to the ones just described at spirit shrines and shrines to gods. One such temple, Wat Sōthǭn Wǭrārām, will serve as an illustrative example.

Wat Sōthǭn Wǭrārām is located about an hour's drive to the east of Bangkok in Cha Chōng Sao Province. When I first visited in the summer of 2007, I was taken by my wife and mother-in-law on the way to Bāng Sǟn, a beach that is popular with local Thai people for its proximity to Bangkok. As a child, my wife and her family, like many others, would regularly go to *wāi phra* (pay respect to the Buddha image) at Wat Sōthǭn on their way to the beach at Bāng Sǟn.

Wat Sōthǭn is a bustling pilgrimage destination, sporting an outsized modern ordination hall (see Figure 1.3) for such a provincial temple and an enormous parking lot for the throngs of visitors that arrive every day. Given that there are nineteen[4] Buddha images found in the main ordination hall, as well as copies of them in a separate hall to accommodate the large crowds, it is quite difficult at first to see what specifically has drawn all these people here. His name is Luang Phǭ Sōthǭn (see Figure 1.4), and although his name is evocative of a Buddhist monk (*Luang Phǭ*, "Reverend Father," is a common term of address used for middle-aged monks), "he" is actually a Buddha image. But this is no ordinary Buddha image, a mere representation of the Buddha suitable for Buddhist worship. He is an individual entity in his own right, with his own personal name and elaborate story of how he came to be created, where he lived in the past, and how he came to reside in Cha

Figure 1.3 The main ordination hall at Wat Sōthǭn, Cha Chə̄ng Sao Province. Photo by Nathan McGovern.

Chə̄ng Sao. And—just like local spirits and the gods—he is widely acclaimed as a *sing saksit* (สิ่งศักดิ์สิทธิ์), a "holy thing" with the power to grant boons.

This status as *sing saksit*, in fact, explains the redundancy and complexity that has been built into Wat Sōthǭn. When I first visited the temple in 2007, a separate hall from the ordination hall had already been built with copies of Luang Phǭ Sōthǭn to accommodate the large crowds coming for worship. On a more recent visit, I found that even this secondary hall with the copies of the Buddha images had been restricted to the most basic worship modes, such as prostrations and applying gold leaf to the images. The reason for this is that many of the worshipers who come to the temple are not there to ask Luang Phǭ Sōthǭn for a boon; rather, they are there because he has already granted them one and they wish to thank him. Luang Phǭ Sōthǭn, like any *sing saksit* in the country, has a reputation for liking certain types of offerings. In particular, Luang Phǭ Sōthǭn is known for liking hard-boiled eggs, and with hundreds of worshipers present at any one time, this leads to a stockpile of thousands of eggs being continuously sold and then offered to him. The volume is so great that this operation has now been moved to a dedicated enclosure just for donating eggs. In addition, worshipers wanting to thank Luang Phǭ for granting them a boon can hire a resident troupe of

Figure 1.4 The original image of Luang Phǭ Sōthǭn. Photo by Nathan McGovern.

Figure 1.5 A traditional Thai dance troupe performing on behalf of worshipers wishing to *kǟbon* (fulfill a vow). Photo by Nathan McGovern.

traditional Thai dancers to perform a dance for him (see Figure 1.5). This would once have been performed directly in front of the Buddha image (or copy thereof), but it has now been moved to a dedicated building across the street. Wat Sōthǭn is not primarily a place to meditate (something that would be quite difficult given the boisterous crowds), nor simply a residence for monks (although they are there), nor even simply a place for laypeople to make merit (although they do). It is, first and foremost, the residence of a "holy thing," a living individual whose power to aid people in their ordinary lives draws them from across the region, the country, and even the world.

Luang Phǭ Sōthǭn, and other Buddha images like him, defy easy attempts to explain away syncretism through reference to the place of gods and spirits as saṃsāric beings in the traditional Buddhist worldview. For Luang Phǭ Sōthǭn is neither a god nor a spirit—he is a Buddha image—and yet he is propitiated for mundane boons in almost exactly the same way as a god or spirit. Moreover, by being identified as a *sing saksit*, a holy thing, he is emically placed in the same conceptual category as gods and spirits. To be clear, *sing saksit* is a clearly defined category in the modern Thai religious imaginary, more so than its literal translation "holy things" implies in English. These are not random "things" that can be described as holy. They are specific statues and shrines with a recognized sacred power that attracts worshipers asking for mundane boons according to the *do ut des* procedure already described. The placement of Buddha images within the category and associated praxis of "holy things" thus, it would seem, effaces the traditional Buddhist distinction between saṃsāric beings and the Buddha.

As if this were not problematic enough for the critique of syncretism, increasingly Thai Buddhists themselves are adopting the language of syncretism, which can take two forms. On the one hand, some Thai Buddhists have enthusiastically embraced the worship of gods like Brahmā that they explicitly call "Hindu" or "Brahmanical." This phenomenon, which I dub "Hindu enthusiasm," is relatively recent and clearly draws on globalized discourses and information networks that allow its adherents to draw upon Hindu imagery, mythology, and ritual in worshiping the gods. Yet it also draws upon a long history in which the imagery, mythology, and ritual involving the gods have not remained statically moored to Pali scriptural paradigms, but instead have been continually updated to follow developments in Hinduism.

Another form that the Thai adoption of the language of syncretism has taken is reformist critiques of traditional Thai Buddhist practice. As I was preparing the final manuscript for this book, I attended the Songkrān (New Year) Festival at the Lao/Thai Buddhist temple near my home in Madison, and a Thai monk at the temple gave a sermon in which he explained the origins of this festival with reference to the "three religions" (*phī*, *phrām*, and *phut*) that have mixed together in Thai and Lao practice. In doing so, he was drawing from a discourse among reformist monks such as P. A. Payutto and Buddhadāsa Bhikkhu that criticizes traditional Thai Buddhism (*sātsanā phut*) as being mixed with non-Buddhist practices from the local spirit religion (*sātsanā phī*) and Brahmanism (*sātsanā phrām*). This trifold schema has also been adopted by secular Thai academics, as exemplified by the recent volume *Phī-Phrām-Phut*, which features an introduction by the eminent historian and public intellectual Nidhi Eoseewong.[5]

As a historian of religion, I remain committed to the position that the theory of religious syncretism is fundamentally flawed. Yet as an observer of Thai Buddhism, I find myself repeatedly confronted with practices for which syncretism is a seductively attractive explanation—not only for myself as an outside observer but also for many Thai Buddhists themselves. The goal of this book is to make sense of this situation. I take my task to be akin to that of an evolutionary biologist explaining why things like eyes and wings can look like they were created by an intelligent designer when in fact they are the product of natural selection. The purpose of this book, to put it quite simply, is to answer the question: If syncretism is so wrong, why does it feel *so* right?

Asking for Boons: Making and Fulfilling Vows

In order to better understand the practice of asking "holy things" for boons and dive into the issue of syncretism it seemingly represents, I will now offer a translation of the short introduction to a popular book titled *Manual for Fulfilling Vows, Asking for Boons, and Increasing Auspiciousness.* This book, which I purchased in a chain bookstore in Bangkok in 2007, is simply one of any number of books published in Thailand, intended for a popular audience, that explain the basic procedures for asking for boons from *sing saksit.* While there is nothing exceptional or definitive about this particular book (other books offer varying lists of "holy things"), it is representative of its genre, and as such it gives a useful entrée into the discourse surrounding "holy things" in Thailand today. This book happens to include Luang Phǭ Sōthǭn, but it gives a comprehensive treatment of no fewer than thirty-six different "holy things," of which Luang Phǭ Sōthǭn is only one:

> Nowadays, because of the need to make a living, and because of various problems one encounters in life, people are increasingly coming to rely on holy [*Saksit*] things for willpower. Therefore, people are seeking support in various holy things by making vows [*kānbonbān*] to them, and when they have gotten what they wanted, many people forget what they vowed because they make vows everywhere that people say is good.
>
> In this book, I therefore will explain in detail all of the places where people like to make vows [*bon*] and the way to fulfill the vows [*kābon*] that one has forgotten about.
>
> So look no further! I'll explain what you need to do to be successful—whatever you want!—where to make a vow and how, how to ask for a boon, as well as how to make a vow to ask for various things—for example, for money, for children, for love, to win the lottery, to get rich, and so on. In particular, I'll explain how to make a vow with various Hindu gods and at holy places in general.
>
> I will begin by explaining how to make a vow to Father Catukhām Rāmathēp, who is really "hot" right now, because there are probably a lot of

> people who want to know what you must make the vow with and how you must make the vow if you make a vow to Father Catukhām Rāmathēp.
>
> First of all, you need to know the way to worship. In the end, I will explain the way to worship that gets results. Keep reading![6]

The first and most important term for understanding the practices described in this passage is *saksit* (ศักดิ์สิทธิ์). *Saksit* is an adjective that serves in modern Thai as the standard translation of "holy" or "sacred." It is not, however, a modern neologism; in accordance with its long genealogy within Thai discourse, which we will explore in more detail in Chapter 4, it refers to a special type of power that inheres in certain people, objects, and supernatural beings. While nowadays it is quite common to refer to Buddha images like Luang Phǭ Sōthǭn as *saksit* or "holy," in older Siamese literature the word *saksit* is quite conspicuously *not* used to describe Buddha images or other Buddhist relics. Unraveling the changes in discourse that have led to this shift in usage will be one of the primary goals of this book.

"Holy things" are relevant in the context of the passage I have translated here because they play a crucial role in the practice the author refers to as *kānbonbān* (การบนบาน, which I have translated as "making a vow"), also known more formally in Thai as *kānbonbānsānklāo* (การบนบานศาลกล่าว). This practice is in turn related to the practice of "asking for a boon" (*kānkhǭphǭn*, การขอพร), which the author does not refer to directly in this passage, but which is nonetheless implied because "making a vow" is precisely the way that one "asks for a boon." The whole practice in question consists of two steps, referred to colloquially by the verbs *bon* (บน) and *kǣbon* (แก้บน). The verb *bon* means "to make a vow." As already mentioned, it follows the logic of *do ut des*, and thus is no different in structure from, say, a Catholic man in an airplane that is about to crash promising the Blessed Virgin that he will become a priest if she delivers him from death. In the Thai practice of *kānbonbānsānklāo*, however, there is no need for any dramatic crisis or a life-altering promise; nearly any need can be fulfilled by making a vow, and the vow usually consists of promising to make a simple offering of food or the like to the *sing saksit* in question once the boon has been granted. The cover of the book whose introduction I have translated here, in fact, lists several common requests made by Thai people in the practice of *kānbonbānsānklāo*: having children, winning the lottery, getting well from an illness, being successful in love, and passing a test.

The verb *kǣbon*, in turn, is used colloquially to refer to "fulfilling the vow." What this means is that, once the boon has been granted, one must return to the "holy thing" to which the vow was made to give it what was promised. This is a crucial step that the author of the passage notes many people may skip if they make many vows to many "holy things" and then forget when they finally receive what they asked for. The book even contains the following "warning" in a starburst pattern on the cover:

Warning!
Have you **made a vow?**
You must fulfill the vow.[7]

When a practitioner first goes to a "holy thing" to ask for a boon and make a vow, he or she will make a small offering (e.g., a candle, incense) as a matter of course in worshiping the image, but the real offering is something that is withheld until the boon requested is actually received. At that point, the practitioner will return to make that offering. Making this offering *after* receiving a boon—like the worshipers at Wat Sōthọn offering hard-boiled eggs or hiring the traditional dance troupe to perform a dance—is what is referred to as *kābon*.

Naturally, sometimes one will not receive what one asked for, and individual practitioners obviously explain this in different ways. Generally speaking, the failure to receive the boon is blamed on a failure to properly propitiate the holy thing in question, or perhaps credited to the holy thing's higher wisdom that sees the boon is bad for the practitioner, rather than blamed on a lack of *khwāmsaksit* ("holiness") in the holy thing itself.[8] However such failures are rationalized, though, there is no need to make the promised offering unless the boon is actually received. Moreover, the practitioner has complete freedom in deciding how much or how little to promise to the image he or she is praying to. Nevertheless, the point in *kānbonbānsānklāo* is to get what one is asking for, and famous images that are commonly worshiped by Thai people all have individual reputations for liking certain things over others, so people tend to promise those things when they go to *bon*. Indeed, explaining what offerings various "holy things" like is one of the purposes of the book I have quoted from here.

"Holy Things" and the Limits of Religious Taxonomy

What, then, are these "holy things" that one goes to to *bon* and *kābon*? As already mentioned, the book discusses a total of thirty-six "holy things," which are listed in Table 1.1.[9] I include the original Thai name of each object;

Table 1.1 A list of all the "holy things" (*sing saksit*) discussed in the book *Manual for Fulfilling Vows, Asking for Boons, and Increasing Auspiciousness*. The original Thai names are listed in the first column; the middle column gives a translation/transliteration of each name; and the column on the right gives my attempt at identifying what sort of "holy thing" each represents (a spirit, a god, a Buddha image, etc.).

Thai Name	English Name	Identity
จตุคามรามเทพ	Catukhām Rāmathēp	Pseudo-Hindu deity
วัดบ้านแหลม	Wat Bān Laem	Buddhist temple
วัดไร่ขิง	Wat Rai Khing	Buddhist temple
หลวงปู่ศุข	Reverend Grandfather Suk	Deceased Buddhist monk
กรมหลวงชุมพร	Krom Luang Chumphọn	Deceased disciple of Rev. Grandfather Suk
หลวงพ่อพุทธโสธร	Reverend Father Phuttha Sōthọn	Buddha image
วัดบางพลีใหญ่	Wat Bang Phlī Yai	Buddhist temple
หลวงพ่อเขาตะเครา	Reverend Father Khao Takhrao	Buddha image
วัดพระศรีรัตนมหาธาตุวรมหาวิหาร	Wat Phra Sī Rattana Mahāthāt Wọramahāwihān	Buddhist temple
พระเจ้าตากสินมหาราช	Phra Cāo Taksin Mahārāt	Deceased king
สมเด็จพระนเรศวรมหาราช	Somdet Phra Naresuan Mahārāt	Deceased king
ศาลเจ้าจีน	Chinese ancestor shrine	Chinese ancestor worship
ศาลพระภูมิ	Shrine to the land spirit	Local spirit cult
ศาลตายาย	Ancestor shrine	Local spirit cult
พระพิฆเนศวร	Vighneśvara (Gaṇeśa)	Hindu deity
ท้าวมหาพรหม	King Mahābrahmā	Hindu deity
พระตรีมูรติ	Trimūrti	Hindu deity
พระสุรัสวดี	Sarasvatī	Hindu deity
พระวิษณุ	Viṣṇu	Hindu deity
พระลักษมี	Lakṣmī	Hindu deity
พระศิวะ	Śiva	Hindu deity
พระแม่อุมา	Mother Umā	Hindu deity
พระแม่กาลี	Mother Kālī	Hindu deity
พระแม่ธรณี	Mother Dharaṇī	Earth goddess, found in accounts of the Buddha's Awakening

Table 1.1 Continued

Thai Name	English Name	Identity
ช้างสามเศียร	Three-headed elephant (Airāvaṇa)	Indra's mount (Hindu)
เจ้าพ่อหลักเมือง	Lord Father of the City Pillar	Local spirit cult
หลวงพ่อโตวัดอินทร์	Reverend Father Tō of Wat In (Somdet Tō)	Deceased Buddhist monk
พระนอนวัดโพธิ์	The Reclining Buddha of Wat Pho	Buddha image
วัดพระแก้วมรกต	The Temple of the Emerald Buddha	Buddhist temple
หลวงพ่อศรีศากยมุนี	Reverend Father Śrī Śākyamuni	Buddha image
รัชกาลที่ 5	Rāma V	Deceased king
สมเด็จพระนางเจ้าสุนันทากุมารีรัตน์	Somdet Phra Nāng Cāo Sunanthākumārīrat	Deceased wife of Rāma V
ศาลเจ้าพ่อเสือ	Shrine to the Lord Father Tiger	Daoist (Chinese)
พุ่มพวง ดวงจันทร์	Phumphuang Duangcan	Deceased country singer
เจ้าแม่เขาสามมุข	The Lord Mother of Sāmmuk Mountain	Local spirit cult
ศาลย่านาค	Shrine to Grandma Nāk	Local spirit cult

an English translation; and my attempt to give an identity to each object (Buddhist, Brahmanical, local spirit cult, or other)[10] when possible. What we immediately see from this table is that the threefold schema (Buddhism, Brahmanism, local spirit cults) is inadequate to the task of analyzing "holy things" in Thailand. To begin with, although certain things are easy to categorize within these three categories (Buddha temples and Buddha images as "Buddhist," Hindu gods as "Brahmanical," and spirit shrines as "local spirit cults"), others are less so. Two of the things in the list are clearly Chinese (Chinese ancestor shrines and a Daoist temple), and thus neither "local" nor of Indian (Buddhist/Brahmanical) origin. Likewise, the list includes three deceased kings and one deceased royal consort, suggesting that perhaps there should be a fourth category, "royal cult." Phumphuang Duangcan, on the other hand, seems to be in a category of her own; she is a deceased country singer with a fan-based cult, much like that of Elvis in the United States.

I want to emphasize, however, that the problems one faces in trying to taxonomize this list of "holy things" cannot be solved simply with a more detailed taxonomy. Any attempt to divide these "holy things" into discrete categories is ultimately arbitrary. This is particularly obvious when considering deceased persons found in the list. Should kings be considered a category of their own? Or should they be considered part of local spirit cults because they are local and their spirits are worshiped in death? Why not consider them Buddhist? After all, famous kings are considered powerful because they are *dhammarājas* who have accumulated great merit (*phūmībun*, ผู้มีบุญ) and have perfected the Buddhist perfections (*phūmībāramī*, ผู้มีบารมี). Likewise, why consider the cults of other deceased persons to be "Buddhist" simply because the person in question was a monk? They are local personages whose spirits are worshiped in death, so why not consider them to be local spirit cults? And what about other deceased persons who do not fit neatly into any category? Should Rāma V's wife be considered part of a separate "royal cult," together with her husband, or should she (and her husband) be categorized as members of local spirit cults? What about the dead country singer? Is hers just another local spirit cult, or is there something that distinguishes her from, say, the famous ghost of Mother Nāk (Mā Nāk)? Perhaps the cults of all deceased persons are simply local spirit cults.

Even the distinction between "real" persons who are now deceased and "mythical" figures (gods, goddesses, and spirits) proves arbitrary. Whatever one decides about Buddhist monks, kings, a royal wife, or a country singer, the cults of some deceased persons—like Sāmmuk, a Juliet-like figure who committed suicide after her lover was forced to marry someone else, and whose spirit now inhabits a mountain bearing her name, and Mā Nāk, the ghost of a woman who died in childbirth and who was famously defeated by the "magical monk" Somdet Tō[11]—clearly do constitute local spirit cults. But the most common spirit cults—those of Phra Phūm (Skt. *bhūmi*: the local land spirit) and *pūyātāyāi* (lit., "grandparents," i.e., the spirits of people who lived on the land in the distant past)—do not involve real historical personages (except generically in the case of the latter). And if the cult of, in particular, Phra Phūm is considered to be a "local spirit cult" just because he is associated with the land and therefore locality, even though he has a Sanskritic name, then why separate him arbitrarily from other Sanskritic gods like Viṣṇu and Brahmā? In theory, the "high Hindu gods" are, unlike Phra Phūm, "translocal," but as we will see, in practice they are worshiped in the same way by Thai Buddhists: in a particular place, with a particular image, and using the same procedures of *bon* and *kābon*.

Likewise, why distinguish deceased Thai monks from Buddha images? This distinction might seem clear from an etic perspective: the spirits of deceased Buddhist monks are worshiped in death, whereas Buddha images are worshiped as representations of the Buddha, an exemplar for all those who are on the path to *nirvāṇa*. A thick description of Thai Buddhist praxis forces one to abandon even this distinction, however. At least within the context of *kānbonbānsānklāo*, Buddha images like Luang Phọ̄ Sōthọ̄n are *not* worshiped because they are "representations of the Buddha"—that is, local instantiations of a translocal deity, the essence of the *dhamma*, or what have you—but because they *individually* are considered to be "holy things," things endowed with *khwāmsaksit*, and therefore efficacious granters of boons. I emphasize "individually" because it is not some hypothetical power of the Buddha or power of the *dhamma* that allows one to get what one asks for in prayer; if this were the case, a Thai person could go to any Buddha image and ask the Buddha for a boon. Rather, Thai people go to *particular* Buddha images in *particular* places to ask for boons, because those Buddha images are each—individually and quite separately from one another—renowned for being very *saksit* and thus efficacious in granting boons. Moreover, each of these famous Buddha images has an individual name, backstory, and preference for certain gifts over others, just as one would expect from an individual god, spirit, or ghost.

Given that the distinctions between Buddha images and monks, between "real" people and "mythical" beings, between gods and spirits, and ultimately between Buddhist, Brahmanical, and "local spirit" cults are so arbitrary—and given that *all* of these "holy things" are treated as individual personalities endowed with *khwāmsaksit* and therefore worshiped as granters of boons—it seems prudent to abandon, at least within the context of our thick description, attempts at categorization and instead regard them as belonging to a *single* category: "holy things," or *sing saksit*, as they are understood by Thai practitioners themselves.

Moving beyond Syncretism

The effort to discern a mixture of religious practices in what emically is considered unified has a long pedigree in the study of Theravāda Buddhism.

Early scholars of Theravāda Buddhist cultures, such as Michael Ames in the case of Sri Lanka and Melford Spiro in the case of Burma, drew a distinction between two religious "components" within the cultures they studied: Theravāda Buddhism proper and another, non-Buddhist component, usually referred to as "animism."[12] Stanley Tambiah understood these Buddhist and non-Buddhist components in a more nuanced way, as belonging to a single religious "field," within which different practices can be discerned, but that nevertheless are inextricably linked to one another, such that any attempt to separate them into "components" is ultimately arbitrary.[13] B. J. Terwiel, on the other hand, distinguished between two "orientations" in Thai religious practice: a popular orientation that is syncretic and an elite orientation that sees Buddhism as separate from and superior to animism.[14]

By far the most influential model of syncretism in Thai religion, however, has been that of anthropologist Thomas Kirsch. Kirsch analyzed Thai religion into *three* components—Buddhism, Brahmanism, and animism—and assigned them distinct geographical and historical origins, thus lending Thai religion what Kirsch calls "complexity."[15] This threefold schema has been particularly influential not only in Western scholarship but also in Thai scholarship, where it is the dominant paradigm—translated as *sātsanā phut* (ศาสนาพุทธ), *sātsanā phrām* (ศาสนาพราหมณ์), and *sātsanā phī* (ศาสนาผี). From there, it has increasingly come to have an influence on popular discourse in Thailand, as I will discuss further in Chapter 6.

More recent scholars of Buddhism have criticized the model of syncretism because it presupposes the autonomous existence of two distinct "religions" that are then mixed. As Robert Sharf has discussed in the context of Chinese religion:

> Buddhism would then be construed as an autonomous religious system that originated in India and assimilated (or was assimilated by) a variety of regional traditions and cults as it traveled across Asia. Thus, there would be Taoist-Buddhist syncretism in China, Bon-Buddhist syncretism in Tibet, Shinto-Buddhist syncretism in Japan, and so on. The problem is that the category of syncretism presupposes the existence of distinct religious entities that predate the syncretic amalgam, precisely what is absent, or at least unrecoverable, in the case of Buddhism.[16]

That which is "precisely what is absent" in the case of Buddhism is a pure, "original" Buddhism, originating in India and then mixing with non-Buddhist religions as it spread to other lands:

> [I]t seems prudent to assume that Buddhism, even in the land of its origin, would have been fully implicated in a wide variety of local religious practices that had little if any scriptural sanction. . . . There is thus little reason to assume that the depiction of Buddhist monastic life found in the scriptures ever bore much resemblance to the situation on the ground. It was, rather, an idealized ideological construct that in all likelihood existed in marked tension with living practice. As Jonathan Z. Smith has cogently argued, the social and cognitive allure of religious systems lies in precisely this gap between the ideal and the actual.[17]

Indeed, recent scholarship on Indian Buddhism has shown that the "pure" Buddhism presupposed by models of syncretism is largely a myth, and that even early Indian Buddhism was just as "syncretic" as contemporary forms of Buddhism outside of India. Richard Cohen, for example, has used archaeological evidence to show that Buddhism as practiced at Ajaṇṭā incorporated local spirit cults,[18] while Robert DeCaroli has used a broad range of art historical evidence, as well as textual evidence from the Pali Canon itself, to show that spirit cults played an important role in even the earliest practice of Buddhism.[19]

Some recent scholars of Thai Buddhism have sought to move beyond the paradigm of syncretism by borrowing the concept of "hybridity" from postcolonial studies. Pattana Kitiarsa has argued that "Thailand's popular beliefs and religiosity in the past few decades have been undergoing a significant degree of 'subtle hybridization,' where religious commodification and capitalist consumerism have been increasingly prominent."[20] Likewise, James Taylor has adopted the term "hybridization" to

> [imply] the emergence of an alternative religious spatiality; one that is embedded in power relationships of centre-periphery and dominant/dominated. . . . Religious hybridization is not so much a singular or unidirectional emergent cultural process, rather a mixing and fusing of various ideas and practices. It may even be anti-hegemonic, undermining the centre and creating something new, different, not even previously noticed, and marked by negotiation of meaning and representation.[21]

Both Pattana and Taylor associate the hybridization of Thai religion with recent history, even as recent as just the past couple of decades, and in particular with *urban* religion. Taylor furthermore associates it with *postmodernity*, which he understands to be endemic to the urban landscape.

The concept of hybridity does have one advantage over that of syncretism—namely, that it implies an autonomy and counterhegemonic power within the hybridized space, as opposed to the relative passivity implied by "syncretism." Nevertheless, I find "hybridization" to be inadequate as a replacement for the model of "syncretism,"[22] for two reasons. First, it reinscribes the very same presupposition that rendered "syncretism" problematic to begin with—that is, that there are two distinct religions that then are mixed or, in this particular parlance, "hybridized." In this respect, the switch from syncretism to hybridization serves as little more than a change in terminology. Second, both Pattana and Taylor associate hybridization with the very recent past and with urban religious space. As we will see in this book, modernity has wrought significant changes in Thai religiosity—including a radical change in the conceptualization of the category *saksit*—but that does not mean that Siamese religion was any less "hybrid" (insofar as such a term makes any sense) prior to the modernizing reforms of the nineteenth century. Modernity and urbanization have brought profound changes, but the solution to scholarly anxiety over perceived mixed categories cannot be found within them.[23]

Justin McDaniel, in his work on the famous eighteenth–nineteenth century Thai monk Somdet Tō, provides a trenchant critique of the model of syncretism that replaces it not merely in name but through a thoroughgoing shift in theoretical outlook. McDaniel refers to his approach as a study of "cultural repertoires" in an effort to take Thai religious practices seriously on their own terms rather than forcing them through the filter of historical, anthropological, sociopolitical, and other scholarly categories. McDaniel writes:

> Instead of seeing a Thai monastery or even Thai image blending essentialized local and translocal, Indic and Southeast Asian, Brahmanic and Buddhist elements, I see these complex lives, rituals, and objects as questioning the very usefulness of metacategories like Buddhism, Brahmanism, animism, local, translocal, Indic, Chinese, Thai, and the like. In my experience and interviews, monks or laypeople prostrating in front of a shrine with statues of General Taksin, Kuan Im, Shakyamuni Buddha, Somdet To, Phra Sanghkhacchai do not see the shrine as a syncretistic stage or themselves as multireligious. They do not process the images separately, with some being local, some translocal, some Buddhist, and some non-Buddhist. . . . I soon realized that it was not only

> scholars who had difficulty in determining what was Hindu, Mahayana, Theravada, superstitious, orthodox, esoteric, folk, and the like. The practitioners and scholars in Thailand had trouble separating practices and objects into these categories. . . . Therefore, I started asking different questions and stopped trying to fit Thai practices into my preconceived categories.[24]

We can thus see McDaniel—by focusing on the local, the vernacular, the emic—as taking one of the "roads . . . not taken in the study of Theravāda Buddhism," as advocated by Charles Hallisey.[25]

In this book, I take a similar approach. Rather than "trying to fit Thai practices into my preconceived categories," I ask what categories Thai people themselves use to explain what they are doing when they worship Brahmā or any other Hindu god, a famous Buddha image like Luang Phọ̄ Sōthọn, or simply the land spirit Phra Phūm in the shrine outside their house. In contemporary Thailand at least, the most important category is singular: all of these and more are "holy things," *sing saksit*, that have the power to grant boons.

Buddhist Inclusivism

It would be a mistake, however, to conclude that ordinary Thai religious actors are simply ignorant of or not concerned with normative categories that might militate against the indiscriminate worship of spirits, gods, and Buddha images as "holy things." After all, Thai people of the current generation are arguably better educated about the normative teachings of Buddhism than any previous generation. All Thai schoolchildren now study Buddhism as one of their compulsory subjects for the twelve years of their primary and secondary education. This is in marked contrast with premodern times—or even the early twentieth century—when such detailed access to the normative teachings of Buddhism would have been limited to males who ordained for many years and were sufficiently privileged to pursue higher study of the *dhamma*. Moreover, as Julia Cassaniti has shown, the "living Buddhism" of ordinary Buddhists is suffused with sophisticated doctrinal concepts and by no means separable from the Buddhism of elites.[26] In spite of this, by all accounts, *sing saksit* and the practice of *kānbonbānsānklāo* have been proliferating, not disappearing.

It is not necessary to appeal to Sharf's tension between normative ideals and living practice to understand why the model of syncretism is problematic. Thai religious actors who practice *kānbonbānsānklāo* are in many cases reasonably or even highly educated and aware of the categories that have led many scholars to see their practice as "syncretistic." They simply do not see their practice as problematic in light of those same categories.

Indeed, syncretism is the solution to a pseudo-problem caused by the projection of Western assumptions about the nature of religion onto Buddhism. Christianity is premised on the assertion that there is only one true God, the God of Israel. From the very beginning, becoming Christian meant abandoning worship of any other beings as gods. In more recent times, due to certain strains in Reformation theology that were then accentuated by Enlightenment rationalism, this aspect of Christianity has been simplified into an effective assertion that other gods simply do not exist. Christianity thus polices its boundaries in a very particular way. As Paul Hacker has observed, this manner of policing boundaries is not generally found in Indian religions. Indian religions such as Buddhism instead practice *inclusivism*—a practice that he contrasted with Christian "tolerance"[27] but that scholars of Indian religion now use in a neutral sense to refer to the way in which Indian religions police their boundaries differently from the rejection of other gods found in the Abrahamic traditions of Judaism, Christianity, and Islam. Inclusivism, simply put, is a technique for dealing with religious difference not by rejecting the God, gods, or important figures of one's rivals but rather by "including" them in a subordinated role.

As Hacker observed, this method for policing boundaries is quite common across the history of Indian religions. Ancient Indian religion as portrayed in the Vedas involved, as in many ancient societies, a variety of gods associated with natural powers and whose harmonious coexistence with humanity could be ensured through proper sacrifice. The *śramaṇa* traditions that arose in the middle of the first millennium BCE valorized the accomplishments of a human being (the Buddha for Buddhists, Makkhali Gosāla for Ājīvakas, the Mahāvīra for Jains) over the gods, but they did not deny the existence or divine status of the gods. Instead, they simply denied their immortality, relegating them to the world of *saṃsāra* just like any other unliberated being.

Buddhists had a particular strategy for dealing with Brahmā, who at that time had come to be recognized by many Brahmans as the Creator of the world and the ultimate soteriological goal. The Buddhists transformed the singular Brahmā into a whole class of deities that one could be reborn as—a high attainment, to be sure, but still short of true Awakening.[28] At the same time, they told stories about a Brahmā who was deluded into thinking he was Creator of the universe until put in his place by the Buddha (*MN* 49; *DN* 1, 11). This strategy of what Alexis Sanderson has called "super-enthronement"[29] was then followed by Vaiṣṇavas and Śaivas.[30] Myths in the *Mahābhārata* and Purāṇas variously made Brahmā a demiurge of either Viṣṇu (*MBh* 3.194.11–12) or Śiva (*MBh* 10.17.10; *KūrmaP* 1.9.5–87; *ŚivaP* 1.6.1–21) and subordinated Viṣṇu and Śiva to each other, according to the sectarian affiliation of the text (e.g., Viṣṇu to Śiva in *KūrmaP* 1.25.64–95 and Śiva to Viṣṇu in *ViṣṇuP* 1.2.57–69). Vaiṣṇavas likewise practiced inclusivistic super-enthronement toward Buddhism by making the Buddha an *avatāra* of Viṣṇu (*GaruḍaP* 1.32). The practice of inclusivism has become such a pervasive aspect of Indian religious culture that, in modern times, the Neo-Vedānta movement has taken it global by claiming that all religions are forms of Hinduism,[31] at the same time serving as an important influence on the rise of modern perennialism, which in different manifestations makes use of overt or crypto-inclusivism.[32]

Buddhism, therefore, comes out of a culture with a long history of inclusivism and in fact has played a central role in that history. Gods and various other beings usually referred to in English as "spirits" (the exact nature of the distinction between which we will examine in more detail in Chapter 2) are therefore not only not surprising in any Buddhist culture; they are required by Buddhism's basic cosmology, which elaborates a vast hierarchy of unliberated beings ranked according to *karma*. Buddhist Modernism, which has arisen only in the past century and a half but has an outsized influence in the West, is an aberration in downplaying or fully denying the existence of gods and other supernatural beings as incompatible with modern conceptions of rationality and science.[33] In traditional Buddhist cultures, the existence of such beings has always been assumed, and there is no need to resort to syncretism or point to a hypothetical indigenous substrate to explain them; one need only point to the normative Buddhist scriptures from India to justify their inclusion within a Buddhist culture of belief and praxis. *Syncretism is a bad explanation for Buddhist cultures not because it privileges the normative over the descriptive but because it fundamentally misunderstands the normative to begin with.*

Inclusivism thus explains why a Thai Buddhist would make a vow and ask the local land spirit or Brahmā for a boon: according to the normative teachings of Buddhism, such beings exist, and although they may be subject to *saṃsāra* and unable to point the way to *nirvāṇa*, they still possess powers beyond the ken of human beings. But inclusivism does not fully explain why a Thai Buddhist would do the same thing with a Buddha image *as if it were a god or spirit*. I am not the first scholar to note that Buddha images are frequently treated not as mere representations of the Buddha but as living *individuals* in their own right. Within the context of Thailand, Donald Swearer has studied in detail the *buddhābhiṣeka* ceremony whereby a new Buddha image is ritually made alive as an instantiation of the Buddha.[34] Angela Chiu has studied the rich tradition of "biographies" of Buddha images in Northern Thailand (Lānnā), which, like Luang Phǫ Sōthǫn, are consistently portrayed as individuals with their own stories and miraculous powers.[35] The treatment of Buddha images as miracle-working individuals is not unique to Thailand; it has also been studied in the context of Japan by Sarah Horton[36] and in the context of China by Koichi Shinohara.[37] I am interested in understanding how such practices and interpretations of Buddha images are possible without resorting to tired models of syncretism that imply that Buddhism has been "tainted" in some way by local spirit beliefs.

The Genealogy of *Saksit*

Within the context of Thailand, the problematic I have posed here—Why are Buddha images treated like living individuals that can be entreated for boons?—can be expressed in another, more fruitful form: Why are Buddha images subsumed under the same category of "holy things" as are spirits, gods, and the like? This formulation of the problematic makes it clear that syncretism is not relevant. The question is not why Buddhism is "mixed" with the worship of gods and spirits—a basic understanding of normative Buddhist doctrine makes this no less surprising than the fact that Buddhists believe in and interact with plants and animals (which are, after all, a part of Buddhist cosmology). Rather, the problem is that Buddha images are included within the same category. Gods and spirits are included within normative Buddhist cosmology, but the whole point of inclusivism is that they are *subordinated* to the Buddha—they are radically different from the Buddha insofar as he has escaped from *ṣaṃsāra* and they have not. What does it mean to treat a Buddha image like a god or spirit when the Buddha is radically different from gods and spirits? Or, put differently, what is a "holy thing," and why is a Buddha image like Luang Phọ̄ Sōthọ̄n considered to be one?

In this book, I will be answering these questions genealogically, in the Nietzschean sense. Since *saksit* is the operative emic category, I want to understand how it, and other related categories, have been deployed, redeployed, and changed over the course of Siamese[38] and modern Thai history. I have translated *sing saksit* as "holy things" and chosen that English phrase as the title for this book because the discourse of "religion" is operative in modern Thailand and *saksit* indeed serves as the standard translation for the Western concept of the "holy" or "sacred."[39] Nevertheless, *saksit* has its own genealogy in Siam quite distinct from that of "holy/sacred" in the West, and even today it carries valences rooted in that indigenous genealogy and only awkwardly and incompletely represented in the modern religious paradigm as "holy" or "sacred."

My primary thesis is that, following McDaniel and Hallisey, we must be ever attuned to local categories, but that doing so paradoxically *increases* the importance of normative and translocal categories that scholars are accustomed to working with, rather than eliminating the need for them. This can be seen in the term *saksit* itself, which, although a local category in the sense that it is a Thai term used in an idiosyncratic way in the Thai language, is also derived from the inherently translocal Sanskrit terms *śakti* (pronounced *sak* in Thai) and *siddhi* (pronounced *sit*). Many, indeed most Thai terms relevant to the study of *kānbonbānsānklāo* are likewise terms of foreign origin used in an idiosyncratic way in Thai, and thus an important methodological problem is how to think about the relationship between the local and the translocal.

On this point, it is worth noting that Southeast Asian Studies has long been dominated by a debate over the nature of the relationship between Southeast Asia and South Asia. This debate was inaugurated by the work of George Coedès, who, in his most influential work, *The Indianized States of Southeast Asia*, presented a model whereby state formation in Southeast Asia in the first millennium was fostered by a process of "Indianization"—or, in the original French, *hindouisation*—whereby Indian cultural forms, especially Sanskrit and various Hindu and Buddhist sects, became dominant in the region.[40] The model of Indianization was then criticized by several scholars, including Michael Vickery,[41] Ian Mabbett,[42] and Oliver Wolters,[43] for effacing local agency. As a result of this criticism, scholars of Southeast Asia now prefer models of "localization" to Indianization.

My own perspective is indebted to the proponents of localization, and I am particularly appreciative of a recent turn to thinking in terms of a broader region of "Southern Asia" that encompasses the Cold War categories of "South Asia" and "Southeast Asia."[44] Nevertheless, it can be detrimental to progress in the field if we get too bogged down in a false dichotomy between localization and Indianization, or between the local and the translocal. Taking my cue from Wolters's apt formula of "foreign materials fading into local statements,"[45] I argue that we should set aside the distinction between local and translocal and instead focus on interacting discourses. Discourses are inherently translocal insofar as they are processes of linguistic communication that derive hegemonic power from their ability to universalize, but their interaction is inherently local insofar as it can only be enacted at particular times and in particular places.

By contextualizing the category *saksit* within a broader web of interacting discourses thus conceptualized, we can understand both why the worship of "holy things" through *kānbonbānsānklāo* is not an example of syncretism and why it can appear as such in the modern world, even in some cases to Thai Buddhists themselves. The broadest context for understanding the category *saksit* is Buddhism writ large. Buddhism, as a discourse, can be understood as simply one implicitly theological system among many. It both delineates "the gods" as a category and defines them vis-à-vis other beings. As such, it participates in, but is not the sole agent of, the social construction of gods and other supernatural beings. Discourses that we now refer to as Hindu also have participated in the social construction of gods. Given the historical relationship between Buddhism and Hinduism in India, as well as the interaction between the Pali *imaginaire* and Sanskrit Cosmopolis in Siam, [46] there has thus been space for Hindu discourses to exercise agency within Siamese/Thai Buddhism. This is not syncretism, however. It is not that Buddhism and Hinduism have "mixed"; rather, both, as theological systems, have participated in the ongoing social construction of the gods.

In premodern Siam, the word *saiyasāt* was used to account for the space in which Hindu discourses could exercise agency within Buddhism. It referred to the knowledge and powers possessed by Brahmans—which were acknowledged as real but subordinated to the soteriological knowledge of Buddhism. This is evinced by the word itself, which means "sleeping knowledge," in contradistinction with the "awakened knowledge" (*phutthasāt*) of Buddhism. The term *saksit*, in turn, was associated with *saiyasāt*. It did not, in premodern Siam, mean "holy," but rather referred to supernatural power that inhered in gods and spirits and was accessible to Brahmans through their specialized knowledge. It rarely if ever was used to refer to Buddha images or specifically "Buddhist" paraphernalia.

This situation changed, however, in the nineteenth century when the Thai language fell under the hegemonic power of Western discourse and absorbed the language of Western modernity. The word *sātsanā* (Skt. *śāsana*), a key term within Pali Buddhism, was mustered to translate the modern secularized concept of "religion," while the word *saiyasāt* was used to translate the antithetical modern concept of "magic" or "the occult." For the most part, vocabulary historically associated with *saiyasāt* was used to translate concepts associated with magic. The term *saksit*, however, was an anomaly: it was used to translate the word "holy." The word *saksit* today is thus, through its modern meaning of "holy," associated with religion (*sātsanā*), while still retaining its historical association with *saiyasāt*, making it simultaneously suspect as "magic."

What might seem an idiosyncratic shift in the meaning of a single word has opened up an entirely new conceptual space for the practice of Thai religion. In particular, it has made it possible for spirits, gods, and Buddha images to be considered together under a single category: "holy things," or *sing saksit*. As we will see, Buddha images, insofar as they are a type of "relic," have always been considered, within the context of Buddhism itself, to be a locus of miraculous power. This was historically unrelated to the concept of inherent power known as *saksit*; rather, it was associated with the theory of *adhiṭṭhāna*, whereby one "resolves" one's accumulated merit to the accomplishment of a miraculous goal. Under the newly unified conceptual regime of "holy things," two fundamentally similar acts have become amalgamated: accessing the supernatural power of a god or spirit to obtain a boon and resolving one's merit before a Buddha image to obtain a boon. And thus the illusion of syncretism has been created. Religions have not "mixed" in this process: gods and spirits have always been a part of Buddhism, and Buddhists have always been able to ask for boons in front of Buddha images. What *have* mixed, or rather been mixed around, are the conceptual categories by which Thai Buddhists understand what they are doing—the result of a long history of interacting discourses (Pali Buddhist, Sanskritic Hindu, and modern Western) on the Siamese/Thai nexus.

The story does not end here, however. The interaction of Siamese Buddhist discourse with the modern Western discourse of religion has not only created the illusion of syncretism from an *etic* perspective; it has also provided the conceptual tools and space for Thai Buddhists to see their own practices as syncretistic. In part, this has simply been a result of the influence of Western scholarly theories of syncretism, seen, for example, in the adoption of the threefold Kirschan model in Thai as *phī phrām phut*. But it is also a result of the modern shift in meaning of the word *saksit* itself. Under its modern definition as "holy," *saksit* can be applied to almost anything in Buddhism, insofar as Buddhism is considered under the modern conceptual regime to be a religion. But the word *saksit* still retains its previous association with *saiyasāt*, which historically referred to what is now known as Hinduism but is now considered suspect under its modern meaning of "the occult." This situation has thus made it easy for Thai Buddhists of a reformist bent to criticize various aspects of Thai Buddhism, however old, traditional, and coherently Buddhist they may be, as "accretions" from Hinduism or local spirit religion. The interaction of Siamese Buddhist discourse with the modern Western discourse of religion has thus not only created the illusion that traditional Siamese Buddhism is syncretistic; it has, in a sense, made modern Thai Buddhism *prima facie* "syncretistic" insofar as it has forced it into the straitjacket of the modern concept of religion.

The story of the genealogy of *saksit* is complicated but also, I would offer, exciting, compelling, and deeply relevant to our understanding of religion in general. In order to make the entry of the reader into the worlds this story traverses as easy as possible, I have divided the book into two parts. In the first part, I trace the history of interacting discourses relevant for understanding *saksit*. I do so telescopically, starting first in Chapter 2 with Buddhism writ large as an implicit theology, turning then in Chapter 3 to the transformation of cosmopolitan formations on the Siamese nexus, and concluding in Chapter 4 by examining the specific place of the word *saksit* within the discourse of *saiyasāt* before and after the shift to modern conceptual categories. In the second part, I deconstruct the syncretistic model of Thai religion piece by piece by problematizing each of the elements of the threefold Kirschan schema. I begin in Chapter 5 by showing that "local religion" or "spirit religion" is a category that lacks specificity. I then show in Chapter 6 how Hindu discourses have exercised agency within Siamese Buddhism without syncretism and how the modern conceptual regime has made possible a new phenomenon of "Hindu enthusiasm" among Thai Buddhists. Finally I return in Chapter 7 to the example of Luang Phọ̄ Sōthọ̄n to demonstrate how the modern unification of Buddha images with gods and spirits as "holy things" has both created the illusion of syncretism and created the possibility for the criticism of traditional Buddhist practices as such.

PART I

CONTEXTUALIZING HOLY THINGS

2

Buddhism as Implicit Theology

The model of syncretism, as I argued in the introduction, is predicated on a misunderstanding of the normative structure according to which Buddhism polices its boundaries. Although it is not an emic term, "inclusivism" aptly describes the way Buddhism deals with rivals or potential rivals—it "includes" them in a subordinated role. The most foundational way Buddhism does so is by including "the gods"—whose existence was taken for granted in India long before the rise of Buddhism—in its cosmology. Gods and other beings deemed "supernatural" in the modern scientific worldview are included in Buddhism's cosmology as saṃsāric beings—beings who are subject to rebirth and therefore subordinate to the Buddha and anyone else who has attained *nirvāṇa*. There thus is no problem posed by the belief in or worship of gods and spirits in Buddhist societies. The perception that this does pose a problem is a result of the projection of implicit Christian norms onto the category of religion. Christianity, as a monotheistic tradition, does not include a multiplicity of gods in the same sense as does Buddhism. This has then been reflected in the construction of a novel "Buddhist Modernism" that downplays or eliminates gods and other supernatural beings to conform to modern Western sensibilities. As long as we recognize that Buddhist Modernism does not speak for Buddhism as a whole, and that Christian exclusivism is not shared by all religious traditions, the problem syncretism is meant to solve simply melts away.

This may seem to settle the issue, but there is actually much more to be learned about the inclusion of gods and spirits in Buddhism through a more thoroughgoing project of comparison between how Buddhism as a discourse creates, re-creates, and acts upon such beings and how Western discourses have done so. Scholars, even in Religious Studies, often bandy about such terms as "god" and "spirit" as if they are obvious, transcultural categories. Nothing could be further from the truth. "God" (even in its lowercase, plural form) is not a universal category. It is a category with a particular history—albeit one that is particularly long and widespread, leading to the impression that it is universal. Moreover, the distinction between "gods" and other

Holy Things. Nathan McGovern, Oxford University Press. © Oxford University Press 2024.
DOI: 10.1093/9780197759912.003.0002

beings now deemed supernatural (often referred to with the catch-all term "spirits") is not obvious. These two interrelated phenomena—the creation and sustenance of "gods" as a category and their demarcation from other types of beings—are a type of cosmological discourse that we can refer to as "theology."

In this chapter, I will argue that Buddhism should be understood as being, at a fundamental level, a theological enterprise. It delineates "god" as a category, defines what it means to be a god, and demarcates gods from other sorts of beings. The interactions with such beings that we are concerned with in this book, therefore, should be seen as central to Buddhist practice rather than peripheral. Furthermore, instead of simply asking how Buddhism polemically "deals with" gods and spirits—as if they are competitors from "other religions"—we should ask, following Bernard Faure, how Buddhist theology, along with other theological discourses, participates in the continual *creation* and *re-creation* of gods and spirits as, yes, socially constructed but also very much real beings.[1]

As I will show, Buddhism, in spite of its key strategic difference from Christianity vis-à-vis the category "god," arose in a cultural landscape that was similar to that in which Christianity arose and intervened upon that landscape in a similarly theological way. The two arose, respectively, near the Western and Eastern ends of the Indo-European cultural sphere and thus were party to the broader "deity discourse" the latter entailed. Moreover, both arose at a time when there were certain monistic tendencies already present in the local discourse about "the gods." Both then intervened by defining the category "god" vis-à-vis other categories of beings. There thus exists a broader similarity between their projects that has been obscured by two accidents of history: (1) the fact that Buddhism's cultural milieu never developed an *explicit* theological discourse paralleling that of the West and (2) the fact that Christianity's own theological project has been radically transformed by modern disenchantment.

In order to illustrate the parallel theological projects of Buddhism and Christianity, I will begin by introducing Jan Assman's useful concept of "implicit theology." After explicating Buddhism's implicit theological project in context, I will show how modern disenchantment has obscured a historically important aspect of theological discourse—the delineation of gods from other beings—that is just as central to Buddhism as it was historically to Christianity. Ultimately, this unpacking of Buddhism's theological project will give us the theoretical tools we need in the rest of the book to understand *both* why syncretism is a problematic model for the Thai propitiation of "holy things" *and* why this practice appears in a modern context to be so self-evidently syncretistic. In doing so, it will also provide an avenue for understanding how Hindu discourses could exercise agency within Buddhism, without taking recourse to the model of syncretism.

Implicit Theologies

Thinking of Buddhism as a theological discourse or theological project might seem uncanny at first glance because the word "theology" is so closely associated with an *explicit* theological discourse that is usually taken to culminate in the theologies of the Abrahamic religions, especially that of Christianity. This explicit theological discourse began with Plato's theorizing about the nature of God or the gods under the rubric of *theologia*, a term that he perhaps coined, continued with Aristotle's privileging of theology as one of the three branches of philosophy, and then through the intermediary of Hellenistic culture was taken up by intellectuals in all three of the Abrahamic traditions. The theologians of the Abrahamic traditions seized on the monistic trends in Platonic, Peripatetic, and later Neoplatonic thought to support, articulate, and think through the claim that the God of Israel is the only true God. Although this complex discourse has defined the horizons of modern thinking about theology, its full history has rarely been told; therefore, I have included a more detailed history of explicit theological discourse in Appendix A.

If we are being pedantic, there has only ever been one (multifaceted but ultimately connected) discourse of theology, namely, the set of discourses that actually use that word and can be traced back in some way to Plato, the philosopher who, as far as we know, first used it. It would be naïve, however, to think that no other such discourses, unconnected to this one, have ever existed, or that Plato created theology *ex nihilo*. The concept of "implicit theology" introduced by Jan Assman is therefore useful to refer to discourses that do similar work to that of theology from Plato onward but never actually call themselves such.[2] Classicists, for example, have fruitfully examined the theologies implicit in ancient Greek religion, dating well before Plato's first use of the word *theologia* itself.[3] Various tellings and retellings of myths (including but not limited to Hesiod's *Theogony*); works of drama, poetry, philosophy, and rhetoric; and even cultic practice embed within themselves various assumptions about the nature of the gods long before Plato wrote his *Republic*. These implicit theologies laid the groundwork for the explicit theology that Plato and those who looked to him for inspiration engaged in.

Ancient Greek sources, of course, are not the only locus of implicit theologies that would lay the groundwork for later explicit theology. Another source of implicit theology that would later have an enormous impact on explicit theological discourse is ancient West Semitic culture. This is the cultural sphere out of which Judaism arose, and thus it serves as an important precursor to Philo of Alexandria's articulation of Jewish thought in Greek theological terms, a project then taken up by Christian and Muslim intellectuals. As scholars of the Hebrew Bible and its historical milieu have shown, Israelite religion was "polytheistic" like that of its neighbors, and the "monotheism" that came to define Judaic religion by the Hellenistic period when Philo lived developed only slowly over centuries.[4] Based on his comparison of the Late Bronze Age Ugaritic literature to the literature of the Hebrew Bible, Mark Smith has shown that Israel was heir to a complex discourse on cosmic forces known by the West Semitic root *'l* (Akkadian *ilu*, Ugaritic *'il*, Hebrew *'ēl*). The etymology of this word is unknown, but the best guess is that it derives from a root that means "to be strong or preeminent," thus meaning something like "power."[5] The most basic distinction among these "powers," reflecting the basic center-periphery distinction in Mesopotamian cosmology, was between anthropomorphic deities and monstrous forces.[6] The former were in turn organized into a four-tiered hierarchy modeled on both a royal court and a patriarchal family. At the top was the leader, himself known as 'Ēl. (This word thus doubled as a broad category and as a proper name.) He was accompanied by his consort Athirat, known in the Bible as Asherah. The next tier was populated by his "children," subsidiary deities often associated with narrower domains of their own, including various natural forces. Baʿal, a warrior and storm god, was associated with this tier, but he was also seen as a bit of an outsider to the family of 'Ēl. The third tier is poorly represented in Ugaritic texts but would be represented by Kothar, a high-ranking royal servant. Finally, the fourth tier was populated by numerous low-ranking divinities who served the other gods, for example as messengers.[7]

Israelite monotheism emerged over the course of many centuries through a collapsing and hollowing out of the divine hierarchy just described. In the Hebrew Bible as it comes down to us, there is one God, known as both 'Ēl and Yahweh, and his divine council is mostly reduced to a broad group of low-ranking beings (i.e., the fourth tier), which are known today through the Greek term *ἄγγελοι* (i.e., angels; lit., "messengers"). The cults of Asherah and Baʿal are known but criticized,[8] and most of the intermediate gods of the second tier are suppressed or reduced to divine forces that are the expression of 'Ēl/Yahweh. This retrospective view of the biblical texts, however, belies a complex historical development. The original god of Israel, it appears, was 'Ēl—reflected in the name of Isra*el* itself. Yahweh was a warrior/storm god from a more southerly origin (the region around Sinai) who was incorporated into the divine council in the second tier as the god specifically responsible for Israel. In time, he became identified with 'Ēl himself, to the point that he took on the latter's attributes and role as chief deity.[9] During the period of the monarchy (first half of the first millennium BCE), there was already a tendency toward monolatry and henotheism in the exaltation of Yahweh as the national god. True monotheism, however, did not arise until the period of the Babylonian Exile in the sixth century BCE. It finds its culmination in the writings of so-called Second Isaiah (Isaiah 40–55), who not only promotes Yahweh from national god to God of the universe but also denies the existence of other gods.[10] As Smith writes, "The loss of identity as a nation changed Israel's understanding of the national god. Looming empires made the idea of a national god obsolete. Moreover, the rise of supranational empires suggested the model of the super-national god."[11]

The explicit theological discourse that later came to play a major role in the three Abrahamic traditions can thus be seen as having been forged by the merger of two implicit theological discourses that had taken similar if not identical trajectories. On the one hand, there was the discourse on *'ēl* found in the Levant, which culminated in the formation of a truly monotheistic Judaism in the sixth century BCE. On the other hand, there was the discourse on *θεός* in Greece, which culminated in Plato's monistic speculations under the rubric of *theologia*. These discourses were by no means identical, and it is not *a priori* obvious that *'ēl* and *θεός* are the same sort of thing, much less that the claims made by Jews (and later Christians and Muslims) about their God were compatible with the theoretical framework of Greek theology. Explicit theology in the Hellenistic period facilitated the difficult work of *translation*, not just of words but of categories of beings from one culture to another. As Mark Smith has shown, this process has been found going back to the most remote times of recorded history, in which various ecumenes have facilitated and even demanded the correlation of deities in one culture to those in others—the God of Israel being no exception.[12]

Even articulating this fact is made difficult, however, by the limits of the English language, which is itself a product of the very process of translation I am attempting to describe. Following Smith, I have chosen the word "deities" due to its rather generic quality in the English language, but ultimately the idea that there is any single category across which something is being translated is _itself_ a product of that very process of translation. Indeed, the word "deity" can be seen as the product of a very old discourse, an implicit theology, that has facilitated translatability across an even greater temporal and geographical expanse than what we have considered so far. That discourse is the broader Indo-European discourse, which stretches across most of Europe as well as Iran and northern India, with some now extinct forays elsewhere (Anatolian in Asia Minor, Tocharian in China). Much of what we now take for granted about "the gods" as a broad category is actually built upon this old and expansive discourse. As reconstructed by linguists, the word _*dyḗus_, which literally refers to the daylight sky, was used to refer to what we would now call a "high god." _*Dyḗus_ was also referred to as _Dyḗus ph_$_2$_tḗr_, or "Father Daylight Sky." This form was preserved in Greek as _Ζεύς Πατήρ_ (Father Zeus), in Latin as _Iuppiter_ (Jupiter), in Sanskrit as _Dyauṣ Pitṛ_, and in Old Norse as _Týr_ (from which we get _Tuesday_). The _vṛddhi_ form of _*dyḗus_, _*deywṓs_, was then used as a broad category for a class of beings, literally "celestials." This form is preserved in Latin as _deus_, in Sanskrit as _deva_, and in Avestan as _daēva_ (which was made demonic instead of divine in the Zoroastrian reform).[13] Modern English preserves the derivative forms _deity_, _divine_, and _divinity_ by way of Latin.

I should emphasize that the theology implied by linguistic reconstructions of Proto-Indo-European was embedded in a _discourse_, and as such was messy, contested, and nonteleological. We should not envision a Proto-Indo-European pantheon determining the course of all Indo-European religion, but rather an ongoing negotiation of cosmology through terms bequeathed by the Proto-Indo-European heritage. For example, it is ironic that although the Greek term _θεός_ from which we get "theology" bears a superficial resemblance to the Latin _deus_ and Sanskrit _deva_, it is actually a false cognate; the most important true cognate is instead in the proper name of the high god Zeus (equivalent to Proto-Indo-European _*Dyḗus_). Likewise, although this complex of Proto-Indo-European vocabulary for what we now call "the gods" does exist in Proto-Germanic, that is not actually where we get the word "god" from. This word, like modern German _Gott_, derives instead from Proto-Germanic _*guđán_, whose etymology is uncertain but may mean one who is "libated" or "invoked," which would refer to the role played by gods in cultic worship.[14] Nevertheless, "god" and all its Germanic cognates and antecedents were brought into conversation with the broader Indo-European discourse of "divinity" and narrower Hellenistic discourse of "theology" through acts of translation as the Germanic peoples came into contact with the Roman world and Christianity.

The Implicit Theology of *Devas* in Vedic India

Buddhism arose in a cultural context that in certain key ways was quite similar to Christianity. The latter, although deriving most immediately from the Semitic context of first-century Judaism, nevertheless spread in a world that was hegemonically dominated by Indo-European cultures, both Hellenistic and Roman. The Roman ecumene preserved the basic Indo-European cosmology of a sky god and his pantheon, forged out of a correlative translation that equated Roman Jupiter with Greek Zeus, as well as various other Roman and Greek gods with one another (and with certain non-Indo-European deities, such as those of the Egyptians). Likewise, the northern Indian ecumene in which Buddhism arose preserved the basic Indo-European cosmology with Indra as the sky god and a variety of other gods below him, as described in the Vedas. At the same time, there was an intellectual trend toward monism in the theology of Plato and Aristotle, which was paralleled in India by certain philosophical speculations that began in the *Ṛg Veda* and found their culmination in the Upaniṣads. The key difference was that this latter theological discourse, which I will outline here, was implicit rather than explicit.

Although the cosmology of the *Ṛg Veda* is overwhelmingly polytheistic, we find hints in its latest stage (Book X)[15] of a single ultimate god or principle behind the universe of multiplicity. For example, hymn X.129 muses about the origins of the cosmos and posits that at the beginning of time, "That one breathed without wind by its own power. There was nothing else beyond that."[16] It continues, "That one which was void, concealed by emptiness, was born by the power of heat."[17] The hymn thus posits a singular origin to the universe, but it ultimately ends on a note of uncertainty:

> Who really knows? Who here shall proclaim it? From where was it born?
> From where is this creation?

The gods are on this side of the creation of this (world). So who knows from where it came into being?
From where this creation came into being, whether it was produced or not—
He who is the superintendent of this (world) in the highest heaven surely knows . . . or maybe he doesn't know.[18]

The implicit theology here is similar to—if more tentative than—those we have already seen. The hymn suggests that there may be a highest god (*deva*)—akin to the 'Ēl of Levantine polytheism or *ὁ θεός* of Greek theology—but it stops short of certainty on this point. In any case, the *devas* (plural) are already being demoted here, insofar as they are said to be part of creation and thus ignorant of its origins.

Hymn X.121 of the *Ṛg Veda* shows a similar interest in identifying a singular, ultimate principle but is more confident in the end that it (he) exists. This is the famous hymn dedicated, as the tradition records, to a god named simply *Ka* (the Sanskrit word for "who?")—an ironic reference to the refrain of all but the last verse: "Which god shall we bestow with the oblation?" The first few of these verses will suffice to illustrate what this hymn is asking about with such a refrain:

The golden embryo came together in the beginning. Born the lord of what had become, he was singular.
He supports the earth and this heaven. Which god shall we bestow with the oblation?
Who is the giver of breath, the giver of strength, whose command all honor, whose command all gods honor,
Whose shadow is immortality, whose shadow is death—which god shall we bestow with the oblation?
Who, completely unique in greatness, became the king of the breathing, blinking, moving (world);
Who is lord of this (world of) two-footed and four-footed (creatures)—which god shall we bestow with the oblation?[19]

The next several verses continue in this vein; what this hymn is clearly seeking is one highest god, the creator and ruler of the universe, who should be the ultimate recipient of the offerings made in the Vedic sacrifice (*yajña*). In this case, however, the hymn ends on a confident note, stating that this god exists and giving him a name:

> Prajāpati, none other than you has encompassed all these who have been born.
> Let what desires we offer to you be ours. We would be lords of riches.[20]

The name Prajāpati here is not actually a name but a title, meaning literally "lord of creatures." Nevertheless, it was taken as a name by the tradition, leading to an elaborate mythology in the Vedas. As Jan Gonda and Greg Bailey have shown, Prajāpati appears frequently in the later Saṃhitā and in the Brāhmaṇa literature, particularly in cosmogonic myths.[21]

The latest stage of Vedic literature, the Upaniṣads, is often seen as a radical departure from earlier Vedic literature but in fact represents a natural continuity of speculations about the sacrifice found in the earlier Brāhmaṇas, only extending them to cosmic proportions by viewing the entire universe as a sacrificial altar.[22] The Upaniṣads know of Prajāpati, but they show an interest in finding the ultimate principle of the universe that is less anthropomorphic than the Prajāpati mythology that had been inspired by the *Ka* hymn. The oldest two Upaniṣads, the *Bṛhadāraṇyaka* of the *Śukla* (White) *Yajur Veda* and the *Chāndogya* of the *Sāma Veda*, both contain monistic speculations centering on two principles: *brahman* and *ātman*. The word *brahman* is derived from the verbal root *bṛh*, which means "to swell," and it refers, going back to the earliest strata of the Veda texts, to sacred speech uttered by *brāhmaṇas* (Brahmans) in their rituals. In the Upaniṣads, concerned as they are with enumerating "connections" (*bandhus*) between the microcosm of the sacrifice and the macrocosm of the universe,[23] *brahman* becomes a cosmic principle encompassing all reality. According to the *Chāndogya Upaniṣad*, "All this is *brahman*. Calmed, one should honor it.... After departing from here, I will reach that."[24] Likewise, the *Bṛhadāraṇyaka Upaniṣad* posits the *brahman* as an ultimate principle: "In the beginning this was just *brahman*. It knew only itself, (thinking,) 'I am *brahman*.' As a result, it became all."[25] This is followed by a short partial cosmogony in which *brahman* progressively creates the gods according to class (*varṇa*), paralleling the social classes of the *varṇa* system, followed by *dharma* (*BĀU* 1.4.11–14).

The word *ātman*, on the other hand, is simply the reflexive pronoun ("self") in Sanskrit. Speculations on the sacrifice in the Brāhmaṇa literature, however, had already treated *ātman* as a noun—referring to *a* or *the* self, an essence that can be built up through sacrifice, perhaps most spectacularly in the form of the bird-shaped sacrificial altar constructed out of bricks in the Agnicayana.[26] Like the *brahman*, the *ātman* too is elevated to a cosmic principle in the Upaniṣads. The *Bṛhadāraṇyaka Upaniṣad* contains a cosmogony (just prior to the *brahman*-based cosmogony cited above), in which *ātman* alone exists in the beginning. It said, "Here I am!" and thus became a human being (*puruṣa*). This *puruṣa* then split in two, creating a man and a woman. They copulated, and thus was created human beings and the other creatures of creation (*BĀU* 1.4.1–4). Perhaps the most famous articulation of the *ātman* in the Upaniṣads, however, is a noncosmogonic story in which Uddālaka Āruṇi teaches his son Śvetaketu through a series of metaphors, including banyan fruit seeds and salt dissolved in water. At the end of each metaphor, he says, "That which is this minuteness—of this self is this all. That is the truth; that is the self. Thus are you, Śvetaketu."[27]

Other passages make it clear that the *brahman* and the *ātman* are in fact identical. In the *Chāndogya Upaniṣad*, Prajāpati himself gives a progressive teaching to Indra about the *ātman*. At the end of each teaching, he speaks the same refrain: "This is the self. . . . This is immortal; this is free from fear; this is *brahman*."[28] Likewise, according to the *Bṛhadāraṇyaka Upaniṣad*:

> This very self is *brahman*—made of consciousness, made of mind, made of breath, made of sight, made of hearing, made of earth, made of water, made of wind, made of space, made of light, made of the lightless, made of desire, made of the desireless, made of anger, made of the angerless, made of *dharma*, made of *adharma*, made of everything. . . .
>
> Now, a man who does not desire—without desire, free of desire, desires attained, whose desire is the self—his breaths do not go up. Being simply *brahman*, he goes to *brahman* too.[29]

This Upaniṣadic theme of *ātman* and *brahman* as monistic principles would much later serve as the basis for the philosophical school of the Advaita Vedānta. Passages such as the one just cited would also serve as the motivation for renunciatory movements in ancient India, modeled in the Upaniṣads by the "going forth" of Yājñavalkya (*BĀU* 2.4) and followed by various *śramaṇa* groups like the Jains, Buddhists, and Ājīvakas, and later by orthodox Brahmanical renunciates known as *saṃnyāsins*.[30]

Although philosophical monism based on the Upaniṣads would be fully articulated in the Middle Ages in Śaṅkara's Advaita Vedānta, the more immediate aftermath of the speculations of the Upaniṣads was, in parallel to Greek theology in the Hellenistic world, theistic. This tendency is already seen in later Upaniṣads such as the *Śvetāśvatara*. This text, which appears to be proto-Śaiva in its repeated invocation of Rudra, speaks like the earlier

Upaniṣads of *brahman* and the *ātman* but subordinates them to God (*deva*), who is explicitly described as one (*ŚU* 1.10: *deva ekaḥ*). Theistic cosmologies and cosmogonies featuring a single supreme deity would of course become common in the epics and Purāṇas, with the *Bhagavad Gītā* embedded in the *Mahābhārata* being the most famous example. These theistic mythologies would become constitutive of two major sectarian movements—Vaiṣṇavism and Śaivism, centering on the worship of Viṣṇu and Śiva, respectively, as supreme deity—followed in time by Śāktism, an offshoot of Śaivism in which the Goddess is worshiped as supreme.

As I have shown in previous work, however, there is evidence that the rise of Vaiṣṇavism and Śaivism was preceded by a period in which Brahmā was worshiped as supreme. Pre-Mahāyāna Buddhist texts know nothing of Vaiṣṇavas and Śaivas but refer to Brahmans who worship Brahmā as the creator of the world and hope to attain soteriological union with him after they die (*DN* 13; *MN* 84). As Greg Bailey has shown, the mythology of Brahmā is in large part a continuation of the Vedic mythology of Prajāpati, and in post-Vedic literature Prajāpati usually appears not as an independent god but as an epithet of Brahmā.[31] Nevertheless, specific evidence for mythologies, cosmologies, and cosmogonies in the Brahmanical literature in which Brahmā is the supreme deity is surprisingly sparse. The best examples are to be found in the *Mārkaṇḍeya Purāṇa* and in the cosmogony at the beginning of the *Mānava Dharmaśāstra*.[32] Both of the epics contain passages that appear to come from a stage when Brahmā was considered supreme, but they have been eclipsed by the prevailingly Vaiṣṇava cast of the epics in the form they come down to us.[33] The relative lack of evidence in Brahmanical literature for a cult of Brahmā as supreme deity is likely due to the fact that Vaiṣṇavas and Śaivas quickly super-enthroned their own deities over Brahmā in imitation of the Buddhist super-enthronement of the Buddha over Brahmā,[34] as I will describe shortly. The result is that classical Hinduism preserved a great deal of mythology about Brahmā, but for the most part within Vaiṣṇava and Śaiva frameworks.

Buddhism's Intervention in Implicitly Theological Discourse in Ancient India

Buddhism intervened in ancient India's implicitly theological discourse—one that was moving in directions similar to those of implicit theological discourses further to the west—but it did so using a slightly different strategy than did Christianity. Building on the work of Philo and other Hellenized Jews, early Christians wedded Judaic monotheism, itself a product of a long Western Semitic discourse on *'ēl*, to Greek theology in order to argue that all of the *θεοί* recognized in Hellenistic discourse did not in fact belong to that category—with the sole exception of the God ('Ēl/Yahweh) of the Hebrew Scriptures, whom they equated with *ὁ θεός* of Greek theology. This strategy served to delegitimize the cultic practices surrounding the gods of the Hellenistic and broader Roman worlds, as well as discredit the stories ("myths" as opposed to "history")[35] surrounding them. Buddhism, however, performed a different maneuver on the Indo-Aryan discourse on *devas*. It recognized the existence of *devas* as a category and incorporated them extensively into its own growing mythology.

We see this already in the early *sūtra* literature. Repeatedly throughout the *sūtras*, the Buddha meets with, is honored by, and/or debates with *devas*. This was such a prevalent theme in the early literature that the compilers of the *Tipiṭaka* (Pali Canon) used the category *deva* to organize *suttas*. The *Sagāthāvagga* of the *Saṃyutta Nikāya* is divided into eleven *saṃyuttas*, four of which are god-themed: the *Devatāsaṃyutta* ("connected with divinities"), the *Devaputtasaṃyutta* ("connected with sons of gods"), the *Brahmasaṃyutta* ("connected with Brahmās"), and the *Sakkasaṃyutta* ("connected with Śakra [Indra]"). Generally speaking, in these *saṃyuttas* and elsewhere in the Canon, the gods, including Indra, show obeisance to the Buddha, marking him as hierarchically superior. Three *suttas* in the *Sakkasaṃyutta* (*SN* 1.11.18–20), in fact, go a step further. In each of these, Sakka joins his hands in reverential salutation to someone or some group, and his charioteer Mātali asks him whom he is honoring, given that he himself is honored by both gods and human beings. In the second of these *suttas*, Indra is honoring the Buddha himself. In the third, however, he is honoring the whole *saṅgha* of *bhikkhus*, and in the first, he honors all those who are virtuous, including Buddhist householders who make merit. In each case, Mātali responds with a standard verse:

> Best indeed in the world
> Are those whom you honor, Sakka.
> I too honor those
> Whom you honor, Vāsava.[36]

Thus does Buddhist inclusivism subordinate the gods not only to the Buddha but in fact to all Buddhists.

The reason for this subordination is illuminated by other passages that make clear that *devas* are impermanent saṃsāric beings just like humans. For example, in the *Sāleyyaka Sutta* (*MN* 41) the Buddha teaches that by acting in accordance with the *dhamma*, one can be reborn among a whole list of different levels of gods. This is a high reward, but other passages make it clear that even the gods do not live forever. For example, in the *Brahmajāla Sutta* (*DN* 1), the Buddha refers to certain "unconscious" *devas* who fall from that realm as soon as they have a perception and are reborn as human beings. Likewise, the cosmogony (so to speak) of the *Aggañña Sutta* (*DN* 27) states that periodically the universe contracts; when it does so, most beings are reborn in the world of Ābhassara Brahmā (a high heaven), and when the universe expands again, most fall away from that world and are reborn here in the human realm. Yet another *sutta* (*AN* 4.123) specifies that a person who masters one of the four *jhānas* (meditative absorptions) will upon death be reborn as a *deva* of a particular realm. The lifespan of each of these four types of *devas* is specified, ranging from one to five eons. At the end of the *deva*'s lifespan, he is reborn in hell, as an animal or as a hungry ghost—unless he had previously attained the state of nonreturner, in which case he simply attains *nibbāna*. In any case, Buddhist *suttas* make clear that *devas* are powerful, blissful beings experiencing the fruits of good karma, but they are not liberated from the cycle of rebirth.

Brahmās represent a special case of how *devas* are treated in the early Buddhist literature. In Brahmanical literature, *Brahmā* is usually treated as the name of a particular individual god, like Viṣṇu or Śiva. In the Buddhist *sūtra* literature, the situation is quite different. Brahmā refers to a *class* of beings, ranked even higher than the *devas*, who can then hold additional individual personal names. The *Brahmasaṃyutta* of the *Saṃyutta Nikāya*, for example, refers to a variety of Brahmās by name: Sahampati,[37] Baka, Subrahmā, Suddhāvāsa, Tudu, and Sanaṅkumāra.[38] Naomi Appleton has argued that this proliferation of Brahmās in the Buddhist imaginary is part of a deliberate polemical strategy.[39] As we saw, the concept of Brahmā, fusing the creator role of Prajāpati with the ultimate goal represented by the principle *brahman*, arose as a single supreme deity presaging (and later overshadowed by) the sectarian movements devoted to Viṣṇu and Śiva. By transforming Brahmā into a whole class of beings, the Buddhists "included" Brahmā but made it impossible for him to be the supreme deity: any particular Brahmā is just one of many and thus cannot be supreme.

This point is underlined by the *Brahmanimantanika Sutta* (*MN* 49), in which the Buddha becomes aware through his clairvoyance that a certain Brahmā named Baka[40] erroneously thinks of his heavenly world that "this, sir, is permanent, this is fixed, this is eternal, this is total, this is not subject to passing away; for this neither is born nor ages nor dies nor passes away nor arises, and other than this there is no further escape."[41] The Buddha then visits Baka in his heaven, tells him that he is wrong, and proves his superiority to Baka by making himself disappear through his supernatural power, a feat that Baka is not able to replicate. The *Brahmajāla Sutta* (*DN* 1) contains an anecdote that explains why Brahmās like Baka think they are supreme. It states that when the universe expands at the beginning of a cosmic cycle, a being is reborn as a Brahmā after falling from the higher Ābhassara realm. It occurs to him that it would be nice for other beings to exist, and quite by coincidence other beings fall from the Ābhassara realm and are reborn as companions of that Brahmā. As a result, that Brahmā erroneously comes to the conclusion, "I am Brahmā, the great Brahmā, the conqueror, the unconquered, the sure-seeing, the almighty, the lord, the maker, the creator, the best, the appointer, the master, father of all that have been and shall be. These beings were created by me."[42] Some of those in the Brahmā's retinue then fall from that state and are reborn as human beings, who are able to remember just their previous life and thus think they were created by a supreme deity called Brahmā. Thus is the cult of Brahmā that existed at the time of early Buddhism explained away—not by denying Brahmā's existence but by denying that he is a singular, omnipotent creator of the universe that one should strive to attain union with as the highest goal.

The cosmology that is implicit throughout the *sutta* literature was codified by the Theravāda tradition in the Abhidhamma. It divides the cosmos vertically into three "worlds": the world of desire (*kāmaloka*), the world of form (*rūpaloka*), and the formless world (*arūpaloka*). This is a clever Buddhist reinterpretation of the old Vedic cosmology of the "triple world," referring to the earth, the sky, and the intermediate region. While still conceived of vertically, the three levels are imbued with moral and soteriological significance. The lowest level includes all those beings who dwell on, below, or just above the earth. That includes (working karmically and to a certain extent physically upward) hell beings, animals, hungry ghosts (*petas*), *asuras* (the antigods parallel to the Titans of Greek tradition), human beings, and *devas*. There are six levels of *devas* in the *kāmaloka*, including the traditional Vedic gods led by Sakka (Indra) in a heaven called Tāvatiṃsa, which refers to their traditional number of "thirty-three." The *rūpaloka* and *arūpaloka* are inhabited by various types of Brahmās. These different levels of Brahmās are in turn mapped onto the four *rūpa jhānas* and four *arūpa jhānas*—three levels for each of the first three *rūpa jhānas*, seven levels for the fourth *jhāna*, and one level for each of the *arūpa jhānas*. Added together, there are thirty-one levels of beings in this Buddhist cosmos, ranked hierarchically according to their karma and mapped along a vertical axis that is both physical, extending upward from earth into the heavens, and soteriological, from ordinary sensual desire upward through the different levels of meditative absorption toward Awakening. Indeed, the total of thirty-one levels falls just one short of the traditionally "complete" number of thirty-two, implying that *nibbāna*, which of course cannot be represented in the cosmology because it is totally beyond it, is the thirty-second.[43]

The Abhidhammic cosmology also is structured horizontally. At the lower (vertical) level, the *kāmaloka*, the world is divided horizontally into "world-spheres" (*cakravāḍas*)[44] that stretch in every direction. Each *cakravāḍa* is a flat disk with a central land mass surrounded by an ocean. The land mass has circular rings of mountains in the center—the Himalayas in our world-sphere—with four continents pointing out from there in the four cardinal directions. The southern continent is Jambudvīpa, which corresponds to the Indian subcontinent in our world-sphere. At the very center of the concentric rings of mountains in the center of the disk is the highest mountain, Mt. Meru. The various levels of *deva*s dwell in heavens extending vertically from Mt. Meru, while the various levels of hell extend vertically below the disk of earth. Brahmās in the higher heavens of the *rūpa-* and *arūpaloka*s rule over multiple *cakravāḍas*, the number increasing as one goes up the vertical hierarchy.[45]

Buddhism thus intervened in the implicit theology of its day in a manner distinctly different from Christianity. Instead of seizing upon the monotheistic/monistic trend in the broader discourse and taking it to its natural conclusion, it went in the opposite direction, preserving and even extending the multiplicity of the gods. Some of the *deva*s mentioned in the Buddhist scriptures (most importantly Sakka = Indra) are well known from the Vedas, but many levels of heaven and their associated classes of gods have clearly been invented. Most important, though, the individual god Brahmā, who was the culmination of the monistic trend in Indian thought up to that time, was fractured into a plethora of different classes of beings who actually take up the vast majority of the cosmological schema (twenty out of thirty-one levels). To reiterate, although modernist forms of Buddhism attempt to argue otherwise, this cosmology, and its embedded theological claims, was central to Buddhism's project. It maps out the workings of karma and the structure of *saṃsāra*, the "world" from which Buddhism promises escape. Gods are not simply mythological creatures that the unenlightened mistakenly believe in; they are real agents in the Buddhist cosmos who interact with the Buddha and in many cases are his devotees. Gods are not immortal, but they are long-lived and powerful. Being reborn as a god is a reward for good karma in this life, a "good destination" (*sugati*) in standard Buddhist parlance. Buddhas themselves live as gods in their second-to-last life in a heaven called Tusita. This was true of the Buddha Sakyamuni, and it is true of Metteyya (Skt. Maitreya), who dwells in Tusita as a god as he awaits his future rebirth as a human being, when he will become the next Buddha.[46]

Modern Disenchantment and Buddhism's Theological Project

In spite of this key difference, however, Buddhism's theological project is on a deeper level quite similar to Christianity's. In a sense the difference between the two is mostly semantic. Both have a singular soteriological goal—represented by God in Christianity and *nirvāṇa* in Buddhism—and both elevate this goal by demoting in some sense the gods of the prevailing Indo-European discourse. This deeper structural similarity has, however, been obscured by a particular movement in modern Western thought—disenchantment—which has radically transformed Christianity's traditional theological project and thus rendered uncanny aspects of Buddhism that are in fact quite similar to premodern Christianity and explicit theological discourse in general.

Although explicit theology from Plato to the Abrahamic traditions shares from the beginning a common thread of interest in singularity, this is not the same as "monotheism" as it is understood today. Plato and Aristotle, for example, spoke about God, but that does not mean they denied the existence of the many gods of Greek mythology. This cosmology of singularity in multiplicity was systematized by the Neoplatonists through their theory of emanation from the One. Even the theologians of the Abrahamic traditions were generally open to multiplicity in ways that differed in little more than semantics from "pagan" theologians. True, they were committed to the principle that the category "god" (expressed in the Hellenistic cultural sphere with the Greek word *θεός*) belonged to only a single being. For this reason, they could not countenance a large pantheon of "gods," but they were perfectly comfortable with a vast hierarchy of angels, whose existence was in fact demanded by scripture.

In addition, although early Christians were labeled "atheists" by their contemporaries because of their refusal to sacrifice to the gods,[47] they did not necessarily deny the *existence* of the gods as such. For example, in his First Letter to the Corinthians, Paul writes, "Look at Israel according to the flesh; are not those who eat the sacrifices participants in the altar? So what am I saying? That meat sacrificed to idols is anything? Or that an idol is anything? No, I mean that what they sacrifice, [they sacrifice] to demons, not to God, and I do not want you to become participants with demons."[48] This category of "demons" became important over time to Christians and subsequently to Muslims as an army serving Satan parallel to the angels of God. Originally, however, this category was, in the Hellenistic world, borrowed from Greek theology in a clever stratagem to *demote*, rather than totally deny, the gods (*θεοί*).[49] The category "demon" (*δαίμων*) has a very old pedigree in Greek literature, referring to veiled forces that work on human beings; as such it could be used to refer to the gods but was not synonymous with "god." Plato, however, established the *daimones* as an intermediate class of beings between human beings and the gods. He also suggested that those who died in war should be honored as *daïmones*, and later Hellenistic grave inscriptions generalized this principle to refer to the dead person in the grave as a *daimon*.[50] The Jewish scholars who created the Septuagint made use of this term to translate a passage from Deuteronomy that is clearly being alluded to by Paul in his admonition to the Corinthians: "They offered sacrifice to demons, to 'no-gods,' / to gods whom they had not known before."[51] This laid the groundwork for the more expansive Christian project of demoting gods to demons, which, as Christianity stamped out its pagan rivals in late antiquity and the early Middle Ages, gave way to a cosmology that included demons as a class of malevolent beings.

Islam inherited from late antique Christianity the basic dualistic distinction between God (Allāh) and angels (*malā'ikah*) on the one hand and the Devil (Iblīs) and the demons (*shayāṭīn*) on the other. It also, however, allowed, as in early Greek theology, for an intermediate class of beings, known in Arabic as *jinn*. This class of beings is not a popular accretion but rather is explicitly referred to in the Qur'an as having been created by God as rational beings in parallel to humans, albeit created out of wind and fire instead of earth and water.[52] Unlike demons and angels, but like human beings, they are morally ambiguous: they have the capacity for both good and evil, and like human beings, they will be held accountable for their actions on the Day of Judgment.[53] They are thus somewhat similar to the older conception of *daimones*.

Although in Christianity the category "demon" shifted to the negative, the idea of morally ambiguous intermediate beings was not lost and continued for over a millennium.[54] As Euan Cameron has convincingly demonstrated, even in the late Middle Ages European Christians lived in a universe densely populated with such beings.[55] Much of the history of Christian theological thought can be seen as an attempt by the intellectual elite to regulate popular beliefs in various spiritual beings. Already in the writings of the late Church Fathers, epitomized especially by Augustine, we see a clear articulation of the view that the gods of paganism are not just demons, but that said demons are evil, allied with the Devil. Nevertheless, Augustine was himself influenced by Neoplatonism, a system that is quite amenable to a multiplicity of types of spiritual beings; his attempt to distinguish sharply between good and evil spirits was thus in large part an aspirational attempt to turn people away from paganism and toward Christianity.[56]

The rediscovery of classical scholarship in Western Europe in the twelfth and thirteenth centuries, in large part through the mediation of Arab sources, led to a retrenchment of the project of absolute cosmological dualism that ultimately resulted, paradoxically, in the disenchantment of the Enlightenment. Because the scholarship that sparked this revolution in Western European thought (e.g., Averroes) tilted Aristotelian, the Scholastic theologians of the era, epitomized by Thomas Aquinas, systematized their theology on the basis of mostly Aristotelian assumptions. These assumptions, as taken up by Aquinas and the Scholastics, required that spiritual beings be incorporeal and severely limited the categories they could belong to, thus reinforcing a rigid distinction between good and evil spirits.[57] Late medieval discourse on "superstition"—an old category going back to pre-Christian Rome, subsequently modified to take on a Christian meaning—used this rigid distinction to reject various popular practices that were not sufficiently in accord with official Church teaching and ritual. If a practice could not be shown to be sufficiently in line with the Church as the representative of Christ on Earth, then it was "superstition"—that is, an appeal to demons. There was no room for a middle ground of popular practices to manipulate or work with morally neutral or ambiguous beings.[58]

The late medieval Scholastic worldview of a strict dichotomy between good and evil spirits, with the concomitant discourse against superstition, paradoxically laid the groundwork for modern disenchantment. First, in the sixteenth century, Luther and the other Reformers took the argument against popular "superstitions" and turned it against the Church itself. That is, starting from the premise that grace is dispensed directly by God to the believer who has faith, they argued that the rituals of the Church were *themselves* superstitious rites that appealed to demons.[59] Then, beginning in the mid- to late seventeenth century, rationalist thinkers went a step further and critiqued the very idea of angels and demons.

The questioning of the existence of angels and demons was in part a continuation of the trend to expand the category of "superstition" to cover an increasingly wide variety of beliefs and practices. But it was also rooted in an older theological backlash against the Aristotelian philosophical premises of Aquinas and the Scholastics. Known as "nominalism," this revolution in Western thought was motivated by a key concern of Christian theology: the need to preserve the omnipotence of God. Nominalists rejected the concept of universals—so-called universals are mere "names" imputed by human beings, thus the moniker "nominalist"—because they limit God's ability to act arbitrarily according to his will. As Michael Allen Gillespie has argued, much of modern Western thought, including modern science and philosophy, can be traced to this late medieval theological dispute.[60] Enlightenment thinkers, building on the nominalist rejection of universals and Protestant critique of Catholicism, delighted in ridiculing Aristotelian categories. One of the most radical of these thinkers, Thomas Hobbes, was thoroughly committed to the Calvinist God of his upbringing[61] but rejected demonology as a relic of paganism and ridiculed the Aristotelian/Thomistic conception of "incorporeal substance" that angels and demons were supposed to consist of as a contradiction in terms.[62]

Although even today the modern Western world has arguably never truly become disenchanted,[63] the *project* or *ideal* of disenchantment has had a powerful influence on the perception and construction of "world religions." For no religion is this more the case than Buddhism. The entire construction of Buddhism as uniquely rational, scientific, and devoid of the supernatural is, as numerous scholars have argued,[64] rooted in the Protestant conception of "true religion" being located in scripture and the Orientalist rejection of actual Asian practice as "decadent." But even insofar as Buddhist Modernism is a product of privileging normative scriptures over actual practice, it is not honest in doing so, for *the Buddhist scriptures themselves* make it clear that the cosmos is populated by gods and other supernatural beings. The idea that "true Buddhism" rejects the existence of supernatural beings is ultimately and irreducibly a projection of a modern Western fantasy, namely the fantasy of disenchantment—which in turn, as I have just shown, is the product of a very specific and historically contingent set of twists and turns in the explicit discourse of theology.

The Cosmological Agency of Buddhist Implicit Theology

Disenchantment has obscured a deep similarity in the theological projects of Christianity and Buddhism: both elevate a singular soteriological goal by demoting "the gods" in the plural, reshaping the cosmology of multiplicity in the process. In Christianity, this was accomplished through a category change: the *θεοί* of Hellenistic discourse were not *θεοί* but *δαιμώνες*. In Buddhism, on the other hand, *deva*s remained as a category, but they were made mortal and thus part of the cycle of *saṃsāra*. Their very multiplicity served to accentuate the vast expanse of *saṃsāra* and thus highlight the exceptionalism of *nirvāṇa*—just as the multiplicity of demons in early Christianity redounded to the glory of the one true God as Jesus and his followers channeled God's power to defeat them. In both cases, the theological project at play is implicated in the classification of a great scheme of different categories of "supernatural" beings in the cosmos. This fact has been obscured by the trend toward a rationalistic rejection of supernatural beings in the modern West, but traditional Christian cosmology was in fact just as complex and characterized by multiplicity as the Buddhist—filled with angels, demons, and other intermediate beings.

Indeed, even though early Buddhists, unlike early Christians, were interested in defining many "gods," they did not define *every* supernatural being as a god. This caveat is important to understanding their theological project, as gods are defined primarily through their association with good karma. Other supernatural beings were defined through association with bad karma. The punishment for the most grievous sins in Buddhism is of course hell, but beings in hell are not so relevant to the daily lives of human Buddhists because they are at a physical distance. More immediately relevant are hungry ghosts (P. *petas*, Skt. *pretas*), who wander the earth with insatiable hunger as a punishment for past greed. The early Buddhist tradition clearly used the twin supernatural types of *devas* and *petas* as examples to encourage the pursuit of merit and avoidance of sin, in accordance with the Buddhist teaching of the *dhamma*. Two books found in the *Khuddaka Nikāya* of the *Sutta Piṭaka*, the *Vimānavatthu* and the *Petavatthu*, respectively contain poems in which individual gods and ghosts explain what meritorious or unmeritorious deeds they committed in their past life that led to their present rebirth.

As in medieval Christianity, however, the mapping of the dichotomous logic of merit and sin in Buddhism onto the cosmos has never been complete. There are several categories of creatures, featured in the early Buddhist scriptures and prominent in the Buddhist imaginaries of countries like Thailand to this day, that are morally ambiguous. The most important of these, both in the Pali texts and in Thai Buddhism, are *yakkhas* (Skt. *yakṣas*) and *nāgas*. The former are anthropomorophic beings that are not human but not quite gods,[65] while the latter are serpentine creatures similar to Chinese dragons. There are many such categories of beings, however, and their precise definition or distinction from one another is not always clear. The cacophony of often ambiguous spirit-deities in Indian Buddhism has been studied extensively by Robert DeCaroli, who argues that the early Buddhist *saṅgha* actively "sought out and absorbed spirit-deities into its fold" as a "methodology for outward expansion, a means of signaling the *saṃgha*'s purity, and as an act of monastic courage and compassion."[66]

Thus, in spite of the key difference in strategy between Buddhism and Christianity in intervening in the prevailing theological discourse, the end result of their theologies is structurally quite similar. In both cases, there is a singular transcendent goal.[67] The rest of the cosmos is then inhabited by a vast array of creatures that are neither human nor animal ("supernatural," according to modern parlance) and are taxonomized in large part, but also incompletely, by the moral concerns of the respective religion. Buddhism is thus just as theological a project as Christianity because it is equally concerned with defining "god"—both what it is and what it is not—as a category derived from Indo-European discourse. And like Christianity it sought to *demote* the gods as a collective, although it accomplished this goal in a different way, not by switching them to a different category but by making them mortal and subject to rebirth. "God" is thus an incredibly important and productive category in Buddhism, both directly through the myths and cults it spreads, reproduces, and encourages, and negatively through the potential to define certain classes of beings as not gods.

Moreover, insofar as other discourses also intervene upon the beings that Buddhist theology classifies as gods (or not), this theological work opens a space for those other discourses to exercise agency within Buddhism. This is, to be clear, not syncretism. It is not that Buddhism "mixes" with other religions; rather, multiple theological discourses, Buddhist and otherwise, have participated in the continual social construction and reconstruction of supernatural beings, and Buddhism's implicit theology *necessarily* intervened upon the objective reality of supernatural beings whose construction it was only one party to out of many. In the next two chapters, I will trace out how this process has played out for Thai Buddhism: first, by situating Siamese Buddhist discourse within the broader context of transforming cosmopolitan structures in Southern Asia, and then by examining the specific way in which non-Buddhist discourses in that broader context have exercised agency within Siamese Buddhist discourse.

3

Situating Siam in History

In Chapter 2, we began with the broadest context for the Thai practice of *kānbonbānsānklāo*: the Buddhist ideological context writ large. In this chapter, we will move to the more immediate cultural context. In a general sense, that cultural context is Thai, but for the purposes of diachronic analysis, it behooves us to be a bit more precise than this. Thailand, after all, is a modern nation-state, and like all nation-states, its historical existence is largely a projection of present-day realities into the past. Contemporary Thai discourse usually divides the country into four regions: the Northern Region, the Northeast Region (Īsān), the Central Region, and the Southern Region. These regions roughly correspond to historical polities that were fused into the modern nation-state of Thailand in the late nineteenth century.

The Northern Region corresponds in large part to the historical kingdom of Lānnā, centered at Chiang Mai. Lānnā flourished from the thirteenth century until 1558, when it was conquered and made a tributary to the Burmese. In the late eighteenth century, as the Siamese reestablished autonomous rule with a new capital at Bangkok, they expelled the Burmese from Lānnā. Over the course of the nineteenth century the latter became increasingly integrated within the Siamese kingdom, which was fashioning itself into a modern nation-state along Western models.

The Northeast Region, known as Īsān, corresponds to a portion of the historical kingdom of Lān Xāng, the bulk of which comprises the modern country of Laos. Lān Xāng flourished from the fourteenth century until the beginning of the eighteenth century, with its capital at Luang Phabāng. In the early eighteenth century, a succession dispute led to the split of the kingdom into two and then three parts: Luang Phabāng, Viang Can (Vientiane), and Campāsak. These kingdoms became vassals of Bangkok during the Siamese restoration of the late eighteenth century. A rebellion in the early nineteenth century led the Siamese to sack Viang Can and force a large proportion of the population to migrate south of the Mekong River, in the region that is now known as Īsān. Siam made an effort in the nineteenth century to incorporate the Lao kingdoms, just as it did with Lānnā. In 1893, however, France sent

Holy Things. Nathan McGovern, Oxford University Press. © Oxford University Press 2024.
DOI: 10.1093/9780197759912.003.0003

gunboats to Bangkok and forced the Siamese to cede claim to the bulk of its Lao holdings, leaving it with only the repopulated region of Īsān, what once would have been southern Lān Xāng.

In this book, I am not concerned primarily with the North and Northeastern regions. Although they, like other regions outside of modern Thailand, have long been the home of speakers of Tai languages, until relatively recently they had a political and cultural existence quite separate from the polity that evolved into the modern nation-state of Thailand. This polity, known until recent times as Siam, corresponded throughout most of its history in large part to what is now known as Central Thailand. Siam emerged in the thirteenth century as a maritime polity centered at Ayutthayā, in the wake of the wane of the Angkorian Empire. Over the course of the fourteenth and fifteenth centuries, Ayutthayā/Siam and a more northerly Tai kingdom at Sukhōthai became fighting and royal-lineage moieties, culminating in the sixteenth century when a Sukhōthai-derived dynasty was established in Ayutthayā and the two kingdoms were fused. The resulting Siamese culture was a fusion of Khmer and Tai culture and of maritime and hinterland orientations. Siam became an increasingly powerful polity in the region, its main rival being the Burmese to the west, resulting in major wars in which Ayutthayā was captured in the sixteenth century and again in the eighteenth century. In the second of these, the Burmese completely sacked Ayutthayā, and the restoration of Siamese suzerainty resulted in the establishment of new capitals first in Thonburī and then in Bangkok. The Chakri Dynasty that was founded in Bangkok still reigns, although a revolution in 1932 established a constitutional monarchy, and the name of the country was changed from Siam to Thailand in 1939.

The Southern Region has a somewhat autonomous culture from that of Central Thailand, as evinced by its unique dialects, but its historical relationship with Siam goes much further back than the Northern Region or Īsān. Several old kingdoms were found on the peninsula, the most important of which was Tāmbraliṅga, centered at Nakhọn Sī Thammarāt, but this city became a semi-autonomous tributary of Ayutthayā early in Siam's history. Evidence points to frequent raids by the Siamese down along the peninsula from the late thirteenth century as far as Malacca. Any claim to suzerainty over the southernmost, Malay-speaking part of the peninsula was lost to the British in the eighteenth and nineteenth century, but several Malaysian sultans maintain Siamese titles of nobility to this day. The northern part of the peninsula, on the other hand, known today as Southern Thailand, has long been home to speakers of Tai dialects and can be considered historically a part of Siam, albeit a somewhat autonomous and culturally distinct one. It is thus less a focus of my study in this book than the Central Region, the geographical center of Siam and home to its historically most important cities, including Sukhōthai, Ayutthayā, and Bangkok.

As I discussed in the introduction, there has been a shift in recent decades in scholarship on Southeast Asia away from the model of Indianization pioneered by George Coedès and toward models of localization. In the wake of this shift, there has also been a shift in scholarship on Theravāda Buddhism away from models of syncretism toward understanding elements of lived Southeast Asian (and Sri Lankan) Buddhism primarily in terms of the Pali *imaginaire*. Coined by Steven Collins in his magnum opus, *Nirvana and Other Buddhist Felicities*, the term "Pali *imaginaire*" refers to "a mental universe created by and within Pali texts, which remained remarkably stable in and within the traditional period, but which moved, as a developing whole, through various times and places within the premodern material-historical world."[1] Several scholars of Theravāda Buddhism, including Justin McDaniel, Christian Lammerts, and Erik Davis,[2] have argued that seemingly anomalous or "syncretistic" aspects of religion in Theravāda Buddhist cultures can in fact best be explained primarily through reference to the Pali *imaginaire*.

At first glance, these two shifts—from Indianization to localization and from syncretism to the Pali *imaginaire*—may appear to be unrelated, or even at cross-purposes.[3] It is indeed true that, to a certain extent, the shift to the Pali *imaginaire* has been a product of a debate over syncretism in Religious Studies at large unrelated to the debate over Indianization in Southeast Asian Studies. Nevertheless, Indianization, as it was articulated by Coedès, provided grist for the syncretistic mill insofar as it put a large emphasis on the historical presence of Hinduism in Southeast Asia, reflected in the original French term used by Coedès, *hindouisation*. The shift toward explaining Southeast Asian Buddhism primarily in terms of the Pali *imaginaire* reflects the downfall of Indianization insofar as it eschews syncretistic explanations of seemingly "Hindu" elements of religion in Theravāda countries as coming from the classical period of Indianization described by Coedès. Indeed, as Brown, Lammerts, and Prapod have aptly shown in their work, much of the region where Theravāda Buddhism is practiced in Southeast Asia today has evidence of Pali Buddhism going back centuries, to the early first millennium.[4] The model proposed by earlier scholars in which there was a sudden shift to Theravāda Buddhism in Southeast Asia in the thirteenth century has been conclusively discredited.[5]

Nevertheless, we should be careful not to allow important critiques of earlier research to efface the value of that research. It is true that evidence for the practice of Pali Buddhism goes back to the first millennium among the Pyu and Burmese in what is now Myanmar and among the Mon Dvāravatī culture in what is now Central Thailand. The same cannot be said, however, for the Khmer culture in Cambodia. In the easternmost region of what is now the Theravāda world, there was a long history of patronage of "Hindu" cults, particularly Śaivism, as well as of Mahāyāna Buddhism. For the Khmer, the late thirteenth century really did witness a shift to Theravāda Buddhism from a theretofore quite different religious culture.[6]

Siam represents a uniquely liminal zone within what came to be the Theravāda Buddhist world. On the one hand, it is located in the heartland of the old Mon Dvāravatī culture, which as just mentioned has evidence for the practice of Pali Buddhism going back to the early first millennium. On the other hand, that same region was heavily influenced by Khmer culture near the end of the Angkorean Empire, from the tenth to the twelfth centuries, evidenced by numerous Khmer monuments found in modern-day Thailand, such as Prāsāt Phimāi and Phnọm Rung.[7] In addition, it had an early relationship with Nakhọ̄n Sī Thammarāt, the center of the old kingdom of Tāmbraliṅga that, like the Khmer, had a long history of patronage of Hindu cults, especially Śaivism. Siam thus presents an interesting case within Theravāda Southeast Asia that both, like Burma to the west, is amenable to explanations from the Pali *imaginaire* and, like Cambodia to the east, complicates attempts to explain its religious culture *solely* in terms thereof.

In this chapter, I will argue that Siam needs to be understood historically as existing on the nexus of transforming cosmopolitan structures. It emerged in the context of a major shift in not just Southeast Asia but Southern Asia at large with the collapse of the Sanskrit Cosmopolis and the concomitant end of what Alexis Sanderson has dubbed the "Śaiva Age." The Sanskrit Cosmopolis was replaced, in much of Southern Asia, with a Persianate Cosmopolis that brought with it Islam. Even among populations that did not convert to Islam and countries that did not become part of the Persianate Cosmopolis, however, the rise of the latter led to significant cultural and religious shifts. In Sri Lanka and much of mainland Southeast Asia, this took the form of the rise of a Pali Cosmopolis, which drew upon the old Pali Buddhist culture of part of that region but also reinvented it by imitating the structure of the collapsing Sanskrit Cosmopolis. I will argue that the unique continuities between the old Sanskrit Cosmopolis and the newer Pali Cosmopolis created a conduit for the influence of an emerging "Hinduism" within the Theravāda Buddhism of early modernity.

The Sanskrit Cosmopolis and the Śaiva World

Although Siam throughout its history has made legitimating and creative reference to the Pali *imaginaire*, the space that it occupies was once part of an older cosmopolitan order of which Southeast Asia was but a part. This cosmopolitan has aptly been dubbed the "Sanskrit Cosmopolis" by Sheldon Pollock. It stretched across both South Asia and Southeast Asia, a superregion that recent scholars have dubbed "Southern Asia," and whose importance has been obscured by its Cold War division into two separate regions.[8] As Pollock emphasizes, the Sanskrit Cosmopolis "did not come into being simultaneously with the appearance of the Sanskrit language."[9] Instead, it began over a thousand years later, around the beginning of the first millennium CE, with two new inventions: *kāvya*, or written literature, and *praśasti*, or inscriptional royal panegyric.[10] Prior to that time, Sanskrit was restricted to the specialized use of Brahmans, and royal inscriptions were issued in local Prakrits.[11] The shift to Sanskrit in its "cosmopolitan" usage was signaled by the ca. 150 CE inscription of Rudradāman, a Western Kṣatrapa ruler in Gujarat.[12] Pollock suggests that the Śakas (Indo-Scythians), of whom the Western Kṣatrapas were a branch, may have appropriated Sanskrit in this novel way precisely because they were outsiders to Indian civilization.[13] The use of Sanskrit as a medium of cosmopolitan communication spread quickly throughout Southern Asia and became standard as such for over a thousand years. To this day, alphabets across this broad superregion, including such geographically separated examples as Tibetan, Devanāgarī (used to write Hindi and Nepali), Sinhala, and Khmer, bear the imprint of the Sanskrit Cosmopolis insofar as they are designed on a Sanskritic model.

Pollock is at pains in his work to argue that the dawn of the Sanskrit Cosmopolis was primarily political and did not have anything to do with religion or Brahmanism. In support of this argument, he points to the use of Sanskrit to write *kāvya* by authors of various religious affiliations in the first millennium,[14] as well as the fact that use of Sanskrit or Prakrit in royal inscriptions in the transitional period of the early first millennium was not correlated with sectarian affiliation (i.e., there exist Buddhist inscriptions in Sanskrit and Brahmanical inscriptions in Prakrit).[15] Johannes Bronkhorst has questioned this conclusion, pointing to the fact that the patronage of Brahmans spread across Southern Asia at roughly the same time that the use of Sanskrit as a cosmopolitan language spread over that same area.[16] He notes that there is a rough (though not complete) correspondence between use of Sanskrit and acceptance of the Brahmanical *varṇa* system—including in Rudradāman's inscription.[17] Further, he argues, following Pollock's observation that Sanskrit *praśasti* appears to have begun among foreign Śakas, that "[t]heir motivation in promoting Sanskrit was presumably a desire to establish themselves as legitimate Indian or at least Indianized rulers, and *to curry the favor of the educated Brahmanical elite*."[18] Moreover, Bronkhorst has convincingly shown that the use of Sanskrit by Buddhist authors (e.g., Aśvaghoṣa in his *Buddhacarita*) is not a sign that the adoption of Sanskrit had nothing to do with Brahmanism, but rather that what he calls the "new Brahmanism" was so successful that its basic premises about the order of society came to be accepted even by Buddhists.[19]

The Sanskrit Cosmopolis, therefore, though certainly geographically widespread and in a sense "ecumenical," was not ideologically neutral. It served to promote and encode a particular view of society. In my own previous work, I have referred to this ideology as "Neo-Brahmanism" (a slight modification from Bronkhorst's "new Brahmanism") to indicate an appeal to older conceptions of Brahmanhood found in the Vedas that was nonetheless radically new. The proponents of Neo-Brahmanism, from the authors of the Dharma Sūtras onward, valorized Sanskrit, knowledge of the Vedas, Vedic ritual, and the *varṇa* system. They also, most importantly, valorized the householder lifestyle and production of children over celibate lifestyles being promoted by *śramaṇa* groups—although ultimately they were forced to make concessions on this point that opened up a space for renunciation within classical Hinduism.[20] The adoption of Sanskrit for use in royal inscriptions should therefore not be seen as a random event, but rather as the culmination of an ideological battle that had been fought since the late first millennium BCE—through the composition of *sūtra* literature to valorize ritual and *varṇa*, through the composition of epics to project these values into a creatively Vedicized past, and through the use of Sanskrit in novel ways to do so.[21]

Indeed, even when looked at over the *longue durée*, the role played by "religion" in the Sanskrit Cosmopolis—insofar as this Western concept applies to the context of medieval Southern Asia—cannot be denied. Both the temporal and the geographical extent of the Sanskrit Cosmopolis correspond in large part to what Sanderson has called "the Śaiva Age." This period, beginning around the fifth century CE, has a slight time lag behind the beginning of the Sanskrit Cosmopolis. Indeed, it can be seen as a transformation in the Neo-Brahmanical project that had impelled the Sanskrit Cosmopolis in the first place. As Sanderson writes, "[W]hile kings continued to accept their role as the guardians of the brahmanical order (*varṇāśramaguruḥ*), their personal religious commitment generally took the form of Buddhism, Jainism, or, more commonly, devotion to Śiva, Viṣṇu, the Sun-God (Sūrya/Āditya), or the Goddess (Bhagavatī)."[22] Of these, Śaivism dominated, which is to say that evidence for the personal allegiance of kings and endowments of temples overwhelmingly favors Śiva and Śaiva institutions. This was true not only in the subcontinent itself but also in Khmer country, Champa, Java, and Bali in Southeast Asia,[23] thus covering the expanse of Southern Asia, making it coterminous with the scope of the Sanskrit Cosmopolis.

Śaiva dominance was seen not only in direct patronage of Śaivism but in the influence that Śaivism had on other sects in the medieval period, taking the form of the pan-sectarian movement that modern scholars retroactively refer to as "Tantra," after the genre of texts that its principles and practices were written in. By far the second most popular object of patronage during the Śaiva Age was Mahāyāna Buddhism, which gave rise to the Tantric Vajrayāna at this time. Sanderson shows that Tantric Buddhism developed through the adaptation of Śaiva and Śākta (the former's more radical offshoot, focusing on the Goddess) models.[24] This adaptation of Buddhism to Śaivism in the medieval period can thus be seen as a continuation of its earlier adaptation to Neo-Brahmanism in antiquity, as described by Bronkhorst. Śaivism itself, although unorthodox in some of its rhetoric, was mostly in conformity with the Neo-Brahmanical project. As Sanderson writes:

> [Śaivism] was careful to insist not only that the Brahmanical scriptures that govern [Brahmanical] observance are exclusively valid in their own domain but also that their injunctions are as binding on Śaivas after their initiation as they were before it if they remained in that domain as active members of society. Śaiva ascetics were allowed a degree of choice in this matter, at least in theory, but householders were not. The religion of the Śaivas, then, was not Śaivism alone but rather Śaivism and Brahmanism, a fact born[e] out not only by their literature but also by biographical data and the epigraphic record of the activities of Śaiva kings.[25]

Śaiva dominance should therefore not be seen as incidental to the Sanskrit Cosmopolis with which it largely coincided nor at odds with the Neo-Brahmanical project that helped to fuel the latter. The Neo-Brahmanical vision of society provided the mundane horizon against which various transcendental sectarian movements, dominated by Śaivism, defined themselves, and the Sanskrit Cosmopolis provided the medium through which this entire ideological system was disseminated.

The continued legacy of the Sanskrit Cosmopolis can be seen in Thailand to this day. One of the most obvious signs of this legacy is the influence of Sanskrit itself on the Thai language. The Thai alphabet, which has a history of over seven hundred years, going back to the earliest Sukhōthai inscriptions in the late thirteenth century, is designed with a large number of redundant letters whose only purpose is to be able to faithfully spell Sanskrit words. This includes letters that are found *only* in Sanskrit and not in Pali, namely *ś* (ศ), *ṣ* (ษ), and the vowel *ṛ* (ฤ). In addition, Thai is replete with words of Sanskrit origin, and although some are spelled according to the Pali version, most (when there is a distinction) use the Sanskrit spelling. Along with Khmer, Sanskrit dominates the special register of language used to speak about kings and royalty, known as *rāchāsap* (Skt. *rājāśabda*). Brahmans to this day play a central role in royal ceremony, especially in the performance of a *Phra Borommarāchāphisēk* (Skt. *paramarājābhiṣeka*), or royal consecration.[26] These Brahmans, perhaps as a legacy of the old dominance of Śaivism, are primarily Śaiva in orientation. The *Rāmakian* (Skt. *Rāmakīrti*), the Thai version of the *Rāmāyaṇa* that was disseminated throughout Southern Asia through the Sanskrit Cosmopolis, continues to exert a heavy influence on Thai literature and art. Although containing certain Buddhist elements, it bears (in distinction to the Vālmīki version) a Śaiva framing in which Viṣṇu is sent to incarnate as Rāma by the supreme lord Śiva.[27] We will have occasion to explore in further detail these and other examples of the influence of Sanskritic discourses on Thai Buddhism and culture in Chapter 6.

The Collapse of the Sanskrit Cosmopolis and the Rise of Persianate and Arabic Cosmopoleis

Both the Sanskrit Cosmopolis and the age of Śaiva dominance came to an end in the first half of the second millennium. This was around the same time that Siam arose as a maritime polity in the wake of the decline of Angkor, itself a major node in the Sanskrit Cosmopolis and medieval Śaivism. According to Pollock, the end of the Sanskrit Cosmopolis was brought about slowly, over the course of about five centuries, through a process of "vernacularization." He conceives of this process as taking place primarily through the agency of literary actors themselves:

> The dominance of Sanskrit in literary and political text production was ended by a conscious challenge from vernacular intellectuals beginning in south India around the ninth century, with the process everywhere more or less complete by the end of the sixteenth. Literary production consisted to a large degree of texts derived from cosmopolitan genres and appropriating many of their formal features. A new aesthetic of Place, *deśī*, moderated these borrowings by balancing them with local forms, while new projects of spatiality—vernacular chrono-tropes that plotted out the domain of vernacular culture, putting culture in place for the first time . . .—began to find expression in literary texts. The primary impetus for vernacularization in most cases was provided by ruling elites, who were increasingly turning to the vernacular as the language of political communication, too.[28]

The impression Pollock gives for the end of the Sanskrit Cosmopolis is therefore of a gradual evaporation of cosmopolitan Sanskrit literary culture into various vernacular literary cultures, which were themselves modeled on their Sanskrit predecessor.

While Pollock's model of vernacularization is convincing from the limited viewpoint of literary agents across Southern Asia, it ignores the broader geopolitical context and therefore reinscribes the universalizing worldview of the Sanskrit Cosmopolis itself. Did nonvernacular cosmopolitanism simply end in Southern Asia in the first half of the second millennium? Was there no desire or need to communicate in a cosmopolitan idiom? Pollock himself admits that in this period "Pali became a medium for the production of a new cosmopolitan cultural order in Burma, Thailand, Cambodia, and Laos"[29]—a point to which we will return shortly—so clearly it cannot be said that cosmopolitanism died in Southern Asia in the second millennium. If Sanskrit could serve as the model for a *new* cosmopolitan order, not just for vernaculars, can vernacularization be a sufficient explanation for the end of the Sanskrit Cosmopolis?

Strikingly absent from Pollock's discussion of the end of the Sanskrit Cosmopolis are Islam and the Islamic elites who came to rule over much of

Southern Asia during the first half of the second millennium. In part, this is likely a reaction against older theories of South Asian history that put inordinate emphasis on Islam and contributed to a broadly Islamophobic narrative of Islam as an aggressive religion and civilizational force—one that has been co-opted to disastrous effect by modern Hindutva. Nevertheless, it is difficult to ignore the fact that the Sanskrit Cosmopolis waned just as the Delhi Sultanate was founded (1206) in the heartland of classical Indian culture, followed by the even more expansive Mughal Empire (founded 1526) that conquered most of the Indian subcontinent, as well as the conversion of (pen)insular Southeast Asia to Islam from the fifteenth century on. Pollock is surely correct in eschewing a narrative of Islam spelling the downfall of classical Indian culture, but in doing so, he risks eliding Muslim actors from South Asian history, which in a different way also feeds into Hindutva fantasies about the Indian past. We can avoid both of these extremes (Islam demonized, Islam ignored), however, if we recognize that it was not some monolithic "Islam" that brought about the end of the Sanskrit Cosmopolis, but rather the introduction of *new* cosmopoleis to Southern Asia, in large part through the efforts of Muslim actors.

To be clear, this is not a semantic trick, replacing "Islam" or "Islamic civilization" with an "Islamic Cosmopolis." *Two* distinct cosmopoleis were introduced to Southern Asia through the agency of Muslim actors in the first half of the second millennium. Moreover, the first and most important of these two was not rooted in Arabic, the language of the Qur'an, but rather in Persian. Richard Eaton writes:

> The Sanskrit world that Pollock describes was, however, only one such formation to have appeared in South Asian history. From about the eleventh to the nineteenth centuries a similar, Persianate world embraced much of West, Central and South Asia. Both expanded and flourished well beyond the land of their origin, giving them a transregional, "placeless" quality. Both were grounded in a prestige language and literature that conferred elite status on its users. Both articulated a model of worldly power—specifically, universal dominion. And while both elaborated, discussed and critiqued religious traditions, neither was grounded in a religion, but rather transcended the claims of any of them.[30]

This "Persianate Cosmopolis," as I will call it, spread into northern South Asia through the military campaigns and political ascendancy of Persianized

Turks in the first few centuries of the second millennium and, I will argue, played a crucial role in the disintegration of the Sanskrit Cosmopolis. A second cosmopolis new to the region, which Ronit Ricci has dubbed the "Arabic Cosmopolis,"[31] spread through maritime trade networks around the Indian Ocean, becoming particularly important for (pen)insular Southeast Asia and within Muslim communities in southern South Asia.

I will begin by describing the rise of the Persianate Cosmopolis in some detail because, even though it was at further remove from Siam than the Arabic Cosmopolis, it was arguably the more important of the two for the history of Southern Asia as a whole in the second millennium and for the fall of the Sanskrit Cosmopolis. The term "Persianate" was originally coined by Marshall Hodgson to refer to "cultural traditions, carried in Persian or reflecting Persian inspiration."[32] This concept has since been expanded by scholars to refer to a wide-ranging "Persianate world," as described by Nile Green: "By the fifteenth century, having gained written form as a fashionable patois of the court poets of tenth-century Bukhara, Persian had become a language of governance or learning in a region that stretched from China to the Balkans, and from Siberia to southern India."[33] Since scholarly work on the Indian corner of the Persianate world has explicitly compared it to Pollock's concept of the Sanskrit Cosmopolis,[34] I prefer to use the term "Persianate Cosmopolis" to maintain a consistent vocabulary with the other cosmopolitan formations we will consider in this chapter.

The Persian of the Persianate Cosmopolis had its origins in the spoken language that developed in the lands of the conquered Sasanian Empire while it was under the Arab rule of the Umayyad and 'Abbāsid caliphates in the seventh and eighth centuries. This language is technically referred to by linguists as "New Persian" to distinguish it from the Old Persian (Avestan) of the Achaemenid and Middle Persian (Pahlavi) of the Sasanian Era.[35] It was profoundly influenced by Arabic but, in part because it was not a related Semitic language, not fundamentally superseded by it. New Persian written in Arabic script first rose to prominence in the ninth century in the breakaway Islamic polities of the Sāmānid and Saffārid dynasties of Khurasan and Transoxiana, at the easternmost edge of the crumbling 'Abbāsid Empire.[36] In a sort of twist on the birth of the Sanskrit Cosmopolis (patronage of Sanskrit by a non-Indian dynasty in India), the birth of the Persianate Cosmopolis thus also displayed its fundamentally cosmopolitan character in being born outside of Persia proper.

The next key link in the spread of Persianate culture was provided by a non-Persian dynasty, the Ghaznavids. The Ghaznavids were ethnic Turks who had become Persianized while serving as slave-soldiers to the Sāmānids. They founded their own dynasty in the late tenth century that spread Persianate culture through an empire that at its height controlled a territory extending through not only Khurasan but also much of what is now Iran, Afghanistan, and Pakistan—thus, to the doorstop of South Asia. Persianate culture was then brought to the heartland of classical Indian civilization when the Ghurids, another Turkic dynasty that was an offshoot of the Ghaznavids, established the Delhi Sultanate in 1206. It ruled consistently over most of North India for the next three hundred years, with periods of suzerainty over parts of South India as well. Its successor, the Mughal Empire (founded in 1526), was also a Persianized state that, at its height, ruled over most of the subcontinent, making South Asia an integral part of the Persianate Cosmopolis right up until the advent of British rule in the eighteenth century.

There are two observations I would like to make about the Persianate Cosmopolis in South Asia. The first is that, while certainly tied up with Islam and propagated primarily through the agency of Muslim actors, this new cosmopolitan formation was in no wise synonymous with "Islam" or "Islamic civilization." The adoption of New Persian as the language of court by the Sāmānid and Saffārid dynasties happened at the periphery of the ʿAbbāsid Caliphate and corresponded with the rise of an "Islamic secularism," in which the worldly power of the sultan was only nominally subordinated to what increasingly was the merely religious authority of the caliph.[37] Moreover, when the Ghaznavids and Ghurids engaged in raids into South Asia in the early second millennium, they were identified in Indian texts not religiously as Muslims but ethnically as Turks (*turuṣka*).[38] Finally, under the Delhi Sultanate and Mughal Empire, Persianate culture had a profound impact on all Indians, both Muslims and (as they came to be referred to in Persian) Hindus. Hindi and the other indigenous languages of modern North India are all Persianized vernaculars,[39] bearing as much imprint from Persian as from their Indo-Aryan roots. The Persianate Cosmopolis was thus truly *Persianate* and not, more vaguely, Islamic.

Second, the Persianate Cosmopolis was truly *cosmopolitan*. The very fact that it arose *outside* of Persia proper and was spread, particularly in South Asia, not by ethnic Persians but by ethnic Turks is testament to this fact.

Moreover, the use of Persian as the language of court in the Delhi Sultanate was not simply a quirk of Indian polity in the bulk of the second millennium; it brought South Asia into conversation with a broader world that stretched for hundreds of years over a vast swath of Eurasia. The fact that Persianate culture was cosmopolitan is a key point because it better explains why the Sanskrit Cosmopolis came to an end than a model of gradual evaporation into vernaculars. The Sanskrit Cosmopolis persisted through much of the first millennium because various rulers across Southern Asia patronized the use of Sanskrit in *praśasti* inscriptions and *kāvya* literature. It came to an end in the second millennium because the most powerful polities in South Asia—who ruled from capitals right in the heartland of old Sanskritic culture—instead patronized Persian. Cosmopolitan culture did not die in South Asia with the end of the Sanskrit Cosmopolis; instead, it transferred from one cosmopolitan formation to another.

Cosmopolitan culture did not die in Southeast Asia at this time either. The most obvious parallel to the rise of the Persianate Cosmopolis in South Asia is the steady conversion of various (pen)insular polities of Southeast Asia to Islam from roughly the fifteenth century on. Indeed, the Islamic connection might lead one to conclude that this process was simply an extension of the spread of the Persianate Cosmopolis, but the reality is a bit more complicated. There is some evidence for the influence of Persian in the Indian Ocean, but the vast majority of evidence points to a greater influence of Arabic, reflected, for example, by a far greater proportion of Arabic than Persian loanwords into Malay.[40] For this reason, in a study focusing on Malay, Javanese, and Tamil, Ricci has characterized the region around the perimeter of the Indian Ocean most tied to maritime trade as an "Arabic Cosmopolis."[41] The existence of these two distinct cosmopoleis in second-millennium Southern Asia thus belies the tired narrative of Islam as aggressor. Yes, military force on the part of outsiders (something not at all new to South Asian history) did play a role in the end of the Sanskrit Cosmopolis, but the invaders were identified primarily by their ethnicity (Turkish); they played a key role in the decline of the Islamic caliphate; and they patronized a language (Persian) that was neither their own nor the prestige language of Islam, Arabic. On the other hand, maritime Southern Asia became part of a cosmopolis that was based on Arabic, but its establishment had nothing whatsoever to do with military force. Muslims were key agents in the end of the Sanskrit Cosmopolis, but a monolithic Islam was not.

The Ripple Effects of the Persianate Cosmopolis and the Rise of the Pali Cosmopolis

The expansion of the Persianate Cosmopolis into Southern Asia had ripple effects throughout the region far beyond the Delhi Sultanate and Mughal Empire, which served in turn as its most important political instantiations over the course of the second millennium. Persianate *political* culture, in particular, had a far wider spread than the specific spread of Persianate literary culture. The Deccan sultanates that ruled in the period of the waning of the Delhi Sultanate and the rise of the Mughal Empire were of course modeled on Persianate forms, but even the Hindu Vijayanagara Empire and Buddhist Siam adopted Persianate forms of court dress and ceremonial.[42] More important, however, are the ripple effects that the Persianate Cosmopolis had on the course of religious life throughout Southern Asia. These ripple effects took three forms. The first and most obvious was conversion of new populations to Islam. The second was the formation of a Hindu identity that, although in continuity with religious practices from the period of the Sanskrit Cosmopolis, increasingly rejected Śaiva in favor of Vaiṣṇava sects and Tantric forms of religiosity in favor of *bhakti*. Finally, and most important for our purposes, the combined ripple effects going on around the region led to the rise of a new cosmopolitan formation, which I will refer to as the "Pali Cosmopolis," that included Siam.

The most obvious effect of the rise of the Persianate Cosmopolis in Southern Asia was the conversion of new populations to Islam. The patterns that conversion followed are complicated, however, and by no means correlate with Islamic polity. Modern Pakistan was formed at Partition out of those parts of British India that were majority Muslim. Much of this country as it exists today corresponds to the easternmost frontier of the original Arab Empire from the time of the Umayyads; thus, there is a very long history of Islamic polity in that region. For centuries, however, Islamic polities—most important, the Delhi Sultanate and the Mughal Empire—ruled over a much broader portion of South Asia, particularly North India. Although this history of Islamic polity did lead to significant conversions to Islam, such that Islam is the largest minority religion in India today, it did not lead to conversions of the majority of the population to Islam (with the significant exception of East Bengal, which became East Pakistan, then Bangladesh). Some of the most significant conversions to Islam, as we have seen, took place far from the Delhi Sultanate and Mughal Empire, in (pen)insular Southeast Asia, and were facilitated by Sufi missionaries and maritime trade networks.

A less direct but nonetheless monumental ripple effect of the Persianate Cosmopolis on religious life in Southern Asia was the rise of an early modern Hindu identity, which went hand in hand with the collapse of the Śaiva world that had dominated the Sanskrit Cosmopolis. Although some scholars have claimed that the British "invented" Hinduism,[43] the word "Hindu" itself belies the crucial and much earlier role that Persianate culture played in the formation of Hindu identity. "Hindu" is a Persian word, like the Western term "India," derived from the name of the Indus River (Skt. Sindhu), and it was used by the Persianate ruling classes to refer to indigenous Indians who did not convert to Islam. As several scholars have convincingly argued, a nascent Hindu culture *avant la lettre* had developed in the classical period of the first millennium, and this was solidified in discourse by the Persianate distinction between Muslims and Hindus. The primary role of the British was to take this preexisting "Hindu" identity and fit it into the modern discourse of "world religions" as "Hinduism."[44]

"Hindu" religiosity in the Persianate period—both within and outside of Islamic polities—bore continuities with religion in the period of the Sanskrit Cosmopolis but also moved in new directions whose legacy continues to be felt today. These changes took two (related) forms. The first was a shift, at least rhetorically, away from Tantric forms of practice and towards *bhakti*, especially in North India. The second was a shift in patronage away from Śaiva and toward Vaiṣṇava institutions in Hindu polities. As Patton Burchett has shown in his recent monograph on the rise of *bhakti*,

> [T]he establishment of the Delhi Sultanate at the beginning of the thirteenth century and the corresponding military and political dominance of Persianized Turks resulted in the collapse of most of the infrastructure sustaining institutionalized and Brahmanical forms of tantric religion. . . . The new, "post-Tantric Age" environment of Sultanate India witnessed the spread of cosmopolitan Persian literary-political culture, the expansive growth of popular Sufism, and, relatedly, the rise of vernacular (Hindavi) literary composition and performance alongside the emergence of a transsectarian North Indian culture of charismatic asceticism. Each of these historical developments . . . was crucial in paving the way for the *bhakti* poets and communities of early modern North India.[45]

This shift from Tantric to *bhakti* forms of religiosity was accompanied by a shift in sectarian fortunes within the emerging world of "Hinduism." Burchett continues:

> Vaiṣṇava devotional forms increasingly took the place of previously dominant tantric Śaiva-Śākta traditions and—owing in no small part to their resonance with Sufi perspectives that had become rooted in Indian soil in the Sultanate period—came to be considered by many Hindus, whether they be kings or peasants, as the most proper and effective way to achieve their various desires.[46]

The Persianate Cosmopolis, in other words, helped to foster a sense of "Hindu" identity in contradistinction with the Islam of its elites, but at the same time disseminated values and norms of religious practice that were reflected within that very "Hindu" identity.

The shift that accompanied the crystallization of Hindu identity was not limited to the North Indian base of Sultanate and Mughal rule. It was reflected more broadly in "Hinduism" and across Southern Asia as a whole. As already mentioned, Vijayanagara, which dominated South India from the fourteenth to the sixteenth centuries, was a Hindu kingdom that nonetheless adopted Persianate forms in court dress and ceremonial. In a similar fashion, although the founding Sangama Dynasty was Śaiva, later kings of Vijayanagara were more favorable to Vaiṣṇavas, thus reflecting the sectarian shift taking place in the North. In Southeast Asia, major centers of Śaiva patronage had, under the aegis of the Sanskrit Cosmopolis, been found in Khmer country, Java, and Champa (modern South Vietnam). With the decline of the Sanskrit Cosmopolis, these regions were incorporated into different cosmopolitan formations. The Khmers were the first to do so, becoming part of an emerging Pali Cosmopolis from the late thirteenth century. Java was host to a late revival of Sanskritic polity, with patronage of Hinduism and Buddhism, under Majapahit from the late thirteenth to the early sixteenth centuries, but it ultimately was incorporated into the Arabic Cosmopolis that emerged in (pen)insular Southeast Asia in the mid-second millennium. Finally, Champa went into decline after its conquest by Đại Việt in the late fifteenth century, and it spent the next few centuries at the cusp of two cosmopolitan formations. On the one hand, its close ties to the maritime world of Southeast Asia drew it toward the Arabic Cosmopolis, and many Chams, including the ruling families, converted to Islam. On the other hand, its progressive domination by Đại Việt, which ultimately conquered the last of the Cham polities in 1832, drew it into the Sinitic cosmopolitan world of that kingdom. Although the process was therefore slow, protracted, and nonlinear, the ultimate result of all these changes outside the immediate sphere of Persianate polity was a fundamental break in the mid- to late second millennium from the pan-Southern Asian Sanskrit Cosmopolis and accompanying Śaiva Age.

This brings us to the third and, for our purposes, most important ripple effect of the rise of the Persianate and collapse of the Sanskrit Cosmpolis: the rise of a new cosmopolitan formation linking Lanka and much of mainland Southeast Asia, which I will refer to as the "Pali Cosmopolis." This term has been used before, in particular by Tilman Frasch, who, however, uses it somewhat differently to refer to a period beginning as early as 500 CE. He thus dates the formation of the Pali Cosmopolis to the systematization of the Pali scriptures through the commentarial work of Buddhaghosa, under the auspices of the Mahāvihāra. By dating the formation of the Pali Cosmopolis to the mid-first century, Frasch is able to argue against the applicability of the Sanskrit Cosmopolis, which he dismisses as "an updated and modified version of the old theory of an 'Indianization' (or 'Hinduization') of Southeast Asia,"[47] to Sri Lanka and part of Southeast Asia.

Frasch's use of a "Pali Cosmopolis" so conceived as an argument against the Sanskrit Cosmopolis does not, however, stand up to scrutiny. To begin with, by placing the origins of the Pali Cosmopolis in fifth- to sixth-century Lanka, he does nothing to improve upon the supposed crypto-Indianization of Pollock's Sanskrit Cosmopolis. The simple fact is that Southeast Asian actors *did* participate for centuries in discourses originating in South Asia. Substituting Lanka for India proper does not really make much of a difference in this respect. The critique of Indianization lies in recognizing Southeast Asians' *agency* in adopting cultural forms that originated in South Asia, not in denial that the Sanskrit, or Pali for that matter, used by Southeast Asians originated in South Asia.

More important, however, the dominance of Sanskrit as a cosmopolitan language through the period studied by Pollock is simply undeniable—with the participation of several Southeast Asian cultures, as we have seen—and was not rivaled by Pali until the early second millennium. This is not to say that Pali did not have any transnational spread in the mid- to late first millennium. It did, through the prestige of the scriptures used by Buddhists in South India, Lanka, and among the Burmese and Mon in Southeast Asia.

Nevertheless, as Steven Collins has shown, this was a dark period for the production of Pali literature, with no significant literary production in that language, other than the *Mahāvaṃsa*, during the thousand years from the latest canonical and para-canonical texts until the "Pali Renaissance" of the early second millennium.[48] Moreover, Lankan Buddhism *itself* was clearly participating in the Sanskrit Cosmopolis in the first millennium. As Jonathan Walters has shown, Lankan kings issued inscriptions in Sanskrit, and Lankan Buddhists, particularly those affiliated with the Abhayagiri Vihāra, were cosmopolitan participants in the wider Buddhist world, including the Mahāyāna that was disseminated through Sanskrit texts.[49]

This situation changed, however, in the early second millennium, and it is to this latter period that we should date the rise of the Pali Cosmopolis. Indeed, Frasch himself recognizes the significance of the eleventh to thirteenth centuries, during which he situates a "great translocation" of the Pali Cosmopolis.[50] The significance of this period is greater than Frasch allows for, however. It witnessed not simply the movement of the center of a cosmopolitan formation from Lanka to Southeast Asia but rather the birth of something substantively new. As Collins notes, "[M]onks in Sri Lanka began to compose *kāvya* in Pali again, more than a thousand years after Pali texts were first composed . . . in a consciously high-literate, Sanskritized manner, deliberately adopting the specifically *kāvya* mode of literary expression."[51] Likewise, as Frasch himself notes, Pali appears, from the number of inscriptions found there, to have become a *lingua franca* in Bagan during this period.[52] In other words, it was in the early second millennium that Pali first began to be used, in practical terms, as a living cosmopolitan language, rather than simply as the language of the ancient "texts," as the term *pāḷi* itself implies.

The impetus for the rebirth of Pali as a cosmopolitan, literary language has usually been identified by modern scholars with King Parākramabāhu's reform of the Lankan *saṅgha* in 1165, in which he forced all monks to reordain in the Mahāvihāra lineage. This had the ironic long-term effect of elevating the anticosmopolitan tradition of the Mahāvihāra to a new cosmopolitan status. As recent research by Alastair Gornall has shown, however, the reality is a bit more complicated. Gornall situates the renaissance of Pali literature not in a single event but in a longer "Reform Era," ca. 1157–1270, that was characterized not so much by royal power as by political fragmentation and chaos in the wake of the Cōḻa invasions. The agency for the new Pali literature lay within the *saṅgha* itself, which, due to this political chaos, was largely inward-looking.[53] Indeed, looked at from a broader historical and geographical angle, it was perhaps inevitable that a previously noncosmopolitan tradition—that of the Mahāvihāra, with its devotion to the Pali scriptures to the exclusion of first-millennium cosmopolitan developments in Sanskrit—would become ascendant at this point in history. As Walters argues, the disruption in North Indian institutions due to Turkic invasions cut off "southern" Buddhist cultures from "northern" ones, leading institutions like the Abhayagiri with a cosmopolitan orientation to lose out to those like the Mahāvihāra that were not dependent on cosmopolitan networks.[54]

Put differently, we can see the rise of the Pali Cosmopolis as resulting from the cosmopolitan vacuum that was created in a certain portion of Southern Asia with the collapse of the Sanskrit Cosmopolis, which in turn was precipitated by the introduction of the Persianate Cosmopolis to North India in the early second millennium. To be clear, this process was not linear or teleological, and it was composed of numerous actors with their own motivations and contradictory historical trends. Parākramabāhu I, for example, had his own idiosyncratic reasons for preferring the Mahāvihāra that had nothing to do with developments in North India, much less the foundation of the Delhi Sultanate, which had not happened yet. The monks who composed new Pali literature during the Reform Era were, as Gornall has shown, driven by inward-looking, local concerns, and not motivated by a desire to create a new cosmopolitan. And the fact that Southeast Asian monks sought reordination in Lanka and that Southeast Asian kings patronized these "Sīhaḷa" lineages, opening up avenues for the dissemination of Reform Era Pali works that would inspire Pali compositions in Southeast Asia, was itself due to idiosyncratic local concerns.[55] Nevertheless, broader regional and historical trends conspired to shape what otherwise would have been random local events and trends into a small but significant cosmopolitan formation rooted in Pali.

The Historical Origins of Siam

Attuned to the broader geopolitical trends across the region, we are now in a position to properly understand why and in what sense Pali Buddhism, or "Theravāda Buddhism," as it is known today,[56] became the primary ideology of the Siamese state. As I already noted at the beginning of this chapter, Siam arose in the area of the first-millennium Dvāravatī culture, with a long history of Pali Buddhism. On the other hand, the Angkorean Empire, which mostly did *not* patronize Pali Buddhism, exercised influence over the region in the centuries just prior to Siam's rise, and Khmer influence is clear in Siamese culture. One could argue (and some have)[57] that Tai elites simply adopted Pali Buddhism under the influence of local Mons, but this ignores the broader geopolitical trends that led to the rise of Pali Buddhism even in the Khmer homeland of the collapsing Angkorean Empire. A major cosmopolitan shift was taking place around the time that Siam arose, and I will now show that Siam arose as an important nexus in that shift.

The standard history of Siam taught to children in Thailand today derives from the "Damrong School," named after Prince Damrong Rajanubhap (1862–1943), the half-brother of King Chulalongkorn (Rama V), founder of the modern Thai education system, and prominent intellectual widely recognized as the "Father of Thai History." According to this standard historiography, the history of Siam is divided into three (technically four) periods corresponding to three (four) "capitals": Sukhōthai, Ayutthayā, (Thonburī), and Bangkok. The Sukhōthai Period corresponds to a kingdom centered at a city of the same name in the northernmost portion of what is now Central Thailand. It was founded in the thirteenth century and reached its height under Rāmkhamhǣng (r. 1279–1298), the author of the oldest inscription extant in the Thai language, which was rediscovered by King Rāma IV in the nineteenth century and is a prized artifact of Thai nationalism.[58] Ayutthayā, in turn, was founded in 1351 by Ū Thǫng (Rāmāthibodi I). Ayutthayā conquered or absorbed Sukhōthai, became the most prosperous kingdom of mainland Southeast Asia, and lasted for over four hundred years. This second period of Siamese history came to an end when Ayutthayā was sacked by the Burmese in 1767. Siamese sovereignty was restored by the Phra Cāo Tāk (Tāksin), who founded a new capital at Thonburī, a bit to the south of Ayutthayā. This third "Thonburī Period" was quite short lived, however, as Tāksin was overthrown in a coup in 1782 by one of his own officials, the Cāo Phrayā Cakrī. The Cāo Phrayā Cakrī moved the capital across the Cāo Phrayā River from Thonburī to Bangkok and, as King Yǭt Fā (posthumously dubbed Rāma I, r. 1782–1809), founded the Chakri Dynasty, which rules to this day. This fourth and current period of Siamese/Thai history is usually referred to as the "Rattanakōsin Period," named after the oldest section of the capital in Bangkok, directly across the river from Tāksin's capital in Thonburī.

There are several problems with this traditional historiography. For our purposes, the most important of these problems is that it does not adequately describe the historical origins of Siam and, in particular, the relationship between Sukhōthai and Ayutthayā. The context in which Siam arose was not so much one of well-defined kingdoms but of city-states known in Tai languages as *müang* (เมือง) and the relationships between them,[59] which were defined by three major processes: (1) marital alliances between the lords of different *müang*; (2) wars of pillage in which the lords of one *müang* sought to obtain wealth, religious relics, and even people from a rival *müang*; and (3) the appointment of children or other relatives by the lords of a powerful *müang* to rule over a less powerful, tributary *müang*. Sukhōthai and Ayutthayā were thus not so much "capitals" of "kingdoms" as they were the two most powerful *müang* that contributed to the formation of Siam, which ultimately became centralized around Ayutthayā beginning in the sixteenth century.

According to the traditional history, which is based on the Luang Prasoet Chronicle, a document written during the reign of King Nārāi (1656–1688), Ayutthayā was founded by Ū Thọng in 1351. There is almost no secure historical information about Ū Thọng, if he even existed, and there is good evidence that the city he supposedly founded existed as early as the thirteenth century and ruled over a country known to outsiders as Siam. Chinese records refer to a polity known as Xiān (暹) as early as 1282/3, Sumatran chronicles refer to Siamese raids in the early fourteenth century, a Buddhist chronicle from Lānnā refers to a city to the south called Ayōdhiyā in the first half of the fourteenth century, and even the Luang Prasoet Chronicle itself says that an important Buddha image was founded outside the city in 1324/5.[60] If there is any significance to the date 1351 recorded as the foundation of Ayutthayā by the Luang Prasoet Chronicle, it may have to do with a power consolidation within the Siamese realm. Chinese accounts record that in 1349 Xiān either submitted to Luóhú or Luóhú submitted to Xiān (with a discrepancy between sources likely due to a scribal error). Luóhú here refers to the neighboring city of Lopburī, which is known from Siamese sources to have played an important role in Ayutthayā's early dynastic history. Chinese sources from after this date refer to Siam not simply as Xiān, but as Xiānluó (暹羅), reflecting the merger.[61] In any case, there is ample evidence that Ayutthayā was not actually "founded" *de novo* in 1351. Siam as a polity was clearly known to outsiders as early as the late thirteenth century, and its central city, named after Rāma's city of Ayodhyā in the Rāmāyaṇa,[62] existed well before 1351.

As recent research has shown,[63] Siam arose as a maritime polity, quite different in nature from inland, agricultural polities such as the classical kingdoms of Angkor and Bagan, or even of contemporaneous Sukhōthai. Ayutthayā was not located in an area good for agriculture, but it was well situated on a river system closely connected to the Gulf of Thailand that allowed it to become a major entrepôt in trading networks stretching from China in the East, across the Southeast Asia archipelago, and onward to ports in South Asia and beyond.[64] Most likely its rise as a trading center was made possible by the decline of Śrī Vijaya, a trading network of ports across Sumatra and the Malay Peninsula that had dominated Southeast Asian trade, with the benefit of Chinese favor, for centuries.[65] Ayutthayā was not simply a passive port, however; numerous sources report that the Siamese were known for raiding and piracy, with attacks up and down the coast of the Malay Peninsula that extended Siamese power as far south as Temasek (modern Singapore). Indeed, maritime attacks to the south appear to have completely dominated Siam's earliest expansionist policy and continued until the late fifteenth century.[66]

In terms of networks between cities, Siam was dominated early on by Ayutthayā in a complex web of relationships with the neighboring cities of Suphanburī and Lopburī, as well as, to a certain extent, Phetburī.[67] These relationships are reflected in the recorded dynastic histories of Ayutthayā, which report a rivalry between lineages from the former two cities in the second half of the fourteenth century.[68] In time, however, Ayutthayā became embroiled in similar cross-city relations with a group of cities farther to the north, known as the "Northern Cities" (เมืองเหนือ). These cities, which included Sī Satcanālai, Phichai, Phitsanulōk, Phicit, and Kamphāng Phet, were dominated from the end of the thirteenth century by Sukhōthai.

It is likely that Ayutthayā became enmeshed in relations with Sukhōthai and the Northern Cities through a combination of factors. First, Ayutthayā sent raiding expeditions into the Northern Cities from the 1370s onward. These were expeditions to obtain goods, religious relics, and, most important, manpower, not to conquer the cities and impose centralized administrative control. At the same time, the Suphanburī lineage in Ayutthayā intermarried with the ruling family of Sukhōthai, which led to closer ties even in peacetime, as well as the movement of large retinues from the north to Ayutthayā to accompany women marrying into the Ayutthayān elite. The relationship between Ayutthayā and the Northern Cities grew to such an extent that, in the early fifteenth century, the kings of Ayutthayā stopped sending their heirs apparent to Suphanburī to rule as *uparāja* (deputy king) and instead sent them to rule in the northern city of Phitsanulōk, a practice that continued for 150 years.[69] Ultimately, the ruling families of Ayutthayā and the Northern Cities became so intertwined that in 1569 Mahāthammarāchā, a northern noble descended from the ruling house of Sukhōthai, ascended to the throne of Ayutthayā, inaugurating a "Sukhōthai Dynasty." The Northern Cities have thus functionally been a part of Siam since the fifteenth century, and the provinces of modern Thailand that correspond to them are considered part of Central Thailand, sharing in the same general culture, today.

Although we take it for granted now that Siam is/was culturally and linguistically Thai, it is likely that that was not the case in its earliest history. The language, culture, and ethnicity of the Siam/Xiān referred to in the earliest sources of the late thirteenth and early fourteenth centuries is unknown. Most likely, as a maritime polity, early Siam was highly cosmopolitan. Many ethnic groups would have lived in Ayutthayā, and it is not necessarily clear which if any language dominated. The region in which Siam arose was the home of the old Dvāravatī culture, in which Mon was spoken, and Mon speakers have played an important role in Siamese life up until modern times. Likewise, various merchant groups from overseas would have settled in Ayutthayā, including Chinese and South Indian Tamils, contributing to the linguistic landscape of early Siam.

However, the most important language by far other than Thai itself in early Siam was Khmer. This is not surprising given that Angkor exercised heavy influence over the region that would become Siam from the tenth to the twelfth centuries. Michael Vickery has argued that Angkor did not so much collapse as devolve in the thirteenth and fourteenth centuries into two new centers—Ayutthayā and Phnom Penh—that were better able to take advantage of changing maritime trade networks.[70] It is possible, therefore, that Khmer was *the* dominant language in early Ayutthayā. Modern Thai includes an enormous vocabulary, as well as some grammatical structures, derived from Khmer, more than any other language in the Tai language family—to such an extent, in fact, that one scholar has dubbed it Khmero-Tai.[71] This heavy infiltration of Khmer into Thai, akin to that of French in Modern English in the wake of the Norman invasion, indicates the existence of a strong relationship between two groups of different language speakers early in Siam's history. Likewise, certain Ayutthayān inscriptions and a text of land grants for the region around the southern city of Phatthalung in the seventeenth century were written in part in Khmer, indicating that Khmer was actively used in early Siamese administration.[72] Indeed, the prestige of Khmer was so great that Pali Buddhist texts in Siam were written exclusively in a version of the Khmer script known as Khǫm until the nineteenth century. The prestige of Khmer is also reflected in the frequent use of Khmer terms, along with Sanskrit, to replace ordinary Thai terms in *rāchāsap* (ราชาศัพท์), the special honorific vocabulary used to this day to talk about the king and the royal family.

How exactly Thai[73] became the dominant language of Siam is not entirely clear, but it must have done so as part of the broader spread of the Tai languages from the late first millennium onward. Linguists have determined that the homeland of the Tai languages is in the region along the border between Guangxi Province in China and northern Vietnam, reflected today in the fact that the greatest density of different Tai languages is found in that region.[74] Chinese military expeditions to subdue the "barbarians" of the South (known in Chinese as 越 *yuè*) in the eighth to tenth centuries led Tai peoples to migrate to the West, with the result that today Tai speakers (the Ahom) are found as far west as Assam in India.[75] The Tai were partially Sinicized, organized into a political structure of *bān* (villages) and *müang* (city-states), the latter of which were led by a warrior aristocracy known as *cāo* (เจ้า), most likely derived from the Chinese word 主 *zhǔ* ("lord, master"). Their ability to establish new *müang* and settle lands already occupied by other peoples was likely a result of, as well as driven by, their wet rice method of cultivation, which was suitable to well-irrigated lowland areas and gave higher yields than other techniques.[76]

The major Tai states of Southeast Asia were not founded until the thirteenth century, however, and this southward expansion of the Tai peoples was likely also driven by Chinese military activity. Under the Mongol rule of the Yuán Dynasty, Chinese forces attacked various states in northern mainland Southeast Asia, including Tai polities and even the great Burmese kingdom of Bagan.[77] Under this pressure, Tai groups moved further south along the river valleys and established *müang* that would become centers of important polities in early modern Southeast Asia. One of these was Chiang Mai, located in what is now Northern Thailand. It was legendarily founded by the Tai *cāo* of Chiang Sǣn, Mangrāi, in 1292 as the capital of the Lānnā kingdom, although the shift of power in that region from the old Mon city of Haribhuñjaya (modern Lamphūn) to the new Tai city Chiang Mai was probably a more complex process than legend suggests.[78] Further south, a Khmer-style city called Sukhōthai came by the middle of the thirteenth century to be ruled by Tai *cāo* who bore Khmer titles.[79] Sukhōthai, as we have seen, became a powerful *müang* in its own right and issued the oldest inscriptions that exist in any Tai language, dating from the late thirteenth century.

Unfortunately, how Tai elites came to power in polities further to the South—Siam in the region of Ayutthayā and the old kingdom of Tāmbraliṅga centered at Nakhọn Sī Thammarāt in the Malay Peninsula—is less clear due to a lack of historical evidence. Most likely, in Ayutthayā it took place through the processes described above, namely through an increasingly symbiotic relationship with the Northern Cities driven by intermarriage and wars of pillage. It is important to note, however, that this process likely did not begin with Ayutthayā *per se*. We know from Ayutthayā's historical documents that the Suphanburī lineage in that city was intermarrying with northern (and thus Tai) elites in the late fourteenth century, but we know virtually nothing about the politics of Suphanburī and Lopburī themselves in that century. It is possible that Tai elites had become involved in the leadership of those cities even earlier than in Ayutthayā. The significance of the middle of the fourteenth century—noted by the Chinese as a merger between Xiān and Luóhú and by the Luang Prasoet Chronicle as the date of Ayutthayā's "foundation"—may even lie in the rise of Tai elites to leadership in Ayutthayā proper, although this is strictly speculative. Phetburī, just at the northernmost part of the Malay Peninsula, was embroiled in the networks of early Siamese *müang* politics but also part of the old Tāmbraliṅga *maṇḍala* centered at Nakhọn Sī Thammarāt, and as such it may have served as a jumping point for the transfer of Tai elites to that latter city in the South.

In any case, it appears that Tai-speaking elites leveraged the network politics of Southeast Asian city-states to become established in most of the regions of what is now Thailand by the end of the fourteenth century. They would have brought with them Tai-speaking commoners from more established *müang* further north—and acquired even more through raids to the north—thus establishing a Tai dialect as a widely spoken language in the cities where they reigned as *cāo*. This Tai dialect then merged with languages already spoken in the area through a process of creolization. In Siam, the most important "indigenous" language that merged with Tai was actually a relative newcomer to the area—Khmer—which had become important in the region in the last couple of centuries of the Angkorean Empire. The resulting language, which is known today as Central Thai, became the standard language of the kingdom of Siam, followed by modern Thailand, and it is the language of discourse studied in this book.

Siam thus arose as a nexus of cosmopolitan change, occupying a liminal position in the expanding Pali Cosmopolis. On the one hand, it was situated on territory of the old Mɔn culture of Dvāravatī, which, like that of the Burmese, had practiced Pali Buddhism from an early date in the first millennium. It was just as ripe as was Burma to its west for incorporation into a Pali Cosmopolis. On the other hand, Siam arose more immediately out of the collapse of the Angkorean Empire, a highly cosmopolitan participant in the earlier Sanskritic world that had exercised a great deal of influence over the land of Dvāravatī for centuries. In practice, Siam was a less prolific participant in Pali literary production not only than Burma to the west but also than the neighboring Tai polity of Lānnā to the north. Chiang Mai indeed became such a renowned center for Pali Buddhist learning that the script used to write the local dialect of Tai Yuan became known as *aksǭn tham*, or "*dhamma* letters."[80] Siam was therefore somewhat peripheral to the spread of Pali cosmopolitan culture among Tai-speaking peoples, but nevertheless participated insofar as Siamese rulers, both in Ayutthayā itself and in its various tributaries, patronized monks (including those of "Sīhaḷa" lineages) who were connected to cosmopolitan Pali networks and works of literature that drew from the Pali *imaginaire*.

Continuities between the Sanskrit and Pali Cosmopoleis

The fact that Siam arose on a nexus of transition from the Sanskrit to the Pali Cosmopolis is significant not only or even primarily because it allowed Siamese discourse to simply draw from both cosmopoleis. Rather, the particular continuities between the Pali Cosmopolis and the Sanskrit Cosmopolis that preceded it, combined with the historical hegemony of the Sanskrit Cosmopolis in the region, paradoxically opened a space for emerging Hindu discourses to exercise agency *within* a Siamese discourse increasingly circumscribed by the Pali *imaginaire*. Although the Sanskrit and Pali Cosmopoleis are distinct, they share deep roots. The Pali language is a slightly Sanskritized version of a Middle Indic vernacular that was spoken around the region of modern Madhya Pradesh slightly after the time of the Buddha.[81] Indeed, it represents an early stage in a process of Sanskritization ("ornamenting" vernacular language in imitation of the language of the

Vedas) that culminated in the widespread adoption of classical Sanskrit in the first millennium. Pali thus is closely related to the classical Sanskrit of the Sanskrit Cosmopolis and shares with it most of its vocabulary, often with only slight differences in spelling.

In addition, the Pali Canon that serves as the foundation for the Pali *imaginaire* is rooted in the same early Indic worldview as the various sectarian movements, including Śaivism, that were promulgated through the Sanskrit Cosmopolis. Pali texts speak often of Brahmans, the Vedas they passed down, their rituals, the gods they worshiped, and the system of *varṇa* they claimed governed society. Of course, the early Buddhist texts do not simply provide a snapshot of early Indian society and religion; they themselves contributed to the development of Indian society and religion that would later be reflected in the Sanskrit Cosmopolis. As I have shown, Buddhists were likely instrumental in the widespread demotion of the god Brahmā from Supreme Deity to demiurge,[82] and Buddhism together with other śramaṇic groups such as the Jains likely played an important role in the widespread acceptance in India of a worldview of *karma*, rebirth, and liberation.

Finally, the Pali Renaissance in the beginning of the second millennium that led to the rise of the Pali Cosmpolis was itself undertaken on Sanskritic models. Much as was the case with what Pollock calls the "cosmopolitan vernaculars" emerging in Southern Asia in the early second millennium,[83] the Pali grammars and literature written at that time were based not solely on the old Pali literature of a millennium before but also on classical Sanskritic models of *vyākaraṇa* and *kāvya*.[84] The rise of the Pali Cosmopolis thus does not represent as much a break with the past cosmopolitan order as does the Persianate Cosmopolis in North India or the Arabic Cosmopolis in the (pen)insular Southeast Asia. Instead, it represents a sort of modified continuity: the same grammatical, literary, and cultural structure as the Sanskrit Cosmopolis that preceded it, but with a new focus on a particular sectarian literature and its idiosyncratic idiom.

At the same time as the Pali Cosmopolis was emerging to fill a cosmopolitan vacuum in Lanka and mainland Southeast Asia, "Hinduism" was emerging as a shared cultural/religious discourse in India. I put "Hinduism" in scare quotes because, as many scholars have pointed out, the use of the word to refer to a "world religion" is remarkably modern, dating only to the era of British colonialism. This has led some to go so far as to argue that Hinduism was in fact *invented* by the British. As other scholars have convincingly argued, however, the roots of a Hindu identity far precede British rule, even if the word "Hinduism" *per se* was not used. We can usefully demarcate a tripartite process. The first part was the development of a shared mythological, ritual, and philosophical idiom in the midst of sectarian differences—what is often etically referred to as "classical Hinduism"—in the first millennium under the auspices of the Sanskrit Cosmopolis. The second was the emergence of a "Hindu" identity—not a fully "religious" identity in the modern sense, but an identity nonetheless—vis-à-vis "Muslim" in the middle of the second millennium under the auspices of the Persianate Cosmopolis. The third and final part was the incorporation of this "Hindu" identity, as "Hinduism," into the emerging globalized discourse of "world religions," under the auspices of European colonialism.

Without discounting the importance of the first stage of this process, which provided much of the content of Hinduism, I want to foreground the second stage, which corresponds chronologically with the height of the Pali Cosmopolis. To begin with, it is in this stage that "Hindu" itself became a term of identity, through its use within Persianate idiom by Turkic Muslim rulers to refer to the peoples of India whom they conquered, their culture, and their non-Islamic religion or religions. More significant, this period saw a shiftfrom the Śaiva/Tantric orientation of the Sanskrit Cosmopolis to a more Vaiṣṇava/*bhakti* orientation, which persists to this day. Likewise, it was also at this time, as Andrew Nicholson and Elaine Fisher have shown, that a discourse of *āstika* unity under Vedānta supremacy and the "sectarianization" of once independent religions through "public theology" emerged.[85] British colonialism did not unify Hinduism, nor did it create for the first time the pressure to conform to iconoclastic monotheistic ideals—even if these tendencies were accentuated by the so-called Hindu Reformers. These trends were all well-established during the centuries of Muslim rule.

There thus was an emerging "Hindu" discourse under the Persianate Cosmopolis—not a cosmopolitan formation in itself but a discourse that, like the Pali Cosmopolis, maintained continuity with the Sanskrit Cosmopolis under the new conditions wrought by an increasingly Persianate world. This discourse was far less broad than the Sanskrit Cosmopolis, however, being confined mostly to modern-day India, and as such it was not directly operative in Siam. Nevertheless, Siam and the Pali Cosmopolis of which it was a part did not exist in isolation. Indeed, the very continuities between the Pali Cosmopolis and the Sanskrit Cosmopolis that preceded it made it possible for "Hinduism" to indirectly exercise agency *within* Pali Buddhism.

The evidence for this can be seen in the fact that Siamese art and literature, while circumscribed by the Pali *imaginaire* and oriented firmly toward the practice of Pali Buddhism, did not confine itself to classical Pali texts, but rather "updated" the Indic world of those texts to reflect developments within Hinduism. As we saw in the previous chapter, Buddhism acts as an implicit theology insofar as it defines gods (*deva*s) as a particular class of beings, trapped within *saṃsāra* but nonetheless powerful agents who have been born in their position due to good karma. Classical Pali texts codified in an elaborate cosmology the existence of the full range of gods recognized in ancient India—with the top god, Brahmā, multiplied into a whole class of beings. The Siamese Buddhist imaginary, however, while looking to the Pali texts as the guiding authority, has never confined itself *exclusively* to characters or "facts" described in the classical Pali texts. It has, from the very beginning, recognized the existence of important Hindu gods—most important, Viṣṇu, Śiva, and Gaṇeṣa—who are not found or emphasized in the classical Pali texts because they became popular objects of devotion only after its codification.[86] Similarly, the iconography of gods in Siam reflects developments in Hinduism; for example, Brahmā is routinely portrayed as having four faces, a feature never mentioned in the Pali Canon because it did not become prominent in Brahmā's mythology until the Purāṇas.[87]

The influence of Hindu discourse on the Siamese is not confined to divine cosmology. Although the story of Rāma is found in the classical Pali texts in the form of the *Dasaratha Jātaka*, the Siamese Thai version of the *Rāmāyaṇa*, the *Rāmakian*, is not drawn from it; it instead represents a variation upon the classical Sanskrit version in which Śiva is portrayed as the Supreme Deity who sends Viṣṇu to incarnate as Rāma.[88] The *Mahābhārata* has played a much less important role in Siamese literature and art, but it is at times referred to,[89] in spite of the fact that it plays no significant role in the *imaginaire* created by the classical Pali texts. Finally, as I have shown elsewhere, actual Hindu Brahmans imported from India have played an important role in the ceremonial of Siamese kingship since at least the Ayutthayā period.[90] In short, Siamese Buddhists, while oriented by the Pali Cosmopolis toward the Pali *imaginaire*, have not viewed that *imaginaire* in isolation but as existing in a broader context that could be informed by Hindu discourses.

Until the nineteenth century, however, when the Thai language absorbed a large vocabulary from English, the word "Hindu" itself was not used in Siamese discourse to refer to those foreign discourses that were appropriated to provide context to the Pali *imaginaire*. Instead, an idiosyncratic Sanskritic word was used, pronounced in Thai as *saiyasāt*. This *saiyasāt* was seen as distinct from, but complementary to, Buddhism, or *phutthasāt*. In the next chapter, I will explore the role played by *saiyasāt* in Siamese literature in order to provide a genealogy of one of its key subsidiary concepts: *saksit*.

4
The Genealogy of the Sacred

So far in Part I we have established two things. The first is that Buddhism has from its very inception acted as an implicitly theological system, defining the gods vis-à-vis other beings and contextualizing them within a cosmology of *saṃsāra*. The second is that Siam has historically existed on a nexus of cosmopolitan transformation, occupying a liminal position in the transition from a pan–Southern Asian Sanskrit Cosmopolis to a more regionally localized Pali Cosmopolis. The continuities between these two cosmopoleis created space within Siamese discourse for broader discourses that were the legacy of the Sanskrit Cosmopolis under the aegis of a new Persianate regime—what we now call "Hinduism"—to continue to operate within the framework of the Pali *imaginaire*. Thus, we must consider the work of Buddhism as an implicit theology, not as a singular act fully accomplished at Buddhism's inception in ancient India but rather as a dynamic process, continuing to evolve in unique ways throughout Siam's history and even in present-day Thailand.

In this chapter, we will explore how Siamese discourse specifically conceptualized and interfaced with the legacy of the Sanskrit Cosmopolis and the continued relevance of Hindu discourses. Although modern Thai has a word for Hinduism, namely *sātsanā hindū* (ศาสนาฮินดู), this is a modern neologism, a product of the colonial encounter and concomitant need to translate the concepts of Western modernity, including the vocabulary of world religions, into Thai. It is constructed, as with all modern Thai terms for world religions, by combining the Sanskrit word *śāsana*—which was idiosyncratically chosen to translate the Western concept of "religion"[1]—with a transliteration of an appropriate word to refer to the particular religion in question. Thus, modern Thai has *sātsanā khrit* (ศาสนาคริสต์) for "Christianity," *sātsanā itsalām* (ศาสนาอิสลาม) for "Islam," *sātsanā phut* (ศาสนาพุทธ) for "Buddhism," *sātsanā sik* (ศาสนาสิข) for "Sikhism," and *sātsanā hindū* (ศาสนาฮินดู) for "Hinduism." Modern Thai also has a word, *sātsanā phrām* (ศาสนาพราหมณ์), which serves as a translation of the English word "Brahmanism." Prior to this modern adoption of Western vocabulary—up to and well into the nineteenth century, that is—Hinduism/

Holy Things. Nathan McGovern, Oxford University Press. © Oxford University Press 2024.
DOI: 10.1093/9780197759912.003.0004

Brahmanism was instead referred to in Siamese discourse using the word *saiyasāt* (ไสยศาสตร์). This word is well-known in modern Thai as referring to the "occult," but as I will show, in premodern Thai it referred more specifically to the knowledge and power associated with Brahmans, a valence that is not entirely lost even in the modern usage.

Saiyasāt, and the interface it has provided between Siamese and Hindu discourses, will prove pivotal to the argument I am advancing in this book because of its close historical association with *saksit*, the term that in modern Thai puts the "holy" in "holy things." In this chapter, I will demonstrate that throughout most of Siamese history the word *saksit* did not, in fact, mean "holy," nor was it a concept associated with Buddhism. It was instead a concept associated with *saiyasāt*, or Brahmanism. In order to demonstrate this, I will first identify when and how the word *saksit* came to be used by nineteenth-century Christian missionaries to translate the Western concept of "holy." Then, through a comprehensive study of an electronic corpus of older Siamese texts that I have assembled, I will show that prior to the nineteenth-century use of *saksit* to translate the concept "holy," it meant something quite different: supernatural power associated with *saiyasāt*.

The end of the chapter will explain how the shift in *saksit*'s semantic categorization took place. In the nineteenth century, the Buddhist term *śāsana* was adapted to refer to the Western concept of "religion," and *saiyasāt* was adapted to refer to the Western concept of "magic." In this process, the word *saksit*, by being used to translate the concept of "holy," was effectively "reassigned" from (to use Western terms) magic to religion or (to use terms more closely approximating native Siamese categories) from Brahmanism to Buddhism. This would have profound effects on Thai religious praxis that manifest in the culture of worshiping *sing saksit* today.

How *Saksit* Became "Holy"

We will ultimately be interested in the discourse of *saiyasāt* because it contained within it the very term that has motivated this book, namely *saksit*. Although in modern Thai *saksit* means "holy" or "sacred," "holy," like "religion" and "magic," is not really an indigenous concept. It is instead the product of the program of translation that took place in the colonial era. The earliest use of the word *saksit* to translate the Western concept of "holy" that I have been able to find is an 1835 translation of the Gospel of Matthew by the American Baptist missionary John Taylor Jones. The verse in question is Matthew 4:5, which is found in the context of Satan's temptation of Christ. The verse reads, "Then the devil took him to the **holy** city [referring to Jerusalem], and made him to stand on the parapet of the temple," or in the original Greek from which Jones made his translation, "Τότε παραλαμβάνει αὐτὸν ὁ διάβολος εἰς τὴν **ἁγίαν** πόλιν, καὶ ἔστησεν αὐτὸν ἐπὶ τὸ πτερύγιον τοῦ ἱεροῦ." Jones translates this same verse as "ครั้งนั้นศัตรูก็ภาพระองค์ไปยังเมืองอันศักดิสิทธิ แลตั้งพระองค์บนยอดวิหาร."[2] Jones uses the word *saksit* to translate the Greek adjective *ἅγιος*, which is equivalent to the Latin *sanctus*. These key terms of the early Christian lexicon are typically translated by the English "holy" or "sacred."[3]

Although I cannot be certain that Jones did not pick up this choice of translation from elsewhere, such as an earlier unpublished Bible translation, his translation was likely the most influential because it became part of the first full translation into Thai to be published, first of the New Testament in 1843, and then of the entire Bible in 1894.[4] *Saksit* has, in any case, become the standard word for the concept of "holy" among Thai Christians, perhaps best evinced by its use in the opening line of the *Sanctus* in the Catholic Mass (thus *Saksit, saksit, saksit!* in place of English "Holy, holy, holy!" or Latin *Sanctus, sanctus, sanctus!*).[5] Through the mediation of the modern discourse of "world religions," the word *saksit* is by extension used in modern Thai to refer to anything that might conceivably be considered "holy" in any religion—whether originally conceived as such or not. As we will see, this includes, significantly, Buddha images.

That *saksit* is not an obvious choice to translate the concept of "holy," and moreover that the concept of "holy" likely did not exist in Thai prior to the nineteenth century, is made clear by the earliest attempts by Europeans to translate Christian texts and concepts into Thai in the late seventeenth century. During the reign of King Nārāi (1656–1688), French Catholic missionaries enjoyed a short period of favor at court and hoped even to convert the king, before Nārāi, nearing death, was ousted in a coup that expelled French military forces and curtailed French missionary activity.[6] Two translations made by French Catholics in this era decline even to attempt to translate the concept of "holy" (Latin *sanctus*) when presented the opportunity. The first is a translation of the *Ave Maria* (the short prayer, usually known by English-speaking Catholics as the "Hail Mary," that is represented by the majority of beads in the rosary) by Simone de la Loubère, a French diplomat who led an embassy to Siam in 1687 and published in

1691 a two-volume account of his experience, titled *Du Royaume de Siam*. The prayer consists of two stanzas, beginning, respectively, with the words *Ave Maria* ("Hail, Mary!") and *Sancta Maria* ("Holy Mary").[7] La Loubère translates every word of the prayer except for these two opening phrases, which he leaves in Latin, and the word *amen* at the end, which he also leaves untranslated.[8]

The second text is a translation of a short excerpt from the Gospel of Luke (1:5–17)—the very first translation of any biblical text into Thai known to exist—made by Bishop Louis Laneau in 1685. It contains the announcement by an angel to Zechariah of the coming birth of John the Baptist. The second half of verse 15 reads, "He will be filled with the **holy** Spirit even from his mother's womb," or in the original Greek, "καὶ πνεύματος **ἁγίου** πλησθήσεται ἔτι ἐκ κοιλίας μητρὸς αὐτοῦ." As in Jones's later translation of Matthew, the Greek adjective *ἅγιος* appears, in this context as part of the key phrase *πνεύμα ἅγιο*, or "Holy Spirit." But like La Loubère, Laneau declines to translate this phrase at all, instead transliterating from the Latin equivalent as *phra sapīritua santǭ* (พระสปีริตุะสันตอ).[9] In this case, the evidence is even more damning: Laneau certainly knew of the word *saksit*, as he uses it just a couple of lines earlier in a different context. He uses it in the phrase *athibodī saksit* (อธิบดีสักสิทธิ), meaning "powerful leader," which appears to be a loose translation of the word *μέγας* in the original Greek or *magnus* in the Vulgate (both meaning "great"), used to describe John.[10] Laneau thus knew the word *saksit*, used it in his translation in a place where the word *holy* does not occur, and chose not to translate at all when the word *holy* did occur. The equivalence between *holy* and *saksit* is clearly a later invention.

The Literary Corpus for This Study

What, then, did the word *saksit* mean prior to being mustered to serve as a translation for the Western concept of "holy"? In order to ascertain the genealogy of *saksit* and related terms, I have gathered a quasi-comprehensive electronic database of Siamese literature stretching from its earliest recorded instances in the late thirteenth century up to the early nineteenth century, including the works of Siam's greatest literary figure, Sunthǭn Phū (1786–1855). It is of course impossible to be fully comprehensive when considering a "literature" spanning hundreds of years, but there are certain relevant parameters here and accidents of history that at least provide a meaningful demarcation that allows us to investigate the genealogy of terms within a broader discourse. By "Siamese," I mean the literature of Siam proper, written in Siamese Thai. There are other literatures written in Tai dialects, the most important being the Lao literature of Lān Xāng and modern Laos and the Yuan literature of Lānnā. The latter in particular is important for the history of Thailand because Lānnā was almost wholly incorporated into the modern nation-state thereof, but it is excluded from this survey as representing, historically, a cultural sphere separate from Siam proper.

Siamese literature thus construed has been canonized to a certain extent in modern Thailand and serves as the curriculum for the teaching of "literature" (วรรณคดี) in Thai schools. Although there are certain limitations to this "canon," it nonetheless serves as a useful roadmap for tracking Siamese discourse diachronically, and I have followed it as such. The first limitation is that this canon is elitist, representing mostly works made under royal sponsorship or by aristocratic authors. The second limitation is that there is a relative lack of texts for all periods up until the founding of the Chakri Dynasty in the late eighteenth century, after which there is an explosion. The reason for this is that, given the humid climate of Southeast Asia, texts generally survive only if there are stable institutions to preserve and recopy manuscripts; in other words, there is no Siamese Dunhuang or Nag Hammadi. The chaos and destruction that accompanied the Burmese sack of Ayutthayā in 1767 and ensuing warfare that disrupted all Siamese institutions—royal and otherwise—ensured that only a certain number of manuscripts from before that time survived. Indeed, the explosion of literary activity during the reign of Rāma I (1782–1809) was in part an effort to recover and reconstruct the literary heritage of the fallen Ayutthayā kingdom.

There are certain mitigating factors in the limitations of the Siamese literary "canon," such as it is, and even advantages that make it useful for tracking the genealogy of terms in Siamese discourse. The biggest advantages are that its relatively small size makes it manageable to work with and that it has, to a very large extent, been digitized, making it accessible to instantaneous word searches. In addition, the "elite" status of the contents of the corpus is to a large extent explained by the disruption lent by the Burmese sack of Ayutthayā and the fact that the effort to preserve Ayutthayā-era literature was itself a royal project. However, we should recognize that this state of affairs does not mean that nonelite discourse from earlier centuries is completely lost to us, only that it has been mediated by elites. The most important case in point is the popular epic *Khun Chāng Khun Phǣn*, which reflects the everyday life of ordinary people in Ayutthayā but was written down under royal patronage in the early Bangkok period.[11] Certain other written works exist that are not ordinarily included as part of the literary "canon," but they pose problems of their own as well.[12]

The largest problem posed by the works of the Siamese literary corpus is dating, which is often uncertain. This is particularly true for the oldest (nonepigraphic) works of Siamese literature, although a scholarly consensus has arisen in recent years as to which works actually come from the early Ayutthayā period (i.e., prior to the first fall of Ayutthayā to the Burmese in the sixteenth century). Datings for works in the latter half of the Ayutthayā period and into the Bangkok period become increasingly certain. Many of the works of the early Bangkok period, however, are commissioned works drawing from older Ayutthayā-era texts, which is a double-edged sword. On the one hand, they give us access to older material that would otherwise be lost; on the other hand, they make that material difficult to date. For the purposes of this book, however, the lack of granularity in the diachronic ordering of Siamese literary sources is not an enormous impediment because I am mostly interested in demonstrating the contrast between the contemporary uses of words and their usage in times prior to the absorption of Western conceptual vocabulary, which did not begin in earnest until the reign of Rāma IV (1851–1868). It is for the same reason that the end of the third reign in Bangkok serves as a rough cutoff for my corpus.

The corpus I have assembled for the purposes of this study consists of ninety-one texts from the Vajirañāṇa Digital Library (ห้องสมุดดิจิทัลวชิรญาณ) at vajirayana.org and forty-two Sukhōthai inscriptions from the Inscriptions in Thailand Database maintained by the Princess Maha Chakri Sirindhorn Anthropology Centre at https://db.sac.or.th/inscriptions/. A full list of the texts and inscriptions included in the corpus, as well as a more detailed discussion of the history of Siamese literature, can be found in Appendix B.

Saksit in Siamese Literature

The word *saksit* in modern Thai is a compound known as a *kham sǫn* (คำซ้อน). *Kham sǫn* are compounds, used less frequently in spoken language[13] but quite commonly in written language, composed of two words that are similar in meaning (or with the second component simply made up) and either alliterative or rhyming. In the case of *saksit*, the two components are the Sanskrit words *śakti* and *siddhi*, which in Thai can each be pronounced as a single syllable by placing a "killer" symbol over the second syllable. The word *śakti* comes from the verbal root *śak*, which means "to be able," and it refers to a "power" or "ability." The word *siddhi* comes from the verbal root *sidh*, which means "to accomplish," and as such it refers to an "accomplishment." The components *sak* and *sit* of *saksit* are therefore similar in their etymological Sanskrit meaning, and together they should refer to "power," "ability," or "accomplishment," which is not quite the same as the modern concept of "holy." As we will see, this is indeed borne out by the precolonial Siamese literary corpus.

Before we turn to the use of *saksit* in this corpus, however, we must recognize that *saksit* is not always or even usually the form in which the word is found. Given that most Siamese literature prior to the introduction of Western literary norms in the nineteenth century (and thus almost all of our corpus) was in verse, Siamese authors often flipped the order of the elements in *kham sǫn* to fit the needs of meter and rhyme in a particular context. Thus, *saksit* is often found (without any apparent difference in meaning) as *sitthisak* (สิทธิศักดิ์). This form has three syllables because it is not written, strictly speaking, as a Thai *kham sǫn*, but rather as a proper Sanskrit compound, or *samāsa*—that is, as *siddhiśakti*, with only the very last syllable suppressed by the Thai "killer" symbol when the final syllable of a Sanskrit/Pali word is short.

Indeed, it appears that *sitthisak* was the original form and that *saksit* was simply the flipped form. There are three reasons for this hypothesis. First, the two forms are not symmetrical. *Sitthisak* is a Sanskrit *samāsa* that one can flip into the Thai *kham sǫn saksit*, but the converse is not true: if the original form were *saksit*, we would expect its flipped form to be *sitsak* rather than *sitthisak*. Second, older texts seem to prefer the form *sitthisak* over *saksit*. The word *sitthisak* appears eight times in Ayutthayā-era texts, including five instances in the early text *Phra Lǭ* and once each in the *Süa Khō*, *Samudraghoṣa*, and *Dutsadī Sangwōi*, all three of which are likely from the reign of Nārāi.[14] The word *saksit*, on the other hand, is found only twice in Ayutthayā-era texts, once in the *Phra Lǭ* and once in the *Kham Chan Klǭm Chāng Khrang Krung Kao*.[15] In addition to an instance in the Thonburī-era *Nirāt Phrayā Mahānuphāp pai Müang Cīn*,[16] the earliest texts produced in Bangkok, those of the first reign, also prefer *sitthisak* to *saksit*. This includes dozens of examples in the *Rāmakian*, eleven in the *Unnarut*, and one in the

Phra Śrī Vijaya Jātaka,[17] as opposed to a single instance of *saksit* in the entire *Rāmakian*[18] and none in the other two texts.

This leads to the third reason for believing that *sitthisak* is the original form, which is that we see an explosion in the use of *saksit* in the works of Sunthǫn Phū, who appears to strongly prefer it to the form *sitthisak*. It appears once each in the *Nirāt Müang Klāng* and the *Sawatdi Raksā Kham Klǫn*; twice each in the *Nirāt Wat Cāo Fā*, *Nirāt Suphan*, and *Khōbut*; six times in *Singkraiphop*; and fifteen times in *Phra Aphaimanī*.[19] By contrast, the form *sitthisak* appears only ten times in the entire Sunthǫn Phū corpus: twice in *Singkraiphop*, seven times in *Phra Aphaimanī*, and once in *Aphainurāt*.[20] The contrast in particular to the *Rāmakian* and *Unnarut* of Rāma I, which are replete with the word *sitthisak* and virtually ignorant of *saksit*, is striking. Indeed, I would argue that Sunthǫn Phū played a significant role in popularizing the use of the form *saksit*. It is perhaps difficult to prove that Sunthǫn Phū was himself the innovator (although he might have been) in preferring the form *saksit*, as other works of his era, especially *Sām Kok* and the various works sponsored or composed by Rāma II, also appear to prefer *saksit*.[21] Nevertheless, given Sunthǫn Phū's unique fame and influence on modern Thai, it seems likely that *his* preference for the form *saksit* would have been decisive in making it the standard form today.

Although it is important to recognize that historically the word *saksit* came from the alternate form *sitthisak*, and that the latter was in fact more prevalent in the past, there is no discernible difference in meaning. In either form, the word, as used in my corpus of old Siamese literature, fits quite awkwardly with the modern concept of "holy" or "sacred." This can be seen from its frequent use to describe *yakṣas*, especially in the *Rāmakian*. As we saw in Chapter 2, *yakṣas* in Buddhist cosmology are at best morally ambiguous creatures, and in the *Rāmakian* they are fairly unambiguously bad, being soldiers in the army of Thotsakan (ทศกัณฐ์, Skt. Daśakaṇṭha)—better known as Rāvaṇa in the Vālmīki version—the enemy who steals Sītā and is pursued by the heroes Rāma and Lakṣmaṇa. Indeed, Thotsakan himself is at times described in the *Rāmakian* as *sitthisak*,[22] which would hardly make sense if the word meant "holy" in the modern sense.[23]

Instead, the words *saksit* and *sitthisak* consistently mean "power" or "powerful." Discerning this meaning is not difficult and does not rely on conjecture. Classical Thai poetry, as with many poetic literatures, often features the stringing together of synonyms for aesthetic purposes or simply to fill out the meter. Thus, we can use the body of attestations of a particular word in the corpus as a sort of "thesaurus" to read off synonyms. At least three words for "power" are found paired with the word *saksit* or *sitthisak*. Two of these are the words *amnāt* (อำนาจ) and *kamlang* (กำลัง), which are common words for "power" in modern Thai.[24] By far the most common synonym paired with *saksit/sitthisak*, however, is *rit* (ฤทธิ์), which comes from the Sanskrit word *ṛddhi*.[25] Although originally coming from the verbal root *ardh*, which means "to prosper," it came to refer to what we might from a modern (and entirely etic) perspective call "supernatural" powers.[26] This is particularly true in Theravāda Buddhism, in which (as Pali *iddhi*) the word refers specifically to a set of eight supernatural powers enumerated in the scriptures: multiplication of one's body, invisibility, passing through walls and other solid objects, diving into the ground, walking on water, levitation, touching the sun and moon, and traveling to distant heavens.[27]

This association with not just any ordinary power, but more specifically what we might call "supernatural" power, is generally characteristic of the use of the words *saksit* and *sitthisak* throughout the corpus. The words are used most commonly to describe a variety of living beings. These living beings include human beings, but the vast majority are nonhuman, "supernatural" beings. Supernatural beings described as *saksit* include, as we saw, *yakṣas*, especially in the *Rāmakian*.[28] In a few cases, specific Indic gods are described as *saksit*.[29] In the vast majority of cases, however, the supernatural being described as *saksit* is what we can generically refer to as a "guardian spirit."[30] These are local spirits associated with a particular physical feature or a place, of the type that we will explore more thoroughly in the next chapter. In most cases, a Sanskritic term is used to refer to them. These terms include *ārak* (อารักษ์, Skt. *ārakṣa*), *thēphārak* (เทพารักษ์, Skt. *devārakṣa*), *thēwā* (เทวา, Skt. *deva*), and *thēwadā* (เทวดา, Skt. *devatā*). All of these terms are some form of one or a combination of two particular Sanskrit words. The first is *deva*, which means "god," but as we saw in Chapter 2, gods in Buddhism are saṃsāric beings of various levels of power and authority. The second is *ārakṣa*, which comes from the verbal root *rakṣ*, "to protect," and therefore refers to their role as guardians. The beings referred to are therefore generally low-level in the cosmic hierarchy. At times a being referred to with the native Tai category *phī*—also implying low status—is used, although this is rare.[31]

Even when human beings are referred to as *saksit*, the implication is that the "power" they possess is not some ordinary strength. This can often be seen in the *type* of human being that is *saksit*. For example, in the *Rāmakian*

Rāma and Lakṣmaṇa are described as *sitthisak*—but these are, no less than in the Sanskrit *Rāmāyaṇa*, no ordinary human beings.[32] Sunthǫn Phū's *Singkraiphop* refers to a Brahman who can fly as *saksit*.[33] Similarly, both *Phra Aphaimanī* and the *Rāmakian* refer to *hōn* (โหร, Skt. *hora*), or astrologers, as *saksit*/*sitthisak*.[34] The very oldest text that refers to a person as *sitthisak*, the *Phra Lǭ*, uses it to describe three "doctors." Although the word *mǭ* (หมอ) by which these three are identified is the ordinary term for a medical doctor in modern Thai, historically it has been used in Tai cultures to refer to a variety of community specialists understood to have powers of healing and divination.[35] In the *Phra Lǭ*, the "doctors" in question are diviners who are in communication with a powerful local spirit.[36]

Indeed, many of the types of human beings who are described as *saksit* are indicative of the second most common referent of the word, which is knowledge. This is sometimes referred to with the generic Thai word *khwāmrū* (ความรู้)[37] but more commonly with the Sanskritic word *wittthayā* (วิทยา, Skt. *vidyā*).[38] The Sanskrit word *vidyā* comes from the verbal root *vid*, "to know," and in modern Thai, *witthayā* is most commonly found as part of the modern Sanskritic neologism *witthayāsāt* (วิทยาศาสตร์, Skt. *vidyāśāstra*), which means "science." However, premodern texts in either Sanskrit or Thai would have known nothing of modern science in referring to *vidyā*. Instead, the most immediate correlate to *vidyā* would have been the Brahmanical scriptures, the Vedas, whose name in fact comes from the very same Sanskrit root. Indeed, this is borne out by the corpus of old Siamese literature, which frequently refers to the Veda (พระเวท) specifically as *saksit*.[39] The association of *saksit* with what we might call *Brahmanical* knowledge is further reinforced by its association with *ākhom* (อาคม, Skt. *āgama*)—the name of the Śaiva scriptures—and *mantras* (มนต์).[40]

The third most common referent of the words *saksit* and *sitthisak* are certain objects, most commonly weapons. These include both swords—referred to variously as *sāng* (แสง), *khan* (ขรรค์), and *dāp* (ดาบ)—and *sǭn* (ศร), or arrows.[41] But these are not ordinary weapons. They are called *saksit* because they have been imbued with supernatural power that makes them more effective. A nonweapon "object"—if we can call it that—that is also called *saksit* illustrates the same concept. In the popular folk tale *Sang Thǫng*, which was formally written down by Rāma II, the hero of the story, Phra Sang, is being cared for by a *yaksī* (ยักษี, a female *yakṣa*), and he discovers among her belongings a magical mask that makes him appear to others to be a *ngǫ* (เงาะ), a member of a dark-skinned indigenous ethnic group that historically lived in the forests of the Malaysian Peninsula.[42] Rāma II refers to this magical form of a *ngǫ* (รูปเงาะ) as *saksit*.[43]

The sum total of instances of the words *saksit* and *sitthisak* in old Siamese literature therefore paints a fairly consistent picture. These words refer to supernatural power. This power inheres in a variety of supernatural beings, although interestingly reference is most often made to low-status beings, such as guardian spirits, as *saksit*, rather than high gods. This may relate to an emphasis on human accessibility, for when human beings are described as *saksit*, they are often specialists with the appropriate knowledge that allows them to access this supernatural power. Human beings thus can access the supernatural power of *saksit* through specialized knowledge, which in turn allows them to imbue particular objects with it, such as weapons, or to perform extraordinary actions, such as the Brahman who flies in *Singkraiphop*, the three "doctors" who can contact a powerful local spirit in *Phra Lǭ*, or Phra Sang, who can appear as a *ngǫ* in *Sang Thǭng*. To speak from an etic, Western perspective, therefore, *saksit* in old Siamese literature not only seems not to be about holiness; it appears to have more to do with "magic" than with "religion." As we will see, this is not an accident.

In fact, one of the most remarkable things about the words *saksit* and *sitthisak* in old Siamese literature is that they are almost never used to refer to Buddha images or anything uniquely "Buddhist" at all. Contemporary Thai Buddhists routinely refer to Buddha images as *saksit* and pray for the power of the Triple Gem and "all holy things" (*sing saksit thang lāi*) to protect them.[44] But such usages are conspicuously absent from old Siamese literature. Indeed, the only possible exceptions to this rule that I have found are in the corpus of Sukhōthai inscriptions, and they are doubtful. The first is a 1384 inscription that appears at first glance to use the word *sitthisak* to describe the Buddha and the Triple Gem:

๑. สิรินโมพุทธายสิทธิ สกกดิเดชะตบะพระ
๒. พุทธพระธรรมพระสงฆจุงเปนมงคลบน
๓. นเทาสรรพานดราย[45]

Note, however, that the words *siddhi* and *śakti* (I use the Sanskrit forms since the original Thai pronunciation is unclear from the orthography) have a space between them and moreover appear to be part of a list that also includes *tejas* and *tapas*. In other words, they appear to be *separate* words in a list of four attributes of the Triple Gem, and this is in fact how Griswold and

Prasert translate the passage: "Good fortune! Homage to the Buddha! May the **success, honor**, glory and austerities of the Buddha, the Dharrma [*sic*] and the Sangha be a charm to relieve us of all danger!"[46] It does not appear, that is, that the word *sitthisak*, with all its valences attested in Siamese literature, is being referenced in this passage. The same can be said of a later, 1420 inscription. Although the Database of Inscriptions in Thailand reads it as describing *nirvāṇa* as a "place that is *saksit*" (สถานที่ศักดิ์สิทธิ์), the original spelling (สถานธิสกกสิง) makes this reading dubious.[47]

The *Saiyasāt* Context of *Saksit*

Overall, then, the evidence shows that the words *sitthisak* and *saksit* were not historically used in Siamese discourse to refer to the modern concept of "holy," such that they might be used to describe anything "religious" (another foreign concept), such as Buddha images or Buddhist personnel. Instead, they referred to supernatural power, which inheres in supernatural beings, can be harnessed by certain human beings with specialized knowledge, and can be applied to objects such as weapons. As we saw in the previous section, the words used to describe the "knowledge" through which *saksit* is harnessed indicate that the knowledge in question was, to use a modern term, "Brahmanical." This includes, most crucially, the words *veda* and *āgama*, which refer to the early Brahmanical and later Śaiva scriptures, respectively.[48]

Modern Thai has translated the word "Brahmanism" as *sātsanā phrām* (ศาสนาพราหมณ์), but this word is predicated on the nineteenth-century mobilization of the word *sātsanā* to mean "religion" and is thus not found in older discourse. This does not mean, however, that older Siamese discourse lacked a similar category for a system distinct from Buddhism that was predicated on the authority of different texts and a different set of personnel, the Brahmans rather than Buddhist monks. That category was *saiyasāt* (ไสยศาสตร์). In modern, standardized Thai spelling, this word is somewhat anomalous but clearly intended to be a Sanskritic compound. The second half of the compound is unproblematic: it is *śāstra*, pronounced *sāt* because of the use of the "killer" symbol to simplify the final consonant conjunct that is unpronounceable in Thai. *Śāstra* comes from the verbal root *śās*, which means "to teach" or "discipline," with the implication that teaching and discipline are inextricably intertwined. The word *śāstra* was used in classical Sanskrit to refer to a genre of literature devoted to systematic inquiry, and it is used in modern Thai and other modern languages that make use of Sanskrit vocabulary (such as Hindi) as a suffix to refer to academic disciplines, in much the same way as *-logy* (from Greek *λόγος*) is used in modern English.

More problematic is the first element of the compound, pronounced *saiya*. The main difficulty lies in the fact that there is not a credible way to read this word as Sanskrit. I am aware of three possible explanations for this word. The first was made by George Coedès, who reads this vowel sign as representing *-ey-*. That would make the first element of the compound a Pali word, *seyya*, meaning "better" or "excellent."[49] I find this suggestion unlikely because Thai possesses a vowel sign (เ-) for the vowel *e*, and it is not the one found here. Moreover, Coedès claims that the word as he reads it was "une designation courante de la religion brahmanique,"[50] but he provides no evidence that this was the case outside of Siamese literature, and I am not aware of any that exists.

The second explanation, made by Michael Wright, is that *saiya* is a corrupt form of *śaiva*, which would essentially make *saiyasāt* mean "Śaivism."[51] This is a very tempting explanation because it fits quite well with the way the word is used, as well as the historical context. Unfortunately, I do not find it convincing because it requires even more linguistic sleight of hand than *seyya*. To have *saiya* be a "corrupt" form of *śaiva*, we would first have to assume that Sanskrit *ś* was converted to Pali *s*, all while the diphthong *ai*—not found in Pali—was retained. In addition, we would have to assume that *v* was anomalously changed to *y*, a phonetic change that is never observed in Thai. Although Sanskrit words are often "misspelled" in older Siamese texts, the misspellings always occur because different Sanskrit letters are pronounced the same way in Thai. This is not the case with *v* and *y*, which are distinct in Thai as in most languages. Sanskrit *v* is consistently represented either by the corresponding Thai letter (ว แหวน), which is pronounced like English *w*, or by the letter corresponding to Sanskrit *b* (พ พาน), which is pronounced like Sanskrit *ph*. Indeed, modern Thai has no difficulty in transcribing the Sanskrit word *śaiva* accurately (ไศวะ), and there is little precedent, even in older texts, for a transcription of a Sanskrit word as corrupt as *saiya* for *śaiva*.

The third explanation,[52] which I favor, is to read *saiya* as corresponding to a word meaning "bed" or "sleep" that is rendered as *śayyā* in Sanskrit and *seyyā* in Pali. The only problem posed by this reading is that the Thai form does not quite correspond to either. It uses *s* instead *ś*, which would seem to indicate that it is Pali, but the use of the vowel *ai* fits better with the Sanskrit spelling than the Pali.[53] Confusion between *s* and *ś* is, however, common in Thai because they are both pronounced as *s*. Moreover, there are other Thai words that use this anomalous spelling with the intended meaning of sleep. The first is *saiyā* (ไสยา), which refers to "sleep" or "bed," and as such must come from the Sanskrit word *śayyā* or Pali *seyyā*. The second is *saiyāt* (ไสยาสน์), which can mean "sleep" or refer to the reclining position of the Buddha, and as such must be intended to render either Sanskrit *śayyāsana* or Pali *seyyāsana*. According to my reading, then, *saiyasāt* is intended to render a Sanskrit/Pali compound that, in Sanskrit spelling, would more properly be spelled *śayyāśāstra*.[54]

Although I am not aware of the use of this compound outside of Siamese literature, it is, like *siddhiśakti*, a plausible neologism. Literally, *śayyāśāstra* would mean "the discipline of sleep," or to be less elegant but perhaps more to the point, "sleeping knowledge." Although this might not at first glance appear to make much sense, I believe that the point of the neologism was to serve as a complement to Buddhism, or *phutthasāt* (พุทธศาสตร์, Skt *buddhaśāstra*).[55] Since the literal meaning of *buddha* is "awakened," *buddhaśāstra* can be read literally as "the discipline of the Awakened" or simply "awakened knowledge." Read in this way, there is a clever play between *saiyasāt* and *phutthasāt*, "sleeping knowledge" and "awakened knowledge."[56] Although there are a variety of ways that one could interpret the implications of this contrast, the most straightforward is to see it as parallel to the *laukika* versus *lokottara* distinction in Buddhism and other Indic systems.[57] That is, *saiyasāt* corresponds to mundane, "worldly" (*laukika*) knowledge, while *phutthasāt* corresponds to "world-transcending" (*lokottara*) knowledge, the knowledge that leads to liberation from *saṃsāra*.

Whether or not my reading of *saiyasāt* is correct, it is clear from actual historical usage that it was intended as a counterpoint to Buddhism and that it referred roughly to what we now call "Brahmanism." The word *saiyasāt* is at times used in tandem with the word *veda*, indicating the Brahmanical connection.[58] There are also variations on the word *saiyasāt* that imply the same connection. One of these is *saiwēt* (ไสยเวท), which is a combination of the word *saiya* from *saiyasāt* and *wēt*, the Thai pronunciation of *veda*. This word is found frequently in the *Rāmakian* and other early Bangkok literature.[59] Aside from intrinsically making the connection between *saiyasāt* and the Brahmanical scriptures, it is at times explicitly identified with the ritual work of Brahmans.[60]

Another term derived from *saiyasāt* is *phētsai* (เพศไสย),[61] a possible neologism used several times by Sunthǫn Phū (and no one else that I am aware of). The second part of this word, *sai*, is taken from *saiyasāt*, while the first part, *phēt*, is the Sanskrit word *veśa*. It is likely, however, that the intended Sanskrit word is *veṣa*, since that fits better with the use of the word in Thai, and there is already confusion between the two words in Sanskrit. The word *veṣa* can refer to a person's dress or their outward appearance in general. In modern Thai, the corresponding word *phēt* usually refers to gender—male or female—with *kathǭi* (กะเทย), or transgender women, sometimes referred to as a "third gender" (เพศที่สาม). I suspect that Sunthǫn Phū invented the word *phētsai* to imply the same sort of binary distinction between Buddhism and Brahmanism as is found between the genders male and female. In any case, context makes clear the link between *phētsai* and Brahmans. In *Singkraiphop* he refers to a Brahman from Rāmarāja[62] who "protects his caste according to the Veda, which is on the side of *phētsai*,"[63] as well as to the knowledge (*vidyā*) of a *yakṣa* that is "*sitthisak*, holding the Vĕda according to *phētsai*."[64] Likewise, twice in the *Phra Aphaimanī* he refers to Brahmans as being on the "side of *phētsai*" (ข้างเพศไสย).[65] Moreover, in the same text, he uses the word *phētphrām* (เพศพราหณ์) as an apparent synonym of *phētsai* (i.e., by replacing *saiya* with *brāhmaṇa*), in both cases linking it specifically with *saiwēt*.[66] Taken together, this evidence shows that *saiyasāt* was understood in the early nineteenth century to refer to what we now call "Brahmanism." Indeed, Sunthǫn Phū seems to have taken a particular interest in *saiyasāt*, referring to it and to Brahmans repeatedly in his works, perhaps because he was himself descended from a Brahman lineage.[67]

Although the word *saiyasāt* is not as prolific in Ayutthayā-era literature,[68] it is not absent. The earliest datable instance of the word,[69] in fact, is in an inscription on the base of a statue of Śiva that was erected by the Cāo Phrayā Thammāsōkkarāt, lord of Kamphǣng Phet, in the year 1510:

ศกัราช ๑๔๓๒ มเมียนกัษตรอาทิตยพาร
เดิอนหก ขีนสิบสีคำได้หษัดฤ // กษเพลารุงแลว
สองนาลิกาจิงเจ้าพรญาศรีธรรมาโศกราช
ปรดิสถานพระอีสวร//เปนเจานีไวใหครองสตัว
สีตีนสองตีนในเมิองกําแพงเพชร แลชวยเลอก //
สาษณาพุท สาษนแลไสยสาษนแลพระเทพกรรม
มิใหหมนใหหมองให
เปนอนันิงอนัดยว

In the year 1432, year of the horse, on Sunday,
in the sixth month, the fourteenth day of the waxing moon, in the *ṛkṣa* of *hasta*,
two *nāḷikā* after dawn, Cāo Phrayā Thammāsōkkarāt
established this Lord Phra Iśvara to rule over the animals,
four-legged and two-legged, in *müang* Kamphāng Phet, and to help uplift
the *sāsanas*, *buddhasāsana* and *saiyasāsana*,[70] and the work of the gods (*devakarma*),
that they might not be sad,
that they might be one and the same.[71]

Thus, we see that even in the early Ayutthayā period, *phutthasāt* and *saiyasāt* were being juxtaposed with one another, with *saiyasāt* associated with "Brahmanism"—in this case, through the erection of a statue of a major Brahmanical god, Śiva.

The erection of this statue of Śiva by a particular *cāo müang*, incidentally, should not be viewed as an isolated incident in Siam's early history. Both the corpus of Sukhōthai inscriptions and the chronicles of Ayutthayā are replete with references to kings erecting statues and other religious edifices dedicated to Śiva and Viṣṇu.[72] In addition, a late fourteenth-century inscription that records a pact between Sukhōthai and the nearby *müang* of Nān explicitly appeals to both Buddhism and Śaivism in the curse for breaking the oath.[73] It appeals to Buddhism by reference to the Buddha, Dharma, and Saṅgha, and it appeals to Śaivism by reference to *saiphākhom* (ไสพาคม), which corresponds to Sanskrit *śaivāgama*. As we have already seen, *ākhom* (Skt. *āgama*) would become a not infrequent word in Siamese literature for the sort of knowledge that might be considered *saksit*. This early inscriptional reference makes explicit what elsewhere is clear from context: that the *āgama*s being referred to are the Śaiva scriptures.[74]

We thus can paint a portrait of a discourse found in Siam prior to the ultimate confrontation with colonial power in the mid-nineteenth century, which I will refer to as the "discourse of *saiyasāt*." This discourse was—intentionally, it seems, based on the play between *saiya* and *buddha*—intended to juxtapose a Brahmanical "other" to Buddhism. It was not necessarily seen as antithetical to Buddhism, however, as evinced by Thammāsōkkarāt's desire for unity between them, the appeal to both in the pact between Sukhōthai and Nān, and the simultaneous patronage of both the *saṅgha* and Brahmans, as well as the latter's gods, by Siamese kings. *Saiyasāt* was understood to be a system of knowledge, with the vocabulary of that knowledge—*vidyā*, *veda*, and *mantra*, not to mention the explicit reference to Brahmans—indicative of the Brahmanical source of that knowledge. Moreover, the inclusion of the word *āgama* in the vocabulary of *saiyasāt* indicates a particular association with Śaivism. This is most likely a legacy of the importance, as we saw in the previous chapter, that Śaivism held in the Sanskrit Cosmopolis, in particular in the Angkorean Empire that was hegemonic for centuries in the territory that would later become Siam.

For our purposes, however, the most important word found in the discourse of *saiyasāt* is *saksit/sitthisak*. As we saw in the previous section, *saksit* and *sitthisak* were used to describe precisely the sorts of knowledge associated with *saiyasāt*, as well as the purveyors of that knowledge. This is not surprising given the genealogy of the constituent terms *siddhi* and *śakti* in Sanskrit. As we saw, these two words come from the verbal roots *sidh*, "to accomplish," and *śak*, "to be able." As such, they are not intrinsically very remarkable words, meaning simply "accomplishment" and "ability/power." Indeed, they are found also in Pali, as *siddhi* and *satti*, but do not play any highly significant role in Pali discourse.

They *do*, however, play a significant role in another discourse, namely the Tantric discourse that thrived in the Sanskrit Cosmopolis, especially within the dominant Śaivism of that age. As André Padoux writes:

> [T]he Tantric vision is that of a world issued from, upheld and completely permeated by, divine energy (*śakti*), which is also present in the human being who can harness and use it (her, rather) for worldly as well as ritual aims and for liberation. . . . The deity, too, when acting, is nearly always conceived as polarized in masculine and feminine, the female pole being that of power (*śakti*), a power that may be auspicious and favorable but also fierce and fearsome—this especially if in the form of a goddess.[75]

Moreover, we can add that this polarity between the masculine and feminine aspects of divinity, the latter labeled *śakti*, has its roots in the Purāṇic myth of Durgā, the goddess who was created by the gods through an amalgamation of their energy (*śakti*) to circumvent a boon that prevented the buffalo demon Mahiṣāsura from being slain by any "man."[76]

Likewise, the word *siddhi* plays a prominent role in Tantric discourse as the term most commonly used to refer to the supernatural powers that can be attained by a Tantric adept. It is true that the quest for such supernatural powers is not unique to Tantric traditions within the broad scope of Indian traditions. Yet in Pali discourse the term ordinarily used for such powers is *iddhi*, corresponding to Sanskrit *ṛddhi*, not *siddhi*. The latter term, together with related terms—*sādhaka* for the initiated adept, *sādhana* for Tantric practice, *siddha* for highly accomplished Tantric master—are on the other hand characteristic of Tantric traditions. This fact, as well as the pairing with the term *śakti* that is central to Tantric traditions, suggests, therefore, that the Thai terms *sitthisak* and *saksit* are taken from the Tantric discourses that were prevalent in the Sanskrit Cosmopolis, rather than from the Pali *imaginaire*.

As we already saw, these two words were used in old Siamese discourse most commonly to describe supernatural beings, including gods. In Chapter 2, I argued that not only are gods and other supernatural beings very much a part of Buddhism, but the definition and constitution of such beings make up Buddhism's "theological" project. Nevertheless, the use of the words *saksit* and *sitthisak* in old Siamese literature appears to associate them more with *saiyasāt* than with *phutthasāt*. In part, this is likely reflective of the role that *siddhi* and *śakti* play in Tantric/Śaiva conceptions of divinity, which are quite foreign to Buddhism's theological project. From the Buddhist perspective, however, it may be reflective of the implied distinction between *saiyasāt* and *phutthasāt* as being one between "mundane" (*laukika*) and "transcendent" (*lokottara*). Gods and other supernatural beings are not foreign to Buddhism—indeed, they are constituted by it—but since they are defined by Buddhism as being trapped in *saṃsāra*, they are associated with the "mundane science," if we may call it that, of *saiyasāt*, with the purveyors of that system of knowledge, the Brahmans, associated in particular with their worship. In this way, we can understand *saiyasāt* not as opposed to Buddhism but as "included" (in Hacker's sense) by it.

Indeed, Erik Davis has made much the same argument with respect to contemporary Cambodia. He argues that "Buddhism creates Brahmanism" through its "deathpower"—its "techniques of conquering, domesticating, and instrumentalizing spirits."[77] His work on Cambodia can be understood as showing a modern, practical manifestation of the broader theological project that I attributed to Buddhism in Chapter 2. I would argue that the category *saiyasāt*, and its associated discourse, is a precolonial Siamese manifestation of the same project. By delineating a *saiyasāt* to be juxtaposed with *phutthasāt*, Siamese Buddhists "create[d] Brahmanism," to use Davis's turn of phrase—but a Brahmanism on Buddhist terms. Indeed, as we have seen, *saiyasāt* is itself likely one of those terms. If, as I have argued, it derives from the Sanskrit term *śayyā*, for "sleep," and was intended as a play against *buddha*, "awake," then *saiyasāt* was constituted to exist within a broader Buddhist worldview as a purely mundane source of knowledge and power. In Tantric Śaivism, *āgama*s are revealed scriptures that teach one not only to attain *siddhi*s but to ultimately attain liberation through access to the divine power or *śakti* that pervades the universe. The same terms may be used in the Siamese discourse of *saiyasāt*, but they are never mustered toward a transcendental goal. That privilege is reserved for Buddhism, the Pali texts, and the *saṅgha*.

Saiyasāt, Magic, and Religion

In modern Thai, there has been a substantive rearrangement of the vocabulary we have explored in this chapter as a result of the colonial encounter in the mid- to late nineteenth century. *Sātsanā* (Skt. *śāsana*), which previously referred primarily to the teaching of the Buddha, has been "secularized" to refer to an abstract concept of "religion" that can then be particularized, with the addition of an appropriate suffix, to refer to a particular religion. *Saiyasāt* and its associated vocabulary, on the other hand, have been used to translate concepts associated with the Western concept of "magic." *Saiyasāt* itself is used to refer to "magic" as a system of knowledge and practice, what is often referred to in English as "the occult." *Ākhom* (Skt. *āgama*), which in Siamese discourse originally referred to the Śaiva scriptures, now means "magic" as manifested in a particular performative act. And *wētmon*—a combination of *veda*, the name of the Brahmanical scriptures, and *mantra*, the word for a verse thereof—now refers to a "spell" or "incantation." Curiously, however, in this process of translation, *saksit*, a word with Tantric valences and primarily associated with *saiyasāt* in older Siamese literature, has made a jump to the newly secularized concept of *sātsanā*. Rather than being marshaled to translate a concept associated with "magic," it has been used to translate the religious concept of "holy" or "sacred."

As Ruth Streicher has shown,[78] the translation of "religion" as *sātsanā* likely had its beginning in missionary efforts to master languages in the region. Early vocabulary lists, including those found in John Leyden's 1810 *Comparative Vocabulary of the Barma, Maláyu and Thái languages* and James Low's 1828 *Grammar of the T'hai Language*, equate the two terms.[79]

Sātsanā for "religion" took time, however, to enter into ordinary Thai usage. It is found as part of the phrase *sātsanā mahamat* for "Islam" in a Thai article published (by Western missionaries) in the *Bangkok Recorder* in 1844.[80] Likewise, the Thai version of the Bowring Treaty (1855) uses *sātsanā* to refer to "Christianity" (*sātsanā khrittō̄n*).[81]

The most influential publication for spreading the new use of the word *sātsanā*, however, was most likely the *Nangsū̄ Sadǣng Kitcānukit* (*หนังสือแสดงกิจจานุกิตย์*), or as Streicher translates the title, the *Elaboration of Major and Minor Matters*. This book, which was published in 1867 by Cāo Phrayā Thipphākǫrawong (Kham Bunnag) and may have received contributions from King Mongkut (Rāma IV), is a lengthy argument for the adoption of a modern Western worldview and its compatibility with Buddhism. Throughout the book, Thipphākǫrawong repeatedly uses the word *sātsanā* to refer to religion in the abstract and, with appropriate suffixes, to refer to particular "world religions."[82] As Streicher argues, Thipphākǫrawong introduces a "Buddhist secular grammar" by replacing the traditional binary of *lokiya* and *lokuttara* with a binary between *loka* ("the world") and *sāsana* (here conceived of as "religion"), mimicking Western secular discourse.[83]

The path through which the language of *saiyasāt* came to be used to translate Western concepts of "magic" is less clear. I have not found relevant translations in the earliest missionary vocabularies, most likely because they are limited in scope to addressing the most basic "religious" concepts and core vocabulary for basic communication. The earliest publication I have found in which "magic" is translated into Thai is the massive Thai-Latin-French-English dictionary of Bishop Jean-Baptiste Pallegoix, published in 1854. He translates *ākhom* (อาคม, Skt. *āgama*) as "Superstitious magical forms; forms taken from sacred books"; *wēt* (written as เวตร์, but clearly intended to correspond to Skt. *veda*) as "Magicial, superstitious formules [*sic*] which work miracles"; *wētmon* (written as เวตร์มนต์) as "Sacred, magic formules"; *witthayākhom* (วิทยาคม, Skt. *vidyāgama*) as "Magical formules"; and even *barōhit* (บะโรหิต, from Skt. *purohita*) as "Augur, soothsayer, magician."[84] Interestingly, however, he translates *saiyasāt* (written as ไศรยสาตร) and *saiphēt* (ไศรยเพท, corresponding to modern spelling ไสยเวท) as "Religious ceremonies of the brahmins."[85] Pallegoix is thus ambiguous in his treatment of *saiyasāt*. On the one hand, he recognizes the very association between the category and the Brahmans that I have argued for in this chapter, and he places it as such under the genus "religion." The vocabulary associated with it, however—all demonstrably tied to Brahmanism—he associates with magic, albeit mixed with occasional references to their being "sacred." This ambiguity—between *saiyasāt* as Brahmanism and *saiyasāt* as magic—remains in Thai usage to this day.

How did this happen? I would argue that the tendency to associate *saiyasāt* with magic was inevitable once *sātsanā* was chosen to translate the concept of "religion." The reason is that there is a certain structural parallel between the binary of *phutthasāt* and *saiyasāt* in precolonial Siamese discourse and the binary of *religion* and *magic* in modern Western discourse. Valerie Flint has shown in her work on early medieval Europe that the category "magic" was used to negotiate and contest which practices were acceptable under a Christian paradigm.[86] During the Reformation, Protestants extended this logic to criticize Catholic rituals (above all the Mass) as *themselves* being "magic" and thus suspect from a Christian perspective.[87] The result in modern discourse is a (fairly problematic) distinction between "religion," understood as socially respectable but primarily a matter of personal belief, and "magic," understood as an amalgam of ridiculous, superstitious practices.

Historically, *saiyasāt* did not do exactly the same work in Siamese discourse. Given the inclusivistic nature of Buddhism, the category *saiyasāt* was not intended to exclude a particular set of practices as improper or "evil" but rather to include them in a subordinated role. We see this in particular in the inscription of Thammāsōkkarāt, who wanted to unite *phutthasāt* and *saiyasāt*. Nevertheless, the subordinate role given to *saiyasāt* in Siamese Buddhism as a purely *laukika* system of knowledge—as I indicated, no space was ever given for Śaiva soteriologies—provided a close-enough parallel to the Western binary between "religion" and "magic." The credibility of this parallel would only have been accentuated by the increasing prestige of Western science, which relegated *saiyasāt* to a position of irrelevance or, worse, ridiculousness. The rise of "science" as the primary category of "true knowledge" during the colonial era forced a sorting of indigenous systems of knowledge and praxis into respectable (but secularized) "religions" on the one hand and disreputable, worthless "magic" on the other.[88] With Buddhism adapted to the "religion" category, *saiyasāt* was inevitably pushed toward the "magic" category.

Why, then, was the word *saksit*, unlike other words associated with *saiyasāt*, summoned to translate a *religious* concept, namely that of the "holy"? As I showed at the beginning of the chapter, it is not obvious that the Western concept of "holy" or "sacred" should be translated by *saksit*, and French Catholic translators in the seventeenth century in fact seemed to regard it as simply untranslatable. As missionary activity in Siam reignited in earnest in the early nineteenth century, however, there was a pressing need to find a way to convey the concept in Thai idiom, especially in biblical translation, and Jones's influential Bible translation was likely pivotal in cementing the equation between the words *holy* and *saksit*. But why did he and others settle on *saksit*?

On this question, we can only speculate, but there is, I suggest, a plausible explanation. Of all the words from the old discourse of *saiyasāt*, *saksit* is the least amenable to translation to the vocabulary of "magic"; it is associated strongly with the gods (among other supernatural beings), so it has a positive connotation that is not easily made negative. Indeed, this association with the gods may have been precisely what made it attractive to missionaries as a translation for *holy*. After all, God in Christianity is holy, and he is a god. That is not to say that Christianity recognizes God as a member of a broader category of gods, but as we saw in Chapter 2, Christianity is a theological project among many in a broad series of theological discourses that continuously constituted and reconstituted, defined and redefined, the category of "god." Buddhism, as we saw, is another such theological project, one that shares a common genealogical root with Christianity via the implicit theology of Indo-European discourse. Even though Christianity and Buddhism disagree about the nature of god(s), there is a shared conceptual framework that allows for the transference of traits from one discourse to another. The result was that, whereas before the encounter with colonialism *saksit* was associated with a *saiyasāt* (Brahmanism) that was "included" by *phutthasāt* (Buddhism), after that encounter *saksit* was transferred to a newly constituted concept of *sātsanā* (religion) that was protected, through the grammar of secularism, from the conquest of *saiyasāt* (magic) by *witthayāsāt* (science).

Summary

In this chapter, I have traced the genealogy of the term *saksit* by situating it in what I call the "discourse of *saiyasāt*" and exploring how it was used in old Siamese literature. As we saw, *saksit* did not originally mean "holy"; instead, it referred to supernatural power that inheres in supernatural beings but can also be accessed by human beings expert in a system of knowledge known as *saiyasāt*. The contextual use of the category *saiyasāt* indicates that it corresponded roughly to what we now call "Brahmanism," although it was a Brahmanism subordinated to Buddhism through inclusivism. *Saiyasāt* provided a link to the old Sanskrit Cosmopolis and was probably necessitated by the enduring legacy and cultural memory in early Siam of the old Sanskrit Cosmopolis and previous predominance of Śaivism. At the same time, it provided precisely the opening within Siamese discourse for continually evolving Hindu discourses to operate within Siamese Buddhist discourse, as we noted in the previous chapter.

The absorption of the vocabulary of Western modernity in the nineteenth century, however, completely reconfigured these categories. The bulk of the "discourse of *saiyasāt*" was marshaled to translate the very loaded concept of "magic," but *saksit* was anomalously transferred to the newly secularized concept of *sātsanā* or "religion." This modern reconfiguration of categories created new possibilities for the use of *saksit* that did not exist before. For our purposes, the most important of these new possibilities is the use of the word *saksit* to describe specifically Buddhist objects like Buddha images, something that was generally not the case in older Siamese discourse. The contemporary discourse of *sing saksit*, "holy things," in Thailand has roots in very old concepts in Siamese discourse but is nonetheless made possible by modernity. By making *saksit* a "religious" concept and Buddhism a "religion," modern Thai discourse has allowed for the delineation of a field of praxis according to parameters—including Buddha images and prominent monks together with local spirits and Indic gods—that were not possible previously. This shift of the conceptual horizons has led both to reconfigurations of practice and to new avenues of discourse and polemic.

Indeed, many of these new avenues of discourse and polemic are predicated on the fact that *saksit* was never fully severed from *saiyasāt*, nor did *saiyasāt* lose its older connection with the knowledge and praxis of the Brahmans. Instead, the conceptual shift introduced a whole series of ambiguities. *Saiyasāt* is suspect insofar as it is "magic," but it can also be valorized as "religion" insofar as it is associated with Hinduism. A Buddha image is *saksit*—a good thing!—because it is a valued "religious" object, but that also opens it, or rather the practices surrounding it, to scrutiny insofar as *saksit* is still associated with *saiyasāt* and therefore (according to the old meaning) Brahmanism/Hinduism or (according to the new meaning) magic. Both are, to the critical eye, problematic in their own way.

In Part II, we shift from the progressive contextualization of the concept of *saksit* found here in Part I to a closer examination of the actors involved: the *sing saksit* themselves. The three chapters of Part II are dedicated, respectively, to the three major categories of *sing saksit* as reflective of Kirsch's schema: spirits, gods, and Buddha images. As I explained in the introduction, however, any attempt at categorizing *sing saksit* is ultimately arbitrary. The danger of organizing the chapters in this way is thus to further reify the problematic model of Thai religion as a syncretistic "mix" of three elements: animism, Hinduism/Brahmanism, and Buddhism. That is of course not my intent. It is instead a convenience, a means for dismantling piece by piece syncretism as a model for Thai religion. In each chapter, I will problematize one of the supposed "components" of Thai religion to show how interacting discourses have conspired to create the illusion of said component in isolation from the other two.

PART II

DECONSTRUCTING THE SYNCRETISM OF HOLY THINGS

5
Spirits

As we saw in the introduction, every schema that has been proposed for syncretic models of religion in Thailand and other Theravāda Buddhist cultures has included at the bare minimum a dichotomy between Buddhism proper and "something else" that is local. That something else is called by various names. In the past it was frequently referred to as "animism," a fraught term with a dubious pedigree in the racist evolutionary theories of religion prevalent in earlier anthropological scholarship.[1] More recently, it tends to be referred to by some variation of "local religion" or "spirit religion," preserving the dichotomy with Buddhism while discarding the racist overtones of "animism." In Thai, it is frequently referred to as *sātsanā phī*, making particular reference to the most important category for supernatural beings in Tai discourses over the *longue durée*. The basic pattern of a dichotomy between Buddhism and "something else," however, is part of a much broader tendency in the study of religion to posit a dichotomy between abstracted "world religions" that are assumed to be universal and various local traditions—"folk religion" or "popular religion," as it is often called—that are not.[2] Indeed, one of the most influential dichotomizations of this type, distinguishing between "Great Tradition" and "Little Tradition," was made by anthropologist Robert Redfield as a general theory of human culture and then applied by his student McKim Marriott to Hinduism in India.[3]

In this chapter, I will use the particular case of Thailand and its predecessor Siam to argue that "local religion," "local spirits," and all such related terms are fundamentally etic concepts produced by universalizing discourses. In the context of Thailand, this phenomenon takes two interrelated forms. On the one hand, Buddhism itself is a universalizing discourse that, as we saw in Chapter 2, acts upon various categories for supernatural beings as part of its implicit theological project. On the other hand, the modern discourse of world religions has abstracted and decontextualized Buddhism to fit a particular Christian paradigm, in such a way as to render uncanny the very presence of supernatural beings within Buddhist societies. My goal in this chapter will be to deconstruct the work done by these universalizing discourses so

Holy Things. Nathan McGovern, Oxford University Press. © Oxford University Press 2024.
DOI: 10.1093/9780197759912.003.0005

as to demonstrate that "local religion" and related terms fundamentally lack specificity. To wit, I will show that it makes little sense to refer to something called "local religion" when ultimately both *everything* and *nothing* about religion is local.

I will begin this chapter by showing that the key components of the "local spirit religion" encountered by Buddhism in Siam and surrounding Tai cultures was not an essential kernel of "Tai" culture but rather an inheritance from an earlier history of contact with China. Next, I will argue that the most important category in this inheritance, the *phī*, was introduced into Buddhist discourse in such a way as to relegate it to a lower cosmological level, contrary to its earlier, more expansive usage. Then I will show how the current array of low-level supernatural beings in modern Thailand was produced through the nexus of interacting cosmopolitan discourses that I described in the Chapter 3. Finally, I will argue that the modern discourse of religion has obfuscated the way in which supernatural beings are constituted by discourse so as to, ironically, reconstitute a certain segment of them in Thai culture as a separate "religion" of "spirits" that has "mixed" with Buddhism.

The Chinese Roots of Tai "Spirits"

Using the methodological tool of reading Buddhist discourse as operating as an "implicit theology," which I presented in Chapter 2, it can be tempting to say that there is a "local" Tai religion, or "native" Tai cosmology, that was encountered by Buddhism and then reconfigured by its implicit theology. This approach risks reconstructing the model of syncretism under a different guise, which is problematic not simply as a matter of principle but because it involves an ahistorical essentialization of pre-Buddhist (or to be more exact, pre–*Pali* Buddhist) Tai culture. Unfortunately, there is little to no historical evidence for Tai culture prior to its contact with Pali Buddhism. Moreover, although initial contact with Pali discourse seems to have been made in the late first or early second millennium as Tai peoples moved south into Southeast Asia and encountered groups (especially the Mon) who already practiced Pali Buddhism, its adoption was so thorough among Tai groups that it is found as far north as the Dai in Yunnan. Nevertheless, it is methodologically obvious that Tai culture could not have existed prior to its dispersal simply as a static, essentialized entity in its apparent "homeland"—the region around the border between Guangxi Province in China and northern

Vietnam.[4] And although it is nearly impossible to trace this "prehistory" of Tai culture in any detail, there is substantial and growing evidence from comparative linguistics that early Tai culture was significantly influenced by Chinese culture.

Hundreds of proto-Tai words have been identified as having distant cognates in Old and Middle Chinese,[5] the classic study by Prapin Manomaivibool identifying a total of 621 examples[6] and a more recent study by Gong Qunhu nearly doubling this number to 1,230 possible cognates.[7] Significantly, this evidence for proto-Tai borrowings from Chinese indicates a long period of contact with Chinese culture(s) rather than a short period of contact just prior to the dispersal of the Tai peoples from the Guangxi region to the south and west from the eighth to tenth centuries. Pittayawat Pittayaporn has demonstrated that the linguistic features of Chinese words that were absorbed into proto–Southwestern Tai range from stages in the Chinese language as old as the period just before Late Han Chinese but no later than Late Middle Chinese, indicating a period of linguistic contact of approximately one thousand years, from the late first millennium BCE to the late seventh century CE.[8]

How are we to account for such a long period of linguistic contact? Since ancient times, the Han Chinese referred to the "barbarians" to the south of the "Middle Country" (中國) as the *bǎi yuè* (百越) or "Hundred Yuè." As with all Chinese terms for frontier "barbarians," the term *yuè* was probably inexact, but it must have included early speakers of Tai-Kadai, the language family from which modern Thai and related Tai languages are derived. In the millennium from the Qín conquest (third century BCE) to the Tang Dynasty (690–705), the region inhabited by the Hundred Yuè was progressively and at times quite forcibly Sinicized. This culminated with the violent suppression of Yuè revolts by the Tang court, corresponding roughly to the time when the Tai peoples began migrating west as far as Assam in India and south into Southeast Asia.[9]

David Holm has further argued that the antiquity of Tai contact with Chinese culture may be explained by taking seriously the origin of the term *yuè* in the name of one of the kingdoms of the early Warring States Period (476–221 BCE). This kingdom of Yuè existed at the far southeastern corner of the ancient Chinese world, along the coast. It conquered the neighboring kingdom of Wú (吳) to its north in 473 BCE. Yuè was in turn conquered by the much larger kingdom of Chǔ (楚) in 333 BCE. Scholars who have studied evidence for the languages of Yuè, Wú, and Chǔ have found a preponderance of loanwords from Tai-Kadai.[10] The elites of these kingdoms fled south during these conquests and the subsequent Qín conquest (221 BCE) that unified China, giving rise to the various kingdoms of the so-called *bǎi yuè* that proved resistant to the centralized rule of subsequent Chinese dynasties over the course of the next millennium.

Holm argues that the Sinified Tai came from precisely the elites of these southern kingdoms as they fled south. He writes:

> I think in all probability that the states on the edge of the sinosphere, including Wu and Yue but also Shu 舒 and Chu, were what you might call multi-ethnic layer cakes, ruled over by partly sinified elites but incorporating a variety of linguistic and occupational groups. These societies showed marked stratification, with aristocratic families and their entourages, household slaves, and bodyguards at the centre, surrounded by a secondary layer of craftsmen, scribes, and suppliers of other important services to the court, and farmer-soldiers providing military service. Scions of collateral branches were put at a safe distance from the court by requiring them to go out and establish satellite houses in new locations. This is very much the kind of Tai polity and confederation that investigators like Georges Condominas found in the peripheral areas of Southeast Asia in the recent past.[11]

A dispersal of Sinicized speakers of proto-Tai languages to the south at the time of the initial Qín conquest, followed by the progressive incorporation of the South into the Chinese imperial state over the course of the next thousand years, would indeed explain the wide chronological range of premodern Chinese loanwords into the proto-Tai languages that they then carried with them into India and Southeast Asia at the end of the first millennium CE.

Whatever the exact scenario that led to the substantial Chinese influence on proto-Tai, it is clear from the specific cognates found that this influence extended to social organization and culture. As we saw in Chapter 3, the basic unit of political organization in Tai cultures is the *müang*, with the "lord" of a *müang* known as a *cāo* or *cāo müang* (เจ้าเมือง). Both of these words come from Chinese. The word *müang* comes from the Chinese character *méng* (盟),[12] which means an "oath" or "union" or "league," thus referring to the political nature of the *müang* as a union of different villages, families, and ethnic groups under the leadership of a single lord.[13] The Tai word for "lord," *cāo*, is in turn derived from the Chinese character *zhǔ* (主), which also refers to a "master" or "lord."[14] Since the Chinese would have dealt with "barbarians" at the periphery of the empire primarily through the leaders of corporate entities, the basic organization of Tai society according to *cāo* and *müang*, or rather *zhǔ* and *méng*, was most likely designed to be legible to Chinese leaders.[15]

Other basic terms for social and political organization were also borrowed from Chinese. The title *khun* (ขุน) is derived from the Chinese character *jūn* (君), which like *zhǔ* can refer to a lord or even a monarch.[16] This title was at one time used as a synonym for *cāo müang*—as exemplified by the Sukhōthai inscriptions, including the famous inscription of Phọ̄ **Khun** Rāmkhamhāng (พ่อ**ขุน**รามคำแหง). It later became a middling title of nobility in Ayutthayā and Bangkok. Likewise, the word *chiang* (เชียง) derives from the Chinese character *chéng* (城), which refers to a "city wall" or "walled city."[17] As the Tai began to build walled cities as the strongholds of their *müang*, they often used the word *chiang* as a prefix to the name of the town. This is seen in Chiang Mai (the erstwhile capital of Lānnā), Chiang Rāi, and Chiang Sāēn in modern Thailand, but also in Chiang Rung (Jinghong in Yunnan, the erstwhile capital of Sipsọ̄ng Pannā), Chiang Tung (Kengtung in the Shan State of Burma), and Chiang Thọ̄ng (Luang Phabāng in Laos).

The Chinese influence on Tai sociopolitical organization, however, was not restricted to such outward-facing terminology, as is demonstrated by comparative linguistics. It also extended to the internal organization of Tai states. Although the evidence is somewhat fragmented, it appears that Tai states typically were organized according to a numerical system of ranks involving progressive authority over larger groups of men and/or rice fields. This is reflected in the Tai Yuan Laws of Mengrāi,[18] in a Sukhōthai inscription,[19] in descriptions of the former political systems of the Tai Dam and Tai Lǖ,[20] and in its most developed form in the system of *sakdinā* (ศักดินา, lit., "rank of rice fields")[21] that was developed in Ayutthayā and inherited by the successor kingdom of Bangkok. As Vickery has convincingly argued, this system of numerical ranking was most likely derived from the Chinese, who also had a numerical system of ranks, counted nominally according to bushels of rice rather than rice fields, for all officials from the emperor's son down. Even aspects of Ayutthayan central administration appear to have been derived from Chinese models, such as the department of Brahmans, which was parallel to the Chinese Censoriate in structure and served a similar judicial function.[22]

Given the deep Chinese influence on Tai sociopolitical structure, it should be little surprise that Chinese influence can also be seen in those aspects of Tai culture that modern discourse deems "religious"—even, more specifically, on Tai "indigenous religion." Since this category has roots in the problematic concept of "animism," a useful starting point is the spirit or spirits that dwell within the (nonpossessed) human body. Scholarly and popular literature often refers to two such spirits. The first is the *winyān* (วิญญาณ), which comes from the Pali word *viññāṇa* (Skt. *vijñāna*) and refers to consciousness, one of the five aggregates (*khandhas*) in Pali Buddhist philosophy. Often the word *winyān* is translated into English as "soul," and this is not an unfair translation insofar as it is understood in Thai culture as animating the body while it is alive, then leaving the body at death and animating another in the process of reincarnation. There exists a persistent misconception among Western scholars and even among some Thai people that the traditional belief about the *winyān* as a transmigrating soul is "wrong" according to Buddhist doctrine. In fact, Pali Buddhist texts make it quite clear that it is the consciousness that transmigrates at death, but like all of the aggregates it is impermanent (*anicca*) and constantly changing, a process rather than a permanent self (*attā*).[23] Therefore, I will not have anything further to say about the *winyān* in this chapter; I mention it here only because it has at times been attributed to some sort of "animistic" influence in spite of being quite standard Buddhist doctrine.

The other type of spirit that dwells in the human body is known as the *khwan* (ขวัญ). This spirit is more relevant for our purposes because it does not derive from Buddhist doctrine. Moreover, it is not singular; according to popular conception, there are a number (often but not always said to be thirty-two) of *khwan* that dwell within a human body, occupying different body parts and organs. The most significant characteristic of *khwan* is their propensity to wander out of the body; this poses a problem, since the flight of *khwan* from the body leads to ill health. One of the most common traditional practices in Tai societies is a rite known as *phithī sū khwan* (พิธีสู่ขวัญ), *phithī riak khwan* (พิธีเรียกขวัญ), or *phithī tham khwan* (พิธีทำขวัญ). This ceremony as practiced by various Tai groups has been studied and described in detail by several scholars.[24] In its simplest form, it consists of a Buddhist monk, lay ritual specialist, or ordinary village elder tying a sacred thread (*sāi sin*, สายสิญจน์) around the person's wrist to bind the *khwan* to the body.

Given that the *winyān* is derived from the Pali *imaginaire*, but the *khwan* is not, scholars often have seen the latter as central to Tai "animism" or "spirit religion." In fact, however, the word *khwan* (ขวัญ) is cognate with the Chinese character *hún* (魂), which, together with the *pò* (魄), is one of the two types of "soul" recognized within traditional Chinese anthropology. The parallels between the Tai *khwan* and Chinese *hún* are by no means exact but bear clear similarities between the cognate terms *per se*. According to early Chinese anthropological understandings going back to the Zhōu Dynasty, the body is animated by two types of soul with different inherent natures: the *hún* goes upward to heaven at death, while the *pò* descends to earth. There were, moreover, multiple *hún* and *pò* souls in a single person, both having a propensity to leave the body, leading to illness or even death. Over time, this basic schema was systematized. The *hún* was correlated with *shén* (神), which are heavenly spirits, and with the active, light, and luminous principle of *yáng* (陽). The *pò*, conversely, was correlated with *guǐ* (鬼), or ghosts, and with the passive, heavy, and dark principle of *yīn* (陰). In addition, the total number of these souls in an individual was set at three *hún* and seven *pò* (三魂七魄). This schema became important to Daoist thought, and Daoists developed rituals to summon wandering *hún* and *pò* in cases of illness.[25]

There are obvious differences between the fully developed Chinese scheme of *hún* and *pò* and Tai beliefs about the *khwan*. To begin with, the *khwan* is not paired with another type of soul cognate with the *pò*, although the *phī* does seem in a sense to take on this role insofar as the *khwan* is associated with life and the *phī* (often) with death.[26] In addition, the traditional number given for *khwan* in the body, often set at thirty-two,[27] does not correspond either to the number of *hún* alone (three) or to *hún* plus *pò* together (ten) in the standardized Chinese schema. Nevertheless, the basic idea of a *multiplicity* of souls is shared between the cultures, as is the idea that these souls have the propensity to wander from the body, causing illness, necessitating rituals to "summon" them back.

On this last point, it is significant that the word for such a ritual specialist, which is *mǭ* (หมอ) in Tai languages, also is derived from Chinese. The word *mǭ* is most commonly used in Thai today to refer to a medical doctor, but prior to the introduction of modern Western medicine in the late nineteenth and early twentieth centuries, *mǭ* referred to a lay ritual specialist. In the traditional village context, *mǭ* would be called upon to treat those who were ill, which explains the modern utilization of the word to mean "doctor." Nevertheless, their purview goes far beyond what we now associate with "medicine," extending into exorcisms, communication with the dead, and general facilitation of interactions with supernatural beings. Different types of *mǭ* are distinguished according to their ritual specialty: for example, *mǭ dū* (หมอดู, astrologer), *mǭ phī* (หมอผี, specialist dealing with *phī*), *mǭ tham* (หมอธรรม, exorcist). Other words may be used to describe such lay ritual specialists (including *phrām* or "Brahman"), but *mǭ* is the most common everyday term, having great flexibility in its ability to take a suffix to indicate the nature of the specialist's expertise. *Mǭ* and related lay ritual specialists have been studied ethnographically in traditional village settings by several scholars, most notably Tambiah and Hayashi.[28] In addition, Condominas has shown that *mǭ* play a much larger role in non-Buddhist Tai Dam society, in which they are a hereditary priesthood that maintain the cult of the *fī* (*phī*) and serve as advisors to the *cāo*.[29] The Chinese cognate of *mǭ* is *wū* (巫), which like the former refers to a traditional ritual specialist.[30]

While there are clear etymological clues linking the Tai *khwan* to the Chinese *hún* and corresponding ritual specialist *mǭ* to the *wū*, the issue of parallels between Tai and Chinese conceptions of "spirits" more broadly is a bit more complicated. Nevertheless, as has already been noted by Anuman Rajadhon, there are clear structural parallels between the praxis of propitiating spirits in the two cultures. The most visible type of spirit in the modern Thai context is known either as the *cāo thī* or Phra Phūm (เจ้าที่, พระภูมิ). The word *cāo thī* is Thai for "lord of the place," while the name Phra Phūm comes from the Sanskrit word *bhūmi*, which means "land" or "earth," thus referring to the same concept. This is the land spirit (see Figure 5.1). The idea behind propitiating a land spirit is that he is disturbed when a human structure is built. If properly served with offerings, he will protect the structure and the people within it. If not properly served with offerings, he has the potential to wreak havoc. This is the basis of the *do ut des* relationship of *kānbonbānsānklāo* that I described in the introduction.

The cult of Phra Phūm or *cāo thī*, the land spirit, parallels closely the Chinese cult of the *tŭdì gōng* (土地公).[31] The *tŭdì gōng*, literally, "duke of the land," is a common deity worshiped throughout Chinese cultures, usually through a simple shrine shared by a village, although, as has been the case in Thailand, individual homes can have such a shrine in more highly urbanized areas.[32] In the fully developed hierarchy of the Chinese pantheon, which parallels the imperial bureaucracy of premodern China, the *tŭdì gōng* is on the diametric opposite end of the spectrum from the Jade Emperor (玉皇). He is one of the lowest "officials" in the bureaucracy, which one interlocutor has compared to a "village chieftain."[33] Like Phra Phūm, the *tŭdì gōng* can

Figure 5.1 A shrine to the land spirit (Phra Phūm) in Phūket. Photo by Nathan McGovern.

be propitiated for boons, according to a *do ut des* transaction that is then extended to other, more exalted deities.[34]

Similarly to the parallel between Thai Phra Phūm and Chinese *tǔdì gōng*, Anuman Rajadhon has also drawn a parallel between the Thai cult of the City Pillar and the "City God," or rather *chéng huáng shén* (城隍神), of Chinese cultures.[35] The former are known in Thai as *lak müang* (หลักเมือง) or sometimes *süa müang* (เสื้อเมือง). The most famous and elaborate such shrine today is, unsurprisingly, found in Bangkok near the Grand Palace (see Figure 5.2), but *lak müang* shrines are found in provincial capitals around Thailand, as well as in Laos and among other Tai ethnic groups outside of Thailand and Laos proper. A *lak müang* shrine consists of a wooden pillar or pillars that stand upright from the ground, with a variable height from a few feet to a couple of meters. For that reason, they are usually referred to in English as "City Pillar" shrines. These pillars are understood to house the guardian spirit of a particular *müang*, known as the *cāo phǭ lak müang* (เจ้าพ่อหลักเมือง). Historical evidence for the establishment of *lak müang* tends to be scanty, but there often exist popular tales around them, including the one in Bangkok, that they involved human sacrifice—that is, that human beings were sacrificed to the *cāo phǭ lak müang* and buried, with the pillars erected over their corpses. In any case, the current distribution of *lak müang* across the Tai-speaking world, as well as the stability of the name for these shrines, indicates that the erection and propitiation of these shrines is a very old Tai practice.[36]

The Chinese *chéng huáng shén*, on the other hand, is, as its name suggests, a god (*shén*) of the city wall (*chéng*) and moat (*huáng*). As such, it may be built on the periphery of a city, and a typical shrine will contain an anthropomorphic image of the deity rather than a pillar as in the Thai *lak müang* shrine. In addition, a *lak müang* shrine is usually found in the center of a city, not at the city wall. Thus, the cultic aspects of the two types of spirit are quite different, complicating any theory of direct borrowing. Nevertheless, the functional similarity invites easy comparisons between *lak müang* and *chéng huáng shén* shrines, with the result that *lak müang* shrines in Thailand, especially the largest one in Bangkok, are particularly popular with Chinese people.[37]

If there are functional similarities in the worship of spirits in Tai and Chinese cultures, this raises the question of a common classification between them. The traditional category used in Tai cultures for supernatural

Figure 5.2 The City Pillar Shrine (*sān lak müang*) in Bangkok. Photo by Nathan McGovern.

beings of a wide variety of functions, statuses, and moral valences is *phī* (ผี), and as we will see shortly, it was only with the influence of Buddhism and the introduction of additional categories through Pali discourse that this category came to be relegated to a more lowly and often malevolent position. This contrasts with the situation in Chinese cultures, in which there is a fairly ancient dichotomy between beneficent spirits, *shén* (神), and ghosts, or *guǐ* (鬼). In addition, neither of these basic terms for supernatural beings is cognate with the Tai word *phī*. Nevertheless, Gong Qunhu has identified the Chinese character *mèi* (魅) as a possible cognate.[38] This character is used in modern Chinese in the word *mèilì* (魅力), which refers to "charm" or "charisma," but in the same sense that in English it can be said that someone with this quality is "enchanting." Indeed, the fact that the radical in this character is the character *guǐ* (鬼), for "ghost," implies that *mèi* originally referred to some sort of supernatural creature.

Other words associated with the Tai word *phī* also suggest a deep etymological connection with Chinese. The word *thǣn* (แถน), which derives from the Chinese word *tiān* (天) for "heaven,"[39] is used in the Tai origin story of Khun Borom (about which more below), together with *phī* as *phī thǣn* (ผีแถน), to refer to beings best described as gods. Another such word is *sāng*, which is often paired with the word *phī* to make *phī sāng* (ผีสาง), with little or no apparent change in meaning. The meaning of *sāng* in the expression *phī sāng* is not immediately clear in modern Thai, with the result that Anuman Rajadhon speculates at length about its possible meanings.[40] A much simpler solution is found if one recognizes, however, that *sāng* is cognate with the Chinese character *sàng* (喪), which has a variety of meanings relating to death, a corpse, a funeral, or the bereavement felt when a loved one dies.[41] The term *phī sāng* is thus likely a frozen form, derived from Chinese, that would originally have referred to a ghost.

Likewise, the expression *phī süa* (ผีเสื้อ) is found several times in the *Traiphūm Phra Ruang* and is particularly associated with the *phī* that inhabits a *lak müang* shrine, also known as a *süa müang*. The expression *phī süa* is no longer commonly used in modern Thai to refer to a type of *phī*; it is instead used nowadays as the common word for "butterfly," possibly by analogy because of the emergence of the butterfly, like a flying ghost, from the "death" of the caterpillar. Nevertheless, the expression clearly has historical importance in Tai cultures. Anuman Rajadhon notes that *süa* is a dialect variant of the word *chüa* (เชื้อ), which refers to a family lineage.[42] The term *phī süa* or *phī chüa* would thus be meaningful as referring originally to an ancestral spirit. Although the ancestral aspect of the Cāo Phǫ Lak Müang has been lost in Thailand, Terwiel notes that, among the Tai Dam, the süa müang is considered to be an ancestral spirit, and the lak müang—that is, the pillar itself—is replaced with each new generation of cāo müang.[43] Moreover, the Tai word chüa is derived from the Chinese character xù (緒), which refers to a "beginning" or "thread," thus "lineage."[44]

To summarize, then, the bulk of key concepts associated with "local Tai spirit religion" are actually derived from Chinese and thus indicative of the historical relationship between Tai and Chinese cultures. These concepts include the spirits that inhabit living human beings (khwan/hún), the spirits that inhabit the world around us (phī/mèi), and the ritual specialists who adjudicate human relationships with such spirits (mǫ/wū). Their modern appearance as uniquely "Tai" therefore cannot be attributed to their origins; instead, it must be accounted for by the unique history of Tai-speaking peoples as they spread into Southeast Asia. What we need, therefore, is not the construct "local Tai spirit religion" but rather the deconstruction of such through thoroughgoing historicization. I will begin this process in the next section by focusing on the concept of phī and how it was intervened upon by Buddhism's implicitly theological discourse.

Historicizing "Indigenous" Tai Spirits

In modern Thai, the word phī is used almost exclusively to refer to malevolent spirits, or "ghosts," as it is usually translated in English. The oldest Siamese historical sources, however—the corpus of Sukhōthai inscriptions that date from the late thirteenth to the mid-sixteenth centuries—record a much more expansive conception of the category phī. In his famous inscription of 1296,[45] King Rāmkhamhǎng enjoins his successors to propitiate the phī who resides in a nearby mountain in order to secure the prosperity of Sukhōthai:

ีมพระขฺพงีผเทพดาในเขาอนนนั่นน
เปนให่ญกว่าฺทกีในีเมองีนัฺ่ขนฺผใดีถีเมอง
ฺสโขไทีนี่แล่ไห้วีดีพลีถกีเมองีนีท่ยงีเมอง
ีนีีดีผีไห้วบ่ีดีพลบฺ่ถกีผในเขาอนนบฺ่คั่มบ่
เกรงีเมองีนี่หาย

> There is Phra Khaphung. The *phī devatā* in that mountain is greater than any other *phī* in this *müang*. If any *khun*[46] holds this *müang* of Sukhōthai and venerates him well, propitiates him correctly, this *müang* will be stable, the *müang* will be well; whoever does not venerate him well, propitiate him correctly, the *phī* in that mountain will not take care of or worry about. This *müang* will be lost.[47]

Clearly, the *phī* of Phra Khaphung is not a mere ghost or malevolent spirit to be avoided or defeated. Instead, he is a powerful guardian whose protection is sought for an entire city-state. Indeed, in this inscription, he is explicitly called both a *phī* and a *devatā*.

A later inscription of 1384 similarly uses the word *phī* to refer to a nonmalevolent class of spirits. In this case, it refers not to guardian spirits but to ancestral spirits:

> อนนนึงโสดพนํไดญูผีพผีแม่ผีแมนํเทดผู๋เปนเมิย๐อนนเปนอนนดบบแม
> ตน๐ได๋ญูผีพีอ๋ายพีญีญผีพีเอื๋อยญูผีลูกผีหลานผู๋เถ๋าผู๋แกแหงตนอนนมา
> ฝากผีตไภญูโสด

> Moreover, Foster-Father exalted the *phī* of his father, the *phī* of his mother, the *phī* of his wife, Foster-Mother Thēt, and of those of his mother's level. He exalted the *phī* of his oldest and second-oldest brothers. He exalted the *phī* of his oldest sister. He exalted the *phī* of the descendants of his own ancestors. He also exalted the *phī* of women who had married into the family.[48]

Again, the *phī* referred to in this passage are not malevolent at all but are literal family members who are exalted in death.

Finally, an inscription of 1393 that records a pact between the *müang* of Sukhōthai and Nān makes copious reference to *phī* as witnesses to and guarantors of the pact. The first part of the inscription is unfortunately fragmentary, but enough survives to show the pivotal role played by *phī* as guarantors:

> ---------- (ส)บดดวยกนนนีจุงใหไดแก---------- (อารกก)ษทงัหลายอ
> นนมีในนําในถํา---------- (ว)งศาหนพรญาผูปู ปูพรญา---------- ปูเริง ปูมุง
> ปูพอง ปูฟาฟฟืน---------- (ผ)ากอง ปูพรญาคําฟู---------- (พร)ญาผากอง
> เทานี ดําพงศกําว---------- (ผี)สิทธิแล แตนีดําพงศ ผีปูผาคํา----------

(ฝู)งผูหวาน ปูขุนจิด ขุนจอด ปูพรญาศ---------- (รีอินทราทิ)
ตย ปูพรญาบาน ปูพรญารามราช ปูไสส---------- (ส)งคราม ปูพรญาเลิไท
ปูพรญางววนำถํ ปู---------- (พร)ญามหาธรรมราชา พงำเมือง พเลิไทย
แ---------- (ลไ)ทผูดีผีชาวเลืองเทานีแล แมผูใดบซีใสให---------- (ผี)มนน
ทงัเสือใหญเซาพูคาเซาผาดานผาแ-------- (ด)งแฝงแม พระสกกพระส
เสิอทานยอางพานสถาน ปูชรมีน หมีนหวย แสนดง ทงัปูเจาพระขพงเซา
ยนนยง พระศรี ผีบางพระสกกดิอารกกษทุกแหง แตงตาดูสองปูหลานรกก
กนน ผีผูใดใครบซีจูงผีฝูงนีหกกกาวนาวคญาเปนพรญาเถิงเถาเปนเจา
อยูยีนหีนตายดงงวนนทนนดงัครยวขยวเหนอเพจีนรกตกอบายเพทนาเสว
ยมหาพีบากญาไดคาดไดพบพระพุทธพระธรรมพระสงฆสกกคาบบาบอนน
ตดดคสงฆจุงใหไดแกผูบซี่ แตนีคำปูหลานสบด ดวยกนน จุงทนนเหน
เปน ปรตยกกษดงัคำกลาวนี . . .

. . . this (oath) sworn between us, let them be . . . all the (guardians)[49] that there are in the water, in the caves. . . . The lineage of the *phrayā* who is the grandfather[50]: Grandfather Phrayā, Grandfather Rō̃ng, Grandfather Mung, Grandfather Phọ̄ng, Grandfather Fā Fū̃n . . . Phā Kọ̄ng, Grandfather Phrayā Kham Fū . . . (Phra)yā Phā Kọ̄ng. The ancestral spirits[51] of the Kāo . . . powerful (*phī*). From here on, the ancestral spirits, the *phī* of Phā Kham . . . (all) the grandchildren: Grandfather Khun Cit, Khun Cọ̄t, Grandfather Phrayā (?) . . . (?) Grandfather Phrayā Bān, Grandfather Phrayā Rāmarāja, Grandfather (?) . . . (Song)khrām, Grandfather Phrayā Lō̃ Thai, Grandfather Phrayā Ngua Nam Thom, Grandfather . . . (Phra)yā Mahādharmarājā, Father Ngam Müang, Father Lō̃ Thai, (?) . . . the Thai nobles of Lüang.[52] If someone is not faithful, let the shining (*phī*), all the great *süa*, of Mt. Phū Khā, Mt. Phā Dān Phā Dāng, hidden in the Phra Sak Phra Sọ̄ River, the *süa* of Thānya-āng Phān Sathān, Grandfather Chọramū̃n, the ten-thousand streams, the hundred-thousand thickets, as well as Grandfather Cāo Phra Khaphong of Mt. Yanyong, Phra Śrī, the *phī* of Bāng Phra Sak, the guardians (*ārakṣa*) of each place watch the two (of us), grandfather and grandson who love each other. If someone is not faithful, may this group of *phī* break his neck. May he not become a *phrayā* even though he be a *cāo* for a long time. May he quickly die within the day. May he see Avīci hell, fall into misery, and consume the great results (of his karma). May he not expect to meet the Buddha, Dharma, or Saṅgha even once. His sin is (equivalent to) breaking the neck of a monk. May this happen to the one who is not faithful. From now on, may the oath that (we), grandfather and grandson, swear to each other be seen clearly as stated here.[53]

This oath, albeit fragmentary, clearly uses the word *phī* in a very expansive sense that includes both land spirits, as in the Rāmkhamhǣng inscription, and ancestral spirits, as in the 1384 inscription. Moreover, all of these supernatural beings classified as *phī* are regarded as powerful beings who can be called upon to enforce the terms of an oath. In this respect, they are not unlike "gods" in various traditions around the world, and as such we can see that older discourses of *phī* in Tai cultures took a form reminiscent of the implicit theologies that we studied in Chapter 2.

A similar oath in which *phī* play a prominent role as guarantors is found in the *Ōṅkān Chǣng Nām*, an early Ayutthayā text that has been used for centuries in the *phithī thū̄ nām phra phiphat sattayā* (พิธีถือน้ำพระพิพัฒน์สัตยา), or water oath ceremony. This is a ceremony in which vassals and royal servants pledge fealty to the king and drink water that has been cursed, using the words of this text, to kill them should they be unfaithful.[54] *Phī* are invoked several times to witness the oath and enforce it should it become necessary. This includes *phī* of the four directions and the air (v. 20: สี่ปวงผีหาวแห่งช่วยดู; v. 21: ผีกลางหาวหารแอ่นช่วยดู), as well as *phī* of the thickets and the "ten thousand caves" (v. 39: ผีดงผีหมื่นถ้ำ). But it also includes *phī phrāi* and other "dark," malevolent *phī* (v. 25: ผีพรายผีชรหมื่นดำช่วยดู), as well as *phī hā*, which cause epidemic disease (v. 44: ล้วนผีห่าผีเหว). There thus is a range of beings encompassed under *phī* similar to that found in the Sukhōthai inscriptions.

The other text from early Ayutthayā in which *phī* play a significant role is the *Phra Lǭ*. This story involves two princesses in one *müang* who decide to seduce the prince of another *müang*, Phra Lǭ, using *saiyasāt* to cast a love spell on him. They consult *mǭ* and finally settle on an adept referred to as Pū Cāo Saming Phrāi (ปู่เจ้าสมิงพราย), who is so powerful that he is practically treated as a supernatural being in his own right.[55] Phra Lǭ's entourage is actively trying to prevent them from casting the spell, so the adept's first two attempts to break their defenses and cast it, using *yantras*, both fail. In his third attempt, he summons *phī* "from the forests, from the waterways, from the caves"[56] and sets them up as an army mounted on a wide variety of wild animals to attack the *phī* defending Phra Lǭ's *müang*. A battle then ensues, in which the soldiers on each side are referred to as "foreign *phī*" (ผีแขก) and "local *phī*" (ผีแดน), the former ultimately winning, allowing the adept working for the two princesses to cast the love spell on Phra Lǭ by tossing an enchanted betelnut into his supply (vv. 140–153). Interestingly, although the word most commonly used to describe the beings in the "spirit army" of this episode is *phī*, the Sanskrit/

Pali word *devatā* is also used (v. 144: เทวดา), and there is every indication that, regardless of the purpose to which they are utilized, these *phī* are an expansive set of morally ambiguous beings dwelling throughout nature, much as in the inscriptions and other texts we have just examined.

Whence, then, the modern relegation of *phī* to the realm of malevolent spirits? This is likely due in part to the modern imposition of the Western distinction between "religion" and "magic," as we explored in Chapter 4, but the seeds for this rigidification of distinctions are found even in early Siamese literature. We see this in those texts that specifically thematize Buddhism—that is, in which Buddhism is not simply reflected as a part of the culture but is the operative legitimizing discourse. The most important such text is the *Traibhūmikathā*, more colloquially known as the *Traiphūm Phra Ruang*, attributed to King Lithai of Sukhōthai in the fourteenth century. This text served as the foundational text in Siamese literature that established the standard Pali Buddhist cosmology of the Triple World (*tiloka*): the world of desire (*kāma-loka*), which includes the plane of earth, the hells below, and the first tiers of heavens above; the world of form (*rūpa-loka*), which includes several tiers of heavens inhabited by Brahmās that correspond to the *rūpa jhānas*; and the formless world (*arūpa-loka*), which includes the highest four tiers of Brahmā heavens that correspond to the *arūpa jhānas*.

Although this text hews quite closely to the standard cosmology given in the Pali Abhidhamma literature and commentaries,[57] it does make some attempt to address Tai cosmological categories. Unsurprisingly, this means that it locates *phī* within the broader Buddhist cosmology. What is surprising, however, given the overwhelming importance of *phī* to Tai cosmologies historically and to this day, is how *little* attention it gives to *phī*. There is a smattering of references to *phī* in the work, usually referred to as *phī süa* (ผีเสื้อ),[58] but for the most part the text categorizes supernatural beings according to Indic categories derived from the Pali *imaginaire*: *devatā*, *yakkha*, *nāga*, *preta*, *garuḍa*, *asura*, and so on.

The most significant reference to *phī süa* is in chapter 3, which deals with suffering ghosts (P. *peta*, Skt. *preta*), one of the three *dugati*s, or bad destinations of rebirth.[59] Although throughout the chapter the Sanskrit word *preta* is usually used, a particular passage effectively equates *phī süa* with them:

เปฺรตลางจำพฺวกทีเป็นเปฺรตตฺริเหตฺปฏิสนฺธินัน กรูพฺระจตฺราริยสจฺจธมฺม
เปฺรตลางจำพฺวกไป้อฺยูแฝงต้นไม้ให้ญ เปฺรตลางจำพฺวกไป้อฺยูแฝงต้นไม้ให้ญ

เปฺรตลางจำพฺวกอฺยูแทบทีราบแลเยามกินอบราบเปนอาหารเลิยงตนเข้า
เปฺรตลางจำพฺวกมีปฺราสาททิพฺยมิเคฺรืองกินนันเยามเป็นทิพฺยดงฺงเทพฺยดา ฯ

ฝูงผิเสือลางจำพฺวกอฺยูในตนไม้ แลเย้ามกินเข้าเป็นอาหาร ฝูงผีเสือ
เป็นตฺรีเหตุปฏิสนฺธิกรู้พฺระจตฺุราริยสัจฺจธมฺมแลฝูงผีทั้งหลายอฺยูในแผ่นดินอัน
ชือว่าปิสาจฺจเฌ้าบตนอฺยู แมนว่าเข้าอฺยูลับต่นไม้รากไม้เนาย ๑ กฺดี คนทัง
หฺลายบฺมีเหนตัวเข้าเลย ฯฝูงเปฺรตแลฝูงผิเสือทังหฺลาย เมือจตาย เข้ากฺลาย
เป็ นมดตเนายดำ ลางคาบเป็นตเขบแล แมฺลงเปาง แมฺลงเมา ลางคาบเป็น
ตักกแตน เป็นเหฺนาน ลางคาบเป็นเนือแลนกแสกเนาย ด่งฺงฝูงนกจิบนก
จาบนัน ลางคาบกลายเป็นเนือเถือน ผิแลว่าเข้าตายใส เนือเข้ากฺลายเป็น
ด่งฺงนันทุกเมือแล ฯ

Some *pretas*, namely those born of the three causes, know the Four Noble Truths. Some *pretas* go to live hidden in large trees. Some *pretas* live close to plains, and they tend to eat things from the plains as food to feed themselves. Some *pretas* have divine palaces. Their food tends to be divine like (that of) *devatās*.

Some *phī süa* live in trees and tend to eat rice as food. Those *phī süa* who are born of the three causes know the Four Noble Truths. And all the *phī süa* that live on the land, which are called *pisācas*, hide themselves. Even if they are hidden by a tree or small root, people do not see them at all. When *pretas* and *phī süa* die, they become little black ants; sometimes they become centipedes, scorpions, and winged insects. Sometimes they become grasshoppers or caterpillars. Sometimes they become deer and small owls, like tailorbirds and ricebirds. Sometimes they become wild deer. If they die, they become like that every time.[60]

While the categories *preta* and *phī süa* are kept nominally separate in this passage, the implication—especially when one considers that the entire chapter is about *pretas*—is that *phī süa* are the same sort of being as *pretas*. Moreover, a particular type of *phī süa* is explicitly equated with the Indic category *pisāca*. Overall, the implication is that *phī süa* effectively *are pretas*, with the corollary that they possess a similarly low ranking in the Buddhist karmic hierarchy. As a result, they suffer the same consequences when they die: rebirth as a variety of lowly animals.

A similar if less systematic placement of *phī* in Buddhist cosmology can be found in another early Ayutthayā text, the *Mahāchāt Kham Luang*, which is a hybrid Pali-Thai rendition of the *Vessantara Jātaka*. Verses of the canonical *jātaka* are interspersed with explanations in Thai, providing a fertile ground for translation and interaction between Pali Buddhist and Thai categories. Although there are a few uses of the word *phī* in this text that gesture toward the more expansive use of the word as a generic class of supernatural beings,[61] in most cases the text explicitly links the word *phī* to a specific Pali category of supernatural being: *yakkha*, *pisāca*, or *bhūta*.[62] All of these beings are ranked low in Pali Buddhist cosmology and range from morally ambiguous (*yakkha*) to consistently malevolent (*pisāca*).

At first glance the inclusion of the Thai category *phī* in Buddhist works that are dominated by Pali categories might seem to be a simple act of translation, as between the Pali and Thai words for "tree" (*rukkha* and *tonmai*, respectively). It is important, however, to recognize the significant work that is being done by translating *phī* in a particular way. The *Traiphūm Phra Ruang* places *phī* in the category of hungry ghosts (*preta*s) and *not* in the category of gods (*deva*s). Given the nature of Buddhist cosmology, this is a hierarchical and ethically laden categorization. Likewise, the *Mahāchāt Kham Luang* tends to associate *phī* with *yakkha*s, *pisāca*s, and *bhūta*s, which are all low-ranked creatures of (at best) ambiguous moral status in the Pali Buddhist hierarchy, and *not* with the more highly ranked gods whose cosmological status is indicative of their moral superiority. This act of translation, then, is not *merely* an act of translation. It is a part of the implicitly theological project of Buddhism as a broader discourse, which, as I argued in Chapter 2, not only defined "gods" as a category *per se* but also delineated them vis-à-vis other, less morally advanced beings, thus placing them high in the cosmic hierarchy. Although not entirely systematic in this respect, the thrust of early Siamese Buddhist discourse was to situate *phī* low in the cosmic hierarchy, thus transforming a landscape of variegated *phī* into one in which Indic terminology, with its associated cosmologies, was used to describe and assess the assortment of living beings, and *phī* was increasingly relegated to the status of low-rank and low-karma "ghosts."[63]

This process was accomplished by the "work" done by Buddhist implicit theology; we can see that this is the case because certain early counterexamples show that it was not inevitable. As I have already shown, the Sukhōthai inscriptions evince an understanding of *phī* as a broad category of beings, many of whom are clearly perceived as high ranked and worthy of propitiation. However, one inscription in particular uses the category *phī* in a way that indicates a uniquely high status. This inscription, which dates to the mid-fourteenth century, refers to the king of Angkor as a *phī fā* (ผีฟ้า),

which literally means "sky *phī*" but in this case can only be interpreted as referring to the king as a god, or *deva* in Sanskrit.[64]

Similarly, older Tai mythology, to the extent that it is preserved in the evidence, clearly intends a godlike status for at least some of the *phī*. This can be particularly well seen in the *Nithān Khun Borom*, an important work of Lao literature that preserves old elements of Tai mythology.[65] Interestingly, although the oldest version of this text dates to 1422,[66] and thus comes from the same era as the *Traiphūm Phra Ruang* of Sukhōthai and displays a similar familiarity with Pali Buddhism, it performs acts of translation between Tai and Pali categories that elevate, rather than lower, the status of *phī*. This text introduces the hero of the story, Khun Borom (ขุนบรม), who brings culture to humankind and becomes the progenitor of the Tai peoples, by first telling the story of a group of supernatural beings called by a variety of terms, all of which could appropriately be translated as "gods":

> **Bho Sādhavo:** listen to me, righteous men who have wisdom. Now I will talk about Phrayā Phī Thaen, who sent down Thāv Khun Borom to be born in our ancient Meuang Lao.
>
> At that time, Phī Thaen sent down Khun Borom Rājā to be born in Meuang Lao, as Phrayā [king]. Hi: [*sic*] as a matter of fact, Lao Kau [ancient Lao people] said that Thaen Fā Kheun is Phrayā In Chau Fā, with long ears pierced by holes. There were other Thaen, such as the Thaen who created rain and wind; the Thaen who created musical instruments to accompany the Lam; the Thaen who created agricultural tools and created the world. They were all Devatā, who lived in Cātummahārājikā. All of them were excellent. Lao of Meuang Lāng in the past called them Phī Fā, Phī Thaen. Actually, they named them wrongly.[67]

These "gods" send the chief god's son, Khun Borom, to rule in a place called Nā Noy Oy Nū, which is probably to be identified with Điện Biên Phủ, known as Müang Thāng (เมืองแถง) in Tai languages.[68] After reigning for twenty-five years, Khun Borom appoints his seven sons to go out to the south and west to establish *müang* of their own, each one of them corresponding to what would later become a prominent Tai kingdom. Although the story is anachronistic and mythical, modern scholars note that the sending off of Khun Borom's seven sons does correspond roughly to the geographical dispersal of the Tai peoples reconstructed from comparative Tai linguistics.[69]

For our purposes, what is interesting is the complex of words used to describe the beings I have called "gods" (to be justified momentarily) in this passage. They are variably called simply *thǣn* (แถน), but also *phī thǣn* (ผีแถน) and *phī fā* (ผีฟ้า). The word *thǣn* has been shown by comparative linguists to be derived from the Chinese word *tiān* (天), which means "sky" or "heaven." Since the Tai word *fā* also means "sky" or "heaven," these three words are essentially synonyms meaning "heavenly *phī*" or, when *thǣn* is used by itself, "celestial." Etymologically speaking, then, these words convey the same sense of "heavenly beings" as does the Proto-Indo-European **deywṓs* from which many Indo-European words for "god" derive, as I discussed in Chapter 2. As it happens, the author of this Lao text unwittingly makes this same connection by equating the *thǣn/phī thǣn/phī fā* with the Pali/Sanskrit category *devatā*. These *devatā* are said to live in Cātummahārājika, the Heaven of the Four Kings. The chief among them, called Thaen Fā Kheun, is moreover identified with Indra (Phrayā In Chau Fā), the king of the gods in the Vedic pantheon and an important god in Pali Buddhist cosmology.[70] Whereas the Siamese Buddhist texts we have already looked at tend to lower the status of *phī*, the *Nithān Khun Borom*, recognizing the intrinsically elevated status of the *phī thǣn* in the story, situates them within Pali Buddhist cosmology at the more elevated status of *devas*. This alternative trajectory thus helps illustrate the real work done by Siamese Buddhism's implicit theology in equating *phī* with *pretas* and other low-ranking beings.

"Local Spirits" in Thailand Today

Due in large part to the work of Buddhism's implicit theology that I just outlined, but also due to the influence of modern Western discourse, the word *phī* is used in modern Thai most commonly to refer to malevolent beings,[71] often but not always the spirits of the dead. For that reason, it is usually taken to correspond to the English word *ghost*. Indeed, given that the *Traiphūm Phra Ruang* many centuries ago equated *phī* with *pretas* in the Buddhist cosmology, and "ghost" (or rather "hungry ghost") became the standard translation for *preta* in the modern period, the identification of *phī* with ghosts was inevitable.

Thailand is famous for its rich culture of "ghost stories," with gruesome accounts of *phī* fueling a significant portion of the Thai movie industry. The various types of *phī qua* "ghosts" have been described in detail by Anuman

Rajadhon,[72] so I will confine myself here to briefly describing the more remarkable and well-known types of *phī* in modern Thailand. One of the most well-known *phī* is the *phī krasū̄* (ผีกระสือ), who lives among human beings as an old and ugly woman. At night, she detaches from the bulk of her body and floats about with only her head and entrails, looking for food. Her preferred food is the entrails of human beings, and thus she is associated with diseases of the digestive tract that cause one to lose weight. Similarly, the *phī pǭp* (ผีปอป), also known as a *phī ka* (ผีกะ) in the Northern region (formerly the kingdom of Lānnā), takes human form and can cause bodily pain to a victim, although he does so not by feeding on the victim at night but by possessing them.

As in many cultures, there is a fear in Thailand of the spirits of people who die violent or unnatural deaths. Traditionally such people were not cremated but buried. A person who dies a violent death (murder, suicide, drowning, etc.) becomes a *phī tāi hōng* (ผีตายโหง), and if they continue to animate the uncremated corpse, they are known as a *phī dip* (ผีดิบ) or "raw *phī*"—what we might refer to in English as a zombie. A woman who dies in childbirth is known more specifically as a *phī tāi thang klom* (ผีตายทั้งกลม) or a *phī phrāi* (ผีพราย). A special substance known as "corpse chin oil" (น้ำมันพราย) can be collected from the corpse of such a woman by holding a lighted candle to its chin. It is believed that by secretly smearing this oil on the object of one's affections, you will make them fall in love with you.[73] On the other hand, the *phī prāi* herself can appear as a human woman and entrap unsuspecting young men into falling in love with her. The most famous such *phī phrāi* is Mǣ Nāk, who lived around two hundred years ago and died in childbirth while her husband was away at war. When her husband returned, she appeared to him as her old self and wreaked havoc on the village while friends, family, and neighbors tried in vain to convince him that his wife was actually dead. After he discovered the truth, her malevolence was fully revealed, and various specialists tried and failed to defeat her, until the famous monk Somdet Tō arrived and defeated her using the power he had through his Buddhist attainment.[74]

Certain *phī* are known primarily for their eccentric forms, much like the *phī krasū̄* that flies about as head and entrails. The *phī kǭng kǭi* (ผีกองกอย) has only one foot and hops around the forest while crying out, *Kǭng kǭi!*, whence his name. Those who travel in the forest must be wary of the *phī kǭng kǭi*, who is known to suck blood from the toes of travelers while they sleep. The *phī lang kluang* (ผีหลังกลวง) approaches travelers in the forest at night in what at first appears to be a normal human form. He will ask someone to scratch his back, revealing that it is hollow and full of worms and millipedes squirming around his intestines.

While in modern Thai the term *phī* has increasingly come to be reserved for malevolent spirits, there are a variety of other types of spirits that are not considered uniformly malevolent and thus are referred to by other names. Of these, the one whose cult is the least institutionalized or commercialized is called *nāng mai* (นางไม้), literally "tree lady," and is a type of spirit that lives in trees.[75] In well-trafficked parts of the forest, such as national parks, but also in cities, one will often find trees that are wrapped with copious amounts of colorful cloth, at times with other offerings, such as food, placed near the tree. The trees targeted for such veneration tend to be large or unusually shaped. The cloth and other offerings are for the female being who is understood to reside in the tree. *Nāng mai* are among the more ambiguous spirits, at times leaning more beneficent and at other times more malevolent. In the latter category are those tree spirits that originated as women who died in childbirth, in which case they may be referred to as *phrāi mai* (พรายไม้), or "tree *phrāi*."

Two other types of spirits have a more institutionalized and commercialized cult in modern Thailand than that of the *nāng mai*. We have already seen one of these types of spirits, Phra Phūm or *cāo thī*, which as the spirit of a place is parallel to the Chinese *tǔdì gōng*. Shrines to Phra Phūm are typically found outside of any building, large or small, in modern Thailand. There is, however, a second type of spirit associated with homes and other buildings, which is known in Central Thailand as *pūyātāyāi* (ปู่ย่าตายาย; see Figure 5.3). Anuman Rajadhon reports that there are some variations on this appellation found in different parts of the country,[76] but the full form found in Central Thailand simply consists of the words for the four types of grandparents: paternal grandfather, paternal grandmother, maternal grandfather, and maternal grandmother, respectively.

Pūyātāyāi are ancestral spirits. It should be noted, however, that, at least in contemporary practice, the ancestral spirits are not conceived of as specific ancestors within a lineage, as in Chinese practice. Rather, they are conceived generically as the spirits of the ancestors who once dwelled in a particular place or in a particular house. This is reflected in the fact that shrines to *pūyātāyāi* generally have within them statuettes of a generic old man and old woman, which can be bought commercially and thus look nearly identical in any such shrine. They do not have the names or images of specific deceased

Figure 5.3 A shrine to the ancestral spirits (*pūyātāyāi*) in Bangkok. Photo by Nathan McGovern.

family members. Moreover, shrines to *pūyātāyāi* are not found only outside of homes, but also outside of institutional buildings such as schools, hospitals, and apartment complexes, where the concept of a specific ancestral lineage could not possibly apply.

Nearly every building in Thailand today has shrines to these two spirits: Phra Phūm, the land spirit, and *pūyātāyāi*, the ancestral spirit. Both are built of an elevated platform with a small shelf in front to make offerings. The shrine to Phra Phūm usually takes the form of a miniature Thai-style palace, with a statue of a Phra Phūm, depicted as a generic deity (*devatā*), placed inside. The shrine to *pūyātāyāi*, on the other hand, usually takes the form of a miniature house, in traditional Thai style, with statues of an old man and woman inside, as already mentioned. It is customary for the owners of the house or representatives of the institution owning a larger building to make offerings of food, drink, flowers, incense, and candles to these shrines every day. In addition, one will find offerings in the form of small statues of servants and traditional dancers, which, unlike the previously mentioned offerings, are left at the shrine permanently. Anuman Rajadhon reports that such offerings are a "stratagem," whereby big promises made in *kānbonbānsānklāo* are rendered in symbolic form.[77]

Although shrines to Phra Phūm and *pūyātāyāi* outside of buildings are ubiquitous in Thailand today, their current form is almost certainly a recent transformation of earlier practices due to urbanization and commercialization in the twentieth century. Vast outdoor stores for the sale of such shrines are a common sight along the highways, and various ritual specialists, from local agents to the royal court Brahmans themselves, advertise services for performing the proper rituals to install such shrines. The epic *Khun Chāng Khun Phǟn*, however, which has its origins in the Ayutthayā period and was written down in its current form in the reign of Rāma II (1809–1824), does not generally speak of permanent shrines, especially with respect to individual houses or buildings. Instead, it refers several times to a *sān phiang tā* (ศาลเพียงตา, lit., "shrine at eye level"), a temporary shrine/altar at which offerings can be made to the gods/spirits for a specific purpose.[78] Often this can include seeking the protection or aid of spirits when traveling, entering the forest, or going into battle, but a particular episode describes in great detail the ritual performed when Khun Chāng builds a betrothal house for Wan Thǫng. This involves a ritual specialist building a *sān phiang tā*, propitiating the gods and spirits, including *phra phūm cāo thī* (พระภูมิเจ้าที่), and overseeing the ritual installation of the posts that would support the house.[79] This episode in the epic is clearly based on traditional practice, as a very similar ritual is described by Terwiel based on his study of a village in Rātburī in the 1960s.[80]

Anuman Rajadhon moreover hypothesizes that the concept of Phra Phūm as it is understood today as connected to houses and other buildings was originally more connected to entire villages.[81] Anuman is surely correct in this hypothesis, as Condominas, based on his fieldwork in rural Laos, found the cult of the *phī bān* to be centered on a village shrine rather than household shrines, a finding echoed by Michael Moerman's fieldwork among the Tai Lü.[82] This development parallels the evolution of the word *bān* (บ้าน) in Thai. Originally, this word meant "village" and was used in tandem with the word *müang*, which, as we have already seen, referred to a city-state. This old meaning of *bān* is still found in contemporary Thai in the expression *bān nǫk* (บ้านนอก), which literally means "outer villages" but in practice is simply a pejorative way of referring to the countryside outside Bangkok. Nowadays, however, the word *bān* by itself means "house," and it has almost completely replaced in everyday usage the previous word for "house," which was *rüan* (เรือน). The increasingly ubiquitous erection of exalted shrines to the land spirit outside of individual buildings and even homes thus parallels the urbanization and complexification of Thai life that took place in the twentieth century.

The specific form that the cult of Phra Phūm takes in Thailand today has also been shaped by its broader historical context: the particular Siamese nexus of transforming cosmopolitan structures on the Khmer frontier that we examined in Chapter 3. According to a popular mythology in Thailand, which is found in manuals for rituals involving Phra Phūm and also recorded by Anuman Rajadhon and Terwiel,[83] there are actually nine Phra Phūm, all of whom are sons of Daśarāja (ทศราช), king of the city of Bālī (กรุงพาลี). Daśarāja was an oppressive king, so Phra Nārāi (พระนารายณ์, Nārāyaṇa, i.e., Viṣṇu) appeared to him in the form of a Brahman to trick him into submission. He requested a grant of land equal to three strides, which Daśarāja gladly granted him. Being a god, Phra Nārāi of course had enormous strides, thus depriving Daśarāja of his kingdom and exiling him to the Himavānta Forest. When Daśarāja begged forgiveness, Phra Nārāi granted him and his sons jurisdiction over different types of places with a right to offerings from human beings. The figure now called Phra Phūm corresponds to the first of these sons, Jayamaṅgala (ชัยมงคล), responsible for the *bān*—that is, the village, or now, house.

This story is derived from a Purāṇic myth about Viṣṇu. In this myth, Bali is king of the *asuras* seeking to defeat the *devas*. Viṣṇu, incarnated as Vāmana, the dwarf, appears to him in the guise of a Brahman and asks for a grant of land equal to three paces. Once Bali agrees, Viṣṇu assumes his divine form and easily traverses the entire triple world in three steps.[84] However, the transition from the Purāṇic to the popular Siamese myth likely was mediated by the Khmer. Cambodians also worship a Krong Pāli, along with Praḥ Phum. The mythology and cult of these figures has been studied extensively by Eveline Porée-Maspero.[85] In the Cambodian version of the story, it is not Viṣṇu but the Buddha who takes three strides to trick Krong Pāli into giving up his kingdom. In addition, the Khmer do not speak of Krong Pāli as having nine sons but instead identify Praḥ Phum as his younger brother. Praḥ Thorni—the earth goddess, corresponding to Nāng Thǫranī in Thailand[86]—is in turn identified as Krong Pāli's wife. Porée-Maspero convincingly argues that all three of these figures are essentially the same, and at times interchangeable in worship, each representing the earth in a different form.[87]

The modern cult of Phra Phūm appears to derive from and simplify this nexus of myths and cultic forms. At core, he is simply a village guardian, transposed to the house through the transformation in meaning of the word *bān*. In that respect, he is basically indistinguishable from the Chinese *tǔdì gōng* and most likely distantly related to the latter. Phra Phūm's mythology, however, is tied to a variation on the Purāṇic myth of Bali, known in Thai as Krung Phālī. The use of this myth to explain the cult of Phra Phūm probably dates to early in Siamese history when Khmer influence was still strong. We know this because the use of the form Krung Phālī as a name, which is found several times in *Khun Chāng Khun Phǣn*,[88] makes sense in Khmer but can be explained only awkwardly in Thai.[89] Nevertheless, the Siamese version of the myth hews more closely to the Purāṇic original by retaining Viṣṇu as the protagonist taking three strides, rather than replacing him with the Buddha, as in the contemporary Cambodian version. It thus most likely reflects an older Khmer version of the myth that was developed under the auspices of the Sanskrit Cosmopolis, prior to the introduction of the Pali *imaginaire* in the thirteenth century. The nexus of interacting discourses is striking: what we have here is a land spirit derived from Chinese practice, explained by a myth learned from the Khmers, itself based on the Purāṇas under the auspices of the Sanskrit Cosmopolis. In the meantime, the Chinese *tǔdì gōng* has been subsumed into a Sinitic pantheon, paralleling the imperial bureaucracy, in which he is a low-ranking representative of the Jade Emperor at the village level.

Although Phra Phūm appears to have followed a historical trajectory from village to house spirit, this is not to say that the house, or *rüan* as it was originally called, was not always understood to be connected with spirits. Anuman Rajadhon describes an old cult of the so-called *phī rüan* (ผีเรือน), which is synonymous with *pūyātāyāi*. In the old practice, the *phī rüan* was understood to protect the welfare of the living residents of the house, and a place in the house would be assigned for his worship. Writing in the mid-twentieth century, Anuman Rajadhon reports:

> The phii ruan or spirit of the house is gradually dying out especially with the city and town people. No vestige of phi ruan is now to be found in their houses except, perhaps, a vague idea that the phi ruan is somewhere in the house. If they want to ask their ancestral spirit to give help in their difficulties, they light one or two joss sticks and place them somewhere in a convenient place where they worship while asking for help. To the younger generation the phiii [*sic*] ruan is a nonentity except in name.[90]

This is decidedly no longer the case in early twenty-first-century Thailand. As I have already described, the cult of *phī rüan*, referred to more ubiquitously as *pūyātāyāi*, is now institutionalized as a shrine in the form of a traditional Thai house, with figurines of an old couple inside it, installed next to the palace-like shrine to Phra Phūm. This historical analysis thus explains the otherwise uncanny doubling of spirit shrines outside of houses and other buildings in modern Thailand.

Indeed, by expanding our historical horizon a bit further, we can understand how *lak müang* shrines relate to Phra Phūm and *pūyātāyāi* as well. As we saw, the Tai concept of *phī süa* likely has its roots in a Chinese conception of an ancestor spirit, and it was from there, rather than the particular cultic practices of the *chéng huáng shén*, that Tai leaders (*cāo*) developed the practices surrounding *lak müang* shrines. Indeed, in spite of having been transformed in modern Thai into mere butterflies, *phī süa*, or ancestral spirits, likely play a central role in Tai conceptions of *phī* writ large. As we have seen, the *Traiphūm Phra Ruang*, insofar as it addresses *phī* at all, deals exclusively with *phī süa* and identifies them as ghosts, spirits of the dead. Moreover, the *pūyātāyāi* spirits of modern Thailand, derived from the old Tai *phī rüan*, are ancestral spirits, represented by an old man and woman.

Condominas reports seeing the same representation for *phī bān*—village spirits—in rural Laos, while conversely Hayashi reports the use of a pillar, like a *lak müang*, in place of "expelled" village spirits in Northeastern Thailand.[91] All of this suggests that *phī* associated with social units—home, village, and *müang*—were all originally ancestral spirits, with cultic differences being mostly incidental.

There are thus significant differences to be expected between the modern forms of Tai and Chinese guardian spirits, the former influenced for the past nearly thousand years by the Pali and even Sanskritic *imaginaires* and the latter shaped by an ever-evolving and complexifying imperial Sinitic *imaginaire* over the past two thousand years. The most significant clear parallel is in the basic division between guardian spirits for local places (village and/or home) and for cities. In addition, the basic procedure for propitiating these supernatural beings for boons follows a similar *do ut des* pattern in which a supplicant asks a favor from the spirit and promises an offering in return if they receive it.

Tai conceptions of the supernatural have thus developed in their own ways, quite differently from those of imperial China, for at least a thousand, and probably closer to two thousand, years. This is what gives the culture of *phī* in modern Thailand its "unique" character—not some putative intrinsic Tai or Thai spirit but rather the particular historical trajectory that Tai discourses have followed over the centuries, as well as the dialectics they have been subject to in the process. We have already seen how this took place with Phra Phūm: the village spirit, endowed with an Indic mythology via the Khmer, now worshiped as a double to the house spirit through the transposition of *bān* from village to house in the midst of modern urbanization and commercialization. Moreover, many of the particular types of malevolent *phī* are likely borrowings from other cultures. The word *phrāi*, used to refer to the spirits of women who have died in childbirth, comes from Khmer, and other types of *phī* now recognized as characteristically "Thai" likely are borrowed from the Khmer or the Mon.[92] Likewise, Thai tree spirits, or *nāng mai*, are so similar to tree spirits found in India[93] that it is nearly impossible to ascertain whether they are a "local" practice or were brought to Southeast Asia through Buddhism or the broader Sanskrit Cosmopolis. Indeed, such a question is probably just as meaningless as asking whether trees themselves are "local" or "Buddhist."

Ultimately, a lack of historical sources makes it difficult to describe in great detail how and when the major constituents of "indigenous Tai spirit religion" were constituted and reconstituted to create the culture of belief and praxis that we observe today. Nevertheless, there is enough evidence available to make it clear that this putative "indigenous religion" can and should be historicized in terms of interacting cultural discourses, including Chinese, Khmer, Mon, and Indian. But this raises an important question: If we wish to identify an "indigenous" or "local" component of Thai religion, and nearly all of it can be traced to other cultures, then is anything in Thai religion actually "local"? When subjected to the critical lens of historical dialectics, the category "local religion" as it applies to modern Thailand or Tai cultures in general completely evaporates.

The Modern Discourse of Religion and the Construction of "Local Religion"

As I noted at the beginning of this chapter, the Western study of Theravāda Buddhism has long sought to distinguish between Buddhism proper and a "local religion" that is somehow separate from Buddhism but always found in Theravāda Buddhist cultures. For Ames, Spiro, and Terwiel, this took the form of a simple dichotomy between Buddhism on the one hand and "animism," "magico-animism," or "supernaturalism" on the other.[94] Tambiah and Kirsch complexified this simple dichotomy by adding Brahmanism to the mix,[95] resulting in the threefold schema that has become common in scholarly and even in popular Thai discourse today. Still, the urge to posit a dichotomy between Buddhism and "something else" is fundamental to all of these models. Moreover, this dichotomizing urge is constitutive specifically of "animism" or "local spirit religion" because this "religion" or "religious component" has no name for itself and lacks all existence as a reified essence in the absence of a putative "Buddhism" to contrast it to.

Where, then, does the dichotomizing urge come from? Simply put, it is a byproduct of the modern discourse of world religions. Insofar as the modern concept of "religion" is predicated on an implicit Christian paradigm, the presence of and interaction with "spirits"—low-level supernatural beings—in Buddhism appears as an anomaly. As Masuzawa has shown,[96] the "discovery" of Buddhism as a perceived parallel to Christianity was central to the construction of "religion" as a universal category. Like Christianity, Buddhism has a founder, is rooted in a historical narrative, is institutionalized, has an ethical orientation, and offers a transcendent soteriology for the human individual. Moreover, this soteriology is advanced through a particular theological project, which we examined in Chapter 2. This project is similar to the theological project of Christianity insofar as it places the founder of the religion and the soteriological goal above "the gods," but it also differs in a key respect. Instead of marking the demotion of the gods by removing them from the category of "god" altogether, as Christianity does, it retains the category of "gods"—along with a whole host of other supernatural beings—but subordinates them to the Buddha by making them impermanent saṃsāric beings subject to karma and rebirth.

Unfortunately, this distinction was not clearly understood by early Western scholars. Moreover, as recent scholarship has shown,[97] the early Western encounter with Buddhism was influenced by a host of Protestant and modernist assumptions. To be sure, Christians of the Middle Ages, if they had embarked on a project to study Buddhism on a scale akin to what actually took place in the nineteenth century, likely would not have found it surprising that Buddhists believe in and interact with a host of supernatural beings. Indeed, as we have already seen, a similarly wide variety of supernatural beings was part of the practical cosmologies of Christians throughout much of Christianity's history, and it is only in the wake of the Reformation, its attack on Catholic "superstition," and the ensuing Enlightenment that Christian monotheism has been transformed into a rejection of the very existence of nearly all supernatural beings (and indeed all for modern atheists).

Thus, when Western scholars began studying Buddhism in earnest in the early nineteenth century, they were of course familiar with religious cultures involving a host of gods and spirits, but they were no longer comfortable with the idea of a soteriologically transcendent religion like Christianity in which gods and spirits existed but played no salvific role. They recognized correctly that gods, ghosts, and the like were not of soteriological significance in Buddhism, but this led them to erroneously conclude that they must be extraneous. In the nineteenth century especially, Orientalism made it easy to dismiss any perceived "accretions" to the "pure" teachings of Buddhism (conceived of as rational and conforming to the emerging modern scientific worldview) as the result of Asian decadence that had corrupted Buddhism. At the same time, certain Asian actors embraced the narrative of a pure Buddhism that was uniquely rational and scientific as a useful polemic against missionary Christianity, and in the process they too became implicated in the construction of a Buddhist Modernism that was free of gods, spirits, and the supernatural.[98]

Ironically, the "animism" that was then constructed in part to explain the "accretions" to "pure Buddhism" was itself less a description of actual "primitive" societies than a projection of an increasingly discredited aspect of the Western philosophical tradition. We see this in the very language used to describe this supposedly "primitive religion." The word "animism" comes from the Latin *anima*, which was used to translate the Greek word *ψυχή* (*psyche*), the "soul."[99] "Psychology," not in its modern sense but in the sense of a theory of the soul,[100] was alongside theology a crucial component of the philosophy of Plato and Aristotle, thus becoming a mainstay of Western thought into the modern period. Aristotle additionally theorized that the *πνεῦμα*, literally "breath," acted as a medium or instrument through which the soul could interact with the material world, including the material body. Later thinkers utilized this idea to theorize the possibility of the soul existing outside of a material body. In late antiquity, for example, Neoplatonists introduced the concept of the *ὄχημα πνεῦμα*, or "breath vehicle," that allows the soul to ascend.[101] More important, however, given the later elevation of Christianity to a central position in Western thought, Paul in 1 Corinthians 15:44 refers to the resurrected body as a *σῶμα πνευματικόν*, or "pneumatic body."[102] Given that the Latin translation of *πνεῦμα* is *spiritus*, however, Paul's phrase is usually translated into English as "spiritual body."[103] It is thus that we get the concept of "spirits"—the very title of this chapter. Spirits are "breath bodies" that allow beings to exist without a material body.

When the rationalizing forces unleashed by the Protestant Reformation increasingly came to question the existence of these "spirits," the groundwork for the theory of animism was laid. Spirits, as a Western category, were distinct from material beings, such as humans and animals—thus, supernatural. But they were lowly creatures, being subsumed within a monotheistic Christian paradigm, and thus conceptually distinct from gods. As the rationalization of the Enlightenment excised these beings from that paradigm, a conspicuous hole was left. Because this *rationalized* Christianity became the hidden paradigm behind the modern concept of "world religions," beings and associated practices in other cultures that appeared to fill that hole begged for categorization. Tylor's theory of animism provided this categorization, and informal concepts such as "spirit religion" that have followed it fulfill the same purpose. Although I have found it unavoidable to use the term given its deep embeddedness in the English language, there are in fact no "spirits" in Thai Buddhism or any traditional form of Buddhism, since none has operated in a thought-world informed by this Aristotelian category.

What there are are living beings and anthropological ontologies that *appear* to be "spiritual" in nature because they fill the gap that was created by the self-destructed Western discourse of traditional "psychology."

The scholarship of the mid-twentieth century that sought to dichotomize or trichotomize Theravāda religious cultures was neither overtly Orientalist nor implicated in a project of Buddhist polemics. Nevertheless, its impulse to separate Buddhism from "something else" was the direct result of a Buddhist Modernist narrative that had become so naturalized as to be invisible. As Robert DeCaroli and others have shown,[104] Buddhism has always, from its very inception in India, involved a host of nonhuman (*amanuṣya*) beings, including gods (*deva*s), but also *yakkha*s, *asura*s, *preta*s, *kinnara*s, *gandhabba*s, *nāga*s, *pisāca*s, and more. The classification of these beings is not entirely consistent, and not all of these beings have a clear role to play in Buddhist cosmology. Their existence is simply assumed, in exactly the same way as is the existence of human beings, elephants, giraffes, dogs, cats, rivers, trees, and mountains.

The movement of Buddhism to lands outside of India (continuing a process that had already played out in India itself) necessitated extensive projects of translation. These projects impinged upon a wide swath of vocabulary and crucially worked in both directions. That is to say, there was a need to translate concepts from the Buddhist scriptural language into the local vernacular—in the case we are examining in this book, from Pali into Thai—but also to translate vernacular concepts or at least situate them within a Buddhist cosmology. The first type of translation was accomplished in Siam and many other Theravāda cultures in large part by simply absorbing Pali vocabulary[105] directly into the local vernacular. The reverse, however, was not the case: local vocabulary was rarely absorbed into Pali discourse, and when it was, generally only with proper names.

The fact that Tai cultures referred to a wide variety of supernatural beings as *phī* posed a dilemma. To be clear, that dilemma was *not*: How do we "mix" the "religion" of *phī* with Buddhism? Rather, the dilemma was: What are *phī*? How should this word be translated? What do *phī* correspond to in Pali Buddhist cosmology? As we have seen in this chapter, there was no consistent answer to this question, but the tendency in Siam was to equate *phī* with low-status beings in Pali cosmology of ambiguous or bad moral capacity. This is most explicit in the *Traiphūm Phra Ruang*, which equates *phī* specifically with *preta*s, or hungry ghosts, a category of supernatural beings that plays a significant role in Buddhist cosmology as a bad rebirth for those whose past karma is tainted by greed. Insofar as *phī* can and at times have been conceived of as more exalted, godlike beings (as in the case of *phī thǟn* and *phī fā*), the relegation of *phī* to low status within Siamese Buddhist discourse is a theological choice. The result in modern Thai discourse is that the word *phī* is usually reserved for ghosts, often malevolent, while Pali and Sanskrit words are used for even moderately more powerful or benevolent beings (*deva* for the gods, *devārakṣa* for guardian spirits, *bhūmi* for the land spirit, etc.).

Now, one might object in defense of syncretism that the very fact that Buddhist discourse had to "translate" the concept of *phī* by situating it within Buddhist cosmology is indicative of a "local religion" separate from Buddhism. But as we have seen in this chapter, this putative "local religion" lacks all specificity. On the one hand, *of course* there is local religion in Siam and other Tai cultures. But this would include not only *phī*, *mǭ*, and ceremonies for calling the *khwan*, but also local artistic and architectural traditions for depicting the Buddha and building Buddhist temples, local traditions of ordination and monastic dress, and so on. In this sense, *everything* is local religion. On the other hand, if we want to exclude everything that has a "foreign" origin from local religion, then *nothing* is local. In this chapter, I have focused on demonstrating that much of what is associated with "indigenous Tai religion" is in fact Chinese in origin. A lack of historical sources makes it impossible to do so in full diachronic detail, but from a methodological perspective doing so is unnecessary. Any element of any culture can, in principle, be traced to some "foreign" origin, because *that is how cultures work.* Cultures are not metahistorical essences; they are (much like the Buddhist conception of the person) continual processes involving a variety of factors and conditions in symbiosis with their environment. A culture can therefore be understood as a name applied to a nexus of various "other" cultures, each bleeding into the next. There can of course be historical continuities within a culture, but the work of "tradition," as Jean-François Bayart has shown, is one of continual (re)invention, responding to the dialectic of identities operative at any moment in history.[106]

Singling out parts of Siamese/Thai religion, or Tai or Theravāda religion more broadly, as "local" does more to obfuscate than it does to clarify. First, it obfuscates the expansiveness of Buddhism as a discourse. Buddhism has something to say about *phī*, for the same reason it has something to say about animals, for the same reason it has something to say about gods and heavens, for the same reason it has something to say about pus and urine, for the same reason it has something to say about joy and suffering. All of these play a role in Buddhism's all-encompassing cosmology and, to varying extents, its soteriology. The word *phī* may be specific to Tai cultures, but insofar as nonhuman beings are assumed by Buddhism as a part of the natural world, they are no more "local" than are *tonmai* (Thai for "trees"), *mānām* (Thai for "rivers"), or *chī* (Thai for "urine"). The only task for Buddhist discourse was to find the correct translation for the term. Buddhism thus did not "mix" with "animism," "local spirit religion," or the like any more than it "mixed" with "local rivers," "local trees," or "local animals." It simply spread to a new geographical location that, like India, had its own unique trees, rivers, animals, and other beings that we would call "supernatural."

Second, singling out certain parts of a religious landscape as "local" ironically obfuscates the way discourse actually operates, instantiated in local actors. Buddhism is not some "thing" from India that "came" to Southeast Asia and "encountered" local religions. Buddhism is a discourse, a process of people talking to one another. At a certain point in history, speakers of Tai languages began participating in this conversation; they entered into the discourse by learning the "language," internalizing its worldview, and communicating with one another in its terms. As with any discourse, Buddhism is not totalizing in the sense of crowding out other discourses, but it does allow local actors to talk in a coherent way about anything that they encounter in their everyday life, including *phī—even if those things are, from a postmodern perspective, themselves constructed by discourse.* Indeed, this insight will be useful to us as we move to the next "component" of Thai religion in the next chapter, namely Brahmanism.

6
Gods

The gods have already figured quite prominently in this book. As I argued in the introduction, the perception that the presence of "Hindu" gods in Buddhism is surprising or a sign of "syncretism" is based on a fundamental misunderstanding of the inclusivistic nature of Buddhism as a religious system. More than that, Buddhism can be understood as advancing an implicit theology, insofar as its cosmology creates a category of "gods" (*devas*) and defines them vis-à-vis other beings. It is therefore not surprising that Indic gods are recognized and worshiped by Thai Buddhists; indeed, it would be surprising if they were not. At the same time, however, it is important to recognize that the complete naturalness of having gods in a Buddhist society such as Thailand's does not mean that the category of "Hinduism" is inapplicable. Indeed, as I argued in Chapter 3, the unique historical existence of Siam on a nexus of transforming cosmopolitan formations, as well as the deep connections between Pali and Sanskrit cosmpoleis, has led to the opening of a space within Thai Buddhism for Hindu discourses to exercise continuing agency. And as I showed in Chapter 4, that space, up until the adoption of Western vocabulary in the late nineteenth century, was encapsulated by the concept and discourse of *saiyasāt*.

Having already established these key methodological principles, my goal in this chapter will be to illustrate *how* exactly Hindu discourses have exercised agency in Siamese and Thai Buddhism without fundamentally altering its Buddhist character. I will take a roughly historical approach, beginning with the literary sources, showing how Siamese literature continued to be influenced by Hindu discourses outside the purview of the Pali *imaginaire*, first in Sukhōthai and Ayutthayā and then in early Bangkok. The latter of these periods was characterized by a refamiliarization of Siamese society with the Indic homeland of Buddhism, but under a new conceptual regime: the modern discourse of world religions, which introduced the category "Hinduism" into Thai vocabulary. This would ultimately have a profound impact on Thai Buddhism, a key turning point in which was the establishment of a shrine to Brahmā, in the style of a Phra Phūm shrine, at

Holy Things. Nathan McGovern, Oxford University Press. © Oxford University Press 2024.
DOI: 10.1093/9780197759912.003.0006

the Ērāwan Hotel in Bangkok in the 1950s. Although Brahmā, unlike Śiva and Viṣṇu, is very much a part of the Pali *imaginaire*, the novelty of building a shrine to him in the style of shrines to *phī*, together with the new discourse of world religions that had introduced the concept of "Hinduism" to the Thai conceptual universe, sparked new forms of Thai Buddhist praxis that thematize "Hinduism" and "Hindu gods" as they are understood today in the global world religions marketplace. I thus end the chapter with an exploration of this phenomenon, which I dub "Hindu enthusiasm," and its place within the worship of "holy things" in Thailand.

Saiyasāt and Extra-Pali Discourses in Sukhōthai and Ayutthayā

As I argued in Chapter 4, the category of *saiyasāt*, juxtaposed with *phutthasāt*, created a space in premodern Siamese discourse for discourses that in retrospect we would dub "Hindu" to hold influence. This was possible because the Pali Buddhism of Siam had always constituted gods as a privileged category in its cosmology, and due to the historical continuities between the emerging Hinduism of the second millennium CE and the divine cosmology that had been written into the Pali *imaginaire* in the late first millennium BCE, Hindu discourses on "the gods" could easily be drawn upon to "update" Buddhist cosmology. Simply put, Siamese discourse on the gods speaks about particular gods and about the gods in general in ways that cannot be derived strictly from authoritative Pali texts.

We see evidence of this pattern in the earliest evidence available, the inscriptions of Sukhōthai. The 1393 pact between Sukhōthai and Nān that we encountered in the previous chapter not only refers to various types of *phī* to witness and enforce the oath; it also invokes a variety of figures that fit more comfortably within Hindu cosmologies than the standard Pali cosmology. Unfortunately, the relevant portion of the inscription is fragmentary, but there is a reference to a Śaiva temple (III.14: ไสพาคมาคร),[1] followed by references to Bhīma, Arjuna, and Yudhiṣṭhira of the *Mahābhārata* (III.15–17), as well as Rāma, Paraśurāma, Balarāma, and Lakṣmaṇa (III.17–18). This is followed by a fragmentary list of lesser deities, some of whom may be derivable from the Pali *imaginaire*, but also including the goddesses Śrī and Umā (III.26). Crucially, however, this section of the inscription is preceded by a discussion of Buddhist relics (III.1–14) and followed by a description of the standard Pali cosmology (III.28–34), so references to the *Mahābhārata* and other deities derived from Hindu discourses are clearly meant to augment, not replace, the operative Pali Buddhist framework.

Another inscription, from the mid-fourteenth century, introduces a similarly interesting amalgam of Pali Buddhism and Hindu mythology not derivable from the Pali *imaginaire*. This inscription describes the king's restoration of a Buddhist temple, which is of course completely unsurprising in the Pali Buddhist context. What follows, however, is a bit more surprising:

> พระกริสพระ . . . หากปรดิสถา ๐ พระกรีสนน๋นคิตนพระมหาสามีศรีสรธาราชจูลามูณีศรีรดดนลง
> กาทิบเปนเจ๋าคิตนพระรามพระนารายเทพจยุดหากทยวในสงสาราภพอนนโทลเกอดไปมาแล
>
> Lord Kṛṣṇa is supposed to have established it. That Kṛṣṇa is Lord Phra Mahāsāmī Śrīśraddhārājaculāmunī Śrīratanalaṅkādīpa, that is, Phra Rāma, Phra Nārāyaṇa, the god, descended from his travels in *saṃsāra*, wandering from birth to birth.[2]

The long title (beginning with "Phra Mahāsāmī") belongs to the king refurbishing the Buddhist temple, and he is identified with Kṛṣṇa, who in turn is identified with Rāma and Nārāyaṇa (i.e., Viṣṇu). The statement being made would thus appear to be that the king, who is restoring the temple in the present, is a reincarnation of Kṛṣṇa, who originally established it (or, more likely, its central *stūpa*) in the past.[3] Again, this statement, while certainly consistent with Buddhist doctrine and its strategy of inclusivism, requires the knowledge and acceptance of the mythology of Kṛṣṇa from outside the Pali *imaginaire*.

Reference to Hindu gods from beyond the Pali *imaginaire* is also found throughout non-inscriptional literature from Sukhōthai and Ayutthayā. Although it hews very closely to the standard Pali cosmology, the *Traiphūm Phra Ruang* of Sukhōthai makes a brief reference to Śiva living on Mt. Kailāśa.[4] A common motif found in several Ayutthayā-era texts is an invocation of Viṣṇu, Śiva, and Brahmā—the three gods of the *trimūrti*—at the beginning. This is found in the *Ōngkān Chāng Nām*, the *Yuan Phāi*, the *Dvādaśamāsa*, and the *Bunnōwāt*.[5] Such an invocation, while not at odds with Buddhist doctrine, nonetheless is not derived directly from the Pali *imaginaire* and instead informed by the epic and especially Purāṇic cosmologies in which the *trimūrti* is developed. In addition, the *Yuan Phāi*, which is a eulogy of King Trailōkkanāt's victory over Lānnā, makes reference, like the Sukhōthai inscriptions we encountered above, to figures from the *Mahābhārata*, comparing the king to Bhīma, Arjuna, and Kṛṣṇa.[6]

To be clear, references to Hindu gods from outside the Pali *imaginaire* are not a mere literary flourish of this era; there is a clear cultic aspect as well. A 1361 Khmer inscription reports that King Mahādhammarājā I of Sukhōthai "erected an image of Maheśvara and an image of Viṣṇu in the Devālayamahākṣetra of this Mango Grove . . . for all the ascetics and brahmins to worship forever."[7] Likewise, we have already seen the 1510 inscription of Cāo Phrayā Thammāsōkkarāt, lord of Kamphāng Phet, dedicating an image of Śiva "to rule over the animals, four-legged and two-legged . . . and to help uplift the *sāsanas*, *buddhasāsana* and *saiyasāsana*."[8] Similar references to the establishment of images and temples to Śiva and Viṣṇu are found in the chronicles of Ayutthayā. In 1575, the Khmer king of Longvek attacked Siam and took away two images of gods, one of them most likely of Viṣṇu, that had earlier been unearthed by King Rāmāthibodī II.[9] In 1601, King Narēsuan received (from origins unspecified) images of Śiva and Viṣṇu.[10] These were presumably set up in a temple or shrine, for the chronicles report that just thirty-five years later King Prāsāt Thọ̄ng moved a preexisting shrine to these two gods to a different location.[11] A royal ceremony during the reign of the same king involved court Brahmans dressing up as Viṣṇu, Śiva, and other gods.[12] King Nārāi rose to power in 1656 by staging a coup against his uncle, King Sī Sutham Rāchā, in retaliation against the latter's "immorality" in attempting to have sex with Nārāi's sister (i.e., his own niece). The chronicles report specifically that Nārāi worshiped Viṣṇu and Śiva in a ceremony on the eve of battle.[13] They also report that during his reign, Nārāi commissioned the casting of four statues of Śiva.[14]

The existence of images of the Hindu gods and temples to them implies ritual specialists to oversee their worship, and indeed we know from various sources that there were Brahmans in the employ of the royal court in Ayutthayā, just as there are today in Bangkok. The *Three Seals Law*, compiled from Ayutthayā-era sources in the reign of King Rāma I, describes an entire department of Brahmans with responsibilities for royal ceremonies, care of royal elephants, astrology, and the judiciary.[15] Moreover, one of the three most significant noble families of Ayutthayā is descended from a Brahman named Sī Watthana, who served in the royal court under King Nārāi.[16] The origins of the Brahmans who served in the royal court of Ayutthayā—and whose descendants serve in the Bangkok court to this day—are not entirely clear, but there is sufficient evidence, in particular in the form of the Tamil *bhakti* hymns they use in their ceremonies, to show that they are descended from actual Indian Brahmans who immigrated to Siam centuries ago.[17]

Two textual sources preserve an account of the origin of the royal court Brahmans that, regardless of its historical accuracy, provides an instructive picture of the role played by Hinduism and Hindu actors in the kingdom of Ayutthayā. The older of the two is *The Short History of the Kings of Siam*, written in 1640 by Jeremias van Vliet, who lived in Ayutthayā for several years as a representative of the Dutch East India Company.[18] The second text is the *Tamnān Phrām Müang Nakhǭn Sī Thammarāt* (*ตำนานพราหมณ์เมืองนครศรีธรรมราช*, "Record of the Brahmans of Nakhǭn Sī Thammarāt"), which is actually a letter compiling several older documents that was sent by the royal court Brahmans in Ayutthayā to the leadership of the southern *müang* of Nakhǭn Sī Thammarāt in 1735.[19] Van Vliet includes the story of the origin of the royal court Brahmans in his account of the reign of Rāmāthibodī II (1491–1529). The *Tamnān Phrām*, on the other hand, includes it as the preamble of the first document attached to the main letter, which (after the initial origin story) is a record of royal pronouncements of laws governing the Brahman community in Nakhǭn Sī Thammarāt.

There are several key differences between the two versions, but the gist of the story goes as follows. During the reign of a king named Rāmāthibodī in Ayutthayā (the *Tamnān Phrām*, unlike van Vliet, records that it was Rāmāthibodī I, the putative founder of Ayutthayā), there is a king with a similar or identical name in a kingdom called Rāmarāja in India.[20] Both of these kings are in fact incarnations of Viṣṇu. In van Vliet's version, the king of Rāmarāja is angered that the king of Ayutthayā has taken the same name as him, so he sends assassins to kill him. Through Viṣṇu's miraculous power, however, they are prevented from doing so, and the king of Rāmarāja sends gifts of friendship to Ayutthayā. In the *Tamnān Phrām* version, the king of Rāmarāja is friendly and sends gifts from the start, although the ambassadors witness a similar display of Viṣṇu's miraculous power in the person of King Rāmāthibodī. In both versions, the upshot is that the king of Rāmarāja sends gifts of Brahmans with knowledge of the "Swing Ceremony" to Siam. In van Vliet's telling, this concludes the story, but the *Tamnān Phrām* version adds that the king of Rāmarāja also sent a statue of Viṣṇu, and the ship carrying the Brahmans and statue is initially shipwrecked near Nakhǭn Sī Thammarāt, which in the context serves to explain why there is a Brahman community in that southern *müang* in addition to the capital.

Elsewhere, I have argued that this story probably records a significant event in which Brahmans were sent from an Indian kingdom, possibly Vijayanagara, to Siam during the reign of Rāmāthibodī II; nevertheless, there likely were transmissions of Brahman lineages other than this one.[21] For our purposes here, the precise historical details lying behind this story are less important than the fact that the story, and the Brahman community it is intended to explain, exist at all. Brahmans of course feature prominently in Pali texts, creating a space for them within the Pali *imaginaire*, and there is no *a priori* reason to find it problematic that Buddhist kings would employ Brahmans in their courts—especially considering that even Buddhist texts portray the employ of Brahmans as an ordinary aspect of the exercise of kingship.[22] What is important to note, however, is that this opens up a space for Hinduism to exercise agency within Buddhism. Buddhism recognizes the gods, and Brahmans are ritual personnel uniquely qualified to oversee the proper worship of the gods on behalf of the state. The Pali *imaginaire* may make space for Brahmans, and the Buddhist culture may have a profound influence on Brahmans after they arrive, but Hindu cultures and Hindu discourses ultimately serve as the source of Brahmans and their rituals to fulfill a Buddhist need.

The Bangkok Restoration and Interest in Hinduism in Prerevolutionary Siam

The destruction of Ayutthayā by the Burmese in 1767 marked a significant break in Siamese history, but it did not in any way diminish the role played by *saiyasāt*, the gods, or Brahmans in Siamese religion. Among the many ways in which Rāma I (r. 1782–1809), founder of the Chakri Dynasty in Bangkok, established a new kingdom for Siam that sought to restore and even improve upon the glories of Ayutthayā, particularly significant were his efforts that gave a prominent place to Brahmanical cult and mythology in the new kingdom. Although, to my knowledge, no written records exist, the oral history of the current court Brahmans holds that their ancestors were brought to the capital by Rāma I from various cities in the South to restore the royal ceremonies, including the Royal Consecration (พระบรมราชาภิเษก, Skt. *paramarājābhiṣeka*), the Trīyampawāi-Trīppawāi,

Figure 6.1 The temple of the royal court Brahmans (Bōt Phrām) in Bangkok. The three sanctuaries are, from left to right, for Śiva (Phra Isuan), Gaṇeśa (Phra Phikkhanēt), and Viṣṇu (Phra Nārāi). In front of the sanctuary to Śiva is a shrine to Brahmā, in the style of the Ērāwan Shrine. Photo by Nathan McGovern.

and the First Plowing Ceremony (แรกนาขวัญ).[23] The Brahman Temple (see Figure 6.1), known by the Sanskrit name *devasthāna* (เทวสถาน), or more colloquially as Bōt Phrām (โบสถ์พราหมณ์), together with the nearby Giant Swing (see Figure 6.2) once used in the Trīyampawāi-Trīppawāi ceremony, were built during Rāma I's reign and stand as living monuments to the effort of the founder of the Chakri Dynasty to restore the worship of the gods using proper Brahman ritual specialists. Although modest in size compared to most Buddhist temples, it consists of three sanctuaries, dedicated to Śiva, Gaṇeśa, and Viṣṇu. Rituals to worship these gods are performed by the Brahmans to this day, most significantly during the fifteen-day Trīyampawāi-Trīppawāi, celebrated annually in December and January, in which the gods Śiva and Viṣṇu are successively invited to earth and given daily offerings.[24]

Rāma I also sponsored two major literary projects that helped to continue and even amplify the space for Hindu mythology in Siamese discourse. The first and more well known was his sponsorship in 1797 of a complete

Figure 6.2 The Giant Swing (*sao chingchā*) in Bangkok that was once used in the royal court Brahmans' Trīyampawāi-Trīppawāi ceremony. In the background is the Buddhist temple Wat Suthat. Photo by Nathan McGovern.

edition of the *Rāmakian* (รามเกียรติ์, Skt. *Rāmakīrti*), the Thai version of the *Rāmāyaṇa*—an ambitious undertaking that went beyond previous kings who sponsored the composition of individual episodes of the epic.[25] Although the story of Rāma is arguably not entirely extraneous to the Pali *imaginaire*, insofar as a version of it is found in the Pali *Dasaratha Jātaka*, the particular version found in the Thai *Rāmakian* is clearly informed by Hindu discourse. It is not the same as the Vālmīki *Rāmāyaṇa*, but it does not hew to a strictly Buddhist narrative frame either, as do the *Dasaratha Jātaka* in Pali and the Lao version of the epic, the *Phra Lak Phra Rām*. Instead, its narrative frame is at least superficially Śaiva—perhaps in keeping with the proclivities of the royal court Brahmans[26]—insofar as Śiva is presented as the supreme god who instructs Viṣṇu and other gods to incarnate, respectively, as Rāma and other characters in the epic.[27]

The second literary project, less well-known and influential than the first, was the sponsorship of the *Unnarut*. This shorter epic is based on an episode from the greater mythology of Kṛṣṇa, without parallel in the Pali tradition, that is narrated most fully in the *Bhāgavata Purāṇa*. In the Sanskrit version, Aniruddha, the son of Pradyumna and grandson of Kṛṣṇa, is kidnaped by a servant of Uṣā, who has fallen in love with him. Uṣā's father, the *asura* Bāna, discovers Aniruddha in Uṣā's room and imprisons him. This leads Kṛṣṇa to attack and defeat Bāna, after which Bāna agrees to the marriage of Uṣā to Aniruddha.[28] In the Thai version commissioned by Rāma I, which is based on older versions written in Ayutthayā, the same basic storyline is followed, but Kṛṣṇa and Aniruddha are collapsed into a single character, the hero Unnarut.

In a seminal article, David Wyatt has argued that, in spite of the common representation of Rāma I's reign as a "restoration" of Ayutthayā, the founder of the Chakri Dynasty actually built something quite new, in what Wyatt refers to as a "subtle revolution."[29] While Wyatt's basic thesis is certainly correct, with respect to religion he takes it a bit in the wrong direction in a way that is relevant for our understanding of the influence of Hindu discourses on Siam. In particular, Wyatt argues, "Rama I seems to have been responsible for beginning that process of 'Buddhaization' . . . by which the Buddhist elements of Siamese religious observance began to gain ground at the expense of the brahmanical and animistic elements."[30] He cites as evidence of this statement a 1782 edict in which Rāma I orders his subjects not to place worship of spirits above the Buddhist Triple Gem, and also orders the destruction of phallic symbols, which Wyatt interprets as referring to Śiva *liṅgas*.

Close examination of this edict, however, belies Wyatt's claim that it is an attack on Brahmanism, much less "animism," or an attempt at a novel "Buddhaization" thereof. First, although Rāma I does advise his subjects not to place *phī sāng thēphārak* (ผีสางเทพารักษ์) above the Triple Gem, such that they forget the role of karma and attribute their fates solely to the workings of spirits, this is standard Buddhist doctrine, and he *also* commands the leaders of cities and villages throughout his kingdom to refurbish the shrines to local spirits and duly worship them. And while he does order the destruction of all phallic symbols (เพศบุรุษลึงค์) that are worshiped, he does not associate them with Śiva, Brahmans, or the worship of the gods in any way. Indeed, his explanation of the practice of worshiping phallic symbols precludes their origin in Śaiva cult practice:

> แรกเหตุนี้จะมีมาเพราะคนพาลกักขะละหยาบช้า แซ่งกระทำเพศอันนี้เยาะเย้ยหญิงแม่มดอันมีมารยาความลอายมิได้เปนเดิม สืบมาหญิงชายผู้หาปัญญามิได้ก็เอาเยี่ยง หย่างนับถือสืบมา เปนที่เทวะดาอันศักสิทธจะชิงชังอีก สมควรแต่กับผีสางอันต่ำศักดิสำหาวเผ่าพาลหยาบช้านั้น
>
> The origin of this is that foolish, crude, and vulgar people made these sexual images to tease and harass women, witches who lack manners and shame. From then on, women and men without wisdom imitated them. The way that people have believed since, that they are also hated by powerful (*saksit*) *devatās*, is only proper with low-ranking, unscrupulous *phī sāng* who are foolish and crude.[31]

Although we do not have to take Rāma I's disdainful "explanation" of the origin of these phallic symbols literally, it is quite clear that he does not associate them with Śiva or the practices of Brahmans in any way.

The reason for this is that he is not talking about Śiva-*liṅgas*.[32] In another work, Wyatt includes a picture of what he calls a "liṅga garden" in modern Bangkok to illustrate what Rāma I had banned and (not surprisingly) failed to eradicate. The phallic symbols in the picture, which I have also observed in my own fieldwork in Thailand, are quite distinct from Śiva-*liṅgas*, which, in most cases, are only vaguely phallic short cylinders emerging vertically from a *yoni* designed to catch and drain liquid offerings.[33] These are instead quite obvious wood carvings of erect penises, long and with an anatomically correct head. They are known in modern Thai not as Śiva-*liṅgas* (ศิวลึงค์) but as *palat khik* (ปลัดขิก). They are not erected in *yonis* and used in anything resembling Śaiva cultic worship; instead, they are worn or displayed to protect one from malign spirits, just as Rāma I explains in his edict. There is absolutely no evidence that Rāma I was opposed to Śiva-*liṅgas* or any other aspect of Brahmanical worship. Indeed, the Brahman Temple whose construction he sponsored includes *liṅgas* within the sanctuary to Śiva.[34]

As even Wyatt himself admits, Rāma I explicitly expressed the desire to reconstruct the court according to the standards of Ayutthayā during the golden age of King Borommakōt (1733–1758).[35] From the evidence I have presented here, that project clearly included rebuilding state sponsorship of the Brahmanical cult of the gods, as well as of mythology informed by Hindu discourses. Moreover, the latter in particular was almost certainly amplified through the ambitious and novel project to compose a complete version of the *Rāmakian*, which in turn would serve as an inspiration for various royal and popular works of art, including masked plays (โขน) and the elaborate mural depicting the *Rāmakian* around the inside wall of Wat Phra Kāo, the Temple of the Emerald Buddha. Where there was a "subtle revolution" à la Wyatt was the broader context in which the restoration and renewal of *saiyasāt* took place. Rāma I oversaw the composition not only of the *Rāmakian* and *Unnarut*, derived from Hindu mythology, but also of the Javanese story *Inao*, the Chinese *Sām Kok* (*The Romance of the Three Kingdoms*), and the Mon chronicle *Rājādhirāja*. As Wyatt approvingly cites, Nidhi Eoseewong has argued that early Bangkok produced a highly cosmopolitan bourgeois literary culture,[36] and this is reflected in the wide variety of literary projects pursued, of which Indic (Buddhist and/or Hindu) were only a part.

Early Bangkok bourgeois literary culture saw its apogee in the reign of Rāma II (1809–1824), who was a renowned poet in his own right and sponsored a number of literati at court, most notably Sunthọ̄n Phū, widely regarded as the Thai language's greatest literary figure. As Nidhi has argued, Sunthọ̄n Phū was a "bourgeois poet laureate," reflecting the cosmopolitanism of the early Bangkok kingdom.[37] Within that context, however, his frequent recourse to Brahmans as literary characters is notable. Indeed, one of the most well-known passages from Sunthọ̄n Phū's work, from his magnum opus *Phra Aphaimanī*, involves a "yogi" rescuing the hero's son, Sut

Sākhǭn, from a "naked ascetic" (ชีเปลือย) who had tricked him and stolen his magic horse:

๏ บัดเดี๋ยวดังหงั่งเหง่งวังเวงแว่ว สะดุ้งแล้วเหลียวแลชะแง้หา
เห็นโยคีขี่รุ้งพุ่งออกมา ประคองพาขึ้นไปจนบนบรรพต
แล้วสอนว่าอย่าไว้ใจมนุษย์ มันแสนสุดลึกล้ำเหลือกำหนด
ถึงเถาวัลย์พันเกี่ยวที่เลี้ยวลด ก็ไม่คดเหมือนหนึ่งในน้ำใจคน

> At that moment, there was a warbling sound. He (Sut Sākhǭn) looked around with a start.
> He saw a yogi burst forth, riding a rainbow. (The yogi) took him up to a mountaintop
> And taught him, "Don't trust people. They're deep and unfathomable.
> "Even a thousand vines tangled together aren't as twisted as one in a person's kindness."[38]

Sunthǭn Phū's fascination with Brahmans was reflective of their continued relevance in early Bangkok, but it was also most likely personal. In his *Nirāt Müang Phet*, a poem about a visit to Phetburī in the South, he speaks about the Brahman community in that city and implies that he himself is descended from them.[39] Phetburī, Nakhǭn Sī Thammarāt, and Phatthalung were the three southern cities from which Rāma I had recalled Brahmans to the capital to perform royal ceremonies. That would make Sunthǭn Phū a close relative of the royal court Brahmans.

Another anonymous work of literature from the same era similarly shows the importance of Brahmans to actual social life and the social imagination in early Bangkok. This short work, called the *Nāng Nopphamāt*, was regarded by early Thai historians as a work of Sukhōthai literature and continues to be known in popular culture for recounting the supposed origins of Lǭi Krathong, which is the Thai version of Diwali. Nidhi, however, has conclusively shown that it is a modern work of fiction, written between 1817 and 1835, and it is possible that it was in part written by King Rāma III (r. 1824–1851).[40] The main character, the eponymous Nopphamāt, is the daughter of a court Brahman in Sukhōthai during its golden age. A significant portion of the book is devoted to describing the royal ceremonies performed by the Brahmans in old Sukhōthai, but as Nidhi has shown, what is actually described is the royal ceremonies as they were performed in early Bangkok.[41]

Nāng Nopphamāt's modern origins are belied in part by the cosmopolitan culture they describe, and in this respect it, like other early Bangkok literature, reflects the shifting landscape in which Brahmans and Brahmanism increasingly are situated not simply as a symbiotic other to Buddhism but as a small part of an increasingly multicultural world.

Whatever groundwork may have been laid by Rāma I's "subtle revolution," the real program of "Buddhaization" that Wyatt, I think, prematurely attributes to him comes with Rāma IV (r. 1851–1868), known in the West as King Mongkut. Mongkut had already embarked on a religious reform campaign while ordained as a monk during the reign of his brother Rāma III, founding the reformist Thammayut Nikāi in 1835.[42] Once he became king in his own right, he was able to put the full force of the state behind a reformist agenda. Although he was certainly not opposed to the Brahmans or their ceremonies, he did make changes to make them more "Buddhist." This consisted of adding "Buddhist" elements to ceremonies, such as the Royal Consecration and Trīyampawāi-Trīppawāi, that previously had primarily consisted of Brahmans making use of Hindu ritual texts.[43] He also separated the court astrologers from the royal court Brahmans, which was the first step in reducing the Brahmans from key government officials to mere religious functionaries.[44]

The role of Brahmans and Brahmanism (or rather *saiyasāt*) in Siamese life was in the end, however, radically changed not so much through any frontal assault but as a byproduct of the Westernizing reforms begun in the reign of King Mongkut and brought to full fruition during the reign of his son, King Chulalongkorn (1868–1910). This in part consisted of an overhaul of the state administration that reduced the Brahmans to ritual functionaries, but, more important, it consisted of a conceptual shift in elite worldviews that resituated Brahmans and their gods within the emerging framework of "world religions."

The most pivotal work in this respect was the *Nangsū Sadāng Kitcānukit*, which we already encountered in Chapter 4. In it, Thipphākǫrawong deploys the term *sātsanā* to present "religion" as a universal phenomenon with different manifestations over the course of history. Instead of the category *saiyasāt*, he creates the term *sātsanā phrām* (สาศนาพราหมณ), which he also at times calls *sātsanā isuan nārāi* (สาศนาอิศวรนารายน์), to refer to Hinduism. This *sātsanā* does not have a privileged position vis-à- vis Buddhism but rather is one among several: *sātsanā phra yēsū khrit* (สาศนาพระเยซูคฤษ) for Christianity, *sātsanā nābī mahamat* (สาศนานาบีมะหะมัด) for Islam, and *sātsanā phra phuttha cāo* (สาศนาพระพุทธเจ้า) or *sātsanā phra samana khōdom* (สาศนาพระสมณะโคดม) for Buddhism. At the same time that Thipphākǫrawong particularized "Brahmanism" as one among several "religions," he also sought to rationalize Buddhism itself, adopting a modern scientific worldview in lieu of the traditional Abhidhamma cosmology.[45] Just as adopting the modern discourse of "religion" rendered the privileged position of *saiyasāt* rhetorically obsolete, so did this reform of cosmology render it substantively so. Whereas before *saiyasāt* was a "worldly" counterpart to *phutthasāt* that had legitimate things to say about the cosmos, the Brahmanism of the *Nangsǖ Sadǣng Kitcānukit* was now just another religion among many, its worldly assertions just as irrelevant to the emerging Buddhist Modernism as its soteriological assertions always had been.

The new position of Brahmanism in Siamese discourse was reflected, if obliquely, in an important book written by King Chulalongkorn, the *Phra Rātchaphithī Sip Sǫng Düan* (*พระราชพิธีสิบสองเดือน*), or *Royal Ceremonies of the Twelve Months*. Based on Chulalongkorn's inside knowledge of palace ceremony and research based on the sources available, this book, originally published in serial format, is a full account of the royal ceremonies celebrated annually by the court under the auspices of the court Brahmans, with the exception of the eleventh lunar month (September–October), which he did not have time to write before his death in 1910. It remains to this day the most valuable source for the study of Siamese court ceremony and the history of the Thai Brahmans. While this book is a testament to the continuing relevance of Brahmans and their ritual in Siamese life—Chulalongkorn certainly did not ban them, and he presents the royal ceremonies as a living institution—the very fact that he felt the need to write the book at all reflects a subtle shift in thinking about them. The *Royal Ceremonies* reads as a sort of antiquary. The Brahmans are no longer powerful government ministers, their rituals routine affairs of state. They are instead relics of a fading past, which needs to be recorded for the benefit of succeeding generations.

The reforms and accompanying shift in worldview that took place in the reigns of Kings Mongkut and Chulalongkorn were alone responsible for transforming *saiyasāt*, worldly complement to *phutthasāt*, into Brahmanism/Hinduism, one world religion among many. This shift was if anything only ratified by the Revolution of 1932, which abolished the absolute monarchy and as a result diminished the role of the royal court Brahmans even further.[46] By adopting the new vocabulary of religion and embarking on a campaign to rationalize and modernize Buddhism, elite Siamese discourse had severed the traditional link between *saiyasāt* and *phutthasāt*. But outside of the realm of the Brahmans and royal court ceremonial, this did not have any immediate effect on popular religious practice. On the contrary, it simply shifted the conceptual horizons for religious practices that continued to develop based on centuries of precedent.

The Ērāwan Shrine and Rise of Brahmā Worship in Thailand

A pivotal event that both illustrated the continuing relevance of the gods to Thai religious practice and served as a prototype for a new way of integrating the gods into that practice was the establishment of a shrine to Brahmā at the Ērāwan Hotel in the middle of the twentieth century. Bangkok's rapid urban development, sparked by the relative economic prosperity of the postwar years, took off in the 1950s. In the early years of that decade, Lt. Gen. Prayūn Phamǭnmontrī, the finance minister in the cabinet of Prime Minister Phibūn Songkhrām, who at that time was the leader of Thailand's military dictatorship, spearheaded the effort to build a large, modern hotel for the benefit of the Thai tourism industry. To that end he founded the United Bangkok Hotel Company, Ltd. (บริษัทสหโรงแรมกรุงเทพฯ จำกัด), whose name was later changed to the United Thai Hotel and Tourism Company, Ltd. (บริษัทสหโรงแรมไทยและการท่องเที่ยว จำกัด).[47] When construction began in 1951, the project was immediately plagued by what could be interpreted either as enormous bad luck or as evidence of graft and mismanagement. Equipment of the wrong size was ordered, construction had to be constantly redone because it was done incorrectly the first time, and a shipment of marble for the hotel's façade sank en route.[48] Construction dragged on for three years, until in 1953 work ground to a halt when some of the construction workers suffered life-threatening accidents.[49]

In order to dispel fears that the ground on which the hotel was being constructed was inhabited by evil spirits, the executive committee in charge of construction consulted Rear Admiral and astrologer Luang Suwichānphāt. He diagnosed the problems as deriving from the choice of the hotel's name. *Ērāwan,* coming from the Sanskrit *Airāvaṇa,* the name of Indra's three-headed elephant-mount, had been selected without Indra's permission. Customary shrines to Phra Phūm and the ancestral spirits had already been erected and duly worshiped, but these were not powerful enough to counteract Indra's anger, so Suwichānphāt recommended that they go to the next highest power after Indra: Brahmā.[50] In accordance with this advice, those in charge of the project worshiped Brahmā, asking for his help and promising (*bon*) to build a shrine to him once construction was completed. Construction was completed without further incident, and the hotel opened on November 9, 1956. Suwichānphāt was brought in once again to advise on placement of the promised shrine, and royal court Brahmans performed the installation ceremony.[51] Thus the Ērāwan Shrine was created—the fruit of the *kābon* of the hotel construction committee for a job well done.[52]

This, at least, is the popular version of the story. When I spoke to an officer who works for the Than Thāo Mahāphrom Foundation, the independent organization that manages the shrine today, he told me that although there were accidents in the construction of the Ērāwan Hotel as in any other construction project, the role of these accidents in the birth of the shrine has been grossly exaggerated in the popular imagination. According to him, the hotel construction committee simply felt that the Ērāwan Hotel, as one of the first big, modern hotels in Bangkok, should have a bigger and better shrine than the ordinary shrine to Phra Phūm, and they went to Suwichānphāt for advice on what sort of shrine to build.[53] Regardless of whether the popular or the official story corresponds more closely to what actually happened, however, it is the popular one that has driven the Ērāwan Brahmā's great success and reputation as a powerful granter of boons. This reputation has spawned all sorts of fantastic stories—some undoubtedly true, others not—both about the statue itself and about the boons it has granted. One of the women selling items for worship outside the shrine made the admittedly partial claim that the Ērāwan statue was the oldest Brahmā statue in the world, and that it had been at its current location *tangtā pūyātāyāi* (lit., "since [the time of our] grandparents").[54] While this story gives the Ērāwan Brahmā the authority of antiquity, other stories memorialize the statue's power in the present day. One such story claims that a nearby building caught fire after a piece of it broke off and fell on the statue, while others claim that actresses have danced naked for Brahmā in order to *kābon*.[55]

Regardless of whether one believes the stories of the Ērāwan Brahmā's power as a granter of boons, the success that has derived from his reputation as such is undeniable. The shrine has always accepted donations, and although these were originally used for maintenance and upkeep, by 1969 they had grown so large that Lt. Gen. Chalōmchai Cāruwat, who at that time was the chairman of the United Thai Hotel and Tourism Company, suggested that the money be donated to hospitals and other charities. The Ērāwan Hotel Brahmā Shrine Fund was set up in July of that year to manage the revenues of the shrine and decide which charities to donate to annually. In 1988, the old Ērāwan Hotel was torn down and replaced by a private hotel, the Grand Hyatt Ērāwan. The shrine was preserved as an independent entity, however, and the Than Thāo Mahāphrom Foundation was established to continue the mission of the old Shrine Fund and manage the day-to-day operations of the shrine.[56] According to information provided by this foundation, more than 60 million Baht, or roughly 1.5 million U.S. dollars, was donated to charities by the foundation in the year 2004.[57]

Today, in far more crowded urban surroundings than when it was built in the 1950s, the Ērāwan Brahmā Shrine (see Figure 6.3) is housed in a small, open-air enclosure at the corner of Thanon Rātchadamnōn and Thanon Phlōncit in the Pathumwan District of Bangkok, not far from Siam Square and Chulalongkorn University. The shrine itself is located at the

Figure 6.3 A view of the complete complex of the Ērāwan Shrine in Bangkok. The actual image of Brahmā is found in a small *sālā* in the center of the complex. The small *sālā* at the back of the complex is a space for the traditional Thai dance troupe that performs on behalf of worshipers who have come to *kābon*. The large white building that dominates behind the complex is the Grand Hyatt Ērāwan Hotel. Photo by Nathan McGovern.

very center of the enclosure and consists of a modest-size gold-leaf plaster statue under a Thai-style *sālā*—which ensemble serves as the prototype for all Brahmā shrines that have been built since this one. Both were designed and constructed by workers at the Handicrafts Division of the Fine Arts Department, a government agency that preserves and promotes traditional Thai arts, literature, and antiquities.[58] At the suggestion of Suwichānphāt, the design for the statue was based on an image commissioned by a certain Aphichāt Chinchōt, a doctor of traditional medicine who had a vision of Brahmā while meditating.[59] Aphichāt had this vision shortly after hearing that a friend's child had gone blind, and so he asked the god—whose identity he did not know at the time—if he could help the child. Brahmā said that the child would be cured after eating morning glory and reciting a *gāthā*. The remedy worked, so Aphichāt went to a famous sculptor to sculpt what he had seen, and he went to one of the royal court Brahmans to identify it. This Brahman identified it as Mahābrahmā, and he recommended that Aphichāt hire several Brahmans to hold a ceremony to invite Brahmā to enter the statue. Aphichāt did so, and he kept the image in his home until its design was made famous when Suwichānphāt asked to copy it to use at the Ērāwan Hotel.[60]

Consistent with such an origin, the Ērāwan statue has an eclectic design that strongly evokes traditional images of Brahmā while not precisely imitating any historical prototype. As one would expect, the god has four faces, but he also has eight arms, unlike most Indian[61] and Thai[62] images of the god, which have only four arms. In seven of his eight hands, the Ērāwan Brahmā carries a staff, a *cakra*, a jug, a mirror, a conch shell, a book of the Vedas, and a rosary, while his eighth hand is making the *jñāna-mudrā*.[63] Of these, the rosary, jug, and Vedas seem to have some traditional association with Brahmā,[64] whereas the other implements may simply be innovations to fill the extra hands. The staff (*daṇḍa*) in particular seems to represent royal power, reflected in the royal *lalitāsana* posture (with one leg up on the seat and the other hanging down) of the deity,[65] as well as in his crown and dress, which imitate that of a traditional Thai monarch.

Around the central shrine is a small fence, surrounded by kneelers at which worshipers can pray and receptacles in which they can place candles, incense, and other offerings. Worshipers are not allowed inside the small fence that surrounds the inner shrine, and therefore major offerings (such as food) must be made via one of the uniformed employees of the Foundation (all male)[66] who work there. These men take the offerings, place them directly in front of the image for a few minutes, and then either give them back to the worshiper if they are wanted as a sort of *prasād* or else take them away. Due to the large volume of worshipers, the central shrine is constantly packed with flower garlands; food offerings; offerings such as statuettes of horses, elephants, dancers, and servants; as well as a cloud of smoke from the incense that is chokingly thick in spite of the fact that the shrine is in the open air. The turnover rate for offerings, therefore, must be fairly rapid, and thus the primary duty of the employees of the shrine is to clear out offerings to make room for new ones.

To one side of the enclosure that marks the outer boundaries of the shrine are two small pavilions—one for a troupe of traditional Thai dancers who, for a fee, will dance on behalf of a worshiper as part of his or her *kǟbon*, and the other for a small shop at which one can buy everything one needs for worshiping at the shrine. According to employees of the shrine, there are two basic procedures worshipers should follow, depending on whether you are there to *bon* (make a vow) or *kǟbon* (fulfill the vow). In the former case, one should go around the image clockwise, offering three sticks of incense and a garland of flowers at each face, plus a candle at the first face. At each face, one should say a prayer to Brahmā, referring to oneself as *lūkchāng* (ลูกช้าง, "elephant cub," a typical way of referring to oneself when addressing a holy thing in prayer) and respectfully making one's request. After making the request and offerings at each face, one should go to a basin of "holy water"[67] located nearby and use a lotus blossom to sprinkle oneself for good luck. The second procedure, which one follows when one is ready to *kǟbon* after receiving a boon, is similar. One should again go around the image clockwise, but this time offering three sticks of incense, one candle, and a set of whatever one had promised Brahmā in return for a boon (e.g., food or statuettes of elephants, horses, or servants) at each face. Then, if one promised to pay for a performance of the Thai dance troupe, one should get in the usually fairly long line to do so. Finally, after at least fifteen minutes or so have passed, one can take back one's offerings if desired and go.[68]

By all accounts—including those found in Thai academic and popular sources, as well as my own personal observations—the Ērāwan Shrine draws worshipers from all walks of life. This is confirmed quantitatively by a survey that was conducted by a Thai student researcher in 2004 with 180 subjects who were solicited at the shrine. Although the data provided by this survey does reveal some patterns in the demographics and motivations of people coming to the shrine, these patterns are generally consistent with the shrine's modern, urban context. Supplicants were found from a variety of age groups and education levels. Nevertheless, respondents skewed young—89% were under the age of forty-five and a full 25.6% were between the ages of twenty-six and thirty. Persons of all education levels, from elementary school to college, were well represented, although graduates of vocational college and university were particularly so (at 22.2% and 26.7%, respectively)—a spread consistent with the sudden increase in education among the Thai populace in the previous generation, coupled with the younger demographic frequenting the shrine.

In terms of profession, there was again a good variety from across the spectrum, but a strong tendency toward the private sectors, with strong representations of private business owners (25%), merchants (19.4%), and private-sector employees (22.2%), and relatively weak representations of civil servants (6.1%) and government contract workers (5.6%). This pattern is consistent with the reasons respondents gave for coming to the shrine. A plurality of worshipers, at 25%, said they came for help with their job or business. This was followed closely by help with physical ailments at 20.6%. Other reasons included emotional distress (18.3%), needing help with one's love life (12.8%) or with school (5.5%), and simply accompanying a friend (10%).[69]

Together, the data reflect the typical contours of traditional *kānbonbānsānklāo*, albeit shaped by the parameters of modern urban life. Worshipers come to the shrine for help with a variety of mundane problems, including health, love, school, and especially money. Given that many of these are the sorts of problems one faces as a young and middle-aged adult—coupled with the fact that the shrine is physically most accessible to younger adults shopping or walking to or from work—the demographic at the shrine skews fairly young. Likewise, the particular reputation of Brahmā for helping with money problems explains the skew in the demographic toward professions in the private sector. These employees are vulnerable to the whims of their employers as they seek to advance in their career, while entrepreneurs are particularly vulnerable to the whims of market forces beyond their control. Government employees and contractors, on the other hand, are poorly represented since their salaries are fixed and their career advancement is relatively predictable. In terms of the particular demographic patterns seen in the worshipers, therefore, the Ērāwan Shrine exemplifies the effects that urbanization have had on the changing religious landscape of Thailand, as has been so aptly demonstrated by scholars such as James Taylor and Pattana Kitiarsa.[70]

Nevertheless, what I would like to emphasize here is that the *manner* of worship at the Ērāwan Shrine, its basic logic, is neither particularly unique nor entirely novel within a Thai religious context. Elephants, possibly because of the shrine's name, are often trumpeted as uniquely special to Brahmā, and indeed the back fence of the shrine is lined with several large elephant statues that have been donated by wealthy worshipers as their *kābon*, but there is of course no traditional connection between elephants and Brahmā, whose mount is a swan.[71] In any case, the presentation of elephants as *kābon*, as well as of horses, servants, and dancers—not to mention the whole practice of *kānbonbānsānklāo* itself—is clearly derived from the much older and broader practice of spirit worship. As the "official" account of its establishment suggests, the Ērāwan Shrine can be described simply as a bigger and more elaborate version of the common, everyday spirit shrine. The central logic of its worship—that of *kānbonbānsānklāo*—is exactly the same as that of an ordinary spirit shrine, as are its placement as a guardian outside of a building and indeed the very offerings that are made to it when a boon is granted.

The most obvious effect of the construction of the Ērāwan Brahmā Shrine and its subsequent reputation as a powerful granter of boons has been the addition of a third model to the repertoire of spirit shrines available to Thai urbanites, on top of shrines to Phra Phūm and to *pūyātāyāi*. Brahmā shrines are much like any other ordinary, private spirit shrine and thus do not have the cast of employees and worshipers that the Ērāwan Shrine has. Nevertheless, they do tend to be slightly larger than ordinary spirit houses, and they are more often found outside of large buildings such as hospitals, hotels, businesses, and government buildings than outside of private homes.[72] I have also encountered Brahmā statues in imitation of the one at the Ērāwan Hotel inside Buddhist temples, such as at Wat Chalǭ in Nonthaburī, where one of the monks told me that a local woman had built it to replace her family's *cēdī* (เจดีย์, a small, *stūpa*-like structure for storing ashes). A copy of the Ērāwan Brahmā has even been built at Bōt Phrām, the temple of the royal court Brahmans near Wat Suthat in Bangkok, which has historically focused exclusively on the worship of Īśvara (Śiva) and Nārāyaṇa (Viṣṇu). The Brahmā shrine was added in 1972, just inside the main gate, in front of the Īśvara temple.[73] According to a Brahman informant, it was built at the request of some laypeople, and it replaced a sculpture of Mount Kailāśa.

The influence of the Ērāwan Brahmā is not limited to Thai society. Copies of it have been built outside of the country as well; I personally have encountered copies of it outside of a hotel in Poi Pet, Cambodia; in and around the city of Taipei in Taiwan; and even outside of Caesars Palace in Las Vegas. The desire to build copies of the shrine in other countries is likely driven by the fact that the original shrine's fame has gone international. The original Ērāwan Shrine no longer draws worshipers from just Bangkok or even Thailand as a whole; it also draws foreign tourists, mostly from around Asia. It is a particularly popular destination for Taiwanese tourists, who are often taken to the shrine by organized Taiwanese tour companies that operate in Thailand. Indeed, when I resided in Taiwan in 2010, I found that the Thai Brahmā—which they refer to as *sìmiàn fó* (四面佛), or "four-faced Buddha"—is fairly well known among Taiwanese people; as testament to the shrine's popularity, I even found an amulet bearing the image of *sìmiàn fó* being sold in 7-Eleven mini-marts in the country.

Hindu Enthusiasm in Contemporary Thailand

Brahmā, as we have already seen, plays an important role in the Pali *imaginaire*, and thus, aside from his Purāṇic-derived iconography with four faces, worship of him in a Buddhist context is not entirely surprising.[74] It is clear, however, that the worship of Brahmā in Thailand is inflected by the modern discourse of world religions, and as such its legacy has been channeled through the category of Hinduism. Aside from the popularity of Brahmā shrines *per se*, the most important legacy of the Ērāwan shrine has been a proliferation of shrines to *other* gods, with an increasing openness to the authority of Hindu discourses in their iconography and even cult. In the vicinity of the Rātprasong Intersection alone, where the Ērāwan Hotel is located, the shrine to Brahmā has inspired a number of high-profile shrines to Hindu gods. This includes shrines to Trimūrti[75] and Gaṇeśa (see Figure 6.4) at Central World, a shrine to Indra at Amarin Plaza, a shrine to Lakṣmī at Gaysorn Village, a shrine to Umā Devī at Big C Supercenter, and a shrine to Viṣṇu riding Garuḍa at the InterContinental Hotel.[76]

While most of the shrines at the Rātprasong Intersection were built by corporate entities in imitation of the Ērāwan Shrine and lack facilities for cultic practice, a number of shrines around Bangkok do provide such facilities and are thronged with worshipers much as the Ērāwan Shrine is. One example is the shrine to Śiva near Central Pin Klao (เทวาลัยพระศิวะปิ่นเกล้า) on the Thonburī side of the Chao Phraya River. It features large statues of

Figure 6.4 A shrine to Gaṇeśa outside of Central World, a large shopping mall in downtown Bangkok. Photo by Nathan McGovern.

Śiva and Umā Devī, as well as facilities for worshiping, including dancers to serve those who wish to *kābon*. Another is the shrine to Gaṇeśa in the Huay Khwang District (เทวาลัยพระพิฆเนศ). It too has facilities allowing for worshipers to *bon* and *kābon*, and it represents an explosion of interest in Gaṇeśa specifically in recent years. There are organizations and individuals that promote the worship of Gaṇeśa as a remover of obstacles, including Phithak Khōwwanchai, a self- styled expert on Gaṇeśa and other Hindu gods who writes books, makes media appearances, and maintains a website at www.siamganesh.com. It has become increasingly common for business enterprises, such as hotels, to erect a shrine to Gaṇeśa alongside or instead of a shrine to Brahmā.[77]

The increase in interest in Hindu gods has had implications for the royal court Brahmans, who at the time of the Revolution seemed destined for obscurity. I have already mentioned that a shrine to Brahmā, in imitation of the Ērāwan Shrine and in response to its popularity, was erected in front of the Śiva temple in the 1970s. Likewise, a ritual dedicated to Brahmā, who previously had no role, was added to the Trīyampawāi-Trīppawāi, the court Brahmans' most important and elaborate annual ceremony, around the same time.[78] Although these accommodations to popular interest in the gods are relatively small, the return in interest in the court Brahmans has been exponential. Quaritch Wales reported in the 1930s that the rituals surrounding the Trīyampawāi-Trīppawāi were sparsely attended.[79] But when I observed the Trīyampawāi-Trīppawāi in 2014–2015, many of the rituals, especially at the key points of the fifteen-day cycle when Śiva, Brahmā, and Viṣṇu are invited to earth and then sent back to heaven, were packed with lay worshipers. Many brought their own statues and amulets of the gods with them to receive the blessings and empowerment associated with the court-sanctioned ritual.

One of the more noticeable of these worshipers was Mēthanī Buranasiri (เมทนี บุรณศิริ), more commonly known by his nickname Nīnō (นีโน่), an actor, singer, and producer who is also the brother of one of the most recently ordained court Brahmans, Tran Buranasiri (ตรัณ บุรณศิริ, nicknamed Cīnō [จีโน่]). Brahman Tran, unlike all of the other court Brahmans, is not the son of an ordained Brahman, but he was able to convince the head Brahman to ordain him after he proved genealogically that he is descended from Sī Watthana (ศรีวัฒน), a Brahman who served in the court of King Nārāi in the seventeenth century and the patriarch of one of the largest and most influential aristocratic families of Siam. I gathered from my interviews that the decision to ordain Tran was somewhat controversial among the Brahmans, and Tran stood out from the other Brahmans in being the only one who expressed any reservation in identifying as a Buddhist. He saw his Brahman lineage and dedication to the Hindu gods as central to his identity, and it was clear, from his brother's presence, that this interest was a family affair. Nīnō, like other worshipers, brought his own statues and amulets of the gods to be blessed, and he capitalized on his own fame and his relationship to a court Brahman to seek more intimate access to the rituals.

Also among the worshipers I witnessed at the Trīyampawāi-Trīppawāi were operators of shrines to Hindu gods who were not simply seeking to have statues blessed for their own use but were cultivating a connection with the temple of the royal court Brahmans to utilize for commercial purposes. Indeed, in speaking with employees of the Brahman Temple, I found that some were disdainful of this tendency of individuals unaffiliated with the royal court Brahmans to capitalize on its fame. One such employee working in the temple office accused such people of misleading and defrauding the public by implying that they were affiliated with the royal court Brahmans when in fact they had no such affiliation beyond having attended a public ritual.

At times independent actors unaffiliated with the royal court Brahmans claim to be Brahmans themselves. This appears to be an old practice, as Tambiah encountered it among traditional *mǭ* in his research in a rural village in the 1960s,[80] but the phenomenon has taken on a new iteration in the age of globalized world religions discourse. For example, in 2015, while visiting the southern city of Nakhǭn Sī Thammarāt, I was introduced to a man who called himself Phī Phrām ("Big Brother Brahman"). He had gathered a group of men, all calling themselves Brahmans, who performed rituals to worship Hindu gods. They took me and my wife to the ruins of the old Śiva shrine in the city and performed a ritual for our benefit, which in form imitated contemporary styles of Hindu *pūjā*. When I asked them how they had learned how to perform these rituals, they said they had learned from the internet. Although they claimed authentic Brahman lineage, and Nakhǭn Sī Thammarāt did indeed at one time have an important Brahman community,[81] from which Rāma I reconstituted the court Brahmans in Bangkok, the actual connection of these contemporary self-styled Brahmans to that community was vague at best. When I asked them for more specifics about their connection to "official" Brahmans, they complained that the royal court Brahmans had neglected their community. They also, however, took us to visit a man in town (not one of their number, but a friend) who showed us pictures of a deceased relative who had been born in Nakhọn Sī Thammarāt and ordained as a court Brahman in Bangkok. He also showed us a very old and battered but treasured copy of the *Tamnān Phrām Müang Nakhọn Sī Thammarāt*, which as we have seen, demonstrates the importance and authority that Brahmans once held in that city.

It is worth noting that while much of the interest in involving "Brahmans" in the worship of the gods in contemporary Thailand tends toward local understandings of that term (royal court Brahmans or self-styled Brahmans), it also has led to engagement with Indian Brahmans who serve expatriate communities. The royal court Brahmans, for example, have held joint rituals with Indian expatriate Brahmans, including for the installation of a Śiva-*liṅga* at their own *devasthāna*.[82] In addition, Hindu festivals with no historical Siamese correlate that are celebrated at Thailand's largest expatriate Hindu temple, the Sri Mahamariamman Temple (popularly known as Wat Khāk Sīlom, วัดแขกสีลม) in Bangkok, draw significant numbers of Thai Buddhists into their orbit as direct participants and through various forms of spiritual bricolage in the vicinity of the temple. This includes the Navarātri festival, studied by Erick White,[83] and the Gaṇeśa Caturthī, referenced by Agarwal and Jones.[84]

Taken together, the things I have described in this section—the proliferation of shrines to Hindu gods, renewed interest in the royal court Brahmans, self-styled Brahmans engaging in ritual bricolage, and patronage of actual expatriate Hindu festivals—represent a new phenomenon in modern Thailand that I will refer to as "Hindu enthusiasm." In coining this phrase, I am inspired by Thomas Tweed's term "Buddhist sympathizer," which he uses to describe Westerners who are interested in and sympathetic to Buddhism but who do not necessarily identify as Buddhists.[85] By "Hindu enthusiasm," I am referring to a similar phenomenon in Thailand, in which religious actors who are themselves Buddhist take an interest in Hinduism that does not necessarily make them "Hindu" *per se*. The cultural basis for this phenomenon is somewhat different from that of the Western Buddhist sympathizer, however. The Western Buddhist sympathizer is playing in a sandbox created by the projection of modernist fantasies onto Buddhism, which serves as a convenient Orientalist "other" to the Western religion, usually Christianity or Judaism, that the sympathizer is familiar with, either personally or culturally. Hindu enthusiasm in Thailand, on the other hand, is a product of the long-standing historical ability of Hindu discourses to exercise agency within Siamese Buddhism through the category of *saiyasāt* and the more recent reconfiguration of this interdiscursive nexus through the introduction of the discourse of world religions.

Hindu enthusiasm in Thailand is made possible by the historical connection between *phutthasāt* and *saiyasāt* in Siam, or, to put it differently, between the Pali and Sanskrit cosmopoleis that have informed Siamese discourse. In a sense, modern Thai Hindu enthusiasts are doing what Siamese Buddhists have always done, which is to draw from Hindu discourses about the gods to elaborate upon or update the Pali Buddhist cosmology that takes the gods very much for granted. The modern discourse of world religions, however, has on the one hand intensified and on the other hand reified and problematized this old practice. The intensification of drawing from Hindu discourses is a simple product of the increased access to those discourses in the age of globalization that it concomitant with the discourse of world religions. In the past, access to new developments in India necessitated the actual movement of knowledgeable personnel and/or texts across an ocean—such as the likely gifting of Brahmans during the reign of Rāmāthibodī II—all at a time when the Sanskrit Cosmopolis was collapsing and the Pali Cosmopolis rising to take its place in Siam's immediate region. Today easy access to "Hinduism" is made possible by international travel, books, the internet, and international education that initiates one into the discourse of "world religions" itself.[86]

World religions discourse, however, has also reified the practice of borrowing from Hindu discourses and, as a side effect, rendered it sufficiently uncanny as to problematize it. Whereas before, borrowings from Hindu discourses—for example, portraying Brahmā with four faces or giving a prominent role to Viṣṇu or Śiva—could fit seamlessly within an otherwise Buddhist cosmological framework, world religions discourse flags this practice as engagement with something that is "Brahmanical" or "Hindu." This reification can take the form, especially within reflective, scholarly discourses, of a wholesale adoption of the Kirschan model of Brahmanism as one of the "components" of Thai religion, or it can take the form of Hindu enthusiasts labeling what they are doing, or the gods they worship, as Brahmanical/Hindu. For example, www.siamganesh.com, the website that serves as a treasure trove of Hindu enthusiasm, describes itself as "the website that collects the most information about knowledge, *gāthās*, pictures, and works of art of Gaṇeśa and 'Brahmanical/Hindu gods.'"[87]

The reification of "Hinduism" or "Brahmanism" within Thai religion also problematizes it, making it a target for critique. For example, the monastic scholar P.A. Payutto, in an essay criticizing the contemporary Thai obsession with *sing saksit*, writes, "We must move beyond an understanding of the supernatural associated with externalized gods—Viṣṇu, Śiva, Indra, Brahmā, and so forth—who personify the power of grasping, conceit, and mental defilements, appealing to them for help."[88] Similarly, Buddhadāsa Bhikkhu, a prominent Thai Buddhist modernist who rejected much of the traditional teaching of Buddhism, including the literal interpretation of the cycle of rebirth, writes the following in defending his interpretation of dependent origination (*paṭiccasamuppāda*) as a purely psychological process in this life:

> The *Visuddhimagga* explains *Paticcasamuppada* in terms of three births.... If Buddhagosa [*sic*] wrote 1,500 years ago, it must mean that the incorrect explanation which he passed on was prevalent more than 1,500 years ago.... Is it possible that there was a worm nibbling at the innards of Buddhism?... Were these people, in fact, explaining it incorrectly in terms of Hinduistic eternalism, or Brahmanism?... In this way, then, Brahmanism could indirectly swallow Buddhism in a flash....
>
> Do you know why Buddhism disappeared from India? Different people say for this, that or the other reason: for example, because foreign enemies came in and oppressed the religion. I don't think that is the case. I think that Buddhism disappeared from India because the followers of Buddhism began to interpret the principles of Buddhism incorrectly, explaining *Paticcasamuppada*, the heart of Buddhism, as a form of having a self. This is, I believe, the *de facto* reason for Buddhism's disappearance from India. Buddhism became simply an appendage of Hinduism.[89]

This sort of thoroughgoing critique of the Buddhist tradition is not simply written in the terms of world religions discourse; it is made possible by that very discourse. Prior to the postcolonial period, it would have been unthinkable for a prominent Siamese monk to reject a Buddhist teaching as fundamental as rebirth. Of course, in doing so Buddhadāsa Bhikkhu is participating in the broader phenomenon of Buddhist Modernism, but it is the terms of world religions discourse, the reification of Brahmanism/Hinduism and identification of it *within* Thai religion, that allow him to construct a theory of the adulteration of Buddhism by a Hindu other. World religions discourse has transformed the erstwhile category of *saiyasāt*—and with it a vast swath of traditional Buddhism—in such a way as to simultaneously inflate it *and* mark it for elimination as "non-Buddhist."

Saiyasāt, the Gods, and the Work of World Religions

As I have argued throughout this book and illustrated in more detail in this chapter, gods have a completely natural place within Buddhism due to its implicit theology, and as such it is not surprising to find mythology and cult surrounding the gods in a Buddhist culture such as that of Siam/Thailand. Because of Siam's historical existence on the nexus of transforming cosmopolitan structures, Siamese discourse has always been able to draw upon Hindu discourses from beyond the Pali *imaginaire* to update and elaborate upon its cosmology. Historically, the category through which Hindu discourses exercised this agency was *saiyasāt*. We thus find many examples of extra-Pali "Hindu" influence on Siamese religion up to the height of the colonial encounter in the nineteenth century: references to the *Mahābhārata* and Purāṇic mythology, worship of gods such as Viṣṇu and Śiva who rose to prominence only after the composition of the Pali Canon, and employment of Brahmans using Tamil *bhakti* hymns at court.

The adoption of the Western discourse of world religions in the nineteenth century, however, transformed Siamese discourse in such a way as to transfigure Thai religious practice and the way modern Thai actors reflect upon it. What had been called *saiyasāt* was now called "Brahmanism" or "Hinduism," a "religion" separate from Buddhism. At the same time, the category *saiyasāt* was repurposed to refer to "magic," a category with a negative connotation vis-à-vis Buddhism. While this did not transform Thai practice in any fundamental way—most Thai Buddhists continue to recognize and worship gods as they have for centuries—it did transform the way Thai Buddhists *conceptualize* what they do, and this, over the long term, has had a significant effect on Buddhist practice.

Whereas before, the gods, as well as the Brahmans who specialize in their worship, were simply a natural part of the Buddhist cosmos, the modern discourse of world religions has reified this aspect of Thai religion, both intensifying it and rendering it sufficiently uncanny as to open it to criticism. The intensification takes the form of what I call Hindu enthusiasm—ordinary Thai Buddhists who do not necessarily have an Indian background taking a heightened interest in worshiping the gods as mediated through Hindu discourses. At the same time, the completely novel perception that the "Hinduism" or "Brahmanism" they are engaging with is separate from Buddhism opens their enthusiasm to critique from reform- and modernist-minded Buddhists.

In this book, I am less concerned with modernist critiques of mainstream religious practice than with mainstream religious practice itself and the way it has been conditioned historically. The reconfiguration of Siamese discourse by the modern discourse of world religions explains *why* we see Hindu enthusiasm as a prominent movement within Thai religion today, but it does not explain in practical terms *how* it arose. For that, we must look to the accidents of history. As I have shown in this chapter, Hindu enthusiasm in its practical forms can to a large extent be traced back to the construction of the shrine to Brahmā at the Ērāwan Hotel in the 1950s. Brahmā is integral to the traditional Pali cosmology, so there is nothing particularly novel about Thai Buddhists worshiping him. The decision to erect a shrine to him in the style of a shrine to Phra Phūm, however, was novel and served as a prototype for the praxis of Hindu enthusiasm that would follow. In choosing to build a "bigger, better" shrine for a "bigger, better" hotel, the founders of the Ērāwan Shrine were simply extending the logic whereby traditional shrines to the *phī bān* and *sān phiang tā* had been standardized into shrines to Phra Phūm for every house and structure in an urban environment. This led to a proliferation of shrines to Brahmā specifically, but also imitation shrines to other "Hindu" gods. The logic of *kānbonbānsānklāo*, which had long been involved in the propitiation of *phī* and low-ranking supernatural beings, provided the paradigm for praxis, albeit in a reproduceable and commercializable urbanized form. At the same time, world religions discourse gave direction to the reproduction of this praxis. Luang Suwichānphāt followed a rather traditional Buddhist logic in recommending a shrine to Brahmā: Indra was angry, so it made sense to go to the next highest god in the traditional Buddhist cosmology, Brahmā. The marking of Brahmā as a "Hindu god," however, has channeled the proliferation of Ērāwan-esque shrines in the direction of "Hindu" gods, irrespective of their importance to or even presence in Pali Buddhist cosmology.

As a result, Hindu gods, often but not always explicitly conceptualized *as Hindu*, have been established as a subcategory under the rubric of *sing saksit*. As we saw in Chapter 4, prior to its modern deployment as a translation of the Western concept of "holy," the word *saksit* referred to the power of *devas* and other supernatural beings, which is what made them potential granters of boons. While Siamese discourse has always been aware of the high gods of Hinduism, and Brahmans have long been employed at court to worship them, there is little evidence prior to the Ērāwan shrine of a popular engagement of them in the *do ut des* practice of *kānbonbānsānklāo*. The gods have always been a part of Siamese Buddhism, but the fetishization of Hindu gods as such and as efficacious granters of boons, as *sing saksit* like the ordinary spirits of houses and trees, is a thoroughly modern Thai phenomenon.

7
Buddha Images

In the previous two chapters, we saw a progression in the modern cultic praxis of *kānbonbānsānklāo* mediated by globalization and commercialization, but simultaneously framed by the changes wrought on Siamese/Thai discourse through the introduction of the concept of world religions. The simple practices of *kānbonbānsānklāo* that were directed toward *phī* of various levels, including the *phī bān* and *phī rüan*, through simple shrines and the temporary *sān phiang tā* were reconfigured through the standardization and commercialization of shrines to Phra Phūm and *pūyātāyāi* in a rapidly urbanizing Bangkok and greater Thailand. This became the model in the 1950s for the Ērāwan Brahmā Shrine, which was conceived as a bigger, better shrine—both physically and in terms of its choice of a highly ranked god as its cult object—for a bigger, better hotel. Although the choice of Brahmā was well within the confines of the Pali *imaginaire*, the introduction of world religions discourse in the late nineteenth century ensured that the fire sparked by the Ērāwan Shrine burned in a particular direction, resulting in the proliferation in shrines to "Hindu" gods and general Hindu enthusiasm that we see in Thailand today. Still, the basic logic according to which Thai practitioners worship these newly popular Hindu gods is that of *kānbonbānsānklāo*, and as such the gods are fully subsumed into the broader category of *sing saksit*, legible as "Hindu" only to those with eyes to see them as such.

Given this trajectory, it is tempting to read the inclusion of Buddha images such as Luang Phọ̄ Sōthọn within the category of *sing saksit* and practice of *kānbonbānsānklāo* as a simple extension of the beliefs and praxis surrounding *phī* to Buddha images. This would represent the ultimate triumph of local or vernacular religion over the elite religion of Buddhism. Indeed, John Clifford Holt offers just this interpretation, albeit in a different Tai context, Laos, in his *Spirits of the Place*:

> [T]his constitutes one of my major assertions, that rather than finding a sustained interpretive Buddhist understanding of *phi* and *khwan* on the

Holy Things. Nathan McGovern, Oxford University Press. © Oxford University Press 2024.
DOI: 10.1093/9780197759912.003.0007

> basis of karma, which was clearly the bedrock principle and interpretive mechanism used by the Sinhala Buddhists in Sri Lanka to explain the relative existences of supernatural beings, the converse is actually more likely to be found among the Lao: Buddhist conceptuality, symbol, and ritual tends to be seen at the popular level of Lao culture through the lenses of the indigenous religious substratum constituted by the cults of *phi* and *khwan*.[1]

Holt refers to the situation he describes as "inspiriting Buddhism" and argues that "Buddhism continues to be understood through the lenses of the spirit cults in Laos."[2]

Before critiquing Holt's argument, it is important to address his geopolitical field of study, which is different from mine in this book. While my study is focused on Siam and the nation-state Thailand that succeeded it, his is Laos, a modern nation-state that was formed through colonialism out of a portion of the erstwhile kingdom of Lān Xāng. Although, as we have seen, Lān Xāng and Siam have deep commonalities arising out of their shared Tai culture, Holt sees a clear distinction between the situation in Laos proper and even neighboring Īsān, the southern portion of the old Lān Xāng kingdom that was incorporated into Siam in the nineteenth century and remains a part of Thailand to this day. Citing the work of Tambiah, Kamala, and especially Hayashi, Holt shows that there has been a concerted effort to assert Buddhist dominance over local spirit cults among Lao communities in Īsān (Northeastern Thailand). He therefore concludes, "It may be a grand overgeneralization, but it seems as though in the tug of war between Buddhism and the spirit cults, Buddhism has seized the upper hand in Thailand, while the spirits remain ultimately vested in Laos."[3]

It may very well be true that certain types of "Buddhacization" have taken place in Thailand that have not taken place in Laos; for example, in Laos, *phī* associated with the land are worshiped aniconically in the form of empty spirit houses, while in Thailand, they are referred to using the Sanskritic name Phra Phūm and are represented iconically by small images placed in the spirit houses. Nevertheless, I think that Holt has exaggerated the difference between Laos and Thailand due to his focus on scholarship on Lao communities in Īsān. If Buddhism in Laos is "inspirited," as Holt calls it, then it is just as much so in Thailand—not only in Īsān but also in central Thailand, the heartland of old Siam. Luang Phọ̄ Sōthọn and the multitude of famous Buddha images throughout Thailand that are propitiated for boons (a practice Holt appears to be unaware of) is testament to this.

Any "battle" between Buddhism and the local spirit cults in Northeastern Thailand is most likely due to central Thai anxieties over the assimilation of the ethnically Lao people of that region into a normatively constructed image of "Thainess" (*khwāmpenkhonthai*, ความเป็นคนไทย) and a concomitant *exaggeration* of the nonnormative qualities of Īsān culture. The people of Īsān are often portrayed negatively in popular Thai culture, referred to as *bānnǭk* (บ้านนอก, "country," in the sense of "uncivilized") or simply "Lao" (intended as a pejorative). Their religious practices are also sometimes portrayed in popular culture as aberrant and *ngomngāi* (งมงาย, "superstitious"); for example, a comedic film produced in 2005 in Thailand called *Luang Phī Thēng* (*หลวงพี่เท่ง*, "Reverend Brother Thēng") portrays a young monk setting up shop as the only resident of a temple in a village in Īsān, trying to win the locals over to the pure teachings of Buddhism while doing battle with the more popular religious figure in town, an unscrupulous spirit medium. In central Thailand, conversely, which tautologically defines cultural normativity, there is less anxiety over the need to assimilate "aberrant" practices to an imagined ideal, and thus the "inspiriting" of Buddhism, if that is indeed what it is, goes on (relatively) unabated.[4]

All of this is to say that, if Holt's thesis about the inspiriting of Buddhism in Laos is correct, then it should be equally true of Siam and in particular of the propitiation of Buddha images as "holy things" for mundane boons. This is, in fact, how such practices are often interpreted. Indeed, a recently scholarly publication in Thai called *Phī Phrām Phut* (lit., "Spirit, Brahman, Buddha") includes an introduction in which the prominent Thai intellectual Nidhi Eoseewong writes, similarly to Holt:

> What I am particularly interested in and would like to talk about is spirit religion and the interaction between spirit religion and Buddhism in Thailand, especially given that Buddhism doesn't stay put in one place but has encountered great changes in the past 200 years. This is because I have the opposite view of most scholars, who hold that Buddhism is the central pith of Thai religion, with spirit religion and Brahmanism being a husk that covers it in some places. I rather think that we understand Thai religion better if we take spirit religion to be the central pith, with Buddhism and Brahmanism being the husk that covers the outside.[5]

Nidhi then argues that when Thai practitioners propitiate a famous Buddha image, they are actually giving offerings to the *phī* or *devatā* that inhabits the

Buddha image, and thus, "[w]orshiping a Buddha image and worshiping a *phī* are the same thing."[6]

In this chapter, I will show that an "inspiriting [of] Buddhism," or a reverse Buddhacization in which Buddhism is read through the lens of local spirit religion, is not a good model for understanding the propitiation of Luang Phǫ Sōthǫn and other Buddha images through *kānbonbānsānklāo*. In particular, it elides both the antiquity and naturalness of such practice in Buddhism as a whole and the role played by modern discourse in shaping the contemporary articulation of this practice. As I will show, Siamese discourse shows a long familiarity with the practice of resolving for miraculous boons at a famous and powerful Buddha image, although until modern times this practice was articulated exclusively in terms dictated by the Pali *imaginaire*. However, the reconfiguration of the category *saksit* in the late nineteenth century to mean "holy" brought this practice into conversation with the similar practice of asking spirits/gods for boons. As a result, what may appear to be an old vestige of the indigenous substratum asserting itself in insufficiently Buddhacized Buddhist contexts is instead a very *modern* phenomenon in which the rhetorical distinctions between the Buddha and his relics on the one hand and powerful saṃsāric beings on the other have been elided by the adoption of a Western category: the "holy."

Early Evidence for the Propitiation of Buddha Images in Siam

Tracing the history in Siam of asking Buddha images for boons, or the general nature of practice surrounding Buddha images and other relics, is made difficult not only by the relative dearth of sources from before the 1767 sack of Ayutthayā but also by the nature of the sources that do survive. Many of our sources are fictional, depicting extraordinary events, and the praxis of Buddhist worship is so mundane and everyday—not only in premodern Siam, but in any Buddhist society at any point in history—that it does not often bear mentioning in works of literature. Nevertheless, there are a few sources that help us glean some idea of how Buddha images and other relics were propitiated in early Siamese history. I will begin with three fragmentary passages from the corpus of Sukhōthai inscriptions and then turn to the *Nirāt Hariphunchai*, a work of early Ayutthayā literature.

The oldest text I have encountered that speaks to the propitiation of a Buddha relic for boons is a mid-fourteenth-century inscription that concerns not a Buddha image but a Buddha footprint (*buddhapāda*). It describes the benefits of worshiping the footprint in broad canonical terms:

กศรีพุทธสํบดดิบ.. คนดงงริแล...... สํบดดินนนอนนึงผีวาเกดเป(น)
.... ญอมไดเสวยสํบดดิ
น.......(จ)กรพรรดิราชไดเปนก...........(แ) ลบมีไดเขนหม..ง
....................(ผิ)วาเกิดท้าวพรบา............ สํบดดิอนนหน
.... รตดิดาย.... ทงง ... เปนพระ ...... เสรถียิพระ
.................ี.... งเมือทิแลวก่จกกได .... เปนสํบดดินนแลมิอยา
เลยผูใดไดขิน(นบ)รอยฝต(น)พระ(พุทธ)เจาเราเถิงเหนี(อจอม)
เขาสูมนกูฏบรรพดนีดวยใจอนนส(ร)(ธา)อนนวาสํบดดิทงงสามอนนนี
.... จกกไดแลมิอย่า

How does one be like that (the attainment of Buddhahood)? ... that attainment. For one thing, if he is born as ... he is likely to enjoy the attainment ... become a *cakravartin* king ... he doesn't get misfortune or sadness.[7] ... [I]f he is born as a king ... the attainment ... as a monk ... rich man. ... When he is there, he will get it ... as that attainment without fail. Therefore, whoever goes up to bow to the footprint of our Lord Buddha on the top of this Sumanakūṭaparvata with a heart of faith [*śraddhā*] that these three attainments[8] ... he will attain them without fail.[9]

This passage, while addressing the rewards of worshiping a Buddha relic, does not take quite the same form as modern *kānbonbānsānklāo*. It does not involve a promise or negotiation, and its rewards relate primarily to future rebirths rather than immediate mundane concerns. It is simply a boilerplate assertion that the merit from worshiping a Buddha relic will lead to good rebirths, such as one can find in Pali texts.

A slightly later inscription, from 1399, describes practices that are somewhat more in line with modern *kānbonbānsānklāo*. In this inscription, written in Thai and Pali, a queen describes her establishment of a *stūpa* and monastery, as well as various gifts she gave for its maintenance. Among the Pali version of this litany, one particular set of gifts is worthy of note:

(taṃ ārā)mikaṃ kūlaṃ *paññāsaparimāṇikaṃ*
sricandavhappamukhañca ....*natthum adāsi sā*
tāḷādikaṃ hi pañcangaṃ- *turiyaṃ saṃkhavaṃsakaṃ*
mahābheriṃ mahātālaṃ

> She gave it fifty families of temple servants, led by Sri Canda . . . and players, instruments for the five types of music, beginning with percussion: conches, bamboo flutes, great drums, great gongs.[10]

Likewise, the Thai version of the inscription indicates that she gave "a full set of musical instruments with horns and conches (for) all the rituals of worship" (พาดถว๋นสำรบักบัแตรสงัขทงักริยาบูชาทงัหลาย).[11] As with the previous inscriptions, the queen in this inscription dedicates the merit from her actions both to her own future good rebirths and Awakening and to her relatives to be free from suffering. Although the exact use of the instruments gifted in this behest is not described, it does appear to make a link between providing musical entertainment and merit-making that can benefit the donor.

A third inscription, dating to 1536, gives a similar extended list of donations made to a Buddhist temple. In particular, it lists the following offerings made specifically to the Buddha image:

> ถวยโคมลายดวงนิงถวย(บร) พนัเลกสิบดวงเปนสำรบักบัลางพานแตงเปน บายศรีบูชาพรเจาตเลิงทองเหลิองดวงนิงคาหาสลิงแต(ง) ใสหมากบูชาพร เจาเลิยนทองสำเรดดวงนิงคาบาดนิงแตงหมยงบูชาพรเจานำเตาทอง สำริดดวงนิงมีฝาคาบาดนิงแตงใสนำบูชาพรเจา

> One large decorated bowl and ten accompanying bowls as a set, with some pedestal trays to put *bāisī*[12] to offer to the Lord. One brass *talüng*, valued at five *salüng*, to put betel nut to offer to the Lord. One bronze *lian*,[13] valued at one *bāt*, to put chewing tea leaves to offer to the Lord. One bronze bottle with a lid, valued at one *bāt*, to put water to offer to the Lord.[14]

Here, then, we find a series of offerings that imply *future* offerings of food to the Buddha image, the closest evidence we have found yet of something like *kānbonbānsānklāo*. The actual way in which these offerings will be made, however, is not specified, so there is no direct evidence of promising offerings in exchange for boons. As with the previous two inscriptions, this inscription ends with a boilerplate expression of the desire for the merit gained to lead to good future rebirths, with wealth and good health.

These Sukhōthai inscriptions provide tantalizing hints at the manner of worshiping Buddha images and relics in old Siam, but by far the most useful source for this purpose is the *Nirāt Hariphunchai*, written in 1517 and recording a Lānnā noble's journey to Haribhuñjaya (now Lamphūn). Because the author of this text is narrating his visit to the city, a large portion of which involves making merit at the old *cēdī* that makes the city a site of pilgrimage, rather than simply recording a donation, we get a detailed look at what practices one actually engaged in at that time when going to *wāi phra* (worship the Buddha image). The overall picture we gain from this text is that at that time one could ask Buddha images and relics for boons in a manner quite similar to but not exactly the same as found at places like Wat Sōthǭn today.

Given that the text is a *nirāt*, and in fact the prototype of the genre in Siamese literature, the *Nirāt Hariphunchai* thematizes the author's longing for his lover, whom he misses while away on a journey. As a result, the "boon" that he asks for repeatedly is to be reunited with his love quickly. He makes this request several times throughout his visit:

ธาราไหลหล่อหื้อ　　เป็นสัตย์ ก็ดี
ก่อเท่าเบิงอันพัด　　พรากซ้ำ
ปัจจุณเผือผลตัด　　สองจาก เจียนรา
พิโยคนุชนี้ล้ำ　　เลิศผู้ใดปะเหียน

The water flows as (an act of) truth
Because I fear that we will be separated further.
(What I do) now is for the fruit to end our separation,
Separation from you, who are great without compare. (v. 125)

ถึงพุทธรูปอั้น　　ยืนยัง
ก่อมก้อเป็นขลงทัง　　สี่ด้าน
ทำบุญเผื่อบุญบัง　　พบแม่ นะแม่
กุโนชพระเจ้าจ้าน　　ค่อยแก้กรรมสนอง

I reach those Buddha images that stand
Low in arches on all four sides.
I make merit in order to meet you.
May the Lord have great compassion to efface my karma in response.
(v. 151)

นานนักชลิ่วแล้ง สาลี
เพียญชน์เรียมนับปี อ่านปั้น
บูชารูปรอยมี ผลมาก นักเอย
ก็เที่ยงลุแก้วหมั้น แม่เอ้ยยาไสลย

For many years there has been a drought and no rice,
No food. I count the years, count the clods.
I offer to the image; there is so much fruit.
It is certain: You need not worry. (v. 154)

พระพุทธสามสี่ห้า หกองค์
สูรส่องไสสีรงค์ หร่ามร้อน
เรียมเห็นเวทนาปลง ใจชื่น ชมเอย
เทียนธูปทูลเจ้าจ้อน จุ่งห้ามโพยภัย

Three, four, five, six Buddhas.
The sun shines brightly, colorfully, glittering, hot.
I see it and feel low, but I am pleased.
I offer candles and incense to the small Lord: May there be no dangers. (v. 157)

ลาพระชินธาตุเจ้า จอมอัฐิ
ถวายคิลาเพียญชน์ภัตร หว่านไหว้
ประจงจอดจักรวัติ ผลเผื่อ ทิพเอย
บัดเดี่ยวขอหื้อให้ แห่งห้องวิวาหา

I take leave of the relics of the Lord Jina, the bone reliquary.
I offer medicine and food and *wāi*.
No need to be a *cakravartin*; let the fruit be for Thip (my lover).
May we get to the bridal chamber right away. (v. 169)[15]

As we can see from these passages, there are two key similarities to modern *kānbonbānsānklāo*. First, the author clearly asks for a boon when worshiping Buddha images and other relics. Moreover, that boon is mundane. He does not resort to stock requests for better rebirths and eventual Buddhahood, or even for general health and prosperity; instead, he asks specifically to be reunited with his lover, exactly the sort of personal and specific request, totally unconnected with Buddhist soteriology, that many Thai practitioners make today of Buddha images and other *sing saksit.* In the last verse quoted above, he even seems to make a sly joke about it, saying that he doesn't need to become a *cakravartin*—the sort of standard request made, for example, in one of the Sukhōthai inscriptions we looked at—he just wants to be reunited with his lover Thip so that they can get married. The second similarity to modern practice is in the type of offerings given. Again, the last verse in particular specifically says that the author gives food and medicine, thus treating the Buddhist relic like a living being.

In spite of these similarities, however, there are some key differences. First, there is extensive discussion of singers, dancers, and other entertainers present at the temple in verses 130 to 140, but there is no indication that they are present to be hired for *ram kābon* (dancing to fulfill a vow) as at Wat Sōthǫn today. Instead, the implication seems to be that they are simply there to entertain—perhaps as part of a temple fair, known in modern Thai as a *ngān wat* (งานวัด). Second, there is no indication whatsoever that there is any process of *bon* and *kābon*—making and then fulfilling a promise in requesting a boon. The author does not promise any future offering; he simply makes his request at the same time as making an offering. He then explains his hope, in nearly every verse, that the merit accrued from his act of devotion will lead to his being reunited with Thip as he desires. In addition, in verse 125, he speaks of his merit-making as an "act of truth," language that we will return to shortly.

The Culture of Buddha Images and Their Miraculous Power in Lānnā

Although the focus of the study in this book is Siam, it is important to recognize that much of the specifically *Buddhist* culture of modern Thailand is rooted not so much in Siam proper as its northern neighbor, Lānnā, which now forms Northern Thailand. Premodern Siamese literature is by no means bereft of Buddhist themes—the *Mahāchāt Kham Luang* of early Ayutthayā, which records the story of Vessantara in a mixture of Pali and Thai being the most important literary example—but the true center of Buddhist learning, literature, innovation, and culture in the broader Tai world for much of the period prior to the nineteenth century was not Ayutthayâ but Chiang Mai. The Lānnā kingdom had its origins in the Tai takeover of a Mon city-state, Haribhuñjaya (modern Lamphūn). In the thirteenth century, a branch of the Tai known as the Yuan expanded under the leadership of its *cāo*, Mangrāi, from its base at Müang Rāo, founding Chiang Rāi in 1263, capturing Haribhuñjaya in 1281, and founding a new capital at Chiang Mai in 1296.[16] The resulting kingdom, culturally a mixture of Tai, Mon, and other indigenous cultures, grew in strength and prosperity until entering what is generally recognized as its golden age in the fifteenth and sixteenth centuries, up until it was conquered by the Burmese in 1558. Lānnā's influence during that period as a center of Buddhist learning was particularly renowned, and that influence was transmitted in large part through texts written in a Mon-derived script known as *aksǫn tham* (อักษรธรรม; lit., "*dhamma* letters").[17] The influence of this Buddhist textual culture spread far beyond Lānnā's direct political sphere, to the extent that Hans Penth has suggested that we can speak of a broader "culture of the region of *dhamma* letters."[18]

One of the innovations of Lānnā's Buddhist textual culture was the development of histories, or *tamnān* (ตำนาน), of particular Buddha images. One of the most well-known and influential of such histories is the *Jinakālamālīpakaraṇa*, a Pali chronicle written in 1527 by the monk Ratanapañña Thera that places the kings of Mon Haribhuñjaya and Tai Lānnā within a broader Buddhist history traced through Laṅkā. It includes detailed histories of four important Buddha images: the Emerald Buddha, the Sikhī Buddha, the Sihing Buddha, and the Sandalwood Buddha.[19] Of these, the Emerald Buddha (พระแก้วมรกฎ, *phra kāo mǫrakot*) and Sihing images continue to be among the most famed Buddha images in Thailand today. The former is found today at Wat Phra Kāo in the Grand Palace in Bangkok and is the palladium of the current Chakri Dynasty. The latter, the Sihing image, has three rival claimants, found in Chiang Mai, Bangkok, and Nakhǫn Sī Thammarāt.

The accounts of the four key Buddha images in the *Jinakālamālīpakaraṇa* are relatively short, but they display several paradigmatic features: they record the (generally mythical) circumstances in which the images were created; they give the images personalized "histories" by recording their travels between different *müang*; and they allude to supernatural powers possessed by the images. These paradigmatic features are found in a wider body of *tamnān* literature coming from Lānnā about famous Buddha images, which has been studied recently by Angela Chiu. She reports that there are over two hundred unique examples of such *tamnān*, most of them written in vernacular languages such as Tai Yuan, but a few in Pali.[20] Chiu's study is based on twenty-four of these *tamnān* found in the collection of the École française d'Extrême Orient at the Princess Maha Chakri Sirindhorn Anthropology Centre in Bangkok.[21] One of the patterns she notes in these texts is a desire to trace the proper lineage of a particular image back to an "authentic" likeness of the Buddha through the display of supernatural power.[22] For example, the *Tamnān Phra Phuttha Sihing* by Bodhiraṃsi reports that the Sihing image, at the behest of the king of Nakhọ̄n Sī Thammarāt, levitated and emitted light of various colors.[23]

Although the *tamnān* studied by Chiu do at times depict Buddha images performing miracles in which devotees receive their specific desires, they do not describe in specific terms a practice akin to modern *kānbonbānsānklāo*, nor do they describe Buddha images with the words *saksit* or *sitthisak*.[24] Nevertheless, they do lay the groundwork in a crucial way for the modern understanding in Thailand of Buddha images as *sing saksit* that can be propitiated for boons through *kānbonbānsānklāo*. That is, they depict Buddha images as *individual beings*, not mere representations of the Buddha, with personal histories, that moreover possess miraculous powers. This particular constellation of understandings of Buddha images is not entirely unique in the Buddhist world, but they were instantiated in the Tai cultural sphere in a particular way through the Lānnā *tamnān* literature. As Chiu writes:

> The Lanna focus on the original production of a statue and the detailed recounting of its history over hundreds of years suggest an understanding of a Buddha statue as capable of having its own biography. Based upon accounts described in existing scholarship, commonalities of motif and theme may be perceived between the Lanna stories and examples from China and Japan, such as the preference for detailed discussion of the origins of an image, attention to its miraculous powers, and the sense of the image as having its own life or at least an autonomous sense of where it should go on its travels. Yet the Lanna style of the extended biography of the travelling statue seems to be without equivalent elsewhere.[25]

As we have already seen, the practice of asking famous Buddha images, like Luang Phọ̄ Sōthọ̄n, for boons depends on the very understanding of Buddha images that was earlier instantiated in *tamnān* emanating from the Buddhist textual culture of Lānnā. One does not simply go to any old Buddha image for a boon. One goes to a *particular* image renowned for granting boons. Luang Phọ̄ Sōthọ̄n, for example, has a name, literally "Reverend Father Sōthọ̄n," that not only distinguishes him from other Buddha images but makes him sound like an individual; he has an individual biography; and he has a reputation for granting boons that lies within his power as an individual, not as a mere representation of the Buddha.

Explaining Miraculous Buddha Relics within the Pali *Imaginaire*

As Chiu suggests, the understanding of Buddha images cultivated in the broader Tai world by the Lānnā *tamnān* literature was in many ways not unique but is found in a variety of Buddhist cultures. This is in part because understanding Buddhist relics in general (of which Buddha images are considered a subset) as individually having the potential to possess miraculous powers has a very old pedigree within Buddhism, including within the Pali tradition. Indeed, the standard canonical explanation for the possibility of such miracles is given by the monk Nāgasena in response to a question by King Milinda in the *Milindapañha*:

> "Venerable Nāgasena, are there miracles at the sepulchral mounds (*cetiya*) of all who have attained complete extinction, or only of some?"
>
> "(At the mounds) of some, Great King, there are; of others there are not."
>
> "Which ones have (miracles), Venerable Sir; which ones do not?"
>
> "Great King, due to the resolution (*adhiṭṭhāna*) of three types of people are there miracles at the sepulchral mounds of those who have attained complete extinction. Which three? Here, Great King, an *arhat*, while still alive, out of compassion for gods and human beings resolves, 'Let there be miracles at the sepulchral mound named such-and-such.' Under the influence of his resolution, there are miracles at his sepulchral mound; thus, there are miracles at the sepulchral mound of one who has attained complete extinction under the influence of the resolution of an *arhat*.
>
> "And further, Great King, divinities out of compassion for human beings display miracles at the sepulchral mounds of those who have attained complete extinction, (thinking,) 'By this miracle the true *dhamma* will be continuously supported, and human beings, pleased, will increase in merit.' Thus, there are miracles at the sepulchral mounds of those who

have attained complete extinction under the influence of the resolutions of divinities.

"And further, Great King, some woman or man, faithful, pleased, intelligent, learned, wise, endowed with intelligence, reflects and throws perfume or garlands or cloth or something else up on the sepulchral mound, (thinking,) 'Let such-and-such (a miracle) happen.' There are miracles at the sepulchral mounds of those who have attained final extinction under the influence of the resolution of even that (ordinary person); thus, there are miracles at the sepulchral mounds of those who have attained final extinction under the influence of the resolutions of human beings.

"These, Great King, are the three types of people under the influence of whose resolutions there are miracles at the sepulchral mounds of those who have attained final extinction.

"If, Great King, there is no resolution by (one of) these (three), then there is no miracle at the sepulchral mound of even one who is without *āsava*s, who possesses the six higher knowledges, who has attained mastery of the mind. Even in the absence (of a miracle), Great King, seeing the conduct (of the one who attained complete extinction) as a miracle, one should focus on (that one's) complete purity, one should go to perfection, one should believe, 'Truly this son of the Buddha has attained complete extinction.'"

"Excellent, Venerable Nāgasena! Therefore, I accept this as (you explain it)."[26]

Clearly, given the context of Buddhist ontology, a natural way to explain something good happening—a boon, if you will—after venerating a relic or Buddha image is that it is the result of the merit accrued through that act of veneration. We have already seen that explanation alluded to several times in the Sukhōthai inscriptions and passages from the *Nirāt Hariphunchai* that we examined earlier. This exchange in the *Milindapañha*, however, goes a step further. It systematizes the capacity of merit-making to lead to wish fulfillment in such a way as to make it possible for a particular object—in this case, relics contained in *cetiya*s, but easily expanded to include Buddha images—to display miraculous powers in perpetuity.

The principle under which the *Milindapañha* effects this systematization is, in Pali, *adhiṭṭhāna*, equivalent to the Sanskrit word *adhiṣṭhāna*. I have translated this word as "resolution," although there is no word in English that quite captures the act of speech or thought that *adhiṭṭhāna* refers to. In

English, a resolution is an act of speech or thought in which one makes a firm commitment to do something or act in a certain way in the future—as with, say, a New Year's Resolution to exercise three times a week or to stop drinking alcohol. The concept of *adhiṭṭhāna*, on the other hand, refers to an act of speech or thought that, through the intrinsic power of making it, comes to pass. It is not a promise to oneself to act in a certain way in the future; it is an act of will that directly effects the desired outcome. The distinction is parallel to that between an order, a speech act that conveys meaning to someone so that they do something, and a spell (or *mantra*), a speech act that directly causes something to occur, whether it conveys meaning or not.

I have framed *adhiṭṭhāna* as a systematization of the potential for merit to produce good outcomes in order to explain miracles. This explanation, however, is only implied in the *Milindapañha* passage. *Arhat*s and divinities are of course intrinsically meritorious because of their high attainment—that is, of *nibbāna* or a high rebirth, respectively. The clearest indication that merit is involved, however, is found in the third case, that of ordinary human beings. Nāgasena tells King Milinda that ordinary men and women can produce miracles through *adhiṭṭhāna*, but note the context: they do so *specifically* when giving offerings to the *cetiya*—that is, when making merit. No such condition is placed on the intrinsically meritorious *arhat*s and divinities, implying that, from a Buddhist perspective at least, ordinary people who lack a large store of merit must produce merit on the spot in order for *adhiṭṭhāna* to be effective, and thus that it is merit, or the workings of good karma, that allow one to "resolve" for miracles to occur.

The fact that merit *can* be used to logically justify *adhiṭṭhāna*, however, does not exhaustively explain why the Buddhist tradition quite early in its history developed such a theory to explain miracles. Choy Fah Kong, in an expansive study of the concept in Theravāda Buddhism, situates *adhiṭṭhāna* in the broader Indian context of belief in the power of true speech, *saccakiriyā*. She shows that the idea that an act of true speech can, through its intrinsic power, cause something to happen has an old pedigree in Indian thought that far predates Buddhism. She traces this concept back to a trope in the *Ṛg Veda* in which a god or gods frees cows by a simple act of truth in uttering their names.[27] A more paradigmatic example, however, can be found in the following verse from the *Atharva Veda*:

samáṃ jyótiḥ sū́ryeṇā́hnā rā́trī samā́vatī |
kṛṇomi satyám ūtáye 'rasā́ḥ santu kṛ́tvarīḥ ||1||

Light is equal to the sun; the night is of the same extent as the day.
I make this true (statement) for help: May the powers be weak! (*AVŚ* 4.18.1)[28]

Here the power of an act of truth is laid out quite starkly: by making true statements about the natural world, the utterer of this *mantra* expects to weaken the supernatural power of his opponent. Kong shows that this old concept of the power of truthful speech was combined with the theory of karma in the Buddhist tradition to allow for the "enhancement" of the good or ill effects of karma. In numerous stories found in the commentary to the *Dhammapada*, the fruits of karma are directed in a particular way because of a "wish" (*patthanā*) made by one of the participants.[29] Although Kong does not make the connection, I would argue that the concept of *adhiṭṭhāna* found in the *Milindapañha*, which functions in a manner quite similar to the "wish" or *patthanā* of the stories of the *Dhammapada* commentary, also involves a creative synergy between the old Indian concept of the power of true speech and the theory of karmic retribution.

Given that the scope of our inquiry in this chapter is the veneration of Buddha images in Siam/Thailand in the second millennium, however, I am less concerned with the precise origins of the concept of *adhiṭṭhāna* than with the fact that it exists as a part of the Pali *imaginaire* for Siamese and now modern Thai discourse to draw from. *Adhiṭṭhāna*, using its Sanskrit spelling, *adhiṣṭhāna*, is in fact a common word in Thai, pronounced *athitthān* (อธิษฐาน). It is usually translated into English as "pray," but it refers to a specific supplicatory type of "prayer" in which one asks for something. It is thus functionally equivalent to the phrase *khọ̄ phọ̄n* (ขอพร), "ask for a boon." We have already seen the word *athitthān* used in the title of the popular book about *sing saksit* that I quoted in the introduction. I translated the title of this book *Manual for Fulfilling Vows, Asking for Boons, and Increasing Auspiciousness.* In the original Thai, however, "asking for boons" is in fact the redundant phrase *athitthān khọ̄ phọ̄n* (อธิษฐานขอพร), which places the functionally equivalent terms *athitthān* and *khọ̄ phọ̄n* in apposition. This apposition, as we will see, will prove pivotal to unraveling the vicissitudes of discourse in Siam/Thailand that have led to the modern agglomeration of Buddha images together with gods, spirits, and more under the category of *sing saksit.*

The word *athitthān* has a long history of use in Siamese literature, going all the way back to the Sukhōthai inscriptions. Moreover, the way in which it is used is consistent with the constellation of associations that I have traced here. On the one hand, it is clearly associated, as Kong has argued, with the belief in the power of truth, as it is often coupled with either the Sanskrit word *satya* or the equivalent Pali word *sacca*.[30] On the other hand, it is also often coupled with a reference to merit, referred to either by the Pali word *puñña* or by a closely related word, such as *kuśala* or *pāramī*.[31] These associations make it clear that the word *athitthān* is operating according to a logic derived from the Pali *imaginaire*, even when the immediate context is not explicitly Buddhist (e.g., a temple, Buddha image, or relic). A passage from Sunthọn Phū's *Phra Aphaimanī* serves to illustrate:

ไม่เห็นฟากเห็นฝั่งเป็นกลางคืน	ทั้งลมคลื่นมิได้หยุดสุดรำพึง
จะเสี่ยงสัตย์อธิษฐานการกุศล	ให้ลมฝนบางเบาพอเข้าถึง
เดชะบุญคุณพระธรรมที่รำพึง	ให้สมซึ่งความประสงค์ที่จงใจ
หกกษัตริย์พัทยาเทพารักษ์	อันสำนักเขาเขินเนินไศล
ขอเชิญช่วยบำบัดกำจัดภัย	การที่ในทะเลลมยมนา
พอสินคำหกกษัตริย์อธิษฐาน	ลมบันดาลเบาบางกลางเวหา
ฝนก็ค่อยน้อยลงทั้งคงคา	เป็นคลื่นกล้าก็ค่อยเบาบรรเทาลง

They could not see the shore; it was the middle of the night.
  The wind and waves did not stop; it was beyond words.
They took a chance on truth, resolved (using) their merit
  That the wind and rain die down enough for them to get where they were going,
(Hoping) the power of their merit, the quality of *dharma* they had spoken,
  Would be sufficient to (attain) what they desired.
The six kings called upon the guardian deities (*devārakṣas*)
  Who dwell in the mountains and hills
To please help eliminate the danger of the windy sea.
As soon as the six kings finished making their resolution,
  The wind died down in the middle of the sky;
The rain slowly decreased across the water,
  And the fierce waves also weakened.[32]

Although no Buddha image, relic, or temple is involved in this passage, and in fact gods are the beings who are prayed to and effect the miraculous calming of the storm, the act of *athitthān*, or "praying," is clearly "Buddhist" insofar as the kings who do it make use of their store of merit to attain their desired end and explicitly hope that that store of merit is sufficient to the task.

In fact, it should be noted that in most cases in which the word *athitthān* is used in old Siamese literature, a Buddha image or relic is not the object of the prayer, while often gods are. This should not be surprising or lead us astray into thinking that *athitthān* is not, within the Siamese context, a fundamentally Buddhist concept. To begin with—and this should go almost without saying at this point—the gods are very much part of Pali Buddhist cosmology, so the act of praying to the gods rather than, say, a Buddha image, does not make it any less Buddhist. More important, though, the concept of *athitthān* is derived from the Pali *imaginaire* and, as we have just seen, clearly embedded in a network of Buddhist concepts, in particular the theory of karma.

In certain texts the context of the *athitthān* is even more immediately Buddhist. For example, a mid-fourteenth-century Sukhōthai inscription that gives the biography of a monk named Śrīśraddhārājaculạ̄muni records that he made *athitthān* on two occasions, both involving Buddha relics broadly construed:

> แมนชิไมกทิงก่ดิแม๋นชิกิงพระสริมหาโพ...แมนชิอี..ก่ดีแมนชิ...สิรพระสริมหาโพธิน(คร)สิงหลนนก่ดีสํเดจพระมหาเถรเปนเจาเอามาป(ลูก)เหนือดินจิงอทิสถานผิวา.........พระพุทธจริงจิงวาใสจุงใหเปนญ่าไดหยวสกกอนนคนน(อทิส)ถานดงัอนนชิใบนิงแ(หง)......จิงขินเปนใบขยวงามหนกกหนาแกกํเปนตนให(หญตน)หลวงสูงงามหนกกหนา
>
> Whether called a *kathing* tree or the branch of a Bodhi tree or . . . or a Sinhala Bodhi . . . Lord Somdet Phra Mahāthera took them and planted them in the ground, resolving, "If . . . really a Buddha, then may they live, may not a single one wither." When he had resolved in that way, a dry leaf . . . became green and very beautiful, and the tree became large, tall, and very beautiful.[33]

Likewise, later in the biography the monk makes a resolution while building a *cēdī* (*cetiya*):

> เมิอจกกสทายปูนในกลางป่า[น]นนหาปูนยากหนกกหนาหาปูนมิไดพระสรีราชจูลามูณีเปนเจ๋าจิง อธิสสถานว่าดงงนี....กูแลญงงจกกไดตรสสแก

สรรเพญุเดญาณเปนพระพุทธจริงวาใส จุงใหพบปูนคน(นกูอธิ)สสถานบดด แมงแหงหนนดายกลายพบโ[ป]งปูนอนิงทายาทหนกกหนาเอามาสทายพระธาดุก่ใหม่เก่าแลวเอามาต่พระพุทธรูบหีนอนนหกกอนนพงงบริบวรณ แล๋ว ปูนก่ญู(งง)เหลิอเลบ ๐ พระมหาธาดุหลวงนน๋นกทำปราดิหารอสสจรรย หนกกหนาแล๋มีพระธาดุ)อนนใหญูลอมหลายแก่ก๋

When they were going to plaster lime, it was very hard to find lime in the middle of the forest. They couldn't find any lime. So Lord Phra Śrīrājacuḷāmuni resolved in this way: "If . . . I will truly attain omniscience and become a Buddha, then may I find lime." As soon as he had resolved this, at that very moment in that spot there appeared a swell of lime. Moreover, it was quite excellent. They took it to plaster the reliquaries, both new and old, and then used it to fix the stone Buddha images that were broken, and there was still lime left over. The primary relic also performed astounding miracles, and there were large relics that gathered together around it.[34]

In both of these examples, the context is thoroughly Buddhist: the person engaging in *athitthān* is a Buddhist monk, the "truth" which allows him to do so is the statement that he will one day become a Buddha, and the miracle that results involves relics—in the first case a Bodhi tree, in the second case actual bone relics in reliquaries.

Examples of *athitthān* embedded in thoroughly Buddhist contexts can be found in later Siamese literature as well. In *Khun Chāng Khun Phǟn*, Sīmālā (the wife of Khun Phǟn's son Phra Wai) does *athitthān* to dissuade the king from executing his wife Sǫifā:

๏ ศรีมาลาฟังคำที่ร่ำว่า น้ำตาหลั่งไหลด้วยใจอ่อน
เห็นสารภาพผิดคิดอาวรณ์ จะผันผ่อนทูลขอดูตามบุญ
เกลือกว่าวาสนามิเคยม้วย กุศลส่งคงจะช่วยมาอุดหนุน
ไม่หมายเอาตอบแรนแทนคุณ จะเอาบุญช่วยกู้ชีวิตไว้
อย่านึกเลยว่าข้าพยาบาท อย่าประมาทภาวนาเอาใจใส่
นางตั้งอธิษฐานด้วยทันใด ขอเดชะข้าได้ทำบุญมา
ปรารถนาจะให้พ้นจากสงสาร เอาทางพระนิพพานภายภาคหน้า
จะช่วยสัตว์ให้พ้นมรณา นางตั้งสัจจาแล้วคลาไคล
ถึงหน้าพระที่นั่งก็บังคม ประนมกรกราบทูลเฉลยไข

Sīmālā listened and tears streamed down as her heart softened.
(Sǫifā) saw her various faults, (so Sīmālā) felt pity.
"I will ask the king for a reprieve and see if I have enough merit.
"If her *vāsanā*s are not such that she should die, sending merit
should help.
"I don't want anything in return. I will use my merit in exchange for
her life.
"Don't think that I am vengeful. Don't be negligent; meditate and focus
the mind."
She immediately made the resolution: "I have made merit.
"I wish to escape from *saṃsāra* and choose the path leading to *nibbāna* in
the future.
"I will help living beings to escape death." After she made this (act of)
truth, she went
Before the throne and prostrated, seeking an answer.[35]

Here, once again, we see a clear complex of three elements: the word *athitthān*, the statement of truth, and the explanation that the resolution will come to fruition if the store of merit is sufficient. In addition, the statement of truth, as with the monk in the Sukhōthai inscription, is simply that Sīmālā will one day attain *nibbāna*. She effectively uses her future attainment of Awakening as collateral against which she is able to take out a "loan" in the present to save Sǫifā's life. Similar examples of *athitthān* embedded in complexes of Buddhist doctrine can be found in Sunthǫn Phū's *Phra Aphaimanī* as well. There we find *athitthān* combined with meditation on the three characteristics (*trailakṣaṇa*, i.e., suffering, impermanent, and not-self), meditative absorption (*jhāna*), recollection of the qualities of the Buddha, and requesting to be reborn as a human being until attaining *nibbāna*.[36]

The concept of *adhiṭṭhāna*, made commonplace in Siamese/Thai discourse as the word *athitthān*, provides a clear Buddhist explanation for how one could ask for a mundane boon when worshiping a Buddha image. Per the explanation given by Nāgasena in the *Milindapañha*, a relic, of which a Buddha image is a type, can display miraculous powers through a resolution made by an *arhat*, a god, or a human worshiper. The miracle is accomplished through the accumulated merit of the person making the resolution, and it is ratified by a statement of truth. Although we have not found many *specific* examples of making *athitthān* at a Buddha image in the Siamese literature, we have found a plethora of other examples, indicating that it has been a part of Buddhist practice in Siam going back centuries, and as such could easily be practiced in temples and at Buddha images (or other relics), even if most recorded examples are made "on the fly," as it were. Indeed, it is worth noting that the passages we saw earlier from the *Nirāt Hariphunchai*, while not using the word *athitthān* specifically, nevertheless imply it. Verse 125 refers to "truth" (*satya*), and subsequent passages refer to merit when the author asks that he be reunited quickly with his lover, all in the context of worshiping at the temple in Haribhuñjaya.

Nevertheless, what we see evidence for in the old Siamese literature is not quite the same as modern *kānbonbānsānklāo*. The practice of asking for boons is present, but it lacks both the method and the concomitant institutional apparatus found today at places such as Wat Sōthǫn. There is no indication that one promises (*bon*) a gift to the Buddha image, with payment made only upon receipt of the boon. And there is likewise no indication of elaborate facilities, such as resident dance troupes, provided for worshipers to *kābon*, or fulfill the vow. Finally, as we already noted in Chapter 4, Buddha images are not referred to in the old literature as *saksit*. Buddha images are said to be powerful and work miracles, but the word *saksit* is reserved for spirits, gods, knowledge associated with *saiyasāt*, and people and objects imbued with that knowledge. How, then, did Buddha images become *saksit* and part of the world of *kānbonbānsānklāo*?

Luang Phǫ Sōthǫn and the Origins of Modern *Kānbonbānsānklāo*

The oldest reference that I am aware of to *kānbonbānsāklāo* at Buddhist temples is found in *Sān Somdet* (*สาส์นสมเด็จ*), a collection of letters between Prince Damrong Rajanubhap (1862–1943) and Prince Narisara Nuwattiwong (1863–1947), both sons of King Mongkut (Rāma IV) who were polymaths and prominent advisors of their half-brother King Chulalongkorn (Rāma V). In a letter to Prince Naris dated February 4, 1941, Prince Damrong writes:

> หม่อมฉันยังจำได้เมื่อเป็นเด็กเคยเจ็บมากครั้งหนึ่ง พอหายขึ้นผู้ปกครอง มีละครชาตรีแก้สินบนที่เฉลียงหน้าพระอุโบสถ วัดพระศรีรัตนศาสดาราม เวลานั้นตัวละครเอกชื่อนายหนู ใช้เครื่องแต่งตัวอย่างละครกรุงเทพฯ ผิดกัน

แต่เพียงตัวเปล่าไม่ใส่เสื้อกับสวมกำไรมือข้างละหลายเส้นอย่างโนห์รา ต่อมาก็เห็นละครชาตรีมักไปเล่นแก้สินบนตามสถานที่ศักดิ์สิทธิ์ เช่นวัดบวรนิเวศ และที่ศาลเจ้าหอกลองเป็นต้น แต่ภายหลังมาเห็นจะเป็นเพราะถูกห้ามมิให้เล่นตามที่นั้นๆ จึงเปลี่ยนประเพณีมาเล่นที่บ้านและเลยเกิดวิธีรับเหมาแก้สินบนดังได้ทอดพระเนตร

I remember that once when I was a child, I got very sick. Once I got better, my guardians had a dance troupe fulfill the vow (*kăsinbon*) at the balcony in front of the *uposatha* (main ordination hall) at Wat Phra Sī Rattanasātsadārām. At that time, the name of the lead dancer was Mr. Nū. He wore a costume like in Bangkok dance. It was only different in that he didn't wear a shirt, and he wore many bracelets on both sides like a *nōrā* dancer. Afterwards, I saw dance troupes who were probably fulfilling vows at holy (*saksit*) places like Wat Bowǫnniwēt and at the shrine of the Lord of the Drum Room, etc. But afterwards I saw that it was forbidden, and they were not allowed to play in those places, so they changed their custom to play at home, and so there arose a way for them to be hired to fulfill vows, as you saw.[37]

This passage is particularly interesting because it indicates that, in the late nineteenth century when Prince Damrong would have been a child, *kānbonbānsānklāo* was taking place not only at certain Buddhist temples but at two of the most prominent royal temples in the country.

The first of these two temples, Wat Phra Kāo (which Damrong refers to by its formal name, Wat Phra Sī Rattanasātsadārām), is the Temple of the Emerald Buddha, the home of the palladium of the Chakri Dynasty. The second, Wat Bowǫnniwēt, is the center of the reformist Thammayut Nikāi monastic sect, founded by King Mongkut, and also home to the famous Phra Phuttha Chinnasī (พระพุทธชินสีห์) image. Both the Emerald Buddha and Phuttha Chinnasī images are renowned today as *sing saksit* that one can propitiate for boons, but their temples do not provide the sort of elaborate facilities to *kābon* that are found at places like Wat Sōthǫn. This would seem to indicate that the elaborate practice of promising offerings to Buddha images and then fulfilling those promises with, for example, dance troupes grew in popularity in Siam at some point in the nineteenth century, perhaps as a fad, and then was stamped out at the most prominent royal temples, most likely under reformist impulses.

Indeed, such a timeframe would broadly coincide with what is known about the history of *kānbonbānsānklāo* at Wat Sōthǫn. The history of the image itself, as with most famous Buddha images, is obscure, hidden by a lack of concrete evidence and patently mythical stories of origin. According to the popular account, Luang Phǭ Sōthǭn is the middle of a group of three "sibling" Buddha images, the older brother being Luang Phǭ Wat Bān Lǣm (หลวงพ่อวัดบ้านแหลม) in Samut Songkhrām and the younger brother being Luang Phǭ Tō Bāng Phlī (หลวงพ่อโตบางพลี) in Samut Prākān. These three images were commissioned in olden times by three brothers somewhere to the north (either Lānnā or Lān Xāng). Using their store of merit, they expressed their intention to the gods that the images go in three different directions and invited gods to reside in each image.[38] As a result, the images had many travels, eventually ending up in Sukhōthai.

When the Burmese attacked Sukhōthai for the last time and destroyed the city (apparently a reference to the Burmo-Siamese War of 1765–1767), the three images miraculously flew to the River Ping and floated down the river for seven days, making their way to the Chao Phraya River and traveling throughout the river system. During their travels, the images stopped at several places and miraculously floated in the air to make their presence known, but when the local people in each place tried to pull them out of the water, they were unable to do so, even when hundreds or thousands of men pitched in. When the images reached the site of the current Wat Sōthǭn (at that time called Wat Hong, วัดหงส์), the local people again tried to pull them out of the water and were unsuccessful. Luang Phǭ Sōthǭn, however, voluntarily floated out of the water and established himself in the temple, making clear his intention to reside there. This took place in the year 1770, which would be a few years after Tāksin restored Siamese suzerainty in the wake of the Burmese destruction of Ayutthayā.[39]

This story, while from a historical perspective impossible to take at face value, displays many of the common tropes found in stories about Buddha images in the broader Tai world. Luang Phǭ Sōthǭn and his siblings were infused with miraculous power through the *athitthān* of those who created it. They then had many travels. Even the particular mode of transport that eventually brought Luang Phǭ Sōthǭn to Chạ Chǭng Sao is reminiscent of classic Buddha image stories, such as that of the Sihing image in the *Jinakālamālī*, which miraculously floated to Nakhǭn Sī Thammarāt after a shipwreck.[40] The wondrous inability of even large groups of men to pull Luang Phǭ Sōthǭn and his siblings from the water is indicative of the Buddha images' inherent power and volition in determining where they will reside.[41]

According to art historical experts, the style of the Luang Phǫ Sōthǫn image indicates a Lao origin, from Luang Phabāng or the Northeastern (Īsān) region of modern Thailand, in either the late Ayutthayā or early Bangkok periods.[42] This accords well with the popular story's claim that the image has a northern origin, as well as with the basic timeframe for when the image might have come to Cha Chōng Sao, although not necessarily with the story's claim that the image is of great antiquity.[43] It is entirely possible that Luang Phǫ Sōthǫn was brought to Cha Chōng Sao in about 1770—most likely as a result of Tāksin's expeditions against the Burmese in the North, rather than by floating down the river.[44] It is also possible that he was brought by Lao war captives who were resettled in the region in the early nineteenth century.[45] In either case, Luang Phǫ Sōthǫn's history *as* Luang Phǫ Sōthǫn, that is, as a Buddha image known by that name in Cha Chōng Sao, goes back no more than about two hundred years, and possibly less.

Although the evidence is scanty, it would appear that the institutionalized practice of *kānbonbānsānklāo* at Wat Sōthǫn, in particular the availability of traditional Thai dance troupes to allow people to *kābon*, has an even shorter history. The style of dance found at Wat Sōthǫn, as with other sites of *kānbonbānsānklāo*, is *lakhǫn chātrī* (ละครชาตรี), which has its origins in southern dance styles influenced by Malay traditions. It most likely was brought to central Siam only in 1832, when the Cāo Phrayā Phra Khlang (Dit Bunnāk) led a campaign against rebellious southern *müang* and resettled war captives, including some expert in dance, in the region of Bangkok.[46] Damrong himself reports, "In the past it would have been because people saw it as something unusual, and they could hire them to play cheaply, so they liked to get *lakhǫn chātrī* to fulfill their vows, until it became a custom."[47] This would imply that the use of *lakhǫn chātrī* to *kābon* that Damrong witnessed at prominent Bangkok temples as a child was a relatively recent "tradition," a fad that took root in the capital in the middle of the nineteenth century and was then suppressed. It was replaced to a large extent by the use of small figurines of *lakhǫn chātrī* dancers to *kābon*,[48] a custom that one will find at nearly any *sing saksit* in Thailand today.

Wat Sōthǫn, being located to the east of Bangkok, was obviously spared the suppression of dance troupes at Buddhist temples that occurred in the capital proper, but it may have been a relative latecomer to the practice as well. Luang Phǫ Sōthǫn gained fame originally not as a general granter of boons but more specifically for his healing powers, in the context of a smallpox epidemic around the turn of the twentieth century. The practice to seek healing at that time, however, was quite different from the commercialized *kānbonbānsānklāo* found at the temple today. Those who were sick with smallpox would create a "medicine" by going to the temple and gathering ashes from joss sticks, dried-up flowers that had been offered to Luang Phọ̄, and drops of wax from candles; they would place these in holy water (น้ำมนต์) from the temple, make a resolution (*athitthān*), and drink it.[49] Among those who suffered from smallpox during the epidemic and benefited from the medicine at Wat Sōthọ̄n were *lakhọ̄n chātrī* dancers. In thanks, the dancers organized a parade to honor Luang Phọ̄ Sōthọ̄n, and this established the custom of using *lakhọ̄n chātrī* dance to *kā̃bon* Luang Phọ̄ Sōthọ̄n.[50] King Chulalongkorn visited the temple in 1908 and wrote about it (the short passage about which is now quoted obsessively in promotional literature about the temple), and he moved the location for the administration of the water oath for officials in the province to Wat Sōthọ̄n as well.[51] All of this served to spread the fame of Luang Phọ̄ Sōthọ̄n across the kingdom, making him a well-known *sing saksit* in Thailand today.

The events surrounding the early twentieth-century smallpox epidemic that catapulted Luang Phọ̄ Sōthọ̄n to national fame are interesting for our purposes for two reasons. First, they demonstrate in a particular instantiation the recent development of the institutional apparatus for *kānbonbānsānklāo*. At the same time, however, they also demonstrate the deep continuities with older Siamese Buddhist custom rooted in the Pali *imaginaire*. The practice that led to the establishment of institutionalized *kānbonbānsānklāo* at the temple was a simple *ad hoc* application of the principle of *athitthān*—which, as we have seen, goes back centuries and has scriptural warrant—to a particular problem in a particular place at a particular time. The "medicine" that worshipers took to cure their smallpox was a concoction of various devotional items that constituted their merit-making—incense, flowers, and candles—infused with the "truth" of the *mantra*s that were used to make the holy water into which they were mixed. The worshipers, in a sense, *ingested* their own *adhiṭṭhāna*.

Indeed, while there is no evidence that the practice of *kānbonbānsānklāo* with Buddha images in its modern form existed prior to the nineteenth century, there is evidence for the sort of *ad hoc* practice witnessed in the smallpox epidemic. Indeed, a very similar practice is reported at a temple in Ayutthayā by Spanish Franciscan missionaries who visited in the late sixteenth century:

> *En este templo del religioso principal había un ídolo muy grande, que tenía una larga cabellera y una concavidad en la cabeza, en la cual, echando agua, la destilaba por la cabellera, y los días de fiesta iban los gentiles con mucha devoción a tomar de aquella agua, que dicen es buena para conservar la salud.*
>
> In this main temple of the religious (i.e., monks), there was a very large idol, which had a wide head of hair and a concavity in the head, into which, when pouring water, it dripped through the hair, and on feast days the Gentiles (i.e., pagans) would go with much devotion to drink this water, which they say is good for preserving health.[52]

The Spanish missionaries who witnessed this practice were of course not aware of the particular rationale behind it, but given the evidence we have seen so far, there is every reason to believe that it was understood by Siamese practitioners through the lens of the canonical concept of *adhiṭṭhāna*. Although the missionaries do not explain in much detail the act of "pouring water" (*echando agua*), this most likely is a reference to the practice of bathing Buddha images (สรงน้ำพระ) that is popular especially during Songkrān (the traditional Thai New Year, in mid-April). The water drunk would thus be the devotional offering that instantiates the merit one resolves for a particular purpose (in this case, health) through *athitthān*. This is the sort of simple practice, involving devotional offerings to make merit that are then "resolved" toward a particular goal, that was transformed in the late nineteenth and early twentieth centuries into a more elaborate practice of promising an offering to be delivered upon receipt of the boon.

The Changing Meaning of *Saksit* and Modern *Kānbonbānsānklāo*

The change that has taken place in the modern era in the way in which Siamese/Thai practitioners interact with Buddha images is in a sense quite subtle but in another sense quite profound. On the one hand, Buddha images have always been considered in Tai cultures to be individual personalities with miraculous powers (just as in other Buddhist cultures), and Siamese Buddhists have always been able to ask for boons when worshiping a Buddha image or other Buddhist relic, such as a *cēdī* (P. *cetiya*). So in that sense nothing has changed. Nevertheless, the conceptual space in which asking Buddha images for boons has changed, and that has had a certain effect on practice as well. Historically, asking a Buddha image or other relic for a boon was firmly rooted in the concept of *adhiṭṭhāna*, taken from the Pali *imaginaire*. The concept of *adhiṭṭhāna* has by no means gone away—Thai people today still routinely say that they *athitthān* when they ask for a boon—but the more dominant conceptual framework has become that of *sing saksit* and the concomitant practice of *kānbonbānsānklāo*, in which one promises an offering ahead of time and then makes that offering if and when the boon is received. Buddha images are now just another type of "holy thing" that one can negotiate with to receive mundane benefits.

This conceptual shift may seem subtle, but it is significant. The canonical concept of *adhiṭṭhāna*, as I have argued, harnesses the Buddhist concept of karma to explain and/or make possible miracles. Good karma, or merit, brings good fruit, and insofar as that merit can be directed to a particular purpose,[53] it stands to reason that, in sufficient quantities, it can be directed toward marvelous wonders. Moreover, as Nāgasena explains in the *Milindapañha*, those who are able to "resolve" in this way are not limited to ordinary human worshipers; they can also include *arhat*s and gods, who have extremely large stores of merit and are thus able to grant miraculous powers to relics in perpetuity. But this conceptual apparatus does not require or even invite negotiation. The merit necessary for the *adhiṭṭhāna* is either sufficient, or it is not. Indeed, many of the historical examples of *adhiṭṭhāna* that we have seen in Siamese literature emphasize the immediacy of results. Negotiation, on the other hand, makes a great deal of sense if one is dealing with a saṃsāric being with the power to grant boons, such as a god or *phī*—the very sorts of beings that are described as *saksit*, that is, powerful, in older Siamese literature.

Indeed, as we have already seen, Buddha images, relics, and personnel were, prior to modern times, conspicuously *not* described as *saksit*. It seems that there was a conceptual distinction made between the miracles made possible by the accumulation and "resolution" of merit within a Buddhist (*phutthasāt*) framework and the power (*saksit*) inherent in gods and other supernatural beings and accessible through the mundane science (*saiyasāt*) of ritual personnel (Brahmans) dedicated to worshiping them. So why did this change in the nineteenth century? Why did Buddha images become *saksit* and concomitantly get drawn into a relatively uniform world of practice in which practitioners negotiate with a variety of "holy things" to receive boons?

Although we lack the sort of robust records of ordinary discourse in the mid- to late nineteenth century that would allow us to see the shift happening in "real time," we have already learned enough in Part I about the general shifts in discourse that took place at the height of colonialism to confidently answer this question. The change that took place was in the word *saksit* itself. Previously it indicated that something or some being was powerful within the context of *saiyasāt*, and as such it could easily have taken on a mostly negative connotation when *saiyasāt* and its associated vocabulary were adapted to translate the Western concept of magic and the occult in the nineteenth century. Instead, however, it was idiosyncratically "moved" to the realm of *sātsanā* (now repurposed as "religion") and used to translate the Western concept of the "holy" or "sacred." In the old conceptual regime, Buddhist relics, including Buddha images, were simply a different sort of thing than gods and spirits. In the modern conceptual regime, on the other hand, under the influence of Western categories, they are all "holy." And if they are all holy, and they all can be propitiated for boons, then why not propitiate them in the same way? In short, the establishment of *sing saksit* as an expansive category including anything with the power to grant boons has opened the conceptual space for the explosive and creative expansion of *kānbonbānsānklāo*.

The argument that practices like *kānbonbānsānklāo* are indicative of an "inspiriting" of Buddhism and represent the reading of Buddhism through the categories and logic of local spirit religion is therefore untenable, or at the very least misses the point. Buddhism has from very early in its history—in India, long before the advent of Siamese history in the thirteenth century—allowed and provided a conceptual framework for the miraculous bestowal of boons upon worshipers of relics. And although the modern configuration of *kānbonbānsānklāo* does bring the practice of asking Buddha images for boons more in line with "local spirit religion," if that category even makes sense, the reconfiguration that led to it was not accomplished by the power of some indigenous "substratum" over elite Buddhist doctrine. On the contrary, it was accomplished through a shift in cosmopolitan formations—a shift that led to the adoption of "religion" and other associated Western categories, such as "holy." This shift in discourse is what effaced erstwhile distinctions between Buddhist relics and powerful (*saksit*) saṃsāric beings. *All* are now *saksit*, that is, holy.

Indeed, there is every reason to believe that changes in discourse due to shifting cosmopolitan formations have influenced the practice of asking for boons in the past—and in the direction of *Buddhism* exerting influence, not vice versa. As we saw, the word *athitthān* is frequently used in older Siamese literature in the context of asking gods or spirits for boons. Nevertheless, this word brings with it the Buddhist conceptual framework of karma. Asking gods and spirits for boons through *athitthān* is not *merely* a negotiation with a powerful but capricious being. It involves the dedication of one's merit in the hope that a being who, while capricious, nevertheless *cares about such things* will look upon you with favor. This is simply another one of the many ways in which Buddhism's implicit theology has exerted influence on mundane cosmology and nonsoteriological practice. In this sense, then, if Buddhism has in any context become "inspirited," it has inspirited itself.

8
Conclusion

I began this book by describing the world of *sing saksit*, or "holy things," in Thailand, in which gods, spirits, Buddha images, and more are propitiated for mundane boons. In doing so, I highlighted a particular *sing saksit*, Luang Phǭ Sōthǭn, because of how seductive a spokesman he appears to be for the old model of syncretism. It is easy to show that Buddhists worshiping gods and spirits is not an example of syncretism. All that is required is to show that Buddhist Modernism is not representative of Buddhism as a whole, that traditional Buddhist cosmology includes a plethora of gods and spirits, and that it is therefore not surprising that Buddhists would propitiate them for mundane boons. Indeed, I routinely teach as much to undergraduate students in Introduction to Buddhism classes. But it is less immediately obvious why propitiating a Buddha image *in the same way as* a local spirit would not constitute some sort of "mixing" of local spirit religion with Buddhism.

I was also motivated to forefront Luang Phǭ Sōthǭn and Buddha images like him because they complicate in an interesting way the critique that scholars of religion have offered of syncretism. This is not to say that the critiques of syncretism are wrong. Rather, those critiques can be taken in a naïve way to imply that everything we see on the ground is simply and unproblematically Buddhist, that etic categories delineating religious "components" of practical religion are just delusional figments of the scholar's imagination, that the only thing that matters is a purported emic perspective from which such distinctions do not matter. I wanted to show not simply that syncretism is a problematic paradigm, which it is, but why, *in spite of that fact*, it is so easy and tempting for an outside scholar—or, increasingly, a Thai Buddhist who is educated in the terminology of world religions—to look at contemporary Thai religious praxis and say, "This is Buddhism, that is Hinduism, that is *phī* worship," and the like.

The solution to this conundrum that I have argued for throughout this book is a model of interacting discourses. This solution is an attractive one to explain the semblance of "religious syncretism" because (1) discourses are not the same as religions, (2) interaction is not the same as "mixing," and yet

(3) the interaction of discourses allows religions (but also cultures in general) to influence one another indirectly, especially if they are closely related. By applying this model of interacting discourses, we find that a focus on emic categories does not eliminate the need for the etic categories; rather, it highlights their importance even more, as the distinction between local and translocal collapses in the everyday exercise of discourse itself.

We see this paradoxical phenomenon perhaps most acutely in the worship of the gods in Thai Buddhism. From the viewpoint of syncretism, this practice is uncanny: Why would a Thai Buddhist worship a Hindu god? The critique of syncretism shows why this thinking is misguided: the Thai Buddhist is not worshiping a "Hindu" god; they are worshiping a Buddhist god. "The gods" are quite simply, and always have been, a part of Buddhist cosmology. They are particularly meaningful within the Buddhist conception of the cosmos because rebirth as a god is the result of good karma. Although the gods are ultimately mortal, they are long-lived and powerful, and as such they can be propitiated for mundane boons.

But this does not mean that it is crazy or meaningless for a scholar—or, again, a modern Thai Buddhist—to look at the gods worshiped in Thai Buddhism and think that the category "Hindu" (or "Brahmanical") somehow applies. Brahmā, Indra, Gaṇeśa, Viṣṇu, and Śiva—all popular gods in Thailand—are indeed Hindu gods. Moreover, while some of them, like Brahmā and Indra, are found in the authoritative texts of the Pali *imaginaire*, others, like Gaṇeśa, Viṣṇu, and Śiva, are not. Their presence and popularity can be explained only through the influence of Hindu discourse.

But this influence is not as surprising or "un-Buddhist" as it might seem. Indeed, this is precisely where attentiveness to emic categories shows the continued relevance of etic categories. Thai Buddhists have always been aware of the close relationship between their own Buddhism and Hinduism, even if the category "Hindu" *per se* entered the Thai language only in the nineteenth century. Prior to that time, Siamese Buddhists used the category *saiyasāt* to express more or less the same idea. The category of *saiyasāt* allowed Siamese Buddhists to recognize the existence of discourses—rooted in the Vedas and Śaiva Āgamas, purveyed by Brahmans—that were relevant to the universe as conceived by Pali Buddhism because they impinged upon the mythology and worship of the gods, a recognized category within that selfsame Buddhist universe. At the same time, it situated those discourses within a solidly Buddhist frame by marking them as *lokiya* (the "sleep discipline" of *saiyasāt*) as opposed to *lokuttara* (the "waking discipline" of *phutthasāt*). This category in turn allowed for Hindu discourses to exercise agency within Siamese Buddhism—by introducing myths, iconography, and even "new" gods not present in the authoritative texts of the Pali *imaginaire*.

This is not syncretism. Buddhism's implicit theology recognizes the gods as a real and natural part of the cosmos. But insofar as the gods are (to take the postmodern, critical perspective of the scholar) socially constructed, *anyone* who talks about the gods has the potential to influence Buddhist perceptions of them—who they are, what they look like, what they have done, and so on. Of course, this "anyone talking about the gods" is limited to those who are talking about "the gods" as a category legible to those operating from within the Pali *imaginaire*. That is why Muslim and Chinese discourses on God or the gods have had far less impact on Siamese conceptions thereof than have Hindu discourses,[1] in spite of the fact that Siamese Buddhists have had just as much or more contact with them over the centuries. As we saw in Chapter 3, the historical relationship between the Pali and Sanskrit cosmopoleis has allowed Hindu discourses to exercise a unique agency within Siamese Buddhism, through the category of *saiyasāt*.

The difference between our critical stance as scholars of religion and the internal logic of the religious discourses we study, I believe, further obscures what is going on here between Siamese Buddhism and Hinduism in such a way as to give rise to the illusion of syncretism. An analogy may therefore be useful to illustrate the point that I am making. Consider the second Jewish Temple, built by King Herod in the first century BCE. This is—or rather was—a real object in the world, whose existence everybody, Jew or Gentile, acknowledges. Indeed, just a few weeks prior to writing these words, I saw with my own eyes and touched with my own hands the last remnant of that Temple, the Western Wall. The Temple has, and since King Herod built it, has always had, an immense significance within Judaism. But that significance changed—radically—when the Romans, led by the future emperor Titus, conquered Jerusalem and destroyed the Temple in 70 CE. Whereas prior to that time Jewish life revolved around sacrifice to God in the Temple, one can without exaggeration say that all of Rabbinic Judaism that followed is organized precisely around the *absence* of the Temple.

The Romans, therefore, through their destruction of the Temple, exercised powerful agency on Jewish self-understanding, understanding of the cosmos, and understanding of the Jewish people's relationship with God. But we would not call this "syncretism." Rather, Judaism always had something to say about a real thing in the real world, the Temple; the Romans destroyed that Temple; and thus Judaism was forced to say new things about it. The situation with the gods shared between Hinduism and Buddhism is not fundamentally different; it only appears different insofar as gods are, under the influence of the Protestant paradigm of religion, viewed as simply a matter of "belief" within particular religions rather than objective realities.

But if we understand the gods as social constructions with a shared reality as such, then the parallel to the Jewish Temple is quite close. Insofar as Buddhist cosmology recognizes the gods as objectively real and Hindu discourses act upon the gods—for instance, by giving Brahmā four faces, by elevating Viṣṇu and Śiva, by telling new stories about the gods in the *Mahābhārata* and the Purāṇas—then it is inevitable that a Buddhist culture sufficiently aware of those Hindu discourses will be forced to adapt its understanding of the gods to the changes wrought by Hindu discourse. And as we have seen, what I have called the "nexus of transforming cosmopolitan formations" has facilitated that awareness, codified in Siamese discourse through the complementary distinction between *saiyasāt* and *phutthasāt.* If anything, the new modern discourse of world religions has only accelerated the ability of Hindu discourses to exercise agency within Thai Buddhism.

The situation posed by *phī* or "local spirits" is parallel to that of the gods, although it plays out in a somewhat different way. While I showed in Chapter 4 that Siamese Buddhists have always had an emic category (*saiyasāt*) corresponding to the etic category "Hinduism," in Chapter 5 I argued that "animism," "local spirit religion," and the like are etic categories that obscure more than they illuminate. When subjected to critical historical analysis, everything about Siamese/Thai religion is local, and so nothing is really local. In any case, there is no emic category corresponding to "animism" or "local spirit religion" prior to the coining of *sātsanā phī* in the modern period to translate those concepts. What we *do* find in older Siamese literature is the category *phī* itself, not as a "religion" but as a fact of nature. Of course, from our critical position as scholars, we do not see *phī* as a fact of nature in the same way as, say, trees, rivers, and animals. We thus understand Tai discourse—however historically contingent it may be on Chinese, Khmer, or other discourses—as bringing *phī* into existence. But insofar as Buddhist discourse has always recognized the existence of beings *like phī*—sentient beings that are neither human nor animal, or what from a modern perspective we might call "supernatural beings"—then *phī*, like any number of "local spirits" across Asia, appear to Buddhist discourse as facts of nature, no different from trees, rivers, and animals.

The nature and cult of *phī* may be somewhat idiosyncratic due to the discourse(s) that have historically been involved in creating them, and Buddhist discourse had to contend with those idiosyncrasies, but that is not syncretism. Buddhist discourse has important things to say about animals (they are a form of rebirth associated with ignorance), and as Buddhism spread throughout Asia, it inevitably encountered and contended with "new" animals that were not present in its Indian homeland, but we do not call this "syncretism." Insofar as Buddhism recognizes beings like *phī* as real, the situation there is no different. The only task for those operating within Buddhist discourse was to determine how to translate the word *phī*—that is, how to categorize it according to Buddhism's implicit theology. As we saw, the tendency within Siamese Buddhist discourse, following the example of the *Traiphūm Phra Ruang*, was to equate them with *preta*s, or hungry ghosts.

Indeed, as I argued at the end of Chapter 5, the *only* reason that we consider the Buddhist interaction with, worship of, or supposed "mixing" with local spirits as something remarkable or worth highlighting at all is that there has been a long trend toward disenchantment in Western thought that has worked to excise such intermediate beings from the Western cosmological imaginary. In so doing, this discourse has rendered the presence of intermediate beings uncanny in anything, but especially Buddhism, that has been dubbed a "religion" and thus implicitly compared to Christianity. If modern Western thought had excised animals instead of spirits from the cosmological imaginary, then it would be "animalism" rather than "animism" that modern scholars would have named as a "component" of religious syncretism with Buddhism.

Ultimately, it is precisely modern discourse, and in particular the modern discourse of world religions, that allows us to explain the specific problematic that I used as an entrée into the world of "holy things" in modern Thailand: the propitiation of Buddha images for mundane boons just like any other "holy thing," whether spirit, god, or the like. As I showed in Chapter 7, the modern practice of *kānbonbānsānklāo* with famous Buddha images like Luang Phǫ Sōthǫn is in a sense very traditional and old and in another sense completely modern and new. The Pali Buddhist concept of *adhiṭṭhāna* has always allowed for Buddhist practitioners to ask for miracles when making merit before Buddha images and other Buddhist relics. We find evidence of such practices in older Siamese literature. What we do not find is the specific practice of negotiation with the Buddha image over an offering in the same manner as with a god or spirit, or the concomitant conceptual amalgamation of Buddha images, gods, and spirits under the rubric of a single category of "holy things."

What accounts for this change? Syncretism does not provide a satisfactory explanation because, even if we accepted the model of syncretism between a putative "local spirit religion" and Buddhism—which I have argued we should not—that "mixing" obviously would have occurred many centuries ago when Buddhism first came to Southeast Asia or, at the very least, was first adopted by Tai-speaking peoples. Instead, the change has been wrought by the introduction of the modern discourse of world religions and its associated vocabulary. As I showed in Chapter 4, the word *saksit* did not always mean "holy." Instead, it referred to the power that inheres in various supernatural beings and that is accessible through knowledge associated with Brahmans. As such, it was associated with *saiyasāt* rather than *phutthasāt*. Under such a conceptual regime, it would make little sense to speak of *phī*, gods, and Buddha images as belonging to a single category of *sing saksit*, and indeed we do not find such a broad categorization until modern times.

When Siam confronted Western modernity in earnest in the nineteenth century, however, a vast vocabulary from the latter's discourse was translated into Thai, just as it was into languages around the world. The Sanskrit word *śāsana* (Thai *sātsanā*) was marshaled to translate the Western concept of religion, and neologisms were created to refer to specific religions in the emerging discourse of "world religions": *sātsanā khrit* for Christianity, *sātsanā phut* for Buddhism, *sātsanā hindū* for Hinduism, and so on. At the same time, the word *saiyasāt* and most of its associated vocabulary was used to translate Western concepts of magic and the occult. The one conspicuous exception was the word *saksit*. Although historically associated with *saiyasāt*, it was used to translate the Western concept of "sacred" or "holy," associated with religion rather than magic. Given that none of these Thai words has truly lost its precolonial meaning, this act of translation created a new conceptual space of "holy things." Gods and spirits are now "holy" because they were always *saksit*. And Buddha images are now *saksit* because, through their association with Buddhism, a "religion," they are holy.

The opening of this new conceptual space might have had little effect on practice were it not for the sympathetic resonance between negotiating with gods and spirits for boons and practicing *adhiṭṭhāna* with a Buddha image or relic. The unification of the two under the conceptual space of "holy things" allows modern Thai practitioners to think of what they are doing with any "holy thing" as fundamentally the same. And this has most likely had certain subtle effects on the praxis of *adhiṭṭhāna* at famous Buddha images, in particular through their incorporation into a highly commercialized industry of *kānbonbānsānklāo.*

Does this blurring of the lines between the way one approaches Buddha images and the way one approaches gods and spirits represent a betrayal of core Buddhist principles? Perhaps, but that is not a question for us as scholars of religion to decide. Rather, it is one for Thai Buddhists to work through themselves. Indeed, the rearrangement of categories effected by modernity has led to a variety of responses and innovations in Thai Buddhism that we have seen in this book: the rise of an industry of *kānbonbānsānklāo* centered on the propitiation of "holy things," the cults of Brahmā and other Hindu gods that have given rise to a wave of Hindu enthusiasm, and a reformist Buddhist backlash that criticizes the propitiation of Buddha images for boons as a form of *saiyasāt.* But we should never lose sight of the fact that even the last of these has itself been made possible by the same modern shift of categories that gave rise to the former two. Buddhists, not just in Siam but even millennia ago in India, have always sought miraculous assistance in their everyday lives at the sites of Buddhist relics. The very modern and idiosyncratically Thai association of this practice with *saiyasāt*—problematic both in a modern sense as "magic" and in a traditional (but also modern) sense as "Hinduism"—is what has opened this actually quite traditional practice to critique.

Why, then, if syncretism is so wrong, does it feel so right? Because, in a sense, a whole lot of mixing *has* been going on—just not of "religions." There has always been a mixing of people and ideas in Siam due to its location on a nexus of transforming cosmopolitan structures and the inevitable interaction of discourses that that historical nexus intensified. But more important, the modern discourse of religion—the same discourse that brought religions into being as such—also scrambled the terms of debate upon which these newly dubbed "religions" operate. The concept of "religion," with all its Western baggage of Christianity, Reformation, and disenchantment, has given us—by which I mean all of us, whether nonnative scholars, tourists, casual observers, or Thai Buddhists themselves—eyes with which to see components "mixed together" in Thai religion. But it has also, in a sense, brought into being the very syncretism it supposedly identifies, by reifying the ingredients necessary for such mixture to even be conceived. It will remain for future generations of scholars to study and theorize the ways in which this fundamental shift in Thai culture—as well as other cultures like it, Buddhist or otherwise—plays out in the decades and centuries to come.

APPENDIX A

Explicit Theology from Plato to the Abrahamic Traditions

Although theology is commonly associated in the modern world first and foremost with Christianity, as an *explicit* discourse theology was invented by Plato in the fourth century BCE. By "invented," I obviously do not mean that Plato was the first to write about God or gods. This is why the qualifier "explicit" is important; the more common existence of *implicit* theology is explored in Chapter 2. Instead, I mean two things. The first is that the earliest attestation of the Greek word *theologia* is in Plato's writings, specifically in the *Republic* (379a).[1] This fact alone might not be of any great import if it weren't for the second fact, which is that Plato himself outlined a theology that would be the basis—either in agreement or in disagreement—for all explicit theologies for centuries to come.[2]

The foundational role played by Plato has been obscured—except for specialists in the field of classics—by the strong association that theology has in modern times with religion (first and foremost Christianity, but also Judaism and Islam), along with the fact that the academic field of philosophy has distanced itself from the central role that theology played in philosophical discourse from the time of Plato up until the Enlightenment. Already in Plato we find a theology resembling in key ways the later theologies of monotheistic religions. In the foundational passage I just cited, Plato writes:

> "[O]n this specific point, what would be the model for a story about matters divine [θεολογίας]?"
>
> "Something like this, I suppose," I said: "I think you should always present the god as he really is, whether you are writing about him in epic, lyric or tragedy."
>
> "That must be the case."
>
> "The god is, of course, good in reality and must be spoken of as such?"
>
> "What do you mean?"
>
> "Well no good quality is harmful, is it?"
>
> "I don't think so."
>
> "Can what is not harmful cause any harm?"
>
> "Of course not."
>
> "Can what causes no harm do anything bad?"
>
> "Again, no."
>
> "Therefore, whatever can do nothing bad cannot be responsible for anything bad?"
>
> "How can it?"
>
> "Now, what about this: a good thing is a beneficial thing, isn't it?"
>
> "Yes."
>
> "And so responsible for our well-being?"
>
> "Yes."
>
> "Good is not responsible for everything, only for those things which are good, not those which are bad?"
>
> "Entirely."

"Then since he is good," I said, "the god cannot be responsible for all things, as most people say. But he is responsible for only a few things for us men, but not for many of them. For we have fewer good things than bad. No one else is to be held responsible for the good things, but for the bad things we must look for any other cause but the god."[3]

Here in this "pagan" philosopher we already see one of the most foundational principles of monotheistic religious theology: the goodness of divine nature. This point is not obvious, and in fact the entire point of the passage is to criticize preexisting Greek literature for not always portraying the gods as good. In addition, the reference to "the god" (ὁ θεός) in this passage, while here perhaps referring to any god out of many in the abstract, prefigures what would become the common use of the same term (θεός with the definite article) to refer to a singular God. Indeed, Plato himself elaborates a theology of a singular and good God in the *Timaeus*. This text, one of Plato's later works, presents a detailed cosmogony in which God (ὁ θεός), as an expression of his inherent goodness, creates the world (κόσμος) and the creatures within it (*Tim.* 29e–48d). This cosmogony is remarkably similar to monotheistic cosmogonies, with one crucial caveat: one of the classes of creatures that God creates is the (plural) gods (θεοί) of Greek mythology (*Tim.* 39e–40a).

Plato's foundational work lay the foundation for a whole discourse of theological debate in ancient Greece, long before the rise of Christianity or even the Hellenistic encounter with Judaism. For our purposes, however, it suffices to focus on Plato's student Aristotle, who is the one thinker whose work on theology (and philosophy in general) came to rival Plato's own. Aristotle regarded theology, physics (natural philosophy), and mathematics as the three branches of philosophy. His theology is elaborated in a collection of writings known as the *Metaphysics*—a title that was first coined by a first-century CE editor in mere reference to the fact that it contains Aristotle's writings "after the *Physics*" (τὰ μετὰ τὰ φυσικά), but which as a category has since taken on a life of its own. The *Metaphysics* is an extended critique of Plato's theory of Forms. Plato had argued that behind every imperfect, changing entity in the world there is a perfect, eternal Form (εἶδος). Thus, famously, there are many chairs that are different from one another in particulars and subject to creation and decay, but behind them is the ultimate form of Chair, which is eternal. Aristotle rejected Plato's characterization of perfect Forms existing separately from individual manifestations; for him, instead, the form of chair, for example, inheres in every individual chair that exists.

Whatever differences Aristotle may have had with his teacher Plato on the question of Forms, he shared a commitment to the budding discourse of theology. In fact, Aristotle dubbed theology one of the three major branches of philosophy and ranked it the highest, the "first philosophy":

> Hence there will be three speculative philosophies: mathematics, physics, and theology—since it is obvious that if the divine is present anywhere, it is present in this kind of entity; and also the most honourable science must deal with the most honourable class of subject.
>
> The speculative sciences, then, are to be preferred to the other sciences, and "theology" to the other speculative sciences. One might indeed raise the question whether the primary philosophy is universal or deals with some one genus or entity; because even the mathematical sciences differ in this respect—geometry and astronomy deal with a particular kind of entity, whereas universal mathematics applies to all kinds alike. Then if there is not some other substance besides those which are naturally composed, physics will be the primary science; but if there is a substance

> which is immutable, the science which studies this will be prior to physics, and will be primary philosophy, and universal in this sense, that it is primary.[4]

In Book XII (Λ) of the *Metaphysics*, Aristotle engages in his fullest exploration of the nature of God. Like Plato, he identifies God with the Good, as well as being an eternal, living being:

> If, then, the happiness which God always enjoys is as great as that which we enjoy sometimes, it is marvelous; and if it is greater, this is still more marvelous. Nevertheless it is so. Moreover, life belongs to God. For the actuality of thought is life, and God is that actuality; and the essential actuality of God is life most good and eternal. We hold, then, that God is a living being, eternal, most good; and therefore life and a continuous eternal existence belong to God; for that is what God is.[5]

The bulk of this book, however, is taken up by Aristotle's exposition, in more theoretical terms, of the concept of the "unmoved mover" (*ὃ οὐ κινούμενον κινεῖ*). This is the idea that there must be a substance that serves as a cause but is not itself caused, in order to prevent infinite regress. Shortly after identifying this substance as God in the passage just cited, Aristotle raises more pointedly the question "whether we should hold that there is one substance of this kind or more than one, and if more than one, how many."[6] In a turn that would ensure his importance to later monotheistic theologians, he concludes that the answer must be one, ending the book poetically with a quote from the *Illiad*: "The rule of many is not good; let one be the ruler."[7]

Ultimately, it would be the actions of Aristotle's contemporary and royal pupil, Alexander the Great, that ensured the long-term relevance of theological discourse. Alexander's conquest of the Achaemenid Empire, including Asia Minor, Mesopotamia, Persia, the Levant, and Egypt, created in its wake a Hellenistic world in which theological discourse thrived. In particular, Plato's and Aristotle's conception of an ultimate principle who is good and the fundamental cause of the world found a sympathetic resonance in the conception held by Jews of a singular all-powerful being who created the world. Although there were always tensions between those who embraced Hellenism and those who opposed it among the Jewish community, Judaism overall was very much a participant in Hellenistic culture in this era. As Daniel Boyarin has argued, this reality has been obscured by the fact that the Rabbis who reorganized Jewish culture after the fall of Jerusalem and destruction of the Second Temple in 70 CE deliberately sought to define Judaism in opposition to Greek culture, which they associated with Christianity.[8] Nevertheless, the engagement of Judaism with Hellenistic culture is evident in the translation of the Hebrew Scriptures into Greek as the Septuagint, which allowed not only for them to be read by increasingly Hellenized Jews, but also for their dissemination to a broader Greek-speaking Gentile public. Moreover, in this era a Hellenized Jew, Philo of Alexandria, became a significant philosopher in his own right.[9] He sought to reconcile Greek philosophy with Jewish scripture, a project that had the long-term effect of establishing a central role for theological discourse in all three of the Abrahamic religions, but especially Christianity. Philo engaged with Greek philosophers extensively in his own work and argued that there were parallels between Greek and Jewish thought due to *logos*, or divine reason, being present in both cultures.[10]

Although memory of earlier engagement with Hellenism and of Philo in particular was repressed in Rabbinic Judaism, the theological encounter between Greek philosophy and the worldview of the Jewish scriptures became central to another first-century Jewish sect, Christianity. In part due to the efforts of Paul, himself a Hellenized Jew who wrote in Greek, to spread the "good news" of God's kingdom to non-Jews, Christianity quickly became a thoroughly Hellenistic movement, with all of the intellectual engagement that implies. Early Christianity's Hellenism is of course well recognized, but its engagement with Greek philosophy has been obscured, for two reasons. On the one hand, opponents going back to the second-century pagan philosopher Galen rejected Christianity as being grounded in antirational faith; on the other hand, there is a certain antiphilosophical rhetoric in the writings of early Christianity's intellectual class, the so-called Church Fathers.

Nevertheless, as George Karamanolis has argued, early Christian writers should be understood as engaging in philosophy just as much as other philosophical sects of the time, such as the Platonists, Peripatetics, and Epicureans. Church Fathers, including Justin Martyr, Tatian, Clement of Alexandria, Tertullian, Origen, Eusebius, Basil of Caesarea, and Gregory of Nyssa, received classical educations and engaged with Greek philosophy in their work. Although their reverence for scripture led them to defend certain nonnegotiable dogmas, starting out from axiomatic truths taken from authority did not place them out of line with other philosophical schools. The intellectual framework of Hellenistic philosophy allowed the Church Fathers to articulate in a universal language the claims made in scripture, settle intra-Christian disputes on the interpretation of scripture, and defend Christianity against its opponents. While some Church Fathers spoke in disparaging terms about philosophy (as did pagan philosophers about them), they also would paradoxically make the claim that Christianity was the best form of philosophy; in any case, the actual intellectual commitments of these early Christian writers belie their engagement with philosophical discourse.[11] Ultimately, the proof is in the pudding: *theology*, a term apparently coined by Plato and praised by Aristotle as the "first philosophy," came to be seen as central to the intellectual project of Christianity, to the point that today it is a category associated more with "religion" than with "philosophy."

At the same time that Christianity was establishing itself in the Roman Empire and Christian thinkers were engaging in their own philosophical project, non-Christian philosophers retrospectively labeled "Neoplatonists" engaged in a synthesis of Hellenic philosophy inspired by Plato's early theological speculations about God and the Good. Starting with Plotinus and his student Porphyry, the Neoplatonists articulated a monistic worldview in which an ineffable substance known as "the One" serves as the cause of all being. The multiplicity of the universe emerges as a series of emanations from the One, resulting in a cosmic hierarchy of beings. This cosmology in turn allows for a soteriology in which the immortal soul attains union with the One through philosophical contemplation. Late Christian philosophers such as Origen and Augustine were influenced by Neoplatonism, and in time Neoplatonism became the primary vehicle through which Christian thinkers engaged with pre-Christian Hellenic philosophy.

Much of the period of Hellenistic cultural synthesis took place under the auspices of Rome, and while the Greek-speaking cultural sphere continued in the Eastern Roman Empire, a Latin-speaking cultural sphere arose in the Western Roman Empire that absorbed much of the cultural synthesis emerging from the Eastern Hellenistic sphere—most important, Christianity. When the Western Empire fell in the fifth century, the Latinate sphere of Western Europe entered a period of intellectual contraction known (misleadingly) as the Dark Ages, during which there was little engagement with Hellenic philosophy. The so-called Dark Ages were not universal, however; philosophical inquiry in the Greek tradition continued unabated in the Byzantine and Sasanian (Persian) empires. When the early Islamic caliphate conquered the Sasanian Empire and much of the Byzantine Empire in the seventh century, the groundwork was laid for an Arab encounter with Hellenic thought and the development of Islamic theology on Hellenic models.

Systematic theology is referred to in Arabic as *kalām*, a word which originally referred in the Qur'an to the "speech" or "word" of God. As an intellectual discipline, it arose early in Islam's history to deal with problems of Qur'anic interpretation, and as in early Christianity, it contained a strain of distrust of Greek philosophy due to the latter's pagan origins. Nevertheless, the Islamic conquest of much of the Hellenistic world brought Islam into contact with philosophical inquiry, and Islamic philosopher-theologians played an important role in the retransmission of Greek thought to Western Europeans in the Renaissance. *Kalām* was arguably always implicitly "philosophical" insofar as Islam is historically predicated on its Jewish and Christian predecessors, which, respectively, entered into and were formed out of Hellenistic theological discourse, as I outlined above. Explicit Islamic engagement with Greek philosophy, however, began with the ninth-century figure al-Kindī. Al-Kindī advocated seeking truth from any source, even non-Islamic ones, and like Jewish and Christian thinkers before him, saw in Platonic, Aristotelian, and Neoplatonic theories of God, the Good, and the One fruitful discourse partners from a monotheistic perspective.[12]

Unlike al-Kindī, who leaned more Aristotelian in his thought and defended the traditional Islamic view of Creation *ex nihilo*, the tenth-century philosopher al-Fārābī embraced Neoplatonism and in particular the Neoplatonic theory of emanation.[13] Islamic Neoplatonism's most famous proponent, however, is al-Fārābī's intellectual heir, Ibn Sīnā, known better in the West by the Latinized name Avicenna. Although by his own admission intellectually indebted to al-Fārābī, Ibn Sīnā was, due to the elegance of his writing, widely regarded as the greatest philosopher of his day. Manuscripts of his works in the Islamicate world were copied and preserved far more completely than those of al-Kindī or al-Fārābī, and translations of "Avicenna's" works into Latin played a pivotal role in reintroducing the West to Aristotle.[14]

The Neoplatonism of al-Fārābī and Ibn Sīnā, and by extension Greek philosophy in general, drew the ire of the great eleventh-century theologian al-Ghazālī. Although his main conclusion was that philosophy is contradictory and worthless, with the implication that human beings can have recourse only to the authority of revelation, al-Ghazālī was extremely well-versed in philosophical reasoning about God and his Creation and used that same reasoning to subvert it.[15] In part due to criticisms from al-Ghazālī and others, Islamic philosophy waned in the 'Abbāsid caliphate, but it experienced a renaissance in al-Andalus (Iberia), where the remnants of the Umayyad caliphate reigned. The most important figure of this renaissance was the twelfth-century philosopher Ibn Rushd, known in the West by the Latinized name Averroes. Much of Ibn Rushd's philosophical project was dedicated to defending the compatibility of philosophy and Islam against al-Ghazālī and other critics. Nevertheless, Ibn Rushd was also a critic of Ibn Sīnā and favored a more Aristotelian position than his Neoplatonic predecessor.[16] Indeed, it was precisely in his Aristotelianism that Ibn Rushd was most influential, for his works were translated shortly after his death and helped to reintroduce the Latinate West to Aristotle, sparking a revolution in Western European thought.

What we normally think of as "theology"—what I am referring to here as "explicit theology"—is thus the product of a coherent discourse that had its beginnings in ancient Greek philosophy and made its way, through the mediation of Hellenistic culture, into the intellectual traditions of the three major Abrahamic religions. It is "explicit" insofar as it refers to itself using the term "theology," coined and/or popularized by Plato. Since this particular discourse has had such an outsized influence on Western intellectual traditions, it is important to recognize its historical particularity in order to appreciate the full range of human discourses beyond it that have and do engage in similar work.

APPENDIX B

Corpus of Siamese Literary Works Consulted

The narrative that Thai children today are taught generally places the origins of the national literature in Sukhōthai. Although this narrative is in part rooted in the problematic Damrong School of Thai history that I described in Chapter 3, there is nonetheless a strong argument to be made for tracing the origins of Siamese literature in this way, even from the perspective of more up-to-date models of Siamese history. The Sukhōthai cultural sphere is home to a rich corpus of inscriptions, the earliest of which, from the late thirteenth century, are the oldest securely datable instances of writing in any Tai dialect. As we saw in Chapter 3, Ayutthayā and Sukhōthai were moieties from the beginning of the fourteenth century, thus becoming increasingly culturally intertwined from a point quite early in their history. In particular, Sukhōthai likely played a pivotal role in the introduction of Tai elites and their language to Siam, a region formerly dominated by Mon and Khmer.

A full corpus of inscriptions found in modern Thailand has usefully been digitized by the Princess Maha Chakri Sirindhorn Anthropology Centre and is available online at the Inscriptions in Thailand Database (https://db.sac.or.th/inscriptions/). I have included in my corpus all the major Sukhōthai inscriptions, exempting minor inscriptions containing only a few words, for a total of forty-two. Other than these inscriptions, there is most likely only one surviving text from Sukhōthai proper: the *Traibhūmikathā*, known also as the *Traiphūm Phra Ruang* (*ไตรภูมิกถา* or *ไตรภูมิพระร่วง*). This text, ascribed to the future Sukhōthai king Lithai around the year 1345, is a comprehensive description of the "three worlds" (*traibhūmi*) of Buddhist cosmology according to authoritative Pali texts.[1] Thai accounts of literary history often still claim that another text, the *Nāng Nopphamāt* (*นางนพมาศ*), a purportedly autobiographical account by a Sukhōthai princess of the same name, dates from the "Sukhōthai period," but as Nidhi Eoseewong has conclusively demonstrated, it is instead a work of historical fiction, written during the reign of Rāma III (1824–1851), most likely in part by the king himself.[2]

Unlike Sukhōthai, Ayutthayā did not produce many inscriptions,[3] so its literature is represented primarily by texts that managed to survive the destruction of the city in 1767. One of the most vexing questions in the study of Ayutthayā-era literature is over which works can be dated to the "early" period—that is, roughly speaking, before the First Siamese-Burmese War, in the sixteenth century. Traditional Thai scholarship placed only a very small number of texts in this early period. The first of these is the *Ōngkān Chāng Nām* (*ลิลิตโองการแช่งน้ำ*), which is used in an oath-taking ceremony in which vassals and royal servants drink water that has been "cursed" to kill them should they break their oath of loyalty.[4] It is traditionally dated to the reign of Rāmāthibodī I (Ū Thǫng), the putative fourteenth-century founder of Ayutthayā. Although this dating is dubious given Rāmāthibodī's semi-mythical status, the text is undoubtedly old. The second is the *Yuan Phāi* (*ลิลิตยวนพ่าย*), a eulogy of battle written shortly after a successful attack by King Borommatrailōkanāt on Lānnā in 1474/5.[5] The third is the *Mahāchāt Kham Luang* (*มหาชาติคำหลวง*), which is a rendition, in a mixture of Pali and Thai, of the "Great

Birth" (*mahājāti*) of the Bodhisatta as Vessantara, based on the last of the canonical Jātaka tales. According to the *Luang Prasōt Chronicle*, this text was composed in 1482/3.[6]

Earlier Thai scholarship portrayed the reign of King Nārāi (1656–1688) as a golden age of Thai literature, attributing a large number of Ayutthayā-era works to officials in his court. The significance of Nārāi's reign was probably overemphasized in earlier scholarship, however, due to the fact that the French and other Westerners were uniquely active in his court, with the result that Nārāi early on and somewhat idiosyncratically earned pride of place in the Western imagination about Siam.[7] More recent scholarship has shown that several works once attributed to Nārāi's reign more likely, based on linguistic features, belong to the "early" period. The first of these is the *Phra Lǭ* (*ลิลิตพระลอ*), an epic about a fictional king who is drawn to another city by a love potion and there killed along with his lovers, which was probably written around 1500.[8] Another is the *Dvādaśamāsa* (*ทวาทศมาสโคลงดั้น*), a poem of lament about the author's dead lover that chronicles the evolution of his grief over the course of the "twelve months" (in Sanskrit, *dvādaśamāsa*) of the year. It was probably written in the late fifteenth century.[9] In addition, Prasert na Nakhorn has dated the *Nirāt Hariphunchai* (*นิราศหริภุญชัย*), which set the standard for the *nirāt* (Skt. *nirāśa*) genre in which a male author goes on a journey and laments the separation from his female lover, precisely to 1517.[10]

Three other texts have been suggested by some scholars to have come from the same "early" period, but their dating is less secure. The first is the *Kamsuan* (*กำสรวลโคลงดั้น*), which, like the *Dvādaśamāsa* and *Nirāt Hariphunchai*, is based on the theme of separation from one's lover.[11] In addition, some scholars have placed two additional works, the *Samudraghoṣa* (*สมุทรโฆษคำฉันท์*), an apocryphal Jātaka tale, and *Aniruddha* (*อนิรุทธ์คำฉันท์*), an eponymous work about Kṛṣṇa's grandson, in the "early" period, possibly in the reign of Rāmāthibodī II (1491–1529).[12] Most scholars, however, continue to date these texts to the reign of Nārāi.

Although, as we have seen, several of the works once dated to the reign of Nārāi in the seventeenth century have now been redated to an earlier period, several others are still believed to have been composed in his court. Two are of particular historical significance. The first is the *Luang Prasōt Chronicle* (*พระราชพงศาวดารกรุงศรีอยุธยา ฉบับหลวงประเสริฐ*), the oldest chronicle of Ayutthayā extant in Thai, and the basis for all later chronicles of Ayutthayā.[13] The second is the *Cintāmaṇī* (*จินดามณี*), the oldest reflexive scholarly work on Thai language and literature.

Several further works are attributed to the late Ayutthayā period, that is, the early eighteenth century prior to the fall of Ayutthayā. It is in this era that we find works by an author whose name, identity, and dates are well established, namely Prince Thammathibēt, the son of King Borommakōt (r. 1733–1758). Thammathibēt was notoriously accused of plotting a coup against his father and sleeping with his concubines, which led to him being executed in 1755. His most famous and influential work is the *Phra Mālai Kham Luang* (*พระมาลัยคำหลวง*), which is a rendition of a popular tale of a monk named Phra Mālai who uses his meditative attainments to travel throughout the Buddhist cosmos, including the different levels of hell and heaven. Although I have not been able to consult this work, I have consulted several of Thammathibēt's other poetic writings.

A small number of works survive from the brief reign of Tāksin (1767–1782), who restored Siamese rule after the Burmese sack of Ayutthayā and ruled from a new capital in Thonburī. The foundation of the Chakri Dynasty, however, with its capital at Bangkok, in 1782 brought an explosion of literary activity. Three major projects sponsored by the court of Rāma I sought to salvage important aspects of the literary heritage of Ayutthayā. The first, the *Kotmāi Trā Sām Duang* (กฎหมายตราสามดวง), or *Three Seals Law*, is a massive edited compilation of laws from Ayutthayā.[14] The second, the *Rāmakian* (บทละครเรื่องรามเกียรติ์), is a polished dramatic script of the Thai version of the epic *Rāmāyaṇa*, based on versions salvaged from Ayutthayā. Finally, *Unnarut* (บทละครเรื่องอุณรุท) is a dramatic rendition of the story of Kṛṣṇa's grandson Aniruddha.

Literary activity if anything increased in the reign of Rāma II (1809–1824), who was an accomplished poet in his own right. He personally wrote scripts for the dramatic performance of five traditional folk tales—*Chaichēt* (บทละครเรื่องไชยเชษฐ์), *Manīphichai* (บทละครเรื่องมณีพิชัย), *Krai Thǭng* (บทละครเรื่องไกรทอง), *Sang Thǭng* (บทละครเรื่องสังข์ทอง), and *Khāwī* (บทละครเรื่องคาวี)—as well as the epic drama *Inao* (บทละครเรื่องอิเหนา), which was derived from Javanese folk tales. Most important, however, he sponsored and contributed to an edition of the folk epic *Khun Chāng Khun Phǣn* (เสภาเรื่องขุนช้างขุนแผน), which, as I mentioned above, is nonelite in origin and is a rich depository of information on ordinary life in Ayutthayā.[15]

A number of prominent court poets were active during the reigns of the first three kings of the Chakri Dynasty in the first half of the nineteenth century. Hon, who served as the Cāo Phrayā Phra Khlang (Minister of the Treasury) under Rāma I, was an accomplished poet who authored many works, but he is most famous for his translation of the Chinese *Romance of the Three Kingdoms* (*Sānguó Yǎnyì* 三國演繹) as *Sām Kok* (สามก๊ก) and of the Mon history *Rājādhirāja* (ราชาธิราช). Prince Paramānuchitchinōrot (1790–1853) was a son of Rāma I who spent most of his life as a monk and authored several poetic works, including the *Talēng Phāi* (ลิลิตตะเลงพ่าย). The Lord of Trang (พระยาตรัง) was, like Paramānuchitchinōrot, also active during the reign of Rāma II and wrote *nirāt* and other poetic works. Finally, although Rāma III was not a prolific author like his father, his reign saw a proliferation of literary writers, including Prince Dēchādisǭn (1793–1859), Prince Wongsāthirātchasanit (1808–1871), the Phra Mahāmontrī Sap (ทรัพย์), Nāi Mī, and two of Siam's earliest known female authors, Khun Phum and Khun Suwan.

By far the most famous, talented, and prolific author of early nineteenth-century Siam, however, was Sunthǭn Phū (1786–1855), who is generally regarded as the greatest writer in all of Thai literary history, with a stature akin to Shakespeare in the English-speaking world. A commoner who was introduced to the palace through his mother, a royal wet nurse, Sunthǭn Phū was recognized as having such outstanding ability that he was appointed a royal poet by Rāma II. His life was turbulent, marked by alcoholism, numerous affairs, and concomitant palace intrigue. He wrote across a variety of genres, including a total of nine works in the *nirāt* genre that was particularly popular at the time. His magnum opus, however, was the *Phra Aphaimanī* (พระอภัยมณี), a fantastical tale, completely of the author's own invention, about the adventures of a prince by the same name. It is the longest Thai poem in existence and took Sunthǭn Phū twenty-two years to write, from 1822 to 1844. Given its length and extraordinary breadth, as well as its historical position on the cusp of the entry of old Siam into the world of colonial politics, it is a particularly rich source for Siamese-language use just prior to the enormous changes wrought by the absorption of Western vocabulary into what is now modern Thai.

Corpus of Sukhōthai Inscriptions Consulted

The following inscriptions were consulted in digital format from the Inscriptions in Thailand Database (https://db.sac.or.th/inscriptions/).

จารึกกฎหมายลักษณะโจร
จารึกกู่บ้านค่ายเจริญ
จารึกคำปูสบถ
จารึกคำอธิษฐาน
จารึกฐานพระพุทธรูปนายทิตไส
จารึกฐานพระพุทธรูปปางลีลา วัดพญาภู (องค์ที่ 1)
จารึกฐานพระพุทธรูปปางลีลา วัดพญาภู (องค์ที่ 2)
จารึกฐานพระพุทธรูปผ้าขาวทอง
จารึกฐานพระพุทธรูปยืนปางประทานอภัย วัดพระธาตุช้างค้ำวรวิหาร
จารึกฐานพระพุทธรูปแม่ศรีมหาตา
จารึกฐานพระอิศวรเมืองกำแพงเพชร
จารึกที่ฐานพระพุทธรูปสุโขทัย (นายญี่บุญ)
จารึกนครชุม
จารึกประวัติการทำสังคายนาและรายนามพระสงฆ์
จารึกป้านางคำเยีย
จารึกป้านางเมาะ
จารึกปูขุนจิดขุนจอด
จารึกพระปิฎก
จารึกพระยาศรียศราช วัดหงส์รัตนารามฯ
จารึกพ่อขุนรามคำแหง
จารึกพ่อขุนรามพล
จารึกลานทองสมเด็จพระมหาเถรจุฑามุณิ
จารึกลานเงินเสด็จพ่อพระยาสอย
จารึกวัดช้าล้อม
จารึกวัดบางสนุก
จารึกวัดบูรพาราม
จารึกวัดป่ามะม่วง (ภาษาไทย) หลักที่ 1
จารึกวัดป่ามะม่วง (ภาษาไทย) หลักที่ 2
จารึกวัดพระยืน
จารึกวัดศรีชุม
จารึกวัดสรศักดิ์
จารึกวัดหินตั้ง
จารึกวัดอโสการาม
จารึกวัดเขมา
จารึกวัดเขากบ
จารึกวัดเขาสุมนกูฏ
จารึกวัดเจดีย์เหลี่ยมเวียงกุมกาม
จารึกอุทิศสิ่งของ
จารึกเจดีย์น้อย
จารึกเชตพน
จารึกเมืองลอง
จารึกแสดงผลกรรมนำสู่นิพพาน

Works of Siamese Literature Consulted

The following works were consulted in digital format at www.vajirayana.org. They are listed in very approximate chronological order according to the period in which they were written, with subheadings for actual or attributed authors when they are known.[16]

Sukhōthai

ไตรภูมิกถา (ไตรภูมิพระร่วง)	*Traibhūmikathā* (*Traiphūm Phra Ruang*)

Early Ayutthayā

โคลงทวาทศมาส	*Dvādaśamāsa*
โคลงนิราศหริภุญชัย	*Nirāt Hariphunchai*
มหาชาติคำหลวง	*Mahāchāt Kham Luang*
ลิลิตยวนพ่าย	*Yuan Phāi*
ราชาพิลาปคำฉันท์	*Rāchāphilāp*
ลิลิตโองการแช่งน้ำ	*Ōngkān Chǣ̄ng Nām*
ลิลิตพระลอ	*Phra Lǭ*

Reign of King Nārāi

คำฉันท์กล่อมช้างครั้งกรุงเก่า	*Kham Chan Klǭm Chāng Khrang Krung Kao*
คำฉันท์ดุษฎีสังเวย	*Dutsadī Sangwœ̄i*
อนิรุทธคำฉันท์	*Aniruddha*

Phra Hōrāthibodī

จินดามณีเล่ม ๑	*Cintāmaṇī* (Book 1)
พระราชพงศาวดารกรุงเก่า ฉบับหลวงประเสริฐอักษรนิติ์	*Luang Prasœ̄t Chronicle*

Phra Mahārātchakhrū

เสือโคคำฉันท์	*Sūa Khō*
คำฉันท์สรรเสริญพระเกียรติสมเด็จพระพุทธเจ้าหลวงปราสาททอง	*Kham Chan Sansœ̄n Phra Kiat*

Somdet Phra Phuttha Cāo Luang Prāsāt Thǭng

สมุทรโฆษคำฉันท์	*Samudraghoṣa*

Reign of King Borommakōt

บุณโณวาทคำฉันท์	*Puṇṇovāda*

Prince Thammathibēt

กาพย์ห่อโคลงนิราศธารโศก	*Nirāt Thān Sōk*

กาพย์ห่อโคลงประพาสธารทองแดง	*Praphāt Thān Thọ̄ng Dǣng*
บทเห่เรือ พระนิพนธ์เจ้าฟ้าธรรมธิเบศร	*Bot Hē Rüa of Prince Thammathibēt*

Thonburī-Era Literature

โคลงยอพระเกียรติพระเจ้ากรุงธนบุรี	*Khlōng Yọ̄ Phra Kiat Phra Cāo Krung Thonburī*
กฤษณาสอนน้องคำฉันท์ฉบับกรุงธนบุรี	*Krütsanā Sọ̄ng Nọ̄ng* (Thonburī edition)
นิราศพระยามหานุภาพไปเมืองจีน	*Nirāt Phrayā Mahānuphāp Pai Müang Cīn*

Bangkok First Reign

Rāma I

บทละครเรื่องรามเกียรติ์	*Rāmakian*
บทละครเรื่องอุณรุท	*Unnarut*
พระราชนิพนธ์นิราศท่าดินแดง	*Nirāt Thā Din Dǣng*

Cāo Phrayā Phra Khlang (Hon)

กากีกลอนสุภาพ	*Kākī Klọ̄n Suphāp*
พระศรีวิชัยชาดก	*Phra Śrīvijaya Jātaka*
ราชาธิราช	*Rājādhirāja*
ลิลิตเพชรมงกุฎ	*Phet Mongkut*
ลิลิตพยุหยาตราเพชรพวง	*Phayuha Yātrā Phet Phuang*
สมบัติอมรินทร์คำกลอน	*Sombat Ammarin*
สามก๊ก	*Sām Kok*
อิเหนาคำฉันท์	*Inao Kham Chan*

Bangkok Second Reign

นิราศนรินทร์	*Nirāt Narin*

Rāma II

เสภาเรื่องขุนช้างขุนแผน	*Khun Chāng Khun Phǣn*
กาพย์เห่เรือ พระราชนิพนธ์รัชกาลที่ ๒	*Kāp Hē Rüa of Rāma II*
บทละครเรื่องไกรทอง	*Krai Thọ̄ng*
บทละครเรื่องไชยเชษฐ์	*Chaichēt*
บทละครเรื่องคาวี	*Khāwī*
บทละครเรื่องมณีพิชัย	*Manī Phichai*
บทละครเรื่องสังข์ทอง	*Sang Thọ̄ng*
บทละครเรื่องอิเหนา	*Inao*

Phrayā Trang

เพลงยาวนมัสการพระบรมธาตุ นิราศไปตรัง	*Phlēng Yāo Namatsakān Phra Bọrommathāt Nirāt Pai Trang*
เพลงยาวพระยาตรัง	*Plēng Yāo of Phrayā Trang*

โคลงกวีโบราณ	*Kawī Bōrān*
โคลงดั้นเฉลิมพระเกียรติพระบาทสมเด็จพ	*Khlōng Dan Chalə̄m Phra Kiat Phra Bāt*
ระพุทธเลิศหล้านภาลัย	*Somdet Phra Phuttha Lə̄tlā Naphālai*
โคลงดั้นนิราศตามเสด็จทัพลำน้ำน้อย	*Nirāt Tām Somdet Thap Lamnām Nǭi*
โคลงนิราศพระยาตรัง	*Nirāt of Phrayā Trang*

Somdet Phra Mahāsommana Cāo Krom Phra Porammānuchit Chinōrot

กฤษณาสอนน้องคำฉันท์	*Krütsanā Sǭn Nǭng*
ปฐมสมโพธิกถา	*Paṭhamasambodhikathā*
ลิลิตตะเลงพ่าย	*Talēng Phāi*
สรรพสิทธิ์คำฉันท์	*Sapphasit*

Sunthǭn Phū

เพลงยาวถวายโอวาท	*Phlēng Yāo Thawāi Ōwāt*
โคลงนิราศสุพรรณ	*Nirāt Suphan*
กลอนบทละครเรื่องอภัยนุราช	*Apainurāt*
กาพย์เรื่องพระไชยสุริยา	*Phra Chai Suriyā*
นิทานคำกลอนเรื่องโคบุตร	*Khōbut*
นิทานคำกลอนเรื่องพระอภัยมณี	*Phra Aphaimanī*
นิทานคำกลอนเรื่องลักษณวงศ์	*Laksanawong*
นิทานคำกลอนเรื่องสิงหไกรภพ	*Singkraiphop*
นิราศเมืองเพ็ชร	*Nirāt Müang Phet*
นิราศเมืองแกลง	*Nirāt Müang Klǣng*
นิราศพระแท่นดงรัง	*Nirāt Phra Thǣn Dong Rang*
นิราศพระบาท	*Nirāt Phra Bāt*
นิราศพระประธม	*Nirāt Phra Prathom*
นิราศภูเขาทอง	*Nirāt Phūkhao Thǭng*
นิราศวัดเจ้าฟ้า	*Nirāt Wat Cāofā*
นิราศอิเหนา	*Nirāt Inao*
บทเห่เรื่องโคบุตร	*Bot Hē Rüang Khōbut*
บทเห่เรื่องกากี	*Bot Hē Rüang Kākī*
บทเห่เรื่องจับระบำ	*Bot Hē Rüang Cap Rabam*
บทเห่เรื่องพระอไภยมณี	*Bot Hē Rüang Phra Aphaimanī*
สวัสดิรักษาคำกลอน	*Sawatdi Raksā*
สุภาษิตสอนสตรี	*Suphāsit Sǭn Sattrī*

Bangkok Third Reign

| ตำหรับนางนพมาศซึ่งเปนท้าวศรีจุฬาลักษณ์ | *Nāng Nopphamāt* |

Rāma III

| บทละครเรื่องสังข์ศิลป์ไชย | *Sang Sinchai* |
| ประชุมเพลงยาวสุภาพ | *Prachum Phlēng Yāo Suphāp* |

Krom Luang Wongsāthirāt Sanit

| โคลงนิราศพระประทม | *Nirāt Phra Prathom* |

จินดามณีเล่ม ๒	*Cintāmaṇī* (Book 2)

Khun Phum

เพลงยาวคุณพุ่มแต่งเฉลิมพระเกียรติ	*Phlēng Yāo Khun Phum Tǣng Chalœ̄m Phra Kiat*
นิราศวังบางยี่ขัน	*Nirāt Wang Bāng Yī Khan*

Khun Suwan

เพลงยาวจดหมายเหตุเรื่องกรมหมื่นอัปสรสุดาเทพประชวร	*Phlēng Yāo Cotmāihēt Rūang Krom Mū̄n Appasǭn Sudāthēp Prachuan*

Nāi Mī (Mū̄n Phrom Somphatsǭn)

กลอนเพลงยาวสรรเสริญพระเกียรติ	*Klǭn Phlēng Yāo Sansœ̄n Phra Kiat*
นิราศพระแท่นดงรัง	*Nirāt Phra Thǣn Dong Rang*

Phra Mahāmontrī (Sap)

บทละครเรื่องระเด่นลันได	*Radēn Landai*

Somdet Phra Cāo Borommawong Thœ̄ Krom Phrayā Dēchādisǭn

ประชุมโคลงโลกนิติ	*Lōkkanit*

Bangkok Fourth Reign

นิราศลอนดอน	*Nirāt Lǭndǭn*
สุภาษิตอิศรญาณ	*Suphāsit Itsarayān*

Phrayā Itsarānuphāp (An)

พระสุธนคำฉันท์ ของพระยาอิศรานุภาพ	*Phra Suthon*
อุเทนคำฉันท์	*Udena*

Notes

Acknowledgments

1. Nathan McGovern, "A Buddhist Cult of Brahmā: Thick Description and Micro-Histories in the Study of Religion," *History of Religions* 55, no. 3 (Feb. 2016): 329–360.

Chapter 1

1. For a broad overview of the concept of syncretism from a (mostly) sympathetic perspective, see Anita Maria Leopold and Jeppe Sinding Jensen, eds., *Syncretism in Religion: A Reader* (London: Routledge, 2014). For a historical genealogy of the term *syncretism*, see "Introduction to Part II," 14–28 of the same volume.
2. For critiques of the concept of syncretism from a general History of Religions perspective, see Robert D. Baird, "Syncretism and the History of Religions," in *Syncretism in Religion*, 48–58; A. J. Drodge, "Retrofitting/Retiring 'Syncretism,'" *Historical Reflections/Réflexions Historiques* 27, no. 3 (Fall 2001): 375–387; Bruce Lincoln, "Retiring Syncretism," *Historical Reflections/Réflexions Historiques* 27, no. 3 (Fall 2001): 453–459; Jonathan Z. Smith, "Syncretism," in *The Harper Collins Dictionary of Religion*, ed. Jonathan Z. Smith and William Scott Green (New York: Harper Collins, 1995), 1042–1043.
3. British Broadcasting Corporation, *The Long Search 3—Buddhism: Footprint of the Buddha—India* (New York: Time-Life Media, 1977), 40:24.
4. For a diagram of the placement of all nineteen images, including Luang Phọ̄ Sōthọn, on the main altar, see จินตนา ธรรมสุวรรณ, "ละครแก้บนหลวงพ่อพุทธโสธร" [The Dance for Fulfilling a Vow to Luang Phọ̄ Sōthọn] (master's thesis, Mahidol University, 2544 [2001]), 41.
5. คมกฤช อุ่ยเต็กเค่ง et al., *ผี-พราหมณ์-พุทธ ในศาสนาไทย* [Spirit Religion, Brahmanism, and Buddhism in Thai Religion] (กรุงเทพฯ: นาตาแฮก, 2564 [2021]).
6. โหรอโยธยา, "บทนำ," [Introduction] in *คู่มือแก้บน อธิษฐานขอพร เสริมมงคง* [Manual for Fulfilling Vows, Asking for Boons, and Increasing Auspiciousness] (หมู่บ้านไอยราเบย์วิว, ชลบุรี: สำนักพิมพ์ยอดมาลา, n.d.), 5–6:

   > ในปัจจุบัน ผู้คนหันมายึดเหนี่ยวสิ่งศักดิ์สิทธิ์เพื่อเป็นกำลังใจในการดำรงชีวิตกันมากขึ้น อันเนื่องมาจากการดำรงชีพและปัญหาต่างๆ มากมาย ดังนั้นผู้คนหันมาหาที่พึ่งจากสิ่งศักดิ์สิทธิ์ต่างๆ ด้วยการบนบานสิ่งศักดิ์สิทธิ์ และเมื่อสมหวังแล้ว หลายๆ ท่านอกจจะลืมไปว่าบนอะไรไว้ เพราะบางคนน่ะ บนซะทุกๆ ที่ๆ ใครๆ ว่าดี
   >
   > ในหนังสือนี้อาจารย์จึงได้แจกแจงสถานที่ที่คนนิยมบนและวิธีการแก้บนที่ตนเองลืมไปแล้ว
   >
   > เอาล่ะนะที่นี้ก็ไม่ต้องกังวลแล้ว ใครอยากได้อะไร ต้องบนที่ไหนอย่างไร และการไหว้พระขอพร ตลอดจนการบนเพื่อขอสิ่งต่างๆ ให้เกิดความสำเร็จ เช่น ให้ได้งาน, การบนขอลูก, การบนขอความรัก, การบนขอให้ถูกหวย รวย ฯลฯ โดยเฉพาะอย่างยิ่งการบนกับองค์เทพต่างๆ เกี่ยวกับเทพพรหมของศาสนาฮินดู หรือตามสถานที่ศักดิ์สิทธิ์ทั่วไป
   >
   > อาจารย์ขอเริ่มจากการบน องค์พ่อจตุคามรามเทพ ที่สุดฮอตในเวลานี้ก่อนเลยนะ เพราะน่าจะมีคนหลายๆ คนที่อยากจะรู้ว่า ถ้าจะบนกับองค์พ่อจตุคามรามเทพนั้นต้องบนด้วยอะไรและบนอย่างไรก่อนอื่นท่านต้องทราบวิธีบูชาท่านก่อนนะ และสุดท้ายอาจารย์จะบอกวิธีบูชาที่ได้ผล ติดตามในหน้าต่อไปนะ

7. คำเตือน! **บน? ไว้แล้ว ต้องแก้บน** (bold and underlining in original).
8. I thank Nanda Raksakhom for this insight.
9. The names in this table are taken from the table of contents of *คู่มือแก้บน*, 7–8.
10. These three categories, as an analytical tool to understand Thai religion, were popularized by the anthropologist Thomas Kirsch, as I will discuss in more detail below. See A. Thomas Kirsch,

"Complexity in the Thai Religious System: An Interpretation," *Journal of Asian Studies* 36, no. 2 (1977): 241–266.

11. See Justin McDaniel, *The Lovelorn Ghost and the Magical Monk: Practicing Buddhism in Modern Thailand* (New York: Columbia University Press, 2011).
12. Michael M. Ames, "Magical-Animism and Buddhism: A Structural Analysis of the Sinhalese Religious System," *Journal of Asian Studies* 23 (1964): 21–52; Melford Spiro, *Burmese Supernaturalism* (Englewood Cliffs, NJ: Prentice Hall, 1967). Ames's preferred term for the non-Buddhist component of Sinhala religion is "magical-animism," while Spiro refers to the same component in Burmese religion as "supernaturalism" or "animism."
13. Stanley Tambiah, *Buddhism and the Spirit Cults of North-East Thailand,* Cambridge Studies in Social Anthropology, no. 2, ed. J. R. Goody (Cambridge: Cambridge University Press, 1970).
14. B. J. Terwiel, *Monks and Magic: An Analysis of Religious Ceremonies in Central Thailand,* Scandinavian Institute of Asian Studies Monograph Series, no. 24 (Lund: Studentlitteratur, 1975), esp. 5.
15. Kirsch, "Complexity in the Thai Religious System."
16. Robert H. Sharf, *Coming to Terms with Chinese Buddhism: A Reading of the* Treasure Store Treatise (Honolulu: University of Hawai'i Press, 2002), 15–16.
17. Ibid., 14–15. Sharf refers in this passage to Jonathan Z. Smith, "The Bare Facts of Ritual," in *Imagining Religion: From Babylon to Jonestown* (Chicago: University of Chicago Press, 1982), 53–65.
18. Richard S. Cohen, "Nāga, Yakṣiṇī, Buddha: Local Deities and Local Buddhism at Ajanta," *History of Religions* 37, no. 4 (1998): 360–400.
19. Robert DeCaroli, *Haunting the Buddha: Indian Popular Religions and the Formation of Buddhism* (Oxford: Oxford University Press, 2004).
20. Pattana Kitiarsa, "Beyond Syncretism: Hybridization of Popular Religion in Contemporary Thailand," *Journal of Southeast Asian Studies* 36, no. 3 (2005): 461.
21. James Taylor, *Buddhism and Postmodern Imaginings in Thailand: The Religiosity of Urban Space* (Surrey: Ashgate, 2008), 38. See note 6 on the same page for references to earlier works in which Taylor also uses the term "hybridization."
22. In this respect, I am in general agreement with Bruce Lincoln ("Retiring Syncretism," 457), who notes that the apparent nonpejorative connotation of "hybridity" is quickly effaced if one switches to "mongrelization," which is based on a similar biological metaphor.
23. As I finish this manuscript, Peter Jackson has offered yet another alternative to syncretism to describe in particular modern Thai religious practice, describing the Thai religious field as an "amalgam": Peter A. Jackson, *Capitalism Magic Thailand: Modernity with Enchantment* (Singapore: ISEAS, 2022), 136–150. While this book provides an excellent ethnography of much of the newest developments in the world of "holy things" in Thailand, at least as they pertain to the pursuit of wealth, I do not find the model of "amalgam" useful from a historical perspective. The purpose of this model is to emphasize heterogeneity and lack of coherence in the final product. This is appealing as a synchronic description of the present, insofar as one takes the reification of "world religions" and other modern categories such as "magic" for granted, but it does nothing to address the fundamental problem with syncretism as a category of historical analysis, namely, that it presupposes pure religions that then mix; indeed, it reinscribes this problematic assumption.
24. McDaniel, *Lovelorn Ghost*, 228–229.
25. Charles Hallisey, "Roads Taken and Not Taken in the Study of Theravāda Buddhism," in *Curators of the Buddha: The Study of Buddhism under Colonialism*, ed. Donald S. Lopez, Jr. (Chicago: University of Chicago Press, 1995), 31–62.
26. Julia Cassaniti, *Living Buddhism: Mind, Self, and Emotion in a Thai Community* (Ithaca, NY: Cornell University Press, 2015).
27. Gerhardt Oberhammer, ed., *Inklusivismus: Eine indische Denkform* (Vienna: Institut für indologie der Universität Wien, 1983).
28. Naomi Appleton, *Shared Characters in Jain, Buddhist and Hindu Narrative: Gods, Kings and Other Heroes* (London: Routledge, 2017), 57–81.
29. Alexis Sanderson, "Maṇḍala and Āgamic Identity in the Trika of Kashmir," in *Mantras et diagrammes rituels dans l'Hindouisme*, ed. André Padoux (Paris: Editions du CNRS, 1986), 181–185.
30. Nathan McGovern, "Brahmā: An Early and Ultimately Doomed Attempt at a Brahmanical Synthesis," *Journal of Indian Philosophy* 40, no. 1 (Feb. 2012): 20–21n56.

31. Richard King, *Orientalism and Religion: Postcolonial Theory, India and "The Mystic East"* (London: Routledge, 1999), 135–142.
32. Aldous Huxley, the author of *The Perennial Philosophy*, was influenced in large part by Vivekānanda's Neo-Vedāntic portrayal of Hinduism. See ibid., 162–163.
33. David L. McMahan, *The Making of Buddhist Modernism* (New York: Oxford University Press, 2008), 4.
34. Donald K. Swearer, *Becoming the Buddha: The Ritual of Image Consecration in Thailand* (Princeton, NJ: Princeton University Press, 2004).
35. Angela S. Chiu, *The Buddha in Lanna: Art, Lineage, and Place in Northern Thailand* (Honolulu: University of Hawai'i Press, 2017).
36. Sarah J. Horton, *Living Buddhist Statues in Early Medieval and Modern Japan* (New York: Palgrave Macmillan, 2007).
37. Shinohara Koichi, "Changing Roles for Miraculous Images in Medieval Chinese Buddhism: A Study of the Miracle Image Section in Daoxuan's 'Collected Records,'" in *Images, Miracles, and Authority in Asian Religious Traditions*, ed. Richard H. Davis (Boulder, CO: Westview, 1998), 141–188.
38. Siam is the name of the kingdom, located in what is now central Thailand and with origins in the thirteenth century, that evolved into the modern nation-state of Thailand. The name was officially changed to Thailand in 1939, a few years after the revolution that ended the absolute monarchy.
39. For a genealogy of the Western concept of the sacred, see Jonathan Z. Smith, "The Topography of the Sacred," in *Relating Religion: Essays in the Study of Religion* (Chicago: University of Chicago Press, 2004), 101–116.
40. George Coedès, *The Indianized States of Southeast Asia*, ed. Walter F. Vella, trans. Susan Brown Cowing (Honolulu: East-West Center Press, 1968).
41. Vickery argued that most of the "Brahmans" in Southeast Asia were actually Southeast Asians who traveled to India and then returned claiming greater status. See Michael Vickery, *Society, Economics, and Politics in Pre-Angkor Cambodia: The 7th–8th Centuries* (Tokyo: Centre for East Asian Cultural Studies for Unesco, 1998), 59.
42. Mabbett argued that so-called Indianization is just an extension of the process of "Sanskritization" or "Brahmanization" taking place in India itself, and that Southeast Asia should therefore not be understood as a separate entity interacting with a monolithic India. See Ian W. Mabbett, "The 'Indianization' of Southeast Asia: Reflections on the Historical Sources," *Journal of Southeast Asian Studies* 8 (1977): 143–161.
43. Wolters argued that as Southeast Asians received "news" through maritime trade, they saw themselves as operating within larger worlds, and their desire to express local concerns in a universal language led to "foreign materials fading into local statements." See O. W. Wolters, "Khmer 'Hinduism' in the Seventh Century," in *East South East Asia*, ed. R. B. Smith and W. Watson (New York: Oxford University Press, 1979), 427–443; O. W. Wolters, *History, Culture, and Region in Southeast Asian Perspectives*, revised ed. (Ithaca, NY: Southeast Asia Program Publications, 1999), 63.
44. On the importance of "Southern Asia" as a geographical unit of analysis, see R. Michael Feener and Anne M. Blackburn, eds., *Buddhist and Islamic Orders in Southern Asia: Comparative Perspectives* (Honolulu: University of Hawai'i Press, 2019), 8–9.
45. Wolters, "Khmer 'Hinduism,'" 63.
46. On the Pali *imaginaire*, see Steven Collins, *Nirvana and Other Buddhist Felicities: Utopias of the Pali Imaginaire* (Cambridge: Cambridge University Press, 1998), 40–89; on the Sanskrit Cosmopolis, see Sheldon Pollock, *The Language of the Gods in the World of Men: Sanskrit, Culture, and Power in Premodern India* (Berkeley: University of California Press, 2006).

Chapter 2

1. As Bernard Faure has argued, even from our critical stance as scholars, we must take gods seriously as real agents. See Bernard Faure, *Gods of Medieval Japan*, vol. 1: *The Fluid Pantheon* (Honolulu: University of Hawai'i Press, 2016), 6–10.
2. Jan Assmann, *The Search for God in Ancient Egypt* (Ithaca, NY: Cornell University Press, 2001), 8–13, 163, cited in Eidinow, *Theologies of Ancient Greek Religion*, 4n7.

3. Eidinow, *Theologies of Ancient Greek Religion*. For a somewhat dated but influential work, see also Werner Jaeger, *The Theology of the Early Greek Philosophers: The Gifford Lectures 1936* (Eugene, OR: Wipf & Stock, 1967).
4. For a review of the literature and outline of the shift in scholarly understanding, see Mark S. Smith, *The Early History of God: Yahweh and the Other Deities in Ancient Israel*, 2nd ed. (Grand Rapids, MI: William B. Eerdmans, 2002), 1–13.
5. Mark S. Smith, *The Origins of Biblical Monotheism: Israel's Polytheistic Background and the Ugaritic Texts* (New York: Oxford University Press, 2001), 6–7.
6. Ibid., 27.
7. Ibid., 44–46.
8. Smith, *The Early History of God*, 43–53.
9. Smith, *Origins of Biblical Monotheism*, 142–146.
10. Ibid., 179.
11. Ibid., 165.
12. Mark S. Smith, *God in Translation: Deities in Cross-Cultural Discourse in the Biblical World* (Grand Rapids, MI: William B. Eerdmans, 2010).
13. Benjamin W. Fortson IV, *Indo-European Language and Culture: An Introduction*, 2nd ed. (Chichister: Wiley-Blackwell, 2010), 25.
14. "God (n.)," *Online Etymology Dictionary*, https://www.etymonline.com/word/god.
15. On the stages of the development of the *Ṛg Veda*, see Michael Witzel, "The Development of the Vedic Canon and Its Schools: The Social and Political Milieu," in *Inside the Texts, Beyond the Texts*, ed. Michael Witzel, Harvard Oriental Series, Opera Minora, vol. 2 (Cambridge, MA: Department of Sanskrit and Indian Studies, Harvard University, 1997), 261–266.
16. *RV* X.129.2: *ānīd avātaṃ svadhayā tad ekaṃ tasmād dhānyan na paraḥ kiṃ canāsa //*.
17. *RV* X.129.3: *tucchyenābhv apihitaṃ yad āsīt tapasas tan mahinājāyataikam //*.
18. RV X.129.6–7: *ko addhā veda ka iha pra vocat kuta ājātā kuta iyaṃ visṛṣṭiḥ / arvāg devā asya visarjanenāthā ko veda yata ābabhūva // iyaṃ visṛṣṭir yata ābabhūva yadi vā dadhe yadi vā na / yo asyādhyakṣaḥ parame vyoman so aṅga veda yadi vā na veda //*.
19. *RV* X.121.1–3: *hiraṇyagarbhaḥ sam avartatāgre bhūtasya jātaḥ patir eka āsīt / sa dādhāra pṛthivīṃ dyāmutemāṃ kasmai devāya haviṣā vidhema // ya ātmadā baladā yasya viśva upāsate praśiṣaṃ yasya devāḥ / yasya chāyāmṛtaṃ yasya mṛtyuḥ kasmai devāya haviṣā vidhema // yaḥ prāṇato nimiṣato mahitvaika id rājā jagato babhūva / ya īśe asya dvipadaścatuṣpadaḥ kasmai devāya haviṣā vidhema //*.
20. RV X.121.10: *prajāpate na tvad etāny anyo viśvā jātāni pari tā babhūva / yatkāmās te juhumas tan no astu vayaṃ syāma patayo rayīṇām //*.
21. Jan Gonda, "The Popular Prajāpati," *History of Religions* 22, no. 2 (Nov. 1982): 129–149; Greg Bailey, *The Mythology of Brahmā* (Delhi: Oxford University Press, 1983), 63–73.
22. Ganesh Umakant Thite, *Sacrifice in the Brāhmaṇa-Texts* (Poona: University of Poona Press, 1975), 2–6.
23. Brian K. Smith, *Reflections on Resemblance, Ritual, and Religion* (Delhi: Motilal Banaarsidass, 1998), 31–32, 72, 194.
24. *ChU* 3.14.1, 4: *sarvaṃ khalv idaṃ brahma taj jalān iti śānta upāsīta / . . . etam itaḥ pretyābhisaṃbhavitāsmīti*. My translation omits the word *jalān*, which appears to have no meaning. Patrick Olivelle, trans. and ed., *The Early Upaniṣads: Annotated Text and Translation* (New York: Oxford University Press, 1998), 544n14.
25. *BĀU* 1.4.10: *brahma vā idam agra āsīt / tad ātmānam evāvet / ahaṃ brahmāsmīti / tasmāt tat sarvam abhavat /*.
26. Herman W. Tull, *The Vedic Origins of Karma: Cosmos as Man in Ancient Indian Myth and Ritual* (Albany, NY: SUNY Press, 1989).
27. *ChU* 6.8.7, 6.9.4, 6.10.3, 6.11.3, 6.12.3, 6.13.3, 6.14.3, 6.15.3: *sa ya eṣo 'ṇimaitadātmyam idaṃ sarvam / tat satyam / sa ātmā / tat tvam asi śvetaketo iti /*.
28. *ChU* 8.7.4, 8.8.3, 8.10.1, 8.11.1: *eṣa ātmeti hovāca / etad amṛtam abhayam etad brahmeti /*.
29. *BĀU* 4.4.5–6: *sa vā ayam ātmā brahma vijñānamayo manomayo prāṇamayaś cakṣurmayaḥ śrotramayaḥ pṛthivīmaya āpomayo vāyumaya ākāśamayas tejomayo 'tejomayaḥ kāmamayo 'kāmamayaḥ krodhamayo 'krodhamayo dharmamayo 'dharmamayaḥ sarvamayaḥ / . . . athākāmayamāno yo 'kāmo niṣkāma āptakāma ātmakāmo na tasya prāṇā utkrāmanti / brahmaiva san brahmāpy eti //*.
30. As I have argued in previous work, the various *śramaṇa* groups can be understood as having pursued Brahmanhood based on Vedic precedents just as much as the householder groups that

successfully arrogated the term "Brahman" to themselves. See Nathan McGovern, *The Snake and the Mongoose: The Emergence of Identity in Early Indian Religion* (New York: Oxford University Press, 2019), esp. 85–132. On the *saṃnyāsa* tradition that arose within "orthodox" Brahmanism, see Patrick Olivelle, trans., *Saṃnyāsa Upaniṣads: Hindu Scriptures on Asceticism and Renunciation* (New York: Oxford University Press, 1992).

31. Bailey, *Mythology of Brahmā*, 63.
32. The *Mānava Dharmaśāstra* comes closest by far to manifesting the Brahmanical theology of Brahmā as Supreme Creator God depicted in the Buddhist sources. Unlike the earlier Dharma Sūtras, Manu begins with a cosmogony, in which Brahmā is born at the beginning of time of a golden egg in the waters and then proceeds to create the universe. Echoing the *Puruṣa Sūkta*, he creates the four *varṇas* from his mouth, arms, thighs, and feet (1.31), and because the mouth is the purest part of his body, Brahmans are said to be the highest class (1.92–93)—precisely the same argument attributed to Brahmans in declaring their supremacy in the Pali Canon. Brahmā is also identified as the highest goal within the context of *saṃsāra*: *etadantās tu gatayo brahmādyāḥ samudāhṛtāḥ / ghore 'smin bhūtasaṃsāre nityaṃ satatayāyini //*, "These (plants) are declared the lowest of destinations that begin with Brahmā in this terrible cycle of beings that continues forever" (1.50). Although Viṣṇu is briefly mentioned (12.121), there is no sign of Vaiṣṇavism in this text, and in fact the title Nārāyaṇa is applied to Brahmā because he is born of the waters (1.10).

    The *Mārkaṇḍeya Purāṇa*, although in its present form clearly a late compilation bearing the influence of sectarianism, appears to be based on an older text that depicts Brahmā as Supreme Deity in much the same manner as the *Mānava Dharmaśāstra*. Chapters 42 to 79 are of particular interest to us because they contain a cosmogony similar to but more elaborate than the one found in Manu. Brahmā is explicitly identified as the primordial God, whose origin is "inscrutable" (42.20: *avyaktajanmanaḥ*). In chapter 42, the Creation of the universe is recounted along Sāṃkhya lines, but with Brahmā identified as the first cause of the process and also later as the *kṣetrajña*, born of an egg in the waters. Subsequent chapters then recount the Creation of the universe in its various manifest forms, with Brahmā taking a personal role in the process. As in Manu, Brahmā is here referred to as Nārāyaṇa due to his birth on the waters (44.3–5); additionally, he is said to have taken the form of a fish, tortoise, and boar (44.7), *avatāras* later associated with Viṣṇu. Although the chapters corresponding to the "original" *Mārkaṇḍeya* are consistent in asserting the supremacy of Brahmā, they seem to possibly be aware of Vaiṣṇavism and Śaivism in a way that Manu and the early Buddhist *sūtras* are not. Brahmā is identified as the Supreme Deity, but he is also said, in language reminiscent of the *trimūrti*, to take the form of Viṣṇu to protect the Creation and of Rudra to destroy it (43.14–19).

33. The *Rāmāyaṇa* is usually understood to be a Vaiṣṇava text, and in its full extant form as disclosed by the Critical Edition, it is difficult not to interpret it as Vaiṣṇava given the frame story in which Rāma is an *avatāra* of Viṣṇu and the terms in which this incarnation is sometimes expressed. For example, when Rāma's divine identity is revealed near the end of the *Yuddha Kāṇḍa* (ch. 105), he is extolled by none other than Brahmā himself as "the imperishable truth of *brahman*" (13: *akṣaraṃ brahmasatyaṃ*), "[without] origin or destruction" (18: *prabhavaṃ nidhanaṃ vā te na viduḥ ko bhavān iti*), "seen in all beings" (18: *dṛśyase sarvabhūteṣu*), and "support [of] beings and the earth with its mountains" (20: *tvaṃ dhārayasi bhūtāni vasudhāṃ ca saparvatām*). Nevertheless, much of the epic, even with the narrative frame of Rāma's divinity, can be read as the product of a pre-Vaiṣṇava theological context in which Brahmā was considered Supreme Deity. In the *Bāla Kāṇḍa*, Brahmā grants the boon to Rāvaṇa that makes it impossible for him to be killed by any other than a man (14.12–14). When Rāvaṇa begins oppressing the earth, the gods go to Brahmā's heavenly court and there ask Viṣṇu to take human form to fight Rāvaṇa (14.16–15.6). Once Viṣṇu leaves to complete his task, Brahmā orders the other gods to take the form of monkeys in order to assist Viṣṇu in his task (ch. 16). Although other verses in the epic, especially in the *Uttara Kāṇḍa*, can be construed as identifying Viṣṇu as Supreme Deity, this basic frame story and certain references to it in the body of the epic seem to imply that while Rāma is indeed an incarnation of Viṣṇu, the latter is simply doing the bidding of the true High God, Brahmā.

    The *Mahābhārata* poses interpretive problems very similar to those of the *Rāmāyaṇa*. It also includes an incarnation of Viṣṇu, in this case Kṛṣṇa, and many portions of the epic speak of him as the Supreme Deity, most famously the *Bhagavad Gītā* found in Book 6, in which Kṛṣṇa reveals himself to Arjuna as the Highest God. To further complicate matters, certain portions of the *Mahābhārata* (e.g., the *Sauptika Parvan*, in which Kṛṣṇa himself extols Śiva as Supreme) alternatively appear to be Śaiva. Nevertheless, certain passages seem to regard Brahmā as the Supreme Deity. In a parallel to the *Rāmāyaṇa*, one example can be found in the first book, in which the Earth goes to Brahmā to complain of being burdened by Asuras, and in response Brahmā orders the gods to be born on Earth to fight against them (1.58.35–59.6). For this reason, over a hundred years ago Hopkins argued that at an earlier stage of the *Mahābhārata* Kṛṣṇa was regarded only as a demigod, with "no evidence of didactic form or of Krishna's divine supremacy," this later being reworked to make Kṛṣṇa an "All-God." E. Washburn Hopkins, *The Great Epic of India: Its Character and Origin* (New York: Charles Scribner's Sons, 1901), 398.

34. McGovern, "Brahmā."
35. King, *Orientalism and Religion*, 39–40.
36. SN I.234: *seṭṭhā hi kira lokasmiṃ, ye tvaṃ sakka namassasi / ahampi te namassāmi, ye namassasi vāsavā ti //.*
37. This name is clearly a title, and although its etymology is unclear, Przyluski has argued that it comes from *sabhā + pati*, thus, "lord of the assembly," implying Brahmā as chief of the gods. See Jean Przyluski, "Brahma *Sahampati*," *Journal asiatique* 205 (1924): 155–163.
38. The name of this Brahmā is prominent in Brahmanical texts as well. He gives a long discourse to the sage Nārada in chapter 7 of the *Chāndogya Upaniṣad*. The *Mahābhārata* (12.327.63–65) names him as one of the six "mind-made sons" (*manasputra*) of Brahmā. He is also named as the author of the *Sanatkumāra Saṃhitā*, which forms part of the *Śiva Purāṇa*.
39. Appleton, *Shared Characteristics*, 65.
40. Richard Gombrich has argued that this name should be taken to mean "heron" and, consistent with the portrayal of herons in Indian literature as foolish, should be understood as satirical. See Richard Gombrich, "A Visit to Brahmā the Heron," *Journal of Indian Philosophy* 29, nos. 1–2 (Apr. 2001): 95–108.
41. *MN* I.326: ***idañhi, mārisa, niccaṃ, idaṃ dhuvaṃ, idaṃ sassataṃ, idaṃ kevalaṃ, idaṃ acavanadhammaṃ, idañhi na jāyati na jīyati na mīyati na cavati na upapajjati. ito ca panaññaṃ uttari nissaraṇaṃ natthī ti.***
42. *DN* I.18: ***aham asmi brahmā mahābrahmā abhibhū anabhibhūto aññadatthudaso vasavattī issaro kattā nimmātā seṭṭho sajitā vasī pitā bhūtabhabyānaṃ. mayā ime sattā nimmitā.***
43. Rupert Gethin, *The Foundations of Buddhism* (Oxford: Oxford University Press, 1998), 115–118.
44. This word, incidentally, is used in modern Thai (as จักรวาฬ) to refer to the modern concept of "the universe."
45. Gethin, *Foundations of Buddhism*, 118–119.
46. Metteyya's future coming as the next Buddha is predicted in *DN* 26, the *Cakkavādasīhanāda Sutta* (III.75–76). The "rule" that all Buddhas in their final birth descend to their mother's womb from Tusita heaven is stated in *DN* 14, the *Mahāpadāna Sutta* (II.12).
47. Ramsay MacMullen, *Christianizing the Roman Empire (a.d. 100–400)* (New Haven, CT: Yale University Press, 1984), 128n12.
48. 1 Cor. 10:18–20, NAB: βλέπετε τὸν Ἰσραὴλ κατὰ σάρκα · οὐχ οἱ ἐσθίοντες τὰς θυσίας κοινωνοὶ τοῦ θυσιαστηρίου εἰσίν; τί οὖν φημι; ὅτι εἰδωλόθυτόν τί ἐστιν, ἢ ὅτι εἴδωλόν τί ἐστιν; ἀλλ' ὅτι ἃ θύουσιν, δαιμονίοις καὶ οὐ θεῷ θύουσιν, οὐ θέλω δὲ ὑμᾶς κοινωνοὺς τῶν δαιμονίων γίνεσθαι.
49. MacMullen, *Christianizing the Roman Empire*, 17–18.
50. Burkert, *Greek Religion*, 179–181, 331–332.
51. Deut. 32:17, NAB. The Septuagint text of this passage reads as follows: ἔθυσαν δαιμονίοις καὶ οὐ θεῷ, θεοῖς, οἷς οὐκ ᾔδεισαν· καινοὶ πρόσφατοι ἥκασιν, οὓς οὐκ ᾔδεισαν οἱ πατέρες αὐτῶν.
52. Amira El- Zein, *Islam, Arabs, and the Intelligent World of the Jinn* (Syracuse, NY: Syracuse University Press, 2009), 13–22, 32.
53. Ibid., 14.
54. On this point, see also David Gordon White, *Daemons Are Forever: Contacts and Exchanges in the Eurasian Pandaemonium* (Chicago: University of Chicago Press, 2021), esp. 6–9. While White's goal in his book is to establish the existence of intermediate beings in the nonelite praxis of Eurasian cultures that can etically be called *daemons* (itself a modern act of scholarly translation), my goal in this chapter is somewhat different: to show how discourse makes possible and in the process intervenes upon such acts of "translation" in the first place.
55. Euan Cameron, *Enchanted Europe: Superstition, Reason, and Religion, 1250– 1750* (Oxford: Oxford University Press, 2010), 41–49.

56. Ibid., 79–85.
57. Ibid., 42, 91–102.
58. Ibid., 103–118.
59. Ibid., 156–173.
60. Michael Allen Gillespie, *The Theological Origins of Modernity* (Chicago: University of Chicago Press, 2008).
61. Ibid., 207–254.
62. Cameron, *Enchanted Europe*, 256–257.
63. See the carefully articulated and researched argument that we have never truly become disenchanted made by Jason Ā. Josephson-Storm, *The Myth of Disenchantment: Magic, Modernity, and the Birth of the Human Sciences* (Chicago: University of Chicago Press, 2017).
64. Philip C. Almond, *The British Discovery of Buddhism* (Cambridge: Cambridge University Press, 1988), 24–28, 33–53; Gregory Schopen, "Archaeology and Protestant Presuppositions in the Study of Indian Buddhism," *History of Religions* 31 (1991): 1–23; King, *Orientalism and Religion*, 143–160; Tomoko Masuzawa, *The Invention of World Religions: Or, How European Universalism Was Preserved in the Language of Pluralism* (Chicago: University of Chicago Press, 2005), 121–146.
65. In Thai culture, *yak* (as the word is pronounced) are conceived of as giants, but this has not always been the case in Buddhist or broader Indic culture.
66. DeCaroli, *Haunting the Buddha*, 186–187.
67. To be clear, I am not making a perennialist claim here. *Nirvāṇa* and God are not the same; indeed, early Buddhist texts ridicule the idea of a Creator God in the person of Brahmā. I am simply showing that the theological projects of Buddhism and Christianity are structurally similar.

Chapter 3

1. Collins, *Nirvana and Other Buddhist Felicities*, 41.
2. McDaniel argues that the category "Hinduism" is not useful in a Thai context: Justin McDaniel, "This Hindu Holy Man Is a Thai Buddhist," *South East Asia Research* 21, no. 2 (2013): 303–332. Christian Lammerts argues that Burmese *dhammasattha* literature should not be understood primarily in terms of Hindu Dharmaśāstra, but rather as properly "Buddhist law": D. Christian Lammerts, *Buddhist Law in Burma: A History of* Dhammasattha *Texts and Jurisprudence, 1250–1850* (Honolulu: University of Hawai'i Press, 2018), 24. In the context of Cambodia, Erik Davis argues that "Brahmanism" is an emic category created by Buddhism itself for use as a foil: Erik W. Davis, *Deathpower: Buddhism's Ritual Imagination in Cambodia* (New York: Columbia University Press, 2016), 22.
3. By "at cross-purposes," I mean that the Pali *imaginaire* could be construed as an agent of Indianization. This, however, would be a misunderstanding of the term as Collins envisioned it. Although it is true that the Pali *imaginaire* was established in texts written early in Buddhism's history in South Asia, Pali texts were also written (and to a certain extent continue to be written) in Southeast Asia. The Pali *imaginaire* was/is a living phenomenon with roots in local places.
4. Robert L. Brown, *The Dvāravatī Wheels of the Law and the Indianization of South East Asia* (Leiden: Brill, 1996); Lammerts, *Buddhist Law in Burma*, 22–29; Prapod Assavavirulhakarn, *The Ascendancy of Theravāda Buddhism in Southeast Asia* (Chiang Mai: Silkworm Books, 2010).
5. For examples of the older narrative, see, for example, Charles F. Keyes, *The Golden Peninsula: Culture and Adaptation in Mainland Southeast Asia* (New York: Macmillan, 1977), 78–82, and Donald K. Swearer, "Buddhism in Southeast Asia," in *Buddhism and Asian History*, ed. Joseph M. Kitagawa and Mark D. Cummings (New York: Macmillan, 1989), 107–129.
6. Ian Harris, *Cambodian Buddhism: History and Practice* (Honolulu: University of Hawai'i Press, 2005), 22–25.
7. Betty Gosling, *Origins of Thai Art* (Bangkok: River Books, 2004), 96–147.
8. Anne Blackburn and R. Michael Feener, "Sufis and *Saṅgha* in Motion: Toward a Comparative Study of Religious Orders and Networks in Southern Asia," in *Buddhist and Islamic Orders in Southern Asia: Comparative Perspectives*, ed. R. Michael Feener and Anne Blackburn (Honolulu: University of Hawai'i Press, 2019), 8–9.
9. Pollock, *Language of the Gods*, 12.

10. Ibid., 39.
11. Ibid., 61–67.
12. Ibid., 67.
13. Ibid., 72.
14. Ibid., 98.
15. Ibid., 116–117.
16. Johannes Bronkhorst, *Buddhism in the Shadow of Brahmanism* (Leiden: Brill, 2011), 51.
17. Ibid., 62–65.
18. Ibid., 63–64, italics in the original.
19. Ibid., 153–170.
20. McGovern, *The Snake and the Mongoose*, 133–164, 211–212.
21. Johannes Bronkhorst, *How the Brahmins Won: From Alexander to the Guptas* (Leiden: Brill, 2016), 42–108.
22. Alexis Sanderson, "The Śaiva Age: The Rise and Dominance of Śaivism during the Early Medieval Period," in *Genesis and Development of Tantrism*, ed. Shingo Einoo (Tokyo: Institute of Oriental Culture, University of Tokyo, 2009), 43.
23. Ibid., 44.
24. Ibid., 124–243.
25. Ibid., 302.
26. On the royal court Brahmans and their role in royal ceremonies, see พระบาทสมเด็จพระจุลจอมเกล้าเจ้าอยู่หัว, *พระราชพิธีสิบสองเดือน* [The Royal Ceremonies of the Twelve Months] (พระนคร: กรมศิลปากร, 2496 [1953]); H. G. Quaritch Wales, *Siamese State Ceremonies: Their History and Function* (Richmond, Surrey: Curzon Press, 1992); Nathan McGovern, "Balancing the Foreign and the Familiar in the Articulation of Kingship: The Royal Court Brahmans of Thailand," *Journal of Southeast Asian Studies* 48, no. 2 (June 2017): 283–303.
27. Frank E. Reynolds, "Ramayana, Rama Jataka, and Ramakien: A Comparative Study of Hindu and Buddhist Traditions," in *Many Rāmāyaṇas: The Diversity of a Narrative Tradition in South Asia*, ed. Paula Richman (Berkeley: University of California Press, 1991), 50–59.
28. Pollock, *Language of the Gods*, 572–573.
29. Ibid., 386.
30. Richard M. Eaton, *India in the Persianate Age: 1000–1765* (Allen Lane, 2019), 11–13.
31. Ronit Ricci, *Islam Translated: Literature, Conversion, and the Arabic Cosmopolis of South and Southeast Asia* (Chicago: University of Chicago Press, 2011).
32. Marhsall G. S. Hodgson, *The Venture of Islam: Conscience and History in a World Civilization* (Chicago: University of Chicago Press, 1974), 2: 293, cited by Nile Green, ed., *The Persianate World: The Frontiers of a Eurasian Lingua Franca* (Oakland: University of California Press, 2019), 3.
33. Green, *The Persianate World*, 1.
34. Eaton, *India in the Persianate Age*, 10–18.
35. This, as Green points out, is a bit of a simplification. New Persian actually has its origins specifically in the dialect of Middle Persian (Dari) that was spoken in the Sasanian capital Ctesiphon-Seleucia and then exported east to Khurasan near the end of the Sasanian Empire. Green, *The Persianate World*, 10.
36. Ibid., 12.
37. Eaton, *India in the Persianate Age*, 14–16.
38. Ibid., 34.
39. Green, *The Persianate World*, 21.
40. Ibid., 28.
41. Ricci, *Islam Translated*.
42. Karashima Noboru, ed., *A Concise History of South India: Issues and Interpretations* (New Delhi: Oxford University Press, 2014), 210; Chris Baker and Pasuk Phongpaichit, *A History of Ayutthaya: Siam in the Early Modern World* (Cambridge: Cambridge University Press, 2017), 127–128.
43. See, for example, Heinrich von Stietencron, "Religious Configurations in Pre-Muslim India and the Modern Concept of Hinduism," in *Representing Hinduism: The Construction of Religious Traditions and National Identity*, ed. Vasudha Dalmia and Heinrich von Stietencron (New Delhi: Sage, 1995), 51–81.
44. See, for example, David N. Lorenzen, "Who Invented Hinduism?," *Comparative Studies in Society and History* 41, no. 4 (1999): 630–659.

45. Patton E. Burchett, *A Genealogy of Devotion:* Bhakti, *Tantra, Yoga, and Sufism in North India* (New York: Columbia University Press, 2019), 309.
46. Ibid., 311.
47. Tilman Frasch, "A Pāli Cosmopolis? Sri Lanka and the Theravāda Buddhist Ecumene, c. 500–1500," in *Sri Lanka at the Crossroads of History*, ed. Zoltán Biedermann and Alan Strathern (London: University College London Press, 2017), 66.
48. Steven Collins, "What Is Literature in Pali?," in *Literary Cultures in History: Reconstructions from South Asia*, ed. Sheldon Pollock (Berkeley: University of California Press, 2003), 649–651.
49. Jonathan Walters, "Buddhist History: The Sri Lankan Pāli Vaṃsas and Their Community," in *Querying the Medieval: Texts and the History of Practices in South Asia*, by Ronald Inden, Jonathan Walters, and Daud Ali (New York: Oxford University Press, 2000), 112–113, 123–125.
50. Frasch, "A Pāli Cosmopolis?," 70–73.
51. Collins, "What Is Literature in Pali?," 649.
52. Frasch, "A Pāli Cosmpolis?" 72.
53. Alastair Gornall, *Rewriting Buddhism: Pali Literature and Monastic Reform in Sri Lanka, 1157–1270* (London: UCL Press, 2020), 36–56.
54. Walters, "Buddhist History," 145.
55. Anne Blackburn, "Sīhaḷa Saṅgha and Laṅkā in Later Premodern Southeast Asia," in *Buddhist Dynamics in Premodern and Early Modern Southeast Asia*, ed. D. Christian Lammerts (Singapore: Institute of Southeast Asian Studies, 2015), 307–332.
56. Scholars have recently come to realize that "Theravāda" was not an important emic category in the so-called Theravāda world until quite recently. See especially Todd LeRoy Perreira, "Whence Theravāda? The Modern Genealogy of an Ancient Term," in *How Theravāda Is Theravāda? Exploring Buddhist Identities*, ed. Peter Skilling, Jason A. Carbine, Claudio Cicuzza, and Santi Pakdeekham (Chiang Mai: Silkworm Books, 2012), 443–571, and other chapters in the same volume. "Pali Buddhism" has thus been adopted by scholars as an etic term to refer to those forms of Buddhism throughout history that take the Pali scriptures as authoritative.
57. Kanai Lal Hazra, *History of Theravāda Buddhism in South-East Asia, with Special Reference to India and Ceylon* (New Delhi: Munshiram Manoharlal, 1981), 134–135; Swearer, "Buddhism in Southeast Asia," 116–117.
58. For the story of the discovery of the inscription, see Barend Jan Terwiel, *The Ram Khamhaeng Inscription: The Fake That Did Not Come True* (Gossenberg: Ostasien Verlag, 2010), 7–12. On its significance for modern Thai nationalism (from a scholar who is skeptical of its authenticity), see Maurizio Peleggi, *Thailand: The Worldly Kingdom* (Singapore: Talisman, 2007), 92, 156–160.
59. Baker and Pasuk, *History of Ayutthaya*, 43.
60. Ibid., 44–46, 48.
61. Ibid., 55.
62. There is ample evidence that the city was originally named after Ayodhyā and would have been pronounced accordingly. The current pronunciation, Ayutthayā, which is taken from the Sanskrit *ayudhyā* ("unconquerable"), was adopted after the first Burmo-Siamese War in the sixteenth century to assert that it was invincible in the face of Burmese aggression. Ibid., xvii.
63. Chris Baker, "Ayutthaya Rising: From Land or Sea?," *Journal of Southeast Asian Studies* 34, no. 1 (Feb. 2003): 41–62.
64. Baker and Pasuk, *History of Ayutthaya*, 47.
65. On the decline of Śrī Vijaya, see O. W. Wolters, *The Fall of Śrī Vijaya in Malay History* (Ithaca, NY: Cornell University Press, 1970).
66. Baker and Pasuk, *History of Ayutthaya*, 48–50.
67. Ibid., 55.
68. Ibid.
69. Ibid., 58–62.
70. Michael Vickery, "Cambodia and Its Neighbors in the 15th Century," Asia Research Centre Working Paper Series, no. 27 (Singapore: Asia Research Institute, National University of Singapore, 2004), 14, 48.
71. Wilaiwan Khanittanan, "Khmero-Thai: The Great Change in the History of the Thai Language of the Chao Phraya Basin," *ภาษาและภาษาศาสตร์* [Journal of Language and Linguistics] 19, no. 2 (2001): 35–50, cited by Baker and Pasuk, *History of Ayutthaya*, 79.
72. Michael Vickery, "A New *Tamnān* about Ayudhya," *Journal of the Siam Society* 67, no. 2 (July 1979): 143.

73. Note that while in English the distinction between the language of modern Thailand (Thai) and the broader language family (Tai) is indicated by the presence or absence of an *h* after the *t*, in Thai the distinction is not usually indicated by a difference in aspiration but by adding the letter *y* (ย) to the end of the word for the modern language of Thailand, which has no effect on pronunciation.
74. Grant Evans, "The Tai Original Diaspora," *Journal of the Siam Society* 104 (2016): 1–25.
75. Baker and Pasuk, *History of Ayutthaya*, 24.
76. Ibid., 29.
77. Ibid., 26.
78. Michael Vickery, "The Lion Prince and Related Remarks on Northern History," *Journal of the Siam Society* 64, no. 1 (Jan. 1976), 373–374.
79. Baker and Pasuk, *History of Ayutthaya*, 34.
80. Hans Penth, *A Brief History of Lānnā: Northern Thailand from Past to Present* (Chiang Mai: Silkworm Books, 2000), 12. On the Buddhist literature of Lānnā, see Daniel M. Veidlinger, *Spreading the Dhamma: Writing, Orality, and Textual Transmission in Buddhist Northern Thailand* (Honolulu: University of Hawai'i Press, 2006).
81. Oskar von Hinüber, *A Handbook of Pāli Literature* (Berlin: Walter de Gruyter, 2000), 5.
82. McGovern, "Brahmā."
83. Pollock, *Language of the Gods*, 380–397.
84. Ibid., 386; Collins, "What Is Literature in Pali?," 649; Gornall, *Rewriting Buddhism*, 3–5.
85. Andrew J. Nicholson, *Unifying Hinduism: Philosophy and Identity in Indian Intellectual History* (New York: Columbia University Press, 2010); Elaine M. Fisher, *Hindu Pluralism: Religion and the Public Sphere in Early Modern South India* (Berkeley: University of California Press, 2017).
86. Among the oldest examples of Siamese literature we find repeated examples. The *Ōngkān Chāng Nām* begins with invocations to Viṣṇu and Śiva and includes a cosmogony derived in part from the Purāṇas. Michael Wright, *Ong-kan Chaeng Nam* (Bangkok: Matichon, 2000), 105, 111, 115. The *Yuan Phāi* begins with an invocation of Brahmā, Viṣṇu, and Śiva, the three members of the Purāṇic *trimūrti*. Chris Baker and Pasuk Phongpaichit, trans. and eds., *Yuan Phai, the Defeat of Lanna: A Fifteenth-Century Thai Epic Poem* (Chiang Mai: Silkworm Books, 2017), 16. And the *Dvādaśamāsa* likewise begins in its first three verses by invoking Brahmā, Viṣṇu, and Śiva, respectively. Chris Baker and Pasuk Phongpaichit, trans. and eds., *Kings in Love: Lilit Phra Lo and Twelve Months, Two Classic Thai Poems* (Chiang Mai: Silkworm Books, 2020), 207–208.
87. McGovern, "Brahmā," 20.
88. Reynolds, "Ramayana, Rama Jataka, and Ramakien."
89. The *Yuan Phāi*, for example, compares the king to Bhīma, Arjuna, and Kṛṣṇa, three of the Pāṇḍava brothers in the *Mahābhārata*. Baker and Pasuk, *Yuan Phai*, 28–29.
90. McGovern, "Balancing the Foreign and the Familiar."

Chapter 4

1. Many languages across Southern Asia use Sanskrit words for prestige vocabulary and thus chose a Sanskrit word to translate *religion*, but which word they chose differs wildly. Many South Asian languages, including Hindi, use the word *dharma*. Burmese uses *bhāṣā*. Thai, Lao, and Khmer use *śāsana*. Sinhala and Malay/Indonesian, on the other hand, use *āgama*, which, as we will see, was instead used to translate *magic* in Thai!
2. J. T. Jones, *The Gospel of Matthew: พระคฤษวงษโดยมัดชาย*, 2nd ed. (n.p., 1839), 11.
3. On the complex history of concepts relating to the modern concept of "the sacred," see Émile Benveniste, "The 'Sacred,'" in *Dictionary of Indo- European Concepts and Society*, trans. Elizabeth Palmer (Chicago: Hau Books, 2016 [1969]), 453– 476. Many Indo- European languages, like English, have two words. English *sacred* comes from Latin *sacer*, which referred to that which was set apart for the gods, while *holy* comes (via German *heilig*) from Gothic *hails*, which referred to health or prosperity.
4. J. T. Jones, *คำภีรมงคลโอวาทอันสำแดงคำสัญาใหม่ ซึ่งพระเยซูคริศเจ้า ให้ประกาษไว้แก่มนุษทั้งปวง แปลออกจากภาษาเฮเลนเปนภาษาไท The New Testament: Translated from the Greek*, 2nd ed. (Bangkok: Union Press, 1850), v; Harald Krahl, "The History of the Translation of the First Siamese Bible" (master's thesis, Columbia International University, 2005), 45, 77.
5. I thank Arthid Sheravanichkul for sharing this information.

6. Baker and Pasuk, *History of Ayutthaya*, 161–170.
7. When discussing this fact with my wife, Nanda Raksakhom, she rightly pointed out that La Loubère may not have translated *sancta* in this context because he considered it to be a fixed title and thus part of Mary's name (just as one can say "Saint Mary" in English). I acknowledge that this could be the case, but it is still telling that La Loubère did not attempt to translate it (the English translation of the *Ave Maria* after all does translate it, as "Holy Mary"); moreover, the next example, in which "holy spirit" is left untranslated, is less amenable to such an explanation because the "holy spirit" is not generally treated as a name.
8. Simone de La Loubère, *A New Historical Relation of the Kingdom of Siam*, trans. A. P. Gen. R. S.S. (London: T. Horne, 1693), 2: 260.
9. E. Hutchinson, "The Earliest Translation of the Gospel into Siamese," *Journal of the Siam Society* 28, no. 2 (1935): 199.
10. Luke 1:15. Vulgate text at "The Latin Vulgate New Testament Bible," vulgate.org, last accessed Jan. 29, 2021.
11. Chris Baker and Pasuk Phongpaichit, trans. and eds., *The Tale of Khun Chang Khun Phaen* (Chiang Mai: Silkworm Books, 2010), 881–910.
12. The most important of these extracanonical texts are *tamnān* (ตำนาน), or local histories, to be distinguished from the official dynastic histories of Ayutthayā that began with the Luang Prasoet Chronicle in the seventeenth century. The *tamnān* genre has been described in detail by Charnvit Kasetsiri, *The Rise of Ayudhya: A History of Siam in the Fourteenth and Fifteenth Centuries* (Kuala Lumpur: Oxford University Press, 1976), 1–11. Their use as historical sources has been criticized by Michael Vickery, "A New *Tāṃnān* about Ayudhya," *Journal of the Siam Society* 67, no. 2 (July 1979): 123–186. For our purposes, historical accuracy is not an issue; the biggest problem is that *tamnān* are often of uncertain date, and many of those known to be of some antiquity do not come from Siam proper.
13. The word *saksit* is a bit of an exception insofar as it is used quite commonly in modern spoken Thai. That is reflective of the fact that it is, in a sense, a "frozen" *kham sǭn* form that has been given a unique meaning independently of its first element—in this case, "holy," which can be expressed in modern Thai only as *saksit*, not as *sak* (ศักดิ์), which is not generally used by itself, nor for that matter as *sit* (สิทธิ์), which has the entirely different meaning of "right" (as in "human rights").
14. In the pages that follow, I will repeatedly be referring to instances of various words that I have found in Siamese literature through searches of digitized texts found on vajirayana.org. Although these digitized texts are taken from printed editions, unfortunately the original page numbers have not been preserved, and I do not in general have access to the particular printed edition used. In addition, there are many printed editions of most of the texts cited here, so page numbers from a particular printed edition will be of limited use for those seeking to check the references. The best way to check the references is to simply search for the word in the digitized version provided by vajirayana.org, as I have done. In some cases, the text has been given standardized verse or chapter numbers. When that is the case, I will provide them in order to narrow searches. The five instances of *sitthisak* in the *Phra Lǭ* are at vv. 53, 101, 150, 152, and 305; the one instance in the *Samudraghoṣa* is in chapter 2; and the one instance in the *Dutsadī Sangwǭi* is in v. 26. *Süa Khǭ* does not have verse or chapter numbers.
15. *Phra Lǭ* v. 364; *Kham Chan Klǭm Chāng Khrang Krung Kao* v. 102.
16. *Nirāt Phrayā Mahānuphāp Pai Müang Cīn* does not have verse or chapter numbers.
17. There are a total of 186 instances of *sitthisak* in the *Rāmakian*. Many of them are part of a standard formula for referring to a *yakṣa* or *yakṣī*, of which the following verse from chapter 1 is an example: เมื่อนั้นหิรันต์สิทธิศักดิ์ยักษา. Aside from this stock formula, *sitthisak* is found in the *Rāmakian* in the following chapters: 1, 2, 3 (x2), 5, 6, 8 (x2), 9, 11, 12, 15, 16, 24, 25, 26 (x2), 29, 42, 44, 47, 48, 49 (x2), 52 (x2), 53, 59, 60 (x2), 61 (x2), 62 (x2), 64 (x3), 66 (x3), 70, 71, 72 (x2), 73, 74, 75, 77, 78, 79, 83, 87 (x2), 91, 93, 95, 99 (x2), 102, 103, 105, 106, 109, 112, 113 (x2), 116, 117 (x2). It is found in *Unnarut* in chapters 5, 13, 16 (x2), 17, 23, 26, 27 (x2), and 28 (x2). The *Phra Śrī Vijaya Jātaka* does not have chapter or verse numbers.
18. *Rāmakian* ch. 11.
19. *Nirāt Suphan* v. 80, 264; *Khōbut* ch. 4 (x2). The other texts do not have chapter or verse numbers.
20. *Singkraiphop* ch. 6 (x2), 7, 14, 17, 18; *Phra Aphaimani* chs. 11, 27, 31, 32 (x2), 41, 42, 43, 69, 75, 100, 107, 112, 115, 130; *Aphainurāt* does not have chapter or verse numbers.
21. *Sām Kok* ch. 26 (x4), 61 (x2), 64, 65, 69; *Inao* chs. 14, 35; *Sang Thǭng* chs. 1, 3; *Khāwī* ch. 1; *Khun Chāng Khun Phǣn* chs. 16, 28, 31.

22. *Rāmakian* chs. 6, 8, 25.
23. For a brief genealogy of the modern concept of the "sacred," see Smith, "Topography of the Sacred."
24. *Rāmakian* chs. 42, 64, 66, 71, 93; *Unnarut* ch. 28.
25. *Khamchan Klọ̄m Chāng Khrang Krung Kao* v. 102; *Rāmakian* chs. 1, 3, 8, 11, 12, 15, 44, 47, 52, 60 (x2), 61, 62 (x2), 64, 66, 72, 73, 78, 87, 95, 102, 105, 112, 113, 116, 117 (x2); *Unnarut* chs. 16, 17, 23, 26, 28; *Inao* chs. 13, 14 (x2), 20, 26 (x2); *Khāwī* ch. 4; *Khun Chāng Khun Phǣn* chs. 16, 30; *Khōbut* ch. 4 (x2); *Singkraiphop* chs. 7, 14; *Phra Aphaimanī* chs. 27, 32 (x2), 41, 43, 69, 100; *Aphainurāt* (no v. or ch. nos.); *Sangsinchai* ch. 2; *Sawatdi Raksā Khạm Klọ̄n* (no v. or ch. nos.).
26. While I will be using the word "supernatural" several times in this chapter, I want to emphasize that I use it purely as an etic term of convenience. The modern scientific worldview clearly marks certain claimed powers, beings, and phenomena as "supernatural"—that is, outside of the realm of what is actually physically possible—and we are all clearly aware of what those are. I do not mean to imply that "supernatural" is useful in any way for understanding the emic categories of premodern Siam, which would not necessarily have distinguished so rigidly between the ability to, say, fight well with a sword (what we would call a natural ability) and, say, imperviousness to bullets granted through an incantation (what we would call a supernatural power).
27. For citations of stock passages where the *iddhi*s are named, see the entry for *iddhi* in T. W. Rhys Davids and William Stede, eds., *Pali-English Dictionary* (London: Pali Text Society, 1921–1925), 121.
28. In addition to the extremely common formula already described, *yakṣas* and *yakṣīs* are also described as *sitthisak* in the *Rāmakian* in chs. 1, 8, 11, 12, 26 (x3), 42, 52, 60 (x2), 64, 66, 87, 91, 102, 112. See also *Unnarut* chs. 5, 26, 27; *Phra Śrī Vijaya Jātaka* (no v. or ch. nos.); *Singkraiphop* chs. 6, 7; *Phra Aphaimanī* ch. 27.
29. *Khamchan Dutsadī Sangwœ̄i* v. 26 (various gods); *Rāmakian* ch. 5 (Viṣṇu). The divine heroes Rāma and Lakṣmaṇa are described as *sitthisak* in *Rāmakian* ch. 70, as well as Lakṣmaṇa specifically in ch. 72, and Hanumān in ch. 78.
30. *Phra Lọ̄* v. 10, 152; *Nirāt Phrayā Mahānuphāp Pai Müang Cīn* (no v. or ch. nos.); *Rāmakian* ch. 11; *Unnarut* ch. 13; *Sām Kok* chs. 61, 64; *Inao* chs. 13, 14 (x2); *Khun Chāng Khun Pǣn* ch. 30; *Singkraiphop* chs. 14, 18; *Phra Aphaimanī* chs. 31, 32 (x3), 41, 88, 89, 102, 115, 127, 130; *Nirāt Müang Klǣng* (no v. or ch. nos.); *Nirāt Wat Cāo Fā* (no v. or ch. nos.); *Nirāt Suphan* (no v. or ch. nos.); *Phlēng Yāo Namatsakān Phra Bọrommathāt Nirāt Pai Trang* (no v. or ch. nos.); *Lōkkanit* v. 379; *Klōng Nirāt Phra Prathom* v. 78.
31. *Phra Lọ̄* v. 150; *Sām Kok* ch. 26; *Phra Aphaimanī* ch. 43.
32. *Rāmakian* chs. 70, 72.
33. *Singkraiphop* ch. 7.
34. *Rāmakian* ch. 49; *Phra Aphaimanī* ch. 112.
35. For a description of the various types of ritual specialists known as *mọ̄* in a modern village context, see Hayashi Yukio, "The Buddhism of Power and *Mo Tham* in Northeast Thailand," in *Practical Buddhism among the Thai-Lao: Religion in the Making of a Region* (Kyoto: Kyoto University Press, 2003), 196–296.
36. *Phra Lọ̄* v. 53.
37. *Sām Kok* ch. 26 (x2).
38. *Khāwī* ch. 1; *Phra Aphaimanī* chs. 42, 107.
39. *Rāmakian* chs. 5, 9, 52, 61, 74.
40. For the word *ākhom* used in tandem with *saksit*, see *Khāwī* ch. 1 and *Sawatdi Raksā Kham Klọ̄n* (no v. or ch. nos.). For the word *mantra* used in tandem with *saksit/sitthisak*, see *Phra Lọ̄* v. 53, 150; *Phra Aphaimanī* chs. 46, 88; *Khāwī* ch. 1; *Singkraiphop* chs. 7, 8.
41. แสง at *Rāmakian* ch. 71; ดาบ at *Khun Chāng Khun Phǣn* chs. 16, 28; ขรรค์ at *Khōbut* ch. 4 (x2); ศร at *Rāmakian* chs. 3, 9, 26, 53, 73, 116.
42. There are a variety of such indigenous peoples in the Malaysian Peninsula who are known by several names, many of them derogatory. The relatively small number who live in the far South of modern Thailand call themselves the Maniq. The term *ngọ* used in the story *Sang Thọ̄ng* is a slang term used in Thai based on the perception that the hair of the Maniq, which is tightly curled, resembles the hairs of a rambutan (Th. *ngọ*).
43. *Sang Thọ̄ng* chs. 1, 3.
44. Thus, for example, a common contemporary blessing is ขออำนาจคุณพระรัตนตรัย ตลอดจน**สิ่งศักดิ์สิทธิ์ทั้งหลาย**ในสากลโลกจงดลบันดาลให้ท่านและครอบครัวประสบแต่ความสุขความเจริญ, "May the power of the virtues of the Triple Gem, as well as of all holy things in the

entire world, bring it about that you and your family experience nothing but happiness and prosperity."

45. The Princess Maha Chakri Sirindhorn Anthropology Centre, "จารึกวัดช้างล้อม ด้านที่ 1," *จารึกในประเทศไทย* [Inscriptions in Thailand], https://db.sac.or.th/inscriptions/inscribe/image_detail/25715.
46. Prasert Ṇa Nagara and A. B. Griswold, *Epigraphic and Historical Studies* (Bangkok: Historical Society under the Royal Patronage of H.R.H. Princess Maha Chakri Sirindhorn, 1992), 234.
47. Princess Maha Chakri Sirindhorn Anthropology Centre, "จารึกลานเงินเสด็จพ่อพระยาสอย ด้านที่ 2," *จารึกในประเทศไทย* [Inscriptions in Thailand], https://db.sac.or.th/inscriptions/inscribe/image_detail/44.
48. The Vedic texts were composed beginning in the late second millennium BCE and continuing throughout much of the first millennium BCE, with the bulk of the literature known to Patañjali in 150 BCE. For a detailed analysis of the evidence, see Michael Witzel, "Tracing the Vedic Dialects," in *Dialects dans les littératures indo-aryennes: Actes du Colloque International organisé par UA 1058 sous les auspices du C.N.R.S. avec le suotien du College de France, de la Fondation Hugot du College de France, de l'Université de Paris III, du Ministre des Affaires Etrangères, Paris (Fondation Hugot) 16–18 Septembre 1986*, ed. Collette Caillat (Paris: College de France, Institut de Civilisation Indienne, 1989), 97–264. On the Śaiva Āgamas, which were written in the first millennium CE, see André Padoux, *The Hindu Tantric World: An Overview* (Chicago: University of Chicago Press, 2017), 31–32.
49. The only support for this reading that I am aware of is an alternative spelling of *saiyasāt* found in the *Cintāmaṇī*, the first treatise on Thai ever written, from the reign of King Nārāi. It begins the word with the Thai letters, not for Pali/Sanskrit *s* but for Sanskrit *ś* and *r* (thus, ไศรย- instead of ไสย-), which makes no difference for the Thai pronunciation but would appear to represent the Sanskrit equivalent of *seyya*, which is *śreyas*. See *Cintāmaṇī* bk. 1, searching for ไศรยสาตร.
50. George Coedès, *Recueil des inscriptions du Siam* (Bangkok: Bangkok Times Press, 1924), 1: 159, cited in Prasert and Griswold, *Epigraphic and Historical Studies*, 636n6.
51. คมกฤช อุ่ยเต็กเค่ง, "ผี พราหมณ์ พุทธ : ไสยศาสตร์ หมุดล่องหนและการเมืองไทย" [Spirit Religion, Brahmanism, and Buddhism in Thai Religion], *มติชนสุดสัปดาห์* (May 1, 2017 [2560]), https://www.matichonweekly.com/column/article_33527.
52. For a brief discussion of these three explanations, see Peter Skilling, "King, *Sangha*, and Brahmans: Ideology, Ritual and Power in Pre-modern Siam," in *Buddhism, Power, and Political Order*, ed. Ian Harris (London: Routledge, 2007), 209–210n28.
53. It is worth noting that the switch from *a* to *e* before double consonants in Pali is itself somewhat anomalous. See Wilhelm Geiger, *A Pāli Grammar*, trans. Batakrishna Ghosh, ed. K. R. Norman (Oxford: Pali Text Society, 1994), 7.
54. This still leaves the problem of the omission of the long *ā* vowel at the end of the first element of the compound. Thai, however, is incredibly loose about the way it renders the final vowel of Sanskrit/Pali words. It is not uncommon, for example, to see masculine words that should end in *-a* instead rendered with *-ā*. An example is the word for "religion" in modern Thai, which comes from the Sanskrit word *śāsana* but is rendered *śāsanā* (ศาสนา).
55. This is an older way of referring to Buddhism. In modern Thai, the standard way of referring to Buddhism is either *sātsanā phut* (ศาสนาพุทธ) or *phutthasātsanā* (พุทธศาสนา). The former follows the pattern for the names of all "world religions" in modern Thai, while the latter is a Sanskrit compound, used uniquely for Buddhism. While *phutthasātsanā* is pronounced differently from the older word *phutthasāt*, the etymological difference is negligible. Both are Sanskritic compounds; in *phutthasātsanā*, the second element is (in Sanskrit) *śāsana*, while in *phutthasāt* it is *śāstra*. But these two Sanskrit words are both derived from the root *śās*, meaning "to instruct and/or discipline," and thus the two derivative nouns are quite similar in meaning.
56. A similar interpretation has been offered by none other than Buddhadāsa Bhikkhu, who, in an entire chapter devoted to criticizing the "superstition" he associates with *saiyasāt*, plays with the distinction between sleep and wakefulness implied by *saiyasāt* and *phutthasāt*. See Buddhadāsa Bhikkhu, *Seeing with the Eye of Dhamma*, trans. Dhammavidū Bhikkhu and Santikaro Upasaka (Boulder, CO: Shambhala, 2022), 94–115.
57. On this distinction, see Paul Williams and Anthony Tribe, *Buddhist Thought* (London: Routledge, 2000), 4.
58. *Rāmakian* ch. 10; *Singkraiphop* ch. 2; *Phra Aphaimanī* ch. 1.
59. *Rāmakian* chs. 1, 4, 7 (x3), 9 (x2), 10, 14 (x3), 105; *Unnarut* chs. 11, 12, 35, 42; *Rājādhirāja* chs. 6, 15; *Inao* ch. 11; *Khun Chāng Khun Phǣn* ch. 16; *Uthēn Khamchan* (no ch. or v. nos.).

60. *Rājādhirāja* chs. 6, 15; *Uthēn Khamchan* (no ch. or v. nos.).
61. *Manī Phichai* (no v. or ch. nos.); *Khāwī* ch. 2; *Singkraiphop* ch. 6 (x3); 7, 18; *Phra Aphaimanī* chs. 5, 6, 22; *Nirāt Müang Klāng* (no v. or ch. nos.).
62. Both the *Record of the Brahmans of Nakhọn Sī Thammarāt* (eighteenth century) and van Vliet's seventeenth-century history of Siam record a story in which Brahmans are sent to Ayutthayā by the king of a kingdom in India called Rāmarāja (รามราช). The identity of this kingdom is not clear, but I have argued that it may be Vijayanagara; see McGovern, "Balancing the Foreign and the Familiar," 291–292.
63. Ch. 6: พระว่าพี่นี้เป็นพราหมณ์รามราช รักษาชาติตามเวทข้างเพศไสย. Note that the use of the word ข้าง ("side") also implies that the word เพศ is setting up a binary.
64. Ch. 7: จึงลวงล่อขอวิชาพญายักษ์ สิทธิศักดิ์ทรงเวทตามเพศไสย.
65. Ch. 5: ดูท่วงทีกิริยามารยาท มิใช่ชาติพราหมณ์เทศข้างเพศไสย. Ch. 6: แล้วปลอบถามพราหมณ์น้อยกลอยสวาท เจ้ารู้สาตราเวทข้างเพศไสย.
66. Ch. 105: ตามตำราไสยเวทข้างเพศพราหมณ์. Ch. 127: ตามคัมภีร์ไสยเวทข้างเพศพราหมณ์.
67. ทวีโรจน์ กล่ำกล่อมจิตต์, *พราหมณ์สมอพลือ* [The Brahmans of Samọ̄ Phlū̆], ed. ล้อม เพ็งแก้ว (เพชรบุรี: เพชรภูมิการพิมพ์, 2556 [2013]), 103–106.
68. Aside from the inscription about to be discussed, it is also found in the *Cintāmaṇī* (bk. 1, spelled ไศรยสาตร) and the *Khamchan Klọ̄m Chāng Khrang Krung Kao* (v. 98).
69. Although the word *saiyasāt* is not found in the version of the *Phra Lọ̄* digitized by vajirayana.org, an alternate version uses the word in v. 139; see Baker and Pasuk, *Kings in Love,* 54.
70. As is typical for older texts, the spelling is inconsistent and "incorrect" by the standards of Pali or Sanskrit. It is clear, however, that the word being intended here is Sanskrit *śāsana* or its Pali equivalent, *sāsana*, not the word *śāstra* that is used in modern texts with standardized spelling. The discrepancy is understandable, however, and makes no difference to my argument in this chapter. First, in Thai *śāsana* or *sāsana* with a "killer" symbol over the *n* would be pronounced in exactly the same way as *śāstra*, that is, as *sāt.* Second, *śāsana* and *śāstra* come from the same verbal root, *śās*, and thus have similar meanings, even if they are used differently in Sanskrit literature. Given that the endings are not pronounced in Thai and variant spellings were common in older literature, this is a distinction without much effective difference.
71. Princess Maha Chakri Sirindhorn Anthropology Centre, "จารึกฐานพระอิศวรเมืองกำแพงเพชร ด้านที่ 1," *จารึกในประเทศไทย* [Inscriptions in Thailand], https://db.sac.or.th/inscriptions/inscribe/image_detail/26013.
72. Cushman, *Royal Chronicles of Ayutthaya*, 79, 189, 220, 229, 243.
73. Prasert and Griswold, *Epigraphic and Historical Studies*, 95 l. 4.
74. The word *āgama* has been used in many different contexts throughout the history of Sanskrit literature. In fact, in Buddhist traditions that preserved their scriptures in Sanskrit, it was used to refer to the four or five major divisions of the *Sūtra Piṭaka.* In the Pali tradition, however, it is more common to refer to the five divisions of the *Sutta Piṭaka* as *nikāyas*.
75. Padoux, *The Hindu Tantric World*, 16.
76. *Mārkaṇḍeya Purāṇa* 78–90, known as the *Devī Māhātmya.*
77. Davis, *Deathpower*, 215–216.
78. Ruth Streicher, "Imperialism, Buddhism and Islam in Siam: Exploring the Buddhist Secular in the Nangsue Sadaeng Kitchanukit, 1867," *Journal of Southeast Asian Studies* 52, no. 1 (Mar. 2021): 12–13.
79. John Leyden, *Comparative Vocabulary of the Barma, Maláyu and Thái Languages* (Serampore: Mission Press, 1810), 126; James Low, *A Grammar of the T,hai, or Siamese Language* (Calcutta: Baptist Mission Press, 1828), 75.
80. Streicher, "Imperialism, Buddhism and Islam in Siam," 13.
81. Ibid.
82. The digitized version on vajirayana.org does not have any subdivisions. Note when searching that the word *sātsanā* is in this book anomalously spelled สาศนา.
83. Streicher, "Imperialism, Buddhism and Islam in Siam," 19–20.
84. Jean-Baptiste Pallegoix, *สัพะ วะจะนะ พาสา ไท Dictionarium Linguae Thai* (Paris: Jussu Imperatoris Impressum, 1854), 8, 861, 49, respectively.
85. Ibid., 691.
86. Valerie I. J. Flint, *The Rise of Magic in Early Medieval Europe* (Princeton, NJ: Princeton University Press, 1991).
87. Cameron, *Enchanted Europe*, 196–210.

88. On the complex interplay between the categories "religion," "science," and "magic" in modern thought, see Randall Styers, *Making Magic: Religion, Magic, and Science in the Modern World* (New York: Oxford University Press, 2004).

Chapter 5

1. The term "animism" was coined by the nineteenth-century anthropologist E. B. Tylor, who presented his theory of a primitive religion called "animism" most fully in Edward B. Tylor, *Primitive Culture: Researches into the Development of Mythology, Philosophy, Religion, Language, Art, and Custom*, 2 vols. (London: John Murray, 1920). For a useful introduction to Tylor's theory of animism, see Daniel L. Pals, *Nine Theories of Religion*, 3rd ed. (New York: Oxford University Press, 2015), 15–48. For a critique of Tylor's theory of animism that places it within its historical context, see David Chidester, *Empire of Religion: Imperialism and Comparative Religion* (Chicago: University of Chicago Press, 2014), 91–123.
2. Cassaniti's *Living Buddhism* has provided an excellent critique recently of a similar tendency to dichotomize between "lived Buddhism" and elite or scholarly Buddhism. My critique here is rather of the tendency to dichotomize between Buddhism and "local religion," but both are manifestations of the same broad theme.
3. Robert Redfield, *Peasant Society and Culture: An Anthropological Approach to Civilization* (Chicago: University of Chicago Press, 1956); McKim Marriott, "Little Communities in an Indigenous Civilization," in *Village India: Studies in the Little Community*, ed. McKim Marriott (Chicago: University of Chicago Press, 1955), 171–222.
4. James R. Chamberlain, "The Origin of the Southwestern Tai," *Bulletin des Amis du Royaume Lao*, nos. 7–8 (1972): 233–244.
5. These cognates, which are present in basic proto-Tai roots and can be discerned only by comparison to Old and Middle Chinese, are to be distinguished from recent loanwords from southern Chinese dialects (such as Hokkien) into Siamese Thai, which are the result of contact with Chinese merchants and immigrant communities in the Ayutthayā and Bangkok periods. For a list of the latter, see Gong Qunhu 龔群虎, *Han-Tai guanxici de shijian cengci* 漢泰關係詞的時間層次 [Temporal Layers in Han-Tai Connecting Words] (Shanghai: Fudan daxue chubanshe, 2002), 257–280.
6. Prapin Manomaivibool, "A Study of Sino-Thai Lexical Correspondences" (PhD dissertation, University of Washington, 1975), 303–356.
7. Gong, *Han-Tai guanxici*, 282–358.
8. Pitayawat Pittayaporn, "Layers of Chinese Loanwords in Proto-Southwestern Tai as Evidence for the Dating of the Spread of Southwestern Tai," *MANUSYA: Journal of Humanities*, special issue no. 20 (2014): 63–64.
9. Baker and Pasuk, *History of Ayutthaya*, 24–26.
10. David Holm, "A Layer of Old Chinese Readings in the Traditional Zhuang Script," *Bulletin of the Museum of Far Eastern Antiquities* 1 (2014): 33.
11. Ibid., 34.
12. Gong, *Han-Tai guanxici*, 321. Throughout I will be transliterating all Chinese characters in pinyin according to their modern Mandarin pronunciation, by which they are most commonly known. At times the resemblance to the modern Thai cognate will be clear, but of course comparative linguists have determined these cognates on the basis of proto-Tai and Old/Middle Chinese pronunciations.
13. Georges Condominas, *From Lawa to Mon, from Saa' to Thai: Historical and Anthropological Aspects of Southeast Asian Social Spaces*, trans. Stephanie Anderson, Maria Magannon, and Gehan Wijeyawardene, ed. Gehan Wijeyawardene (Canberra: Department of Anthropology, Research School of Pacific Studies, Australian National University, 1990), 90, notes the transition from *müang* as an alliance of agricultural villages to a more urbanized situation where the *müang* is capital of a city-state.
14. Prapin, "A Study of Sino-Thai," 304; Gong, *Han-Tai guanxici*, 357.
15. Wyatt, *Thailand*, 7.
16. Prapin, "A Study of Sino-Thai," 318; Gong, *Han-Tai guanxici*, 311.
17. Prapin, "A Study of Sino-Thai," 307; Gong, *Han-Tai guanxici*, 287.

18. A. B. Griswold and Prasert ṇa Nagara, "Epigraphic and Historical Studies, No. 17: The Judgments of King Măṅ Rāy," *Journal of the Siam Society* 65, no. 1 (1977): 147–148, cited by Baker and Pasuk, *History of Ayutthaya*, 42n118.
19. Princess Maha Chakri Sirindhorn Anthropology Centre, "จารึกกฎหมายลักษณะโจร," *จารึกในประเทศไทย* [Inscriptions in Thailand], https://db.sac.or.th/inscriptions/inscribe/detail/118. Prasert and Griswold, *Epigraphic and Historical Studies*, 109–144, argue that this is an Ayutthayan inscription, and thus that reference to numerical ranks is simply reflective of the Ayutthayan system and not the system practiced in Sukhōthai, which they take to be more egalitarian. Vickery, on the other hand, argues, convincingly to my mind, that this inscription is reflective of Sukhōthai policy and that any resemblance to Ayutthayan law is reflective of influence in the other direction. Michael Vickery, "The Constitution of Ayutthaya," http://michaelvickery.org/vickery1996constitution.pdf, 6, 53–54.
20. Vickery, "Constitution of Ayutthaya," 51–52.
21. For a detailed exposition of the *sakdinā* system in its latest, most developed form, in early Bangkok, see Akhin Rabibhadana, *The Organization of Thai Society in the Early Bangkok Period, 1782–1873* (Ithaca, NY: Southeast Asia Program, Department of Asian Studies, Cornell University, 1969), 77–122.
22. Vickery, "Constitution of Ayutthaya," 54–56.
23. Steven Collins, *Selfless Persons: Imagery and Thought in* Theravāda *Buddhism* (Cambridge: Cambridge University Press, 1982), 103–104, 213–214.
24. Tambiah, *Buddhism and the Spirit Cults*, 223–251; Junko Iida, "Tying the Hand: Life-Sustaining Technique in Northern Thailand," *Asia* 71, no. 1 (2017): 305–326; Nancy Eberhardt, *Imagining the Course of Life: Self-Transformation in a Shan Buddhist Community* (Honolulu: University of Hawai'i Press, 2006), 28–45.
25. Farzeen Baldrian-Hussein, "*Hun* and *po*," in *The Encyclopedia of Taoism*, ed. Fabrizio Pregadio (Oxford: Routledge, 2008), 1: 521–523. For a study of an early, Han Dynasty ritual to "summon" the wayward *hún* back to the body at death, see also Ying-Shih Yü, "'O Soul, Come Back!' A Study in the Changing Conceptions of the Soul and Afterlife in Pre-Buddhist China," *Harvard Journal of Asiatic Studies* 47, no. 2 (Dec. 1987): 363–395.
26. For this very reason, it is tempting to hypothesize that the words *phī* and *pò* are cognates, but they are not. The Middle Chinese form of *pò* is *phaek*, and the Old Chinese reconstruction is **pʰˤrak*. Both forms end with a velar stop that could easily be reproduced in Tai phonology but conspicuously is not in the word *phī*. See William H. Baxter and Laurent Sagart, "Baxter-Sagart Old Chinese reconstruction, version 1.1," http:// ocb axte rsag art.lsait.lsa.umich.edu/BaxterSagartOCbyMandarinMC2014-09-20.pdf, 83.
27. The number thirty-two, in fact, almost certainly comes not from Chinese but from Indian culture, via the Pali *imaginaire*. Thirty-two is considered to be an auspicious number in Indian thought. There are thirty-two gods (plus Indra) in Tāvatiṃsa Heaven, there are thirty-two marks of a Great Man (*mahāpurisa*), and the total number of levels in the Abhidhamma cosmology is thirty-one (*nibbāna* implicitly bringing the total to thirty-two). See Gethin, *Foundations of Buddhism*, 126.
28. Ibid., 271–279; Hayashi, *Practical Buddhism*, 196–303.
29. Condominas, *From Law to Mon*, 68–69.
30. Prapin, "A Study of Sino-Thai," 328; Gong, *Han-Tai guanxici*, 342.
31. เสฐียร โกเศศ, *เมืองสวรรค์และผีสางเทวดา* [The Heavenly City and *Phī Sāng Devatā*] (n.p.: แพร่พิทยา, 2503 [1960]), 321–323.
32. I have seen *tǔdì gōng* shrines as niches in the exterior walls of individual homes in the New Territories of Hong Kong.
33. British Broadcasting Corporation, *The Long Search 11: Taoism—A Question of Balance* (New York: Time-Life Media, 1978), 8:30.
34. The procedure for propitiating a deity, whether a *tǔdì gōng* or a god in a community temple, for boons in the Chinese world is similar to *kānbonbānsānklāo* in Thailand in being *do ut des* and cash-on-delivery; however, Chinese worshipers make use of an additional technology of propitiation that is not found in Thailand. This is called *jiǎobēi* (筊杯), often referred to as "moon blocks" in English, which are a pair of wooden blocks, each in a roughly half-moon shape, with one side flat and the other side rounded. The supplicant asks the deity a question and then throws the two blocks to the ground like dice. If one block has the flat side up and the other the rounded side up, the answer is yes. If both have the rounded side up, the answer is no. And

if both have the flat side up, such that the blocks are rocking on their rounded side, the answer is "laughing," which can be interpreted in a variety of ways. *Jiăobēi* can be used for a variety of divinatory purposes, but in the context of asking for a boon, they allow the worshiper to negotiate with the deity up front over the terms of the transaction rather than simply promising an offering for a boon and simply waiting to see if the deity follows through.

35. เสฐียร, *เมืองสวรรค์และผีสางเทวดา* [The Heavenly City and *Phī Sāng Devatā*], 323–324.
36. The phenomenon of *lak müang* shrines across the Tai world has been studied by B. J. Terwiel, "The Origin and Meaning of the Thai 'City Pillar,'" *Journal of the Siam Society* 66, no. 2 (1978): 159–171. For a brief description of the Bangkok City Pillar shrine, see Guelden, *Into the Spirit World*, 89–91.
37. Terwiel, "Origin and Meaning of the Thai 'City Pillar,'" 163–164.
38. Gong, *Han-Tai guanxici*, 321.
39. Prapin, "A Study of Sino-Thai," 347.
40. เสฐียร, *เมืองสวรรค์และผีสางเทวดา* [The Heavenly City and *Phī Sāng Devatā*], 347–349.
41. Gong, *Han-Tai guanxici*, 331.
42. เสฐียร, *เมืองสวรรค์และผีสางเทวดา* [The Heavenly City and *Phī Sāng Devatā*], 332.
43. Terwiel, "Origin and Meaning of the Thai 'City Pillar,'" 167.
44. Prapin, "A Study of Sino-Thai," 308.
45. Some scholars have argued that the Rāmkhamhǣng inscription is a fake, although this theory has not gained wide acceptance. Vickery, one of the foremost proponents of the theory that it was faked, in particular points to the passage I am about to discuss as an example of possible copying from other inscriptions from the Sukhōthai corpus: Michael Vickery, "Piltdown 3: Further Discussion of the Ram Khamhaeng Inscription," *Journal of the Siam Society* 83 (1995): 162–165. Although I do not subscribe to the theory that the Rāmkhamhǣng inscription is a fake, my argument is not seriously impeded even if it is, given that its treatment of *phī* is consonant with that of other Sukhōthai inscriptions that I will discuss below.
46. The word *khun* (ขุน) later in Siamese history became a middling title of nobility, but here it is a synonym for a *cāo müang*. As I will discuss below, it appears to have borrowed from a Chinese title.
47. Princess Maha Chakri Sirindhorn Anthropology Centre, "จารึกพ่อขุนรามคำแหง ด้านที่ 3," *จารึกในประเทศไทย* [Inscriptions in Thailand], https://db.sac.or.th/inscriptions/inscribe/image_detail/50.
48. Princess Maha Chakri Sirindhorn Anthropology Centre, "จารึกวัดช้างล้อม ด้านที่ 2," *จารึกในประเทศไทย* [Inscriptions in Thailand], https://db.sac.or.th/inscriptions/inscribe/image_detail/25716. Translation of this passage is made difficult by the fact that a variety of familial terms are used in the list, but the syntax does not always make it clear to whom their familial relationship is defined. In addition, the nature of what specific action toward the *phī* is being described in this passage is somewhat ambiguous. The verb used is *yǭ*, spelled here ญ but in modern Thai as ยอ, which means "to lift up," thus my translation "exalt." I am attempting to be somewhat literal with this translation to preserve the ambiguity, but probably what is implied is some sort of worship. The word *yǭ* is often used in the phrase *yǭ kǭn* (ยอกร), which literally means to "lift up hands" but is a synonym of the word *wai* (ไหว้), which refers to the common sign of respect in Thai and many Southern Asian cultures of pressing one's palms together. When the object of the *wai* is a supernatural being or Buddha image, then worship is implied. Griswold and Prasert, on the other hand, translate *yǭ* as "help," which strikes me as neither particularly clear nor particularly close to the word's literal meaning: Griswold and Prasert, *Epigraphic and Historical Studies*, 238.
49. Assuming the emendation is correct, the word here would correspond to Sanskrit *ārakṣa*.
50. The word is *pū* (modern Thai ปู่), which is the paternal grandfather. The notes for this passage in the Inscriptions in Thailand Database (cited below) indicate that this word, which is repeated throughout the list of ancestors that follows, is used instead of the word *phǭ* (พ่อ), which literally means "father." In either case, the word used as a prefix in this way is not meant literally, but simply as a sign of seniority.
51. "Ancestral spirits" here translates *dam phong* (ดำพงศ). The word *dam* (ด้ำ in modern Thai) refers to supernatural beings akin to *phī*, while *phong* is the Sanskrit word *vaṃśa*, for "lineage."
52. This reading is uncertain; I am following the reading into modern Thai given by the Inscriptions in Thailand Database. For a discussion of this phrase, see Griswold and Prasert, *Epigraphic and Historical Studies*, 86n21.

53. Princess Maha Chakri Sirindhorn Anthropology Centre, "จารึกปู่ขุนจิดขุนจอด ด้านที่ 1," *จารึกในประเทศไทย* [Inscriptions in Thailand], https://db.sac.or.th/inscriptions/inscribe/image_detail/24717.
54. For a description of this ceremony, see Wales, *Siamese State Ceremonies*, 193–198.
55. For a discussion of the meaning and significance of this name/title, which they translate as "Old Lord Tiger Spirit," see Baker and Pasuk, *Kings in Love*, 188–189.
56. V. 144: หากันมาแต่ป่า มาแต่ท่าแต่น้ำ มาแต่ถ้ำคูหา.
57. See Gethin, *The Foundations of Buddhism*, 112–132.
58. In modern Thai, this word means "butterfly," but in older texts it refers (as the name suggests) to a type of *phī*. The reason why the word came to be used to refer to butterflies is unclear, but I suspect it has to do with the fact that butterflies emerge (with wings, no less!) from the "death" of caterpillars. This might evoke the emergence of *phī süa* from the deaths of ancestors, since, as I will discuss below, the descriptor *süa* appears to mark this type of *phī* as an ancestral spirit.
59. The other two are hell and the animal realm. These three *dugati*s are correlated with the three poisons: greed (*lobha*) with hungry ghosts, anger (*dosa*) with hell, and delusion (*moha*) with animals.
60. *Traibhūmikathā* ch. 3. Note that as of June 2021, when I accessed the website, there is an error involving the reduplication of lines in the digital version of this passage on varjirayana.org; I have emended it to eliminate the reduplication here.
61. *Jūjaka Kaṇḍha*: ทุยิฏฐนฺเต นวมิยํ ยุยวแม่บูชาผีเก้าค่ำ กาเถ้าพร่ำมากิน ก่อนฤๅ; ปนุถสกุณํ ยชิสฺสามิ ก็จะให้เป็นพลี บูชาผีที่ป่านี้. *Kumāra Kaṇḍha*: ปพฺพตานิ วนานิ จ อีกเขาถ้ำน้ำเถื่อน ผีฟ้าเกลื่อนกลางหาว อยู่นั้นน. (Here and below semicolons divide separate passages.) These passages refer to the worship of low-level but seemingly benevolent spirits.
62. *Vanapraveśana Kaṇḍha*: อมนุสฺเส จ เภรวสทฺเทมิคปกฺขิโน จ ปฏิกฺกมาเปตฺวา อันว่าพระพิศวกรรม ก็ยงง**ไปศาจผีเสื้อ**เนื้อแลนก อันมีเสียงต่รดกพึงภึ่ต บมิให้กึ๋ดให้ก้อง บมิให้ร้องระงี่มี่ระงม ก็ขับหนีจากอาศรม พระศรีสรรเพ็ชญ์ ที่ท้าวธเสด็จอยู่นั้นน. *Kumāra Kaṇḍha*: มํ เอว แต่น้อยนารถชาลิ พฺราหฺมณสฺส แก่พราหมณ์**ผีเผ่ายักษ์**; **ยกฺโข** พฺราหฺมณวณฺเณน เถ้านี้รอย**ผีเสื้อ** เยียอเคื้อคูคนดีไส้ พ่ออา ข่าทิตุํ ตาต เนติ โน ภาตูไป่เปนภักษ์ มนนจะหักคอกินเลือดแล นียมานา **ปีสาเจน** เถ้ามราญควาน**ผี**ปั่ง ท้าวธอย่าส่งตูไปรา พ่ออา. *Mahārāja Kaṇḍha*: นียมานา **ปีสาเจน** บพิตร ท้าวธบเอ็นดูตูผู้ลูก ละ**ผี**ผูกเผือไป บอยู่เลอย; **มหาภูต**คณาลโย ที่ฝูงมารฝูงมาหทงง**ผีห่าผีเหว ผีท้องเลว**หลายภาค อารักษ์มากนานา. *Chakkhattiya Kaṇḍha*: อติวิย ปมาณาติกฺกนฺตสฺส เถ้ากลีลาภโลภ แบมือลโมบมักได้ สมพยาธิไร้รูปร่าง พ่างบรางควานผีป่า **ผีภูต** ห่าเหวโหง ขึ้นจับโลงเหลือกตาหลอกลูก ตูแล ฯ. (Note, however, that this last *kaṇḍha* was rewritten in the early Bangkok period.)
63. In this respect, Siamese Buddhist discourse accomplished through the mere act of translation much the same goal as did Tibetan Buddhist discourse more dramatically with the story of Padmasambhava subjugating local spirits so that Buddhism could be established in the country. See, for example, Matthew T. Kapstein, *The Tibetans* (Maiden, MA: Blackwell, 2006), 111.
64. Princess Maha Chakri Sirindhorn Anthropology Centre, "จารึกวัดศรีชุม ด้านที่ 1," *จารึกในประเทศไทย* [Inscriptions in Thailand], https://db.sac.or.th/inscriptions/inscribe/image_detail/25594. See Griswold and Prasert, *Epigraphic and Historical Studies*, 381.
65. On the widespread existence of this origin myth among the Tai, with Khun Borom, son of the *thǣn*, becoming the progenitor of the major Tai ethnic groups, see Condominas, *From Lawa to Mon*, 37, 43–44.
66. Souneth Phothisane, "The Nidān Khun Borom: Annotated Translation and Analysis" (PhD dissertation, University of Queensland, 1996), 29.
67. Ibid., 123–124.
68. Ibid., 130n154.
69. David Wyatt, *Thailand: A Short History*, 2nd ed. (Chiang Mai: Silkworm Books, 2003), 9.
70. The juxtaposition of Cātummahārājika as the residence of the *phī thǣn* and Indra as their leader is a bit confusing from the perspective of Pali Buddhist cosmology. The eponymous "four great kings" of Cātummahārājika are the four *lokapāla*s, who guard the four cardinal directions and lead armies of lower-level supernatural creatures. In the North is Vessavaṇa, king of the *yakkha*s. In the South is Virūḷhaka, king of the *kumbhanda*s. In the East is Dhataratțha, king of the *gandhabba*s. And in the West is Virūpakkha, king of the *nāga*s. Situating the *phī thǣn* in this, the very lowest of the heavenly worlds in Pali Buddhist cosmology, is thus somewhat consonant with the trend to associate *phī* with creatures low in the cosmic hierarchy, such as *yakkha*s, in texts like the *Mahāchāt Kham Luang*. Indra, however, known more commonly as Sakka in Pali texts, is king of the gods in the *next* highest heaven, Tāvatiṃsa, the Heaven of the Thirty-Three.

On the other hand, Pali texts sometimes refer to Sakka as a *yakkha*, and the "confusion" between categories here may be a feature of ambiguity present already in the Pali tradition. On this latter point, see the entry on *yakkha* in Rhys Davids and Stede, *Pali-English Dictionary*, 546. On the general ambiguity between different categories of supernatural beings in early Buddhist texts, see also DeCaroli, *Haunting the Buddha*.

71. To be clear, even today the word *phī* can be and sometimes is used in its older sense to refer to any of the more benevolent sorts of spirits described in this section. Nevertheless, the *tendency* is toward using it more exclusively to refer to malevolent "ghosts." Certainly, that is the image that first comes to mind when bringing up the topic of *phī*.
72. Anuman Rajadhon, *Popular Buddhism in Siam and Other Essays on Thai Studies* (Bangkok: Thai Inter- Religious Commission for Development and Sathirakoses Nagapradipa Foundation, 1986), 103–124.
73. Ibid., 113–114; Marlane Guelden, *Thailand: Into the Spirit World* (Bangkok: Asia Books, 1995), 117–119.
74. For a brief description of the significance of Mā̃ Nāk in Thai culture, see Guelden, *Into the Spirit World*, 77–81. For a scholarly analysis of the mythology and praxis surrounding Mā̃ Nāk and her ultimate defeat by Somdet Tō, see McDaniel, *Lovelorn Ghost*.
75. See Guelden, *Into the Spirit World*, 74–75.
76. Anuman Rajadhon, *Popular Buddhism in Siam*, 120–121.
77. Ibid., 130–131.
78. *Khun Chāng Khun Phā̃n* chs. 2, 6, 16, 20, 30.
79. Traditional Thai houses were built of wood and elevated on posts so as to allow floodwaters to flow under them during the rainy season.
80. *Khun Chāng Khun Phā̃n* ch. 12. For a translation, see Baker and Pasuk, *Khun Chang Khun Phaen*, 246–248. For the modern description of the ritual, see Terwiel, *Monks and Magic*, 142–152, cited by Baker and Pasuk, *Khun Chang Khun Phaen*, 246n8.
81. Anuman Rajadhon, *Popular Buddhism*, 131.
82. Georges Condominas, "*Phībān* Cults in Rural Laos," in *Change and Persistence in Thai Society: Essays in Honor of Lauriston Sharp*, ed. G. William Skinner and A. Thomas Kirsch (Ithaca, NY: Cornell University Press, 1975), 254n6; Michael Moerman, "Ban Ping's Temple: The Center of a 'Loosely Structured' Society," in *Anthropological Studies in Theravada Buddhism*, by Manning Nash (New Haven, CT: Southeast Asian Studies, Yale University, 1966), 138. Note, however, that shrines outside of homes in urban areas are now found in Laos; see John Clifford Holt, *Spirits of the Place: Buddhism and Lao Religious Culture* (Honolulu: University of Hawai'i Press, 2009), 18. This may be due to influence from Thailand.
83. Anuman Rajadhon, *Popular Buddhism*, 131; Terwiel, *Monks and Magic*, 171–172. There are many popular manuals about Phra Phūm in Thailand; an example is แก้ว สุพรรโณ, *ศาลพระภูมิ: เกร็ดความรู้และแนวปฏิบัติบูชาศาลพระภูมิเพื่อให้เกิดสิริมงคลแก่ทุกคนในครอบครัว* [Shrines to Phra Phūm: Bits of Knowledge and the Method for Worshiping Phra Phūm to Create Auspiciousness for Everyone in the Family] (กรุงเทพฯ: สำนักพิมพ์ไพลิน, 2545 [2002]).
84. Versions of the myth of Vāmana defeating Bali can be found throughout the Purāṇas, including at *Bhāgavata Purāṇa* 8.18–8.23. A presumably early version can be found in canto 270 of book 3 (*Vana Parvan*) of the vulgate of the *Mahābhārata*, but not in the Critical Edition. For an English translation of the myth, see Cornelia Dimmit and J. A. B. van Buitenen, eds. and trans., *Classical Hindu Mythology: A Reader in the Sanskrit Purāṇas* (Philadelphia: Temple University Press, 1978), 80–82. The myth is an elaboration of the early reference to Viṣṇu's three strides at *RV* 1.22.18.
85. Eveline Porée- Maspero, "Krŏṅ Pāli et rites de la maison (Suite)," *Anthropos* 56, nos. 3–4 (1961): 548–628; Eveline Porée- Maspero, "Krŏṅ Pāli et rites de la maison (Suite et fin)," *Anthropos* 56, nos. 5–6 (1961): 883–929.
86. Nāng Thǫranī, her name taken from the Sanskrit *dharaṇī*, which means "earth," is a figure found in popular versions of the tale of the Buddha's Awakening in Theravāda Southeast Asia. When the Bodhisatta calls upon the earth to witness to his virtue in the face of Māra's assault, the earth, in anthropomorphic form as Nāng Thǫranī, actually washes away Māra's army by wringing a flood of water from her long hair. This scene is a popular theme of Buddhist art in Thailand and surrounding questions. For a study of Nāng Thǫranī, see Elizabeth Guthrie, "A Study of the History and Cult of the Buddhist Earth Deity in Mainland Southeast Asia" (PhD dissertation, University of Canterbury, 2004).
87. Porée-Maspero, "Krŏṅ Pāli et rites de la maison (Suite et fin)," 884.

88. *Khun Chāng Khun Phǣn* chs. 2, 27, 34.
89. The Khmer word *kroṅ* can mean "king" or "city," but the cognate Thai word *krung* (กรุง) can mean only "city." The Thai version of the myth thus gives him a different name, Daśarāja, and says that he is king of "Krung Phālī"—thus making the latter the name of a city/kingdom rather than the supernatural being who is the object of offerings. As Terwiel (*Monks and Magic*, 173) notes, "The Cambodian honorific title *krŏṅ* may have been misunderstood by the Thais as referring to *krung*, 'city,' 'metropolis.'"
90. Anuman Rajadhon, *Popular Buddhism*, 124.
91. Condominas, "*Phībān* Cults," 258; Hayashi, *Practical Buddhism*, 93–95.
92. Anuman Rajadhon, *Popular Buddhism*, 106, 109–110.
93. For an exhaustive study of the worship of tree spirits in India, see David L. Haberman, *People Trees: Worship of Trees in Northern India* (New York: Oxford University Press, 2013).
94. Ames, "Magical-Animism and Buddhism"; Spiro, *Burmese Supernaturalism*; Terwiel, *Monks and Magic*, 5.
95. Tambiah, *Buddhism and the Spirit Cults*; Kirsch, "Complexity in the Thai Religious System."
96. Masuzawa, *Invention of World Religions*, 121–146.
97. Almond, *The British Discovery of Buddhism*, 24–28, 33–53; Schopen, "Archaeology and Protestant Presuppositions"; King, *Orientalism and Religion*, 143–160; Masuzawa, *Invention of World Religions*, 121–146.
98. McMahan, *Making of Buddhist Modernism*.
99. Anya P. Foxen, *Inhaling Spirit: Harmonialism, Orientalism, and the Western Roots of Modern Yoga* (New York: Oxford University Press, 2020), 44. My discussion of animism in this paragraph is heavily informed by the insights of Foxen in chapter 1 of her book, "Hot Souls, Pneumatic Bodies, and Interplanetary Journeys," 43–67.
100. Here I am inspired (pun intended) by Foxen when she writes that "ensouled anthropology [might] perhaps [be] better termed 'psychology' in its more original sense" (ibid., 46).
101. Ibid., 58.
102. Ibid., 45.
103. Ibid., 44.
104. DeCaroli, *Haunting the Buddha*; Cohen, "Nāga, Yakṣiṇī, Buddha."
105. This is in fact a simplification, given that Sanskritic discourses, as we saw in Chapter 3, also were operative throughout Southeast Asia, and as a result Indic vocabulary, even when it pertained directly to Buddhism, often was absorbed into Thai in its Sanskrit form.
106. Jean-François Bayart, *The Illusion of Cultural Identity*, trans. Steven Rendall, Janet Roitman, Cynthia Schoch, and Jonathan Derrick (Chicago: University of Chicago Press, 2005).

Chapter 6

1. This is the tentative reading provided by Griswold and Prasert, *Epigraphic and Historical Studies*, 82, 90n41.
2. Princess Maha Chakri Sirindhorn Anthropology Centre, "จารึกวัดศรีชุม ด้านที่ 2," *จารึกในประเทศไทย* [Inscriptions in Thailand], https://db.sac.or.th/inscriptions/inscribe/image_detail/25595.
3. Griswold and Prasert, *Epigraphic and Historical Studies*, 394n137, note that another possible interpretation is that the verb *praditsathān* (ประดิษฐาน, written ปรดิสถา in the inscription) should instead be taken to mean "restore," thus referring to the restoration of the temple in the present. I find this interpretation less likely because the normal meaning of *praditsathān* is to establish and not to restore.
4. *Traibhūmikathā* ch. 9: ในเจามเข้าไกฺรลาศนันแล ว่ามีเมืองอันนึงเทียรเยามเงิอนแลเทาง แลมีฝูงกิณรีอฺยูแหงนันบานเมืองแหงนั่นสนุกนินักหฺนา ดฺ่งงเมืองไตฺรตฺรึงสาสฺวรรค แลเมอง นันพฺระศปรเสฐร ธ อฺยูนันแล.
5. *Yuan Phāi* vv. 1, 32–33; *Dvādaśamāsa* vv. 1–3. The *Ōngkān Chǣng Nām* and *Bunnōwāt* do not have verse or chapter numbers.
6. *Yuan Phāi* vv. 34, 38–40.
7. Translated in Griswold and Prasert, *Epigraphic and Historical Studies*, 491.
8. Princess Maha Chakri Sirindhorn Anthropology Centre, "จารึกฐานพระอิศวรเมืองกำแพงเพชร ด้านที่ 1," *จารึกในประเทศไทย* [Inscriptions in Thailand], https://db.sac.or.th/inscriptions/inscribe/image_detail/26013.

9. Cushman, *Royal Chronicles*, 79.
10. Ibid., 189.
11. Ibid., 220.
12. Ibid., 223.
13. Ibid., 229.
14. Ibid., 243.
15. Chris Baker and Pasuk Phongpaichit, trans. and eds., *The Palace Law of Ayutthaya and the Thammasat: Law and Kingship in Thailand* (Ithaca, NY: Southeast Asia Program Publications, Cornell University, 2016), 108–111.
16. Baker and Pasuk, *History of Ayutthaya*, 229–230.
17. McGovern, "Balancing the Foreign and the Familiar," 288–290.
18. Van Vliet, *Short History*, 65–68.
19. *ตำนานพราหมณ์เมืองนครศรีธรรมราช* [Record of the Brahmans of Nakhọn Sī Thammarāt] (นครศรีธรรมราช: ศูนย์วัฒนธรรมภาคใต้ วิทยาลัยครูนครศรีธรรมราช, 2525 [1982]), 1–4.
20. The *Tamnān Phrām* does not specifically state that Rāmarāja is in India, but it is implied. Van Vliet (*Short History*, 65), however, states even more specifically that Rāmarāja is on the Coromandel coast. The identity of Rāmarāja is not clear, but I have argued that it may refer to Vijayanagara. See McGovern, "Balancing the Foreign and the Familiar," 292n40.
21. McGovern, "Balancing the Foreign and the Familiar," 291–292.
22. Bronkhorst, *Buddhism in the Shadow of Brahmanism*, 153–170.
23. Kanjana Suwanwong, "Ways of Life, Rituals and Cultural Identity of Court Brahmins in Thai Society: A Case Study of Bangkok Devasthan Botsbrahmana" (master's thesis, Chulalongkorn University, 2539 [1996]), 95–96; *จดหมายเหตุการบูรณปฏิสังขรณ์ เทวสถาน สำหรับพระนคร* [Record of the Restoration of the Devasthāna for Bangkok] (กรุงเทพ: เทวสถาน สำหรับพระนคร, 2557 [2014]), 17.
24. On this festival, see พระบาทสมเด็จพระจุลจอมเกล้าเจ้าอยู่หัว, *พระราชพิธีสิบสองเดือน* [The Royal Ceremonies of the Twelve Months] (กรุงเทพฯ: แสงดาว, 2556 [2013]), 106–128; Wales, *Siamese State Ceremonies*, 238–255; Priyawat Kuanpoonpol, "Court Brahmans of Thailand and the Celebration of the Brahmanic New Year," *Indo-Iranian Journal* 33, no. 1 (1990): 21–51; Nathan McGovern, "The Trīyampawāi-Trīppawāi of Thailand and the Tamil Traditions of Mārkaḻi," *Journal of the Siam Society* 108, no. 2 (2020): 123–148.
25. David Wyatt, *Studies in Thai History: Collected Articles* (Chiang Mai: Silkworm Books, 1994), 163.
26. The predominantly Śaiva orientation of the Thai Brahmans is suggested by the much larger size of the sanctuary for Śiva in their temple, as well as the fact that the Trīyampawāi, which is dedicated to Śiva, dominates in the Trīyampawāi-Trīppawāi festival, while the Vaiṣṇava Trīppawāi is much shorter and clearly a pale copy of the former. See McGovern, "Balancing the Foreign and the Familiar," 290.
27. Reynolds, "Ramayana, Rama Jataka, and Ramakien."
28. Christopher R. Austin, *Pradyumna: Lover, Magician, and Scion of the Avatāra* (New York: Oxford University Press, 2019), 76–78.
29. Wyatt, *Studies in Thai History*, 131–172.
30. Ibid., 156.
31. *กฎหมายตราสามดวง* [The Three Seals Law], พระราชกำหนดใหม่ 35. See *ประมวลกฎหมายรัชกาลที่ 1 จุลศักราช 1166 พิมพ์ตามฉะบับหลวงตรา 3 ดวง* [Collection of the Laws of the First Reign, *Chula* Era 1166, Printed According to the Royal Copy of the Three Seals] (กรุงเทพฯ: คณะนิติศาสตร์ มหาวิทยาลัยธรรมศาสตร์, 2529[1986]) 3: 420.
32. It is true that Rāma I uses the Sanskrit word *liṅga* as part of a larger phrase (เพศบุรุษลึง, lit., "sign of the male sex") to refer obliquely to a penis, which may be what confused Wyatt. Although in English we have a tendency to associate the word *liṅga* exclusively with the Śiva-*liṅga*, the word actually has a broader usage, both in Sanskrit and in Thai. Its most basic meaning is "mark" or "sign," and it is as such that it can be used to refer obliquely to a penis. The Śiva-*liṅga* is an even more specific use, and by no means implied every time the word *liṅga* appears.
33. It is true that the Śiva-*liṅga* began as an anatomically correct representation of the erect penis. However, it quickly evolved into a much more stylized symbol of the god Śiva, such that it would be very unusual in modern times to find a Śiva-*liṅga* carved in a highly anatomically correct fashion (i.e., with a head, etc.). On this history, see Gritli v. Mitterwallner, "Evolution of the *Liṅga*," in *Discourses on Śiva: Proceedings of a Symposium on the Nature of Religious Imagery*, ed. Michael W. Meister (Philadelphia: University of Pennsylvania Press, 1984), 12–31.

34. ไมเคิล ไรท์, *ฝรั่งอุษาคเนย์* [Southeast Asian *Farang*], ed. สุจิตต์ วงษ์เทศ (กรุงเทพฯ: ศิลปวัฒนธรรม, 2542 [1999]), 201.
35. Wyatt, *Studies in Thai History*, 155.
36. Ibid., 171. For a published version of Nidhi's ideas that Wyatt cites, see Nidhi Eoseewong, "Bourgeois Culture and Early Bangkok Literature," in *Pen and Sail: Literature and History in Early Bangkok*, ed. and trans. Chris Baker et al. (Chiang Mai: Silkworm Books, 2005), 3–151.
37. Nidhi Eoseewong, "Sunthon Phu: Bourgeois Poet Laureate," in *Pen and Sail*, 153–198.
38. *Phra Aphaimanī* ch. 25.
39. สุจิตต์ วงษ์เทศ, "บิดาสุนทรภู่ ไม่อยู่บ้านกร่ำ เมืองแกลง" [The Father of Sunthọ̄n Phū Did Not Live in Village Kram of Klāng], *มติชนออนไลน์*, June 10, 2562 [2014], https://www.matichon.co.th/prachachuen/daily-column/news_1532578.
40. Nidhi, "The World of Lady Nophamat," in *Pen and Sail*, 227–254.
41. Ibid., 230–232.
42. Wyatt, *Thailand*, 160–162.
43. Wales, *Siamese State Ceremonies*, 255.
44. Personal communication, Brahman Tran Buranasiri.
45. Nidhi, "The World of Lady Nophamat," in *Pen and Sail*, 251–253.
46. One of the most iconic festivals celebrated by the Brahmans, the Swing Festival that once formed part of the Trīyampawāi- Trīppawāi, was discontinued after its last performance in 1934, just two years after the Revolution; see *เทวสถาน (โบสถ์พราหมณ์)-เสาชิงช้า* [*Devasthāna*: Cultural Heritage of Thailand] (2550 [2007]), 77. The immediate aftermath of the Revolution was a sharp curtailment of the ceremonial role of the king, but this was reversed in the prime ministership of Sarit Thanarat (1957–1963); see Chris Baker and Pasuk Phongpaichit, *A History of Thailand* (Cambridge: Cambridge University Press, 2005), 176–177.
47. สุชาดา กิตติตระกูลกาล, "ศาลท่านท้าวมหาพรหมโรงแรมเอราวัณ: การแสดงเชิงพิธีกรรมยุคโลกาภิวัฒน์" [The Shrine of King Mahābrahmā at the Erawan Hotel: Showing the Manner of Ritual in the Age of Globalization] (master's thesis, Thammasat University, 2540 [1997]), 71–72.
48. Ibid., 72, 82.
49. Ibid., 72.
50. Ibid., 73.
51. I was told of the Brahmans' involvement by one of the Brahmans at Bōt Phrām.
52. สุชาดา, "ศาลท่านท้าวมหาพรหม" [Shrine of King Mahābrahmā], 73.
53. This "official" version of the story, albeit acknowledging that Luang Suwichānphǎt suggested building a shrine to Brahmā to correct an earlier astrological error in laying the foundation stone of the hotel, is also found in a small informational booklet in English available at the office of the Than Thāo Mahāphrom Foundation: "Than Thao Mahaphrom Foundation: Erawan Hotel."
54. This is the literal meaning, but given the fact that she said it was the oldest Brahmā statue in the world, it seems she meant that it had been there since the time of her ancestors in the distant past.
55. สุชาดา, "ศาลท่านท้าวมหาพรหม" [Shrine of King Mahābrahmā], 103–104.
56. "Than Thao Mahaphrom Foundation: Erawan Hotel."
57. "รายงานผู้ตั้งกองทุนและรายการบริจากมูลนิธิทุนท่านท้าวมหาพรหมโรงแรมเอราวัณ"[Report on Investors and Report on Donations to the Foundation for King Mahābrahmā at the Erawan Hotel] (2004), informational booklet in Thai available at the Foundation's office.
58. "Than Thao Mahaphrom Foundation: Ērāwan Hotel."
59. สุชาดา, "ศาลท่านท้าวมหาพรหม" [Shrine of King Mahābrahmā], 81.
60. ปรมัตถ์, *พลังเหนือพลัง* [Power over Power] (Bangkok: Thonban, 1983), 327–328.
61. Trilok Chandra Majupuria, *Erawan Shrine and Brahma Worship in Thailand* (Bangkok: Tecpress Service, 1993), 49.
62. Dhanit Yupho, *Brahma with Four Faces* (Bangkok: Department of Fine Arts, 1967), 5–6.
63. Majupuria, *Erawan Shrine*, 91.
64. Dhanit Yupho quotes two Sanskrit texts that describe the implements that Brahmā should have. The first, whose title is not given, says that the god should be holding two spoons (ritual ladles?) and a gourd, with the Vedas placed in front of him. The second, from the thirteenth-century *Viṣṇudharmottara* of Hemādri, says that he should carry a water jug and a rosary. Yupho, *Brahma with Four Faces*, 18–19.
65. Majupuria, *Erawan Shrine*, 89.

66. Women are not deemed worthy to handle offerings to the god. สุชาดา, "ศาลท่านท้าวมหาพรหม" [Shrine of King Mahābrahmā], 85.
67. When I asked one of the employees of the shrine where the water comes from (thinking perhaps it had been blessed by a famous monk or Brahman), he said, "The water hose."
68. สุชาดา, "ศาลท่านท้าวมหาพรหม" [Shrine of King Mahābrahmā], 92–93.
69. ฤทัยรัตน์ ศิลธรรม, "อิทธิพลความเชื่อเรื่องสิ่งศักดิ์สิทธิ์ที่มีต่อคนไทยในปัจจุบันศึกษากรณี: ท่านท้าวมหาพรหมเอราวัณ" [The Influence of Beliefs about Holy Things on Thai People Today, a Study of King Mahābrahmā Ērāwan] (senior undergraduate thesis, College of Religious Studies, Mahidol University, 2547 [2004]), 84–136. Note that one major demographic disparity among the respondents was according to gender: the worshipers surveyed skewed female by a factor of two to one. This may possibly be explained by the time of day when the survey was administered, but also by a tendency, found in many religious traditions, for women to participate more actively than men in at least certain religious practices.
70. Pattana, "Beyond Syncretism"; Taylor, *Buddhism and Postmodern Imaginings*.
71. Ibid., 101.
72. Kelly Davidson, "Spirit House Worship in Bangkok's Modern Context" (master's thesis, Chulalongkorn University, 1996), 75.
73. The date for the installation is found in a short Thai-language informational brochure available at Bōt Phrām.
74. I am careful here to say "not entirely," but there is nonetheless a certain novelty to it. I have found no evidence of focused worship of Brahmā in Siam/Thailand prior to the construction of the Ērāwan Shrine. Brahmā plays an important role in Pali Buddhist cosmology, but recall that Brahmās are in fact an entire *class* of being in that cosmology. Early *sutta*s ridicule the pretensions of *particular* Brahmās to omnipotence, although later Abhidhammic cosmology did give a singular role to a Brahmā that rules over our particular world-system. This would appear to justify the worship of Brahmā in the singular within a Pali Buddhist context. See Gethin, *Foundations of Buddhism*, 114.
75. This particular statue depicts the *trimūrti*—Brahmā, Śiva, and Viṣṇu—combined as a single figure. Interestingly, it has gained a reputation for helping in matters of love and thus is popular with young lovers and those looking for love.
76. For a short study of the shrines at this intersection, see Justin McDaniel, "The Gods of Traffic: A Brief Look at the Hindu Intersection in Buddhist Bangkok," *Journal of the International Association of Buddhist Universities* 2, no. 1 (2017): 49–57.
77. For additional studies about the increased interest in Gaṇeśa in recent years, see Arratee Ayuttacorn and Jane M. Ferguson, "The Sacred Elephant in the Room: Ganesha Cults in Chiang Mai, Thailand," *Anthropology Today* 34, no. 5 (2018): 5–9; Ruci Agarwal and William J. Jones, "Ganesa and His Cult in Contemporary Thailand," *International Journal of Asia-Pacific Studies* 14, no. 2 (2018): 122–138; Jane M. Ferguson and Arratee Ayuttacorn, "Accessories Make the Elephant: Buddhist Thais Worship Ganesha, Indian-style," *Asian Studies Review* 45, no. 4 (2021): 656–673, doi:10.1080/10357823.2020.1870212.
78. Kanjana, "Ways of Life," 87.
79. Wales, *Siamese State Ceremonies*, 248.
80. Tambiah, *Buddhism and the Spirit Cults*, 252–259.
81. On this community, see มานะ ช่วยชู, "ตัวตนและการธำรงความเป็นพราหมณ์นครศรีธรรมราช Self and Maintenance of Nakhon Si Thammarat Brahmins" (master's thesis, Walailak University, 2548 [2005]).
82. *เทวสถาน: มรดกวัฒนธรรมบนแผ่นดินไทย* [*Devasthāna*: Cultural Heritage of Thailand] (กรุงเทพฯ: เทวสถาน สำหรับพระนคร, 2555 [2007]), 139. I thank Phra Mahārātchakhrū Phithī Sī Wisutthikhun (Chawin) for giving me this commemorative book as a gift.
83. Erick White, "Staging Hinduism in the Bangkok Metropolis: Religious Pluralism in an Urban Thai Buddhist Milieu," in *The Blooming Years: Kyoto Review of Southeast Asia*, ed. Pavin Chachavalpongpun (Kyoto: Center for Southeast Asian Studies, Kyoto University, 2017), 280–288.
84. Agarwal and Jones, "Ganesa and His Cult."
85. Thomas A. Tweed, "Night-Stand Buddhists and Other Creatures: Sympathizers, Adherents, and the Study of Religion," in *American Buddhism: Methods and Findings in Recent Scholarship*, ed. Duncan Ryūken Williams and Christopher S. Queen (Richmond, Surrey: Curzon Press, 1999), 74, cited by McMahan, *Making of Buddhist Modernism*, 268.

86. The changes brought by globalization are acknowledged even by practitioners themselves. Pandara Theerakanond, a Thai self-styled Brahman who has founded a "Ganesha Museum" near Chiang Mai, reports that learning about Gaṇeśa was difficult only a few decades ago:

"Back then, we didn't have computers or websites. So, the only way to learn about Ganesha was to travel to India. Back then, there was only one kind of package tour to India; it was related to Buddhist sites. If you went on one of those tours, you wouldn't visit Ganesha. You would visit only Lord Buddha" (quoted from Ferguson and Ayuttacorn, "Accessories Make the Elephant," 7).
87. เว็บที่รวมข้อมูล ความรู้ คาถา รูปภาพ และงานศิลปะ . . . ของพระพิฆเนศและ "องค์เทพพราหมณ์-ฮินดู" ไว้มากที่สุด.
88. Swearer, *Becoming the Buddha*, 241.
89. Buddhadāsa Bhikkhu, *Paticcasamuppada: Practical Dependent Origination*, trans. Steve Schmidt (Chaiya: Suan Mokkhabalarama, 1992), 66–68.

Chapter 7

1. Holt, *Spirits of the Place*, 20.
2. Ibid., 250–251.
3. Ibid., 257.
4. A reviewer pointed out, quite rightly, one very crucial difference between Buddhism in Thailand and Buddhism in Laos: the founding of the reform-oriented Thammayut order and the over-one-hundred-year centralization of the *sangha* in Thailand, which was not paralleled in Laos and whose influence in the latter has been limited due to colonization, war, and communist rule. I certainly do not mean to argue that these centralization efforts do not exist, nor that their construction of a "normative" Buddhism is without significance in certain contexts. I concur, however, with Justin McDaniel, who argues that "the central Thai government's sponsorship of ecclesiastical examinations, suppression of local religious practice, and training of Thammayut missionaries have had limited effect in standardizing Buddhism practice and learning over the past century." McDaniel, *Lovelorn Ghost*, 6.
5. นิธิ เอียวศรีวงศ์, "พุทธ-พราหมณ์-ผี หรือ ผี-พราหมณ์-พุทธ" [Buddhism, Brahmanism, and Spirit Religion or Spirit Religion, Brahmanism, and Buddhism], in *ผี-พราหมณ์-พุทธในศาสนาไทย* [Spirit Religion, Brahmanism, and Buddhism in Thai Culture], by คมกฤช อุ่ยเต็กเค่ง et al. (กรุงเทพฯ: นาตาแฮก, 2564 [2021]), 21: ที่ผมสนใจเป็นพิเศษและอยากนำมาชวนคุยก็คือศาสนาผี และปฏิสัมพันธ์ระหว่างศาสนาผีกับพุทธในเมืองไทย โดยเฉพาะเมื่อพุทธก็ไม่ได้หยุดนิ่งอยู่กับที่ แต่เผชิญความเปลี่ยนแปลงอย่างมโหฬารในช่วง 200 ปีที่ผ่านมา ทั้งนี้เพราะผมมีความเห็นตรงกันข้ามกับนักวิชาการทั่วไปที่ถือเอาพุทธศาสนาเป็นแกนกลางของศาสนาไทย โดยมีผีและพราหมณ์เป็นเปลือกห่อหุ้มอยู่บ้าง ผมกลับคิดว่าจะเข้าใจศาสนาไทยได้ดีกว่า หากถือเอาศาสนาผีเป็นแกนกลาง โดยมีพุทธและพราหมณ์เป็นเปลือกห่อหุ้มอยู่ภายนอก.
6. Ibid., 23: กราบพระกับกราบผีจึงเป็นเรื่องเดียวกัน. Similar sentiments are also expressed by Sisakra Wallibhotama in ศรีศักร วัลลิโภดม, "เมืองไทยทูเดย์: ไม่มีพุทธแต่มีผีกับไสย" [Thailand Today: There is No Buddhism, but There Is Spirit Religion and *Saiyasāt*], in *พุทธศาสนาและความเชื่อในสังคมไทย* [Buddhism and Belief in Thai Society] (กรุงเทพฯ: มูลนิธิเล็ก-ประไพ วิริยะพุนธุ์, 2560 [2017]), 225–231.
7. For the reading of เขน, see Griswold and Prasert, *Epigraphic and Historical Studies*, 561n32.
8. The three attainments (*sampatti*) are rebirth as a human being (*manussa*), rebirth in the realm of the gods (*devaloka*), and *nibbāna*. See Rhys Davids and Stede, *Pali-English Dictionary*, 690.
9. Princess Maha Chakri Sirindhorn Anthropology Centre, "จารึกวัดเขาสุมนกูฏ ด้านที่ 1," *จารึกในประเทศไทย* [Inscriptions in Thailand], https://db.sac.or.th/inscriptions/inscribe/image_detail/25612.
10. Princess Maha Chakri Sirindhorn Anthropology Centre, "จารึกวัดอโสการาม ด้านที่ 2," *จารึกในประเทศไทย* [Inscriptions in Thailand], https://db.sac.or.th/inscriptions/inscribe/image_detail/25707. Note that I am reading *kūlaṃ* as *kulaṃ* and *natthum* as *naṭam*, following Griswold and Prasert, *Epigraphic and Historical Studies*, 64n77.
11. Princess Maha Chakri Sirindhorn Anthropology Centre, "จารึกวัดอโสการาม ด้านที่ 1," *จารึกในประเทศไทย* [Inscriptions in Thailand], https://db.sac.or.th/inscriptions/inscribe/image_detail/25706.
12. A *bāisī* (บายศรี) is a traditional form of offering made in Tai cultures, constructed out of banana or other leaves that are folded and sewn together into a beautiful, often roughly conical form.

13. The identity of the *talüng* and *lian* are unknown. Griswold and Prasert, *Epigraphic and Historical Studies*, 649n23–24, hypothesize that they refer to a cover-box and tray, respectively.
14. Princess Maha Chakri Sirindhorn Anthropology Centre, "จารึกวัดเขมา ด้านที่ 1," *จารึกในประเทศไทย* [Inscriptions in Thailand], https://db.sac.or.th/inscriptions/inscribe/image_detail/25696.
15. The edition of the *Nirāt Hariphunchai* digitized on vajirayana.org includes two side-by-side versions of each verse: one taken from a Chiang Mai manuscript and the other from a manuscript in the National Library. I quote the latter version here. Although the translation is my own, I thank Chris Baker for sharing his soon-to-be-published translation (with Pasuk Phongpaichit) of the *Nirāt Hariphunchai*, which I consulted.
16. Hans Penth, *Brief History of Lān Nā: Northern Thailand from Past to Present* (Chiang Mai: Silkworm Books, 2014), 11–12.
17. For a comprehensive overview of Buddhist textual culture in Lānnā during its golden age, see Veidlinger, *Spreading the Dhamma*.
18. Penth, *Brief History of Lān Nā*, 13.
19. Ratanapañña Thera, *The Sheaf of Garlands of the Epochs of the Conqueror, Being a Translation of* Jinakālamālīpakaraṇaṃ, trans. N. A. Jayawickrama (London: Luzac, 1968), 120–126, 139–145, 155–158, 174–180.
20. Chiu, *Buddha in Lanna*, 9.
21. Ibid., 17.
22. Ibid., 182–183.
23. Ibid., 37.
24. Personal communication with Angela Chiu, July 8, 2020.
25. Chiu, *Buddha in Lanna*, 31.
26. *Mp.* 5.3.7: *bhante nāgasena, sabbesaṃ parinibbutānaṃ cetiye pāṭihīraṃ hoti, udāhu ekaccānaṃ yeva hotī ti? ekaccānaṃ, mahārāja, hoti, ekaccānaṃ na hotī ti. katamesaṃ, bhante, hoti, katamesaṃ na hotī ti? tiṇṇannaṃ, mahārāja, aññatarassa adhiṭṭhānā parinibbutassa cetiye pāṭihīraṃ hoti. katamesaṃ tiṇṇannaṃ? idha, mahārāja, arahā devamanussānaṃ anukampāya tiṭṭhantova adhiṭṭhāti evaṃnāma cetiye pāṭihīraṃ hotū ti, tassa adhiṭṭhānavasena cetiye pāṭihīraṃ hoti, evaṃ arahato adhiṭṭhānavasena parinibbutassa cetiye pāṭihīraṃ hoti.*

    puna caparaṃ, mahārāja, devatā manussānaṃ anukampāya parinibbutassa cetiye pāṭihīraṃ dassenti iminā pāṭihīrena saddhammo niccasampaggahito bhavissati, manussā ca pasannā kusalena abhivaḍḍhissantī ti, evaṃ devatānaṃ adhiṭṭhānavasena parinibbutassa cetiye pāṭihīraṃ hoti.

    puna caparaṃ, mahārāja, itthī vā puriso vā saddho pasanno paṇḍito byatto medhāvī buddhisampanno yoniso cintayitvā gandhaṃ vā mālaṃ vā dussaṃ vā aññataraṃ vā kiñci adhiṭṭhahitvā cetiye ukkhipati evaṃnāma hotū ti, tassapi adhiṭṭhānavasena parinibbutassa cetiye pāṭihīraṃ hoti, evaṃ manussānaṃ adhiṭṭhānavasena parinibbutassa cetiye pāṭihīraṃ hoti.

    imesaṃ kho, mahārāja, tiṇṇannaṃ aññatarassa adhiṭṭhānavasena parinibbutassa cetiye pāṭihīraṃ hoti.

    yadi, mahārāja, tesaṃ adhiṭṭhānaṃ na hoti, khīṇāsavassapi chaḷabhiññassa cetovasippattassa cetiye pāṭihīraṃ na hoti, asatipi, mahārāja, pāṭihīre caritaṃ disvā suparisuddhaṃ okappetabbaṃ niṭṭhaṃ gantabbaṃ saddahitabbaṃ suparinibbuto ayaṃ buddhaputto ti. sādhu, bhante nāgasena, evametaṃ tathā sampaṭicchāmī ti.
27. Choy Fah Kong, Saccakiriyā: *The Belief in the Power of True Speech in Theravāda Buddhist Tradition* (Singapore: Choy Fah Kong, 2012), 11.
28. The translation is my own, but this verse is cited by ibid.
29. Ibid., 129–134.
30. *Rāmakian* chs. 4, 8, 104, 107, 111; *Unnarut* chs. 28, 29, 30, 38; *Inao* chs. 5, 26; *Khun Chāng Khun Phǣn* chs. 27, 32, 36, 42; *Sang Thǫng* chs. 3, 4; *Singkraiphop* chs. 2, 11, 12; *Laksanawong* chs. 2, 3, 6; *Phra Aphaimanī* chs. 7, 31, 44, 92, 97, 125, 132; *Suphāsit Sǫn Sattrī* (no v. or ch. numbers); *Paṭhamasambodhikathā* (no v. or ch. numbers); *Klōng Nirāt Phra Prathom* v. 15.
31. บุญ (*puñña*): *Unnarut* ch. 25; *Khun Chāng Khun Phǣn* chs. 3, 42; *Sang Thǫng* ch. 3; *Singkraiphop* ch. 12; *Phra Aphaimanī* ch. 31. กุศล (*kuśala*): *Singkraiphop* ch. 12; *Phra Aphaimanī* chs. 14, 92, 125, 132 (x3). บารมี (*pāramī*): *Rājādhirāja* ch. 8; Princess Maha Chakri Sirindhorn Anthropology Centre, "จารึกวัดเขากบ ด้านที่ 2," *จารึกในประเทศไทย* [Inscriptions in Thailand], https://db.sac.or.th/inscriptions/inscribe/image_detail/25692.
32. *Phra Aphaimanī* ch. 92.

33. Princess Maha Chakri Sirindhorn Anthropology Centre, "จารึกวัดศรีชุม ด้านที่ 1," *จารึกในประเทศไทย* [Inscriptions in Thailand], https://db.sac.or.th/inscriptions/inscribe/image_detail/25594.
34. Princess Maha Chakri Sirindhorn Anthropology Centre, "จารึกวัดศรีชุม ด้านที่ 2," *จารึกในประเทศไทย* [Inscriptions in Thailand], https://db.sac.or.th/inscriptions/inscribe/image_detail/25595.
35. *Khun Chāng Khun Phǟn* ch. 42.
36. *Phra Aphaimanī* chs. 106, 113, 119, 132, respectively.
37. *Sān Somdet*, วันที่ ๔ กุมภาพันธ์ พ.ศ. ๒๔๘๔ ดร.
38. Although the version of the story I am citing does not specifically use the word *athitthān*, it is fairly obvious from the description that that is what is being described here.
39. จินตนา, "ละครแก้บนหลวงพ่อพุทธโสธร" [The Dance for Fulfilling a Vow to Luang Phō̜ Sōthō̜n], 47–49.
40. Ratanapañña, *Sheaf of Garlands*, 122, cited by Stanley J. Tambiah, "Famous Buddha Images and the Legitimation of Kings: The case of the Sinhala Buddha (Phra Sihing) in Thailand," *Res: Anthropology and Aesthetics* 4, no. 1 (1982): 9.
41. Chiu, *Buddha in Lanna*, 31.
42. จินตนา, "ละครแก้บนหลวงพ่อพุทธโสธร" [The Dance for Fulfilling a Vow to Luang Phō̜ Sōthō̜n], 50.
43. This is uncertain because, while the image as it appears today is probably no more than a few hundred years old, it is always possible that the exterior was thoroughly restored at some point over an older original.
44. On the role that Buddha images played in the politics of this era, see วิราวรรณ นฤปิติ, *การเมืองเรื่องพระพุทธรูป* [The Politics of Buddha Images] (กรุงเทพฯ: มติชน, 2560 [2017]).
45. จินตนา, "ละครแก้บนหลวงพ่อพุทธโสธร" [The Dance for Fulfilling a Vow to Luang Phō̜ Sōthō̜n], 51–52.
46. Ibid., 67.
47. *Sān Somdet*, วันที่ ๔ กุมภาพันธ์ พ.ศ. ๒๔๘๔ ดร: เดิมก็จะเป็นเพราะคนเห็นเป็นของแปลก และหาไปเล่นได้ด้วยเงินโรงถูกๆ จึงชอบหาละครชาตรีไปเล่นแก้สินบนจนเลยเป็นธรรมเนียม.
48. *Sān Somdet*, วันที่ ๑๖ ธันวาคม พ.ศ. ๒๔๘๐ ดร: เมื่อหม่อมฉันยังเป็นเด็กได้เคยเห็นเล่นละครชาตรีแก้สินบนที่หน้าพระอุโบสถวัดพระศรีรัตนศาสดาราม และได้ยินว่าที่วัดบวรนิเวศก็เคยมีละครแก้บนพระชินศรี เพิ่งห้ามเมื่อในรัชกาลที่ ๕ ประเพณีที่ไทยเราเล่นละครแก้สินบนแต่ก่อนเห็นจะชุกชุม จึงมีผู้คิดทำตุ๊กตาเรียกว่าละครยกสำหรับขายคนจนให้แก้สินบน.
49. จินตนา, "ละครแก้บนหลวงพ่อพุทธโสธร" [The Dance for Fulfilling a Vow to Luang Phō̜ Sōthō̜n], 47.
50. Ibid., 68–69.
51. Ibid., 47, 49. For an example of a guidebook of *sing saksit* that quotes a passage about the temple taken from one of Chulalongkorn's writings, see ทศพล จังพานิชย์กุล, ed., *สิ่งศักดิ์สิทธิ์คู่บ้านคู่เมือง: ภาคกลาง* [Holy Things of the Country] (กรุงเทพฯ: คอมม่า, 2549 [2006]), 31. In addition, a simple Google search of the phrase กลับมาแวะวัดโสธร will produce numerous hits of websites promoting Luang Phō̜ Sōthō̜n that quote the passage. I have not, however, been able to trace the original source of the quotation.
52. Marcelo de Ribadeneira, *Historia de las Islas del Archipiélago Filipino y Reinos de la Gran China, Tartaria, Cochinchina, Malaca, Siam, Cambodge y Japón*, ed. Juan R. de Legísma (Madrid: La Editorial Católica, 1947), 175.
53. On the antiquity of the concept of the transfer of merit in Buddhism, see Schopen, "Archaeology and Protestant Presuppositions," and Gregory Schopen, "Two Problems in the History of Indian Buddhism: The Layman/Monk Distinction and the Doctrines of the Transference of Merit," *Studien zur Indologie und Iranistik* 10 (1985): 9–47.

Chapter 8

1. Though not none. As McDaniel notes (*Lovelorn Ghost*, 226), Christian objects, for example, can at times be treated as "holy things" in Thailand, and this is undoubtedly facilitated by the melding of the concept of *saksit* to the concept of "holy" as part of modern world religions discourse. More common is the treatment of Chinese gods as *sing saksit*, as evinced by the book on *sing saksit* I quoted from in the introduction. This is surely the result of modern Chinese

immigration to Thailand, which has resulted in a substantial proportion of the Thai population today being of Chinese ancestry. It is also facilitated by the lack of a theological impediment (i.e., monotheism) to seeing the Chinese gods as simply more gods among many, as is required by the Theravāda Buddhist worldview. Nevertheless, the overwhelming preference for "Hindu" gods within the gambit of "holy things" is clearly indicative of the agency played by Hindu discourses within Siamese/Thai Buddhism that I have demonstrated in this book.

Appendix A

1. Julia Kindt, "The Story of Theology and the Theology of the Story," in *Theologies of Ancient Greek Religion*, ed. Esther Eidinow, Julia Kindt, and Robin Osborne (Cambridge: Cambridge University Press, 2016), 22–23, esp. n34.
2. Walter Burkert, *Greek Religion*, trans. John Raffan (Cambridge, MA: Harvard University Press, 1985), 321.
3. Plato, *Republic* 379a–c:

   ὀρθῶς, ἔφη: ἀλλ᾽ αὐτὸ δὴ τοῦτο, οἱ τύποι περὶ θεολογίας τίνες ἂν εἶεν;

   τοιοίδε πού τινες, ἦν δ᾽ ἐγώ: οἷος τυγχάνει ὁ θεὸς ὤν, ἀεὶ δήπου ἀποδοτέον, ἐάντέ τις αὐτὸν ἐν ἔπεσιν ποιῇ ἐάντε ἐν μέλεσιν ἐάντε ἐν τραγῳδίᾳ.

   δεῖ γάρ.

   οὐκοῦν ἀγαθὸς ὅ γε θεὸς τῷ ὄντι τε καὶ λεκτέον οὕτω;

   τί μήν;

   ἀλλὰ μὴν οὐδέν γε τῶν ἀγαθῶν βλαβερόν: ἦ γάρ;

   οὔ μοι δοκεῖ.

   ἆρ᾽ οὖν ὃ μὴ βλαβερὸν βλάπτει;

   οὐδαμῶς.

   ὃ δὲ μὴ βλάπτει κακόν τι ποιεῖ;

   οὐδὲ τοῦτο.

   ὃ δέ γε μηδὲν κακὸν ποιεῖ οὐδ᾽ ἄν τινος εἴη κακοῦ αἴτιον;

   πῶς γάρ;

   τί δέ; ὠφέλιμον τὸ ἀγαθόν;

   ναί.

   αἴτιον ἄρα εὐπραγίας;

   ναί.

   οὐκ ἄρα πάντων γε αἴτιον τὸ ἀγαθόν, ἀλλὰ τῶν μὲν εὖ ἐχόντων αἴτιον, τῶν δὲ κακῶν ἀναίτιον.

   παντελῶς γ᾽, ἔφη.

   οὐδ᾽ ἄρα, ἦν δ᾽ ἐγώ, ὁ θεός, ἐπειδὴ ἀγαθός, πάντων ἂν εἴη αἴτιος, ὡς οἱ πολλοὶ λέγουσιν, ἀλλὰ ὀλίγων μὲν τοῖς ἀνθρώποις αἴτιος, πολλῶν δὲ ἀναίτιος: πολὺ γὰρ ἐλάττω τἀγαθὰ τῶν κακῶν ἡμῖν, καὶ τῶν μὲν ἀγαθῶν οὐδένα ἄλλον αἰτιατέον, τῶν δὲ κακῶν ἄλλ᾽ ἄττα δεῖ ζητεῖν τὰ αἴτια, ἀλλ᾽ οὐ τὸν θεόν.

   Translation from Plato, *Republic: Books 1–5*, trans. Chris Emlyn-Jones and William Preddy, Loeb Classical Library Plato V (Cambridge, MA: Harvard University Press, 2013), 201–203. I have modified the translation slightly (changing "a" to "the" when appropriate) to explicitly reflect the use of the definite article when speaking about "the god." The translators note, "'The god,' with definite article, is a literal translation; rather than attribute monotheism to Plato at this stage, Reeve, n. ad loc, would describe this use of the article as a 'universal quantifier' (e.g., 'The squirrel is an animal which hibernates.'). However, S.'s description here implies a radical critique of Greek polytheism and may to some extent anticipate Plato's later theological ideas" (202–203n70).
4. Aristotle, *Metaphysics* 1026a19–30: ὥστε τρεῖς ἂν εἶεν φιλοσοφίαι θεωρητικαί, μαθηματική, φυσική, θεολογική (οὐ γὰρ ἄδηλον ὅτι εἴ που τὸ θεῖον ὑπάρχει, ἐν τῇ τοιαύτῃ φύσει ὑπάρχει), καὶ τὴν τιμιωτάτην δεῖ περὶ τὸ τιμιώτατον γένος εἶναι. αἱ μὲν οὖν θεωρητικαὶ τῶν ἄλλων ἐπιστημῶν αἱρετώταται, αὕτη δὲ τῶν θεωρητικῶν. ἀπορήσειε γὰρ ἄν τις πότερόν ποθ᾽ ἡ πρώτη φιλοσοφία καθόλου ἐστὶν ἢ περί τι γένος καὶ φύσιν τινὰ μίαν (οὐ γὰρ ὁ αὐτὸς τρόπος οὐδ᾽ ἐν ταῖς μαθηματικαῖς, ἀλλ᾽ ἡ μὲν γεωμετρία καὶ ἀστρολογία περί τινα φύσιν εἰσίν, ἡ δὲ καθόλου πασῶν κοινή) : εἰ μὲν οὖν μὴ ἔστι τις ἑτέρα οὐσία παρὰ τὰς φύσει συνεστηκυίας, ἡ φυσικὴ ἂν εἴη πρώτη ἐπιστήμη: εἰ δ᾽ ἔστι τις οὐσία ἀκίνητος, αὕτη προτέρα καὶ φιλοσοφία πρώτη,

καὶ καθόλου οὕτως ὅτι πρώτη. Translation from Aristotle, *Metaphysics: Books 1–9*, trans. Hugh Tredennick, Loeb Classical Library Aristotle XVII (Cambridge, MA: Harvard University Press, 1933), 297–299.

5. Aristotle, *Metaphysics* 1072b25–30: εἰ οὖν οὕτως εὖ ἔχει, ὡς ἡμεῖς ποτέ, ὁ θεὸς ἀεί, θαυμαστόν: εἰ δὲ μᾶλλον, ἔτι θαυμασιώτερον. ἔχει δὲ ὧδε. καὶ ζωὴ δέ γε ὑπάρχει: ἡ γὰρ νοῦ ἐνέργεια ζωή, ἐκεῖνος δὲ ἡ ἐνέργεια: ἐνέργεια δὲ ἡ καθ᾽ αὑτὴν ἐκείνου ζωὴ ἀρίστη καὶ ἀΐδιος. φαμὲν δὴ τὸν θεὸν εἶναι ζῷον ἀΐδιον ἄριστον, ὥστε ζωὴ καὶ αἰὼν συνεχὴς καὶ ἀΐδιος ὑπάρχει τῷ θεῷ: τοῦτο γὰρ ὁ θεός. Translation from Aristotle, *Metaphysics, X–XIV, Oeconomica, Magna Moralia*, trans. Hugh Tredennick and G. Cyril Armstrong, Loeb Classical Library Aristotle XVIII (Cambridge, MA: Harvard University Press, 1935), 151.
6. Aristotle, *Metaphysics* 1073a14–15: πότερον δὲ μίαν θετέον τὴν τοιαύτην οὐσίαν ἢ πλείους, καὶ πόσας. Translation from ibid., 153.
7. Aristotle, *Metaphysics* 1076a: οὐκ ἀγαθὸν πολυκοιρανίη: εἷς κοίρανος ἔστω. Translation from ibid., 175. The quotation is of Homer, *Iliad* II.204.
8. Daniel Boyarin, *The Jewish Gospels: The Story of the Jewish Christ* (New York: New Press, 2012).
9. Werner Jaeger, *Early Christianity and Greek Paideia* (Cambridge, MA: Belknap Press of Harvard University Press, 1961), 30–31.
10. George Karamanolis, *The Philosophy of Early Christianity* (London: Routledge, 2014), 47.
11. Ibid., 2–18.
12. Majid Fakhry, *A History of Islamic Philosophy*, 3rd ed. (New York: Columbia University Press, 2004), 67–95.
13. Ibid., 111–132.
14. Ibid., 132–166.
15. Ibid., 223–239.
16. Ibid., 280–302.

Appendix B

1. Frank E. Reynolds and Mani B. Reynolds, trans., *Three Worlds According to King Ruang: A Thai Buddhist Cosmology* (Berkeley: Group in Buddhist Studies, UC Berkeley, 1982), 5.
2. Nidhi Eoseewong, "The World of Lady Nophamat," in *Pen and Sail: Literature and History in Early Bangkok*, ed. and trans. Chris Baker et al. (Chiang Mai: Silkworm Books, 2005), 227–254.
3. Baker and Pasuk, *History of Ayutthaya*, 43, 58.
4. Wright, *Ong-kan Chaeng Nam*.
5. Baker and Pasuk, *Yuan Phai*, 1.
6. Richard D. Cushman, trans., *The Royal Chronicles of Ayutthaya*, ed. David K. Wyatt (Bangkok: Siam Society, 2006), 18, cited by Baker and Pasuk, *Kings in Love*, 266n3.
7. Baker and Pasuk, *History of Ayutthaya*, 171–172.
8. Baker and Pasuk, *Kings in Love*, 175.
9. Ibid., 265–269.
10. ประเสริฐ ณ นคร, *โคลงนิราศหริภุญชัย* [*Nirāt* of Haribhuñjaya] (กรุงเทพฯ: สตรีสาร, 2503 [1960]), ฉ-ช.
11. ชลดา เรืองรักษ์ลิขิต, *วรรณคดีอยุธยาตอนต้น: ลักษณะร่วมและอิทธิพล The Early Ayudhya Poetry: Characteristics and Influence* (Bangkok: Department of Thai, Fine Arts, Chulalongkorn University, 2544 [2001]), 147–165.
12. Ibid., 192–259. On *Samudraghoṣa*, see also Thomas John Hudak, trans., *The Tale of Prince Samuttakote: A Buddhist Epic from Thailand* (Athens: Ohio University Center for International Studies, 1993), xiii–xv.
13. On the Luang Prasoet Chronicle, see Ian Hodges, "Time in Transition: King Narai and the Luang Prasoet Chronicle of Ayutthaya," *Journal of the Siam Society* 87, nos. 1–2 (1999): 33–44. This chronicle, along with all Ayutthayā chronicles written in Thai, is translated in Cushman, *Royal Chronicles of Ayutthaya*. Note, however, that the oldest extant history of Ayutthayā, dating to 1640, is actually written in Dutch: Jeremias Van Vliet, *The Short History of the Kings of Siam*, trans. Leonard Andaya, ed. David K. Wyatt (Bangkok: Siam Society, 1975).
14. For a translation of two important parts of the *Three Seals Law*, the Palatine Law (กฎมณเฑียรบาล) and the *Thammasāt* (ธรรมศาสตร์), along with a useful introduction to the *Three Seals Law* and scholarship on it, see Baker and Pasuk, *Palace Law*.

15. Baker and Pasuk, *Khun Chang Khun Phaen*, 922–946.
16. Although my periodization of these works is informed by the latest scholarship, as outlined above, I have also benefited from a Thai textbook on the history of literature, published by the Thai Department of Education, that gives a more traditional periodization: สุคนธ์ ดวงพัตรา, *ประวัติวรรณคดี* [History of Literature], 2 vols. (กรุงเทพฯ: สำนักงานคณะกรรมการศึกษาขั้นพื้นฐาน กระทรวงศึกษาธิการ, 2555 [2012]).

Bibliography

Note: This bibliography includes all secondary sources and translations of primary sources consulted. For primary sources consulted, see "Transliteration, Transcription, and Translation" in the frontmatter, as well as Appendix B.

Agarwal, Ruci, and William J. Jones. "Ganesa and His Cult in Contemporary Thailand." *International Journal of Asia-Pacific Studies* 14, no. 2 (2018): 122–138.

Akhin Rabibhadana. *The Organization of Thai Society in the Early Bangkok Period, 1782–1873.* Ithaca, NY: Southeast Asia Program, Department of Asian Studies, Cornell University, 1969.

Aland, Barbara, Kurt Aland, Johannes Karavidopoulos, Carlo M. Martini, and Bruce M. Metzger. *The Greek New Testament.* 4th revised ed. Stuttgart: Deutsche Bibelgesellschaft, 1998.

Almond, Philip C. *The British Discovery of Buddhism.* Cambridge: Cambridge University Press, 1988.

Ames, Michael M. "Magical-Animism and Buddhism: A Structural Analysis of the Sinhalese Religious System." *Journal of Asian Studies* 23 (1964): 21–52.

Anuman Rajadhon. *Popular Buddhism in Siam and Other Essays on Thai Studies.* Bangkok: Thai Inter-Religious Commission for Development and Sathirakoses Nagapradipa Foundation, 1986.

Appleton, Naomi. *Shared Characters in Jain, Buddhist and Hindu Narrative: Gods, Kings and Other Heroes.* London: Routledge, 2017.

Aristotle. *Metaphysics: Books 1–9.* Translated by Hugh Tredennick. Loeb Classical Library Aristotle XVII. Cambridge, MA: Harvard University Press, 1933.

Aristotle. *Metaphysics, X–XIV, Oeconomica, Magna Moralia.* Translated by Hugh Tredennick and G. Cyril Armstrong. Loeb Classical Library Aristotle XVIII. Cambridge, MA: Harvard University Press, 1935.

Arratee Ayuttacorn and Jane M. Ferguson. "The Sacred Elephant in the Room: Ganesha Cults in Chiang Mai, Thailand." *Anthropology Today* 34, no. 5 (2018): 5–9.

Assmann, Jan. *The Search for God in Ancient Egypt.* Ithaca, NY: Cornell University Press, 2001.

Austin, Christopher R. *Pradyumna: Lover, Magician, and Scion of the Avatāra.* New York: Oxford University Press, 2019.

Bailey, Greg. *The Mythology of Brahmā.* Delhi: Oxford University Press, 1983.

Baker, Chris. "Ayutthaya Rising: From Land or Sea?" *Journal of Southeast Asian Studies* 34, no. 1 (Feb. 2003): 41–62.

Baker, Chris, and Pasuk Phongpaichit. *A History of Ayutthaya: Siam in the Early Modern World.* Cambridge: Cambridge University Press, 2017.

Baker, Chris, and Pasuk Phongpaichit. *A History of Thailand.* Cambridge: Cambridge University Press, 2005.

Baker, Chris, and Pasuk Phongpaichit, trans. and eds. *Kings in Love: Lilit Phra Lo and Twelve Months, Two Classic Thai Poems.* Chiang Mai: Silkworm Books, 2020.

Baker, Chris, and Pasuk Phongpaichit, trans. and eds. *The Palace Law of Ayutthaya and the Thammasat: Law and Kingship in Thailand.* Ithaca, NY: Southeast Asia Program Publications, Cornell University, 2016.

Baker, Chris, and Pasuk Phongpaichit, trans. and eds. *The Tale of Khun Chang Khun Phaen.* Chiang Mai: Silkworm Books, 2010.

Baker, Chris, and Pasuk Phongpaichit, trans. and eds. *Yuan Phai, The Defeat of Lanna: A Fifteenth-Century Thai Epic Poem*. Chiang Mai: Silkworm Books, 2017.

Baldrian-Hussein, Farzeen. "*Hun* and *po*." In *The Encyclopedia of Taoism*, edited by Fabrizio Pregadio, 1: 521–523. Oxford: Routledge, 2008.

Baxter, William H., and Laurent Sagart. "Baxter-Sagart Old Chinese Reconstruction, Version 1.1." http://ocbaxtersagart.lsait.lsa.umich.edu/BaxterSagartOCbyMandarinMC2014-09-20.pdf.

Bayart, Jean-François. *The Illusion of Cultural Identity*. Translated by Steven Rendall, Janet Roitman, Cynthia Schoch, and Jonathan Derrick. Chicago: University of Chicago Press, 2005.

Benveniste, Émile. *Dictionary of Indo-European Concepts and Society*. Translated by Elizabeth Palmer. 1969; Chicago: Hau Books, 2016.

Blackburn, Anne. "Sīhaḷa Saṅgha and Laṅkā in Later Premodern Southeast Asia." In *Buddhist Dynamics in Premodern and Early Modern Southeast Asia*, edited by D. Christian Lammerts, 307–332. Singapore: Institute of Southeast Asian Studies, 2015.

Blackburn, Anne, and R. Michael Feener. "Sufis and *Saṅgha* in Motion: Toward a Comparative Study of Religious Orders and Networks in Southern Asia." In *Buddhist and Islamic Orders in Southern Asia: Comparative Perspectives*, edited by R. Michael Feener and Anne Blackburn, 1–19. Honolulu: University of Hawaiʻi Press, 2019.

Bodhi, Bhikkhu, trans. *The Connected Discourses of the Buddha: A New Translation of the* Saṃyutta Nikāya. 2 vols. Boston: Wisdom, 2000.

Bodhi, Bhikkhu, trans. *The Numerical Discourses of the Buddha: A Translation of the* Aṅguttara Nikāya. Boston: Wisdom, 2012.

Boyarin, Daniel. *The Jewish Gospels: The Story of the Jewish Christ*. New York: New Press, 2012.

British Broadcasting Corporation. *The Long Search 11: Taoism—A Question of Balance*. New York: Time-Life Media, 1978.

Bronkhorst, Johannes. *Buddhism in the Shadow of Brahmanism*. Leiden: Brill, 2011.

Bronkhorst, Johannes. *How the Brahmins Won: From Alexander to the Guptas*. Leiden: Brill, 2016.

Brown, Robert L. *The Dvāravatī Wheels of the Law and the Indianization of South East Asia*. Leiden: Brill, 1996.

Buddhadāsa Bhikkhu. *Paticcasamuppada: Practical Dependent Origination*. Translated by Steve Schmidt. Chaiya, Thailand: Suan Mokkhabalarama, 1992.

Buddhadāsa Bhikkhu. *Seeing with the Eye of Dhamma*. Translated by Dhammavidū Bhikkhu and Santikaro Upasika. Boulder, CO: Shambhala, 2022.

Burchett, Patton E. *A Genealogy of Devotion:* Bhakti, *Tantra, Yoga, and Sufism in North India*. New York: Columbia University Press, 2019.

Burkert, Walter. *Greek Religion*. Translated by John Raffan. Cambridge, MA: Harvard University Press, 1985.

Cameron, Euan. *Enchanted Europe: Superstition, Reason, and Religion, 1250–1750*. Oxford: Oxford University Press, 2010.

Cassaniti, Julia. *Living Buddhism: Mind, Self, and Emotion in a Thai Community*. Ithaca, NY: Cornell University Press, 2015.

Chamberlain, James R. "The Origin of the Southwestern Tai." *Bulletin des Amis du Royaume Lao*, nos. 7–8 (1972): 233–244.

Charnvit Kasetsiri. *The Rise of Ayudhya: A History of Siam in the Fourteenth and Fifteenth Centuries*. Kuala Lumpur: Oxford University Press, 1976.

Chidester, David. *Empire of Religion: Imperialism and Comparative Religion*. Chicago: University of Chicago Press, 2014.

Chiu, Angela S. *The Buddha in Lanna: Art, Lineage, and Place in Northern Thailand*. Honolulu: University of Hawaiʻi Press, 2017.

Coedès, George. *The Indianized States of Southeast Asia*. Edited by Walter F. Vella. Translated by Susan Brown Cowing. Honolulu: East-West Center Press, 1968.

Coedès, George. *Recueil des inscriptions du Siam*. Vol. 1. Bangkok: Bangkok Times Press, 1924.

Cohen, Richard S. "Nāga, Yakṣiṇī, Buddha: Local Deities and Local Buddhism at Ajanta." *History of Religions* 37, no. 4 (1998): 360–400.

Collins, Steven. *Nirvana and Other Buddhist Felicities: Utopias of the Pali Imaginaire*. Cambridge: Cambridge University Press, 1998.

Collins, Steven. *Selfless Persons: Imagery and Thought in* Theravāda *Buddhism*. Cambridge: Cambridge University Press, 1982.

Collins, Steven. "What Is Literature in Pali?" In *Literary Cultures in History: Reconstructions from South Asia*, edited by Sheldon Pollock, 649–688. Berkeley: University of California Press, 2003.

Condominas, Georges. *From Law to Mon, from Saa' to Thai: Historical and Anthropological Aspects of Southeast Asian Social Spaces*. Translated by Stephanie Anderson, Maria Magannon, and Gehan Wijeyawardene. Edited by Gehan Wijeyawardene. Canberra: Department of Anthropology, Research School of Pacific Studies, Australian National University, 1990.

Condominas, Georges. "*Phībān* Cults in Rural Laos." In *Change and Persistence in Thai Society: Essays in Honor of Lauriston Sharp*, edited by G. William Skinner and A. Thomas Kirsch, 252–277. Ithaca, NY: Cornell University Press, 1975.

Cushman, Richard D., trans. *The Royal Chronicles of Ayutthaya*. Edited by David K. Wyatt. Bangkok: Siam Society, 2006.

Davidson, Kelly. "Spirit House Worship in Bangkok's Modern Context." Master's thesis, Chulalongkorn University, 1996.

Davis, Erik W. *Deathpower: Buddhism's Ritual Imagination in Cambodia*. New York: Columbia University Press, 2016.

DeCaroli, Robert. *Haunting the Buddha: Indian Popular Religions and the Formation of Buddhism*. Oxford: Oxford University Press, 2004.

Dhanit Yupho. *Brahma with Four Faces*. Bangkok: Department of Fine Arts, 1967.

Digital Pali Reader. https://www.digitalpalireader.online/.

Dimmit, Cornelia, and J. A. B. van Buitenen, eds. and trans. *Classical Hindu Mythology: A Reader in the Sanskrit Purāṇas*. Philadelphia: Temple University Press, 1978.

Drodge, A. J. "Retrofitting/Retiring 'Syncretism.'" *Historical Reflections/Réflexions Historiques* 27, no. 3 (Fall 2001): 375–387.

Eaton, Richard M. *India in the Persianate Age: 1000–1765*. Allen Lane, 2019.

Eberhardt, Nancy. *Imagining the Course of Life: Self-Transformation in a Shan Buddhist Community*. Honolulu: University of Hawai'i Press, 2006.

El-Zein, Amira. *Islam, Arabs, and the Intelligent World of the Jinn*. Syracuse, NY: Syracuse University Press, 2009.

Evans, Grant. "The Tai Original Diaspora," *Journal of the Siam Society* 104 (2016): 1–25.

Fakhry, Majid. *A History of Islamic Philosophy*. 3rd ed. New York: Columbia University Press, 2004.

Faure, Bernard. *Gods of Medieval Japan*. Vol. 1: *The Fluid Pantheon*. Honolulu: University of Hawai'i Press, 2016.

Feener, R. Michael, and Anne M. Blackburn, eds. *Buddhist and Islamic Orders in Southern Asia: Comparative Perspectives*. Honolulu: University of Hawai'i Press, 2019.

Ferguson, Jane M., and Arratee Ayuttacorn. "Accessories Make the Elephant: Buddhist Thais Worship Ganesha, Indian-Style." *Asian Studies Review* 45, no. 4 (2021): 656–673. doi:10.1080/10357823.2020.1870212.

Flint, Valerie I. J. *The Rise of Magic in Early Medieval Europe*. Princeton, NJ: Princeton University Press, 1991.

Fortson, Benjamin W., IV. *Indo-European Language and Culture: An Introduction*. 2nd ed. Chichister: Wiley-Blackwell, 2010.

Foxen, Anya P. *Inhaling Spirit: Harmonialism, Orientalism, and the Western Roots of Modern Yoga*. New York: Oxford University Press, 2020.

Frasch, Tilman. "A Pāli Cosmopolis? Sri Lanka and the Theravāda Buddhist Ecumene, c. 500–1500." In *Sri Lanka at the Crossroads of History*, edited by Zoltán Biedermann and Alan Strathern, 66–76. London: University College London Press, 2017.

Geiger, Wilhelm. *A Pāli Grammar*. Translated by Batakrishna Ghosh. Edited by K. R. Norman. Oxford: Pali Text Society, 1994.

Gethin, Rupert. *The Foundations of Buddhism*. Oxford: Oxford University Press, 1998.

Gillespie, Michael Allen. *The Theological Origins of Modernity*. Chicago: University of Chicago Press, 2008.

Gombrich, Richard. "A Visit to Brahmā the Heron." *Journal of Indian Philosophy* 29, nos. 1–2 (Apr. 2001): 95–108.

Gonda, Jan. "The Popular Prajāpati." *History of Religions* 22, no. 2 (Nov. 1982): 129–149.

Gong Qunhu 龔群虎. *Han-Tai guanxici de shijian cengci* 漢泰關係詞的時間層次 [Temporal Layers in Han-Tai Connecting Words]. Shanghai: Fudan daxue chubanshe, 2002.

Gornall, Alastair. *Rewriting Buddhism: Pali Literature and Monastic Reform in Sri Lanka, 1157–1270*. London: UCL Press, 2020.

Gosling, Betty. *Origins of Thai Art*. Bangkok: River Books, 2004.

Göttingen Register of Electronic Texts in Indian Languages. 2020. https://gretil.sub.uni-goettingen.de/gretil.html.

Green, Nile, ed. *The Persianate World: The Frontiers of a Eurasian Lingua Franca*. Oakland: University of California Press, 2019.

Griswold, A. B., and Prasert ṇa Nagara. "Epigraphic and Historical Studies, No. 17: The Judgments of King Măṅ Rāy." *Journal of the Siam Society* 65, no. 1 (1977): 137–160.

Griswold, A. B., and Prasert Ṇa Nagara. *Epigraphic and Historical Studies*. Bangkok: Historical Society under the Royal Patronage of H.R.H. Princess Maha Chakri Sirindhorn, 1992.

Guelden, Marlane. *Thailand: Into the Spirit World*. Bangkok: Asia Books, 1995.

Guthrie, Elizabeth. "A Study of the History and Cult of the Buddhist Earth Deity in Mainland Southeast Asia." PhD dissertation, University of Canterbury, 2004.

Haberman, David L. *People Trees: Worship of Trees in Northern India*. New York: Oxford University Press, 2013.

Hallisey, Charles. "Roads Taken and Not Taken in the Study of Theravāda Buddhism." In *Curators of the Buddha: The Study of Buddhism under Colonialism*, edited by Donald S. Lopez Jr., 31–62. Chicago: University of Chicago Press, 1995.

Harris, Ian. *Cambodian Buddhism: History and Practice*. Honolulu: University of Hawaiʻi Press, 2005.

Hayashi Yukio. *Practical Buddhism among the Thai-Lao: Religion in the Making of a Region*. Kyoto: Kyoto University Press, 2003.

Hazra, Kanai Lal. *History of Theravāda Buddhism in South-East Asia, with Special Reference to India and Ceylon*. New Delhi: Munshiram Manoharlal, 1981.

Hinüber, Oskar von. *A Handbook of Pāli Literature*. Berlin: Walter de Gruyter, 2000.

Hodges, Ian. "Time in Transition: King Narai and the Luang Prasoet Chronicle of Ayutthaya." *Journal of the Siam Society* 87, nos. 1–2 (1999): 33–44.

Hodgson, Marhsall G. S. *The Venture of Islam: Conscience and History in a World Civilization*. Vol. 2. Chicago: University of Chicago Press, 1974.

Holm, David. "A Layer of Old Chinese Readings in the Traditional Zhuang Script." *Bulletin of the Museum of Far Eastern Antiquities* 1 (2014): 1–45.

Holt, John Clifford. *Spirits of the Place: Buddhism and Lao Religious Culture*. Honolulu: University of Hawaiʻi Press, 2009.

Hopkins, E. Washburn. *The Great Epic of India: Its Character and Origin*. New York: Charles Scribner's Sons, 1901.

Horton, Sarah J. *Living Buddhist Statues in Early Medieval and Modern Japan*. New York: Palgrave Macmillan, 2007.

Hudak, Thomas John, trans. *The Tale of Prince Samuttakote: A Buddhist Epic from Thailand*. Athens: Ohio University Center for International Studies, 1993.

Hutchinson, E. "The Earliest Translation of the Gospel into Siamese." *Journal of the Siam Society* 28, no. 2 (1935): 197–200.

Iida, Junko. "Tying the Hand: Life-Sustaining Technique in Northern Thailand." *Asia* 71, no. 1 (2017): 305–326.

Jackson, Peter A. *Capitalism Magic Thailand: Modernity with Enchantment.* Singapore: ISEAS, 2022.

Jaeger, Werner. *Early Christianity and Greek Paideia.* Cambridge, MA: Belknap Press of Harvard University Press, 1961.

Jaeger, Werner. *The Theology of the Early Greek Philosophers: The Gifford Lectures 1936.* Eugene, OR: Wipf & Stock, 1967.

Jamison, Stephanie W., and Joel P. Brereton. *The* Ṛg Veda: *The Earliest Religious Poetry of India.* 3 vols. New York: Oxford University Press, 2014.

Jones, J. T. *The Gospel of Matthew: พระคฤษวงษโดยมัดชาย.* 2nd ed. n.d., n.p., 1839.

Jones, J. T. *คำภีรมงคลโอวาทอันสำแดงคำสัญาใหม่ ซึ่งพระเยซูคริศเจ้า ห็ประกาษไว้แก่มนุษทั้งปวง แปลออกจากภาษาเฮเลนเปนภาษาไท The New Testament. Translated from the Greek.* 2nd ed. Bangkok: Union Press, 1850.

Josephson-Storm, Jason Ā. *The Myth of Disenchantment: Magic, Modernity, and the Birth of the Human Sciences.* Chicago: University of Chicago Press, 2017.

Kanjana Suwanwong. "Ways of Life, Rituals and Cultural Identity of Court Brahmins in Thai Society: A Case Study of Bangkok Devasthan Botsbrahmana." Master's thesis, Chulalongkorn University, 2539 [1996].

Kapstein, Matthew T. *The Tibetans.* Maiden, MA: Blackwell, 2006.

Karamanolis, George. *The Philosophy of Early Christianity.* London: Routledge, 2014.

Karashima Noboru, ed. *A Concise History of South India: Issues and Interpretations.* New Delhi: Oxford University Press, 2014.

Keyes, Charles F. *The Golden Peninsula: Culture and Adaptation in Mainland Southeast Asia.* New York: Macmillan, 1977.

Kindt, Julia. "The Story of Theology and the Theology of the Story." In *Theologies of Ancient Greek Religion,* edited by Esther Eidinow, Julia Kindt, and Robin Osborne, 12–34. Cambridge: Cambridge University Press, 2016.

King, Richard. *Orientalism and Religion: Postcolonial Theory, India and "The Mystic East."* London: Routledge, 1999.

Kirsch, A. Thomas. "Complexity in the Thai Religious System: An Interpretation." *Journal of Asian Studies* 36, no. 2 (1977): 241–266.

Kong, Choy Fah. Saccakiriyā: *The Belief in the Power of True Speech in Theravāda Buddhist Tradition.* Singapore: Choy Fah Kong, 2012.

Krahl, Harald. "The History of the Translation of the First Siamese Bible." Master's thesis, Columbia International University, 2005.

La Loubère, Simone de. *A New Historical Relation of the Kingdom of Siam.* Translated by A. P. Gen. R. S.S. Vol. 2. London: T. Horne, 1693.

Lammerts, D. Christian. *Buddhist Law in Burma: A History of* Dhammasattha *Texts and Jurisprudence, 1250–1850.* Honolulu: University of Hawai'i Press, 2018.

Leopold, Anita Maria, and Jeppe Sinding Jensen, eds. *Syncretism in Religion: A Reader.* London: Routledge, 2014.

Leyden, John. *Comparative Vocabulary of the Barma, Maláyu and Thái Languages.* Serampore: Mission Press, 1810.

Lincoln, Bruce. "Retiring Syncretism." *Historical Reflections/Réflexions Historiques* 27, no. 3 (Fall 2001): 453–459.

Lorenzen, David N. "Who Invented Hinduism?" *Comparative Studies in Society and History* 41, no. 4 (1999): 630–659.

Low, James. *A Grammar of the T,hai, or Siamese Language.* Calcutta: Baptist Mission Press, 1828.

Mabbett, Ian W. "The 'Indianization' of Southeast Asia: Reflections on the Historical Sources." *Journal of Southeast Asian Studies* 8 (1977): 143–161.

MacMullen, Ramsay. *Christianizing the Roman Empire (a.d. 100–400).* New Haven, CT: Yale University Press, 1984.

Majupuria, Trilok Chandra. *Erawan Shrine and Brahma Worship in Thailand.* Bangkok: Tecpress Service, 1993.

Marriott, McKim. "Little Communities in an Indigenous Civilization." In *Village India: Studies in the Little Community*, edited by McKim Marriott, 171–222. Chicago: University of Chicago Press, 1955.

Masuzawa, Tomoko. *The Invention of World Religions: Or, How European Universalism Was Preserved in the Language of Pluralism.* Chicago: University of Chicago Press, 2005.

McDaniel, Justin. "The Gods of Traffic: A Brief Look at the Hindu Intersection in Buddhist Bangkok." *Journal of the International Association of Buddhist Universities* 2, no. 1 (2017): 49–57.

McDaniel, Justin. "This Hindu Holy Man Is a Thai Buddhist." *South East Asia Research* 21, no. 2 (2013): 303–332.

McDaniel, Justin. *The Lovelorn Ghost and the Magical Monk: Practicing Buddhism in Modern Thailand.* New York: Columbia University Press, 2011.

McGovern, Nathan. "Balancing the Foreign and the Familiar in the Articulation of Kingship: The Royal Court Brahmans of Thailand." *Journal of Southeast Asian Studies* 48, no. 2 (June 2017): 283–303.

McGovern, Nathan. "Brahmā: An Early and Ultimately Doomed Attempt at a Brahmanical Synthesis." *Journal of Indian Philosophy* 40, no. 1 (Feb. 2012): 1–23.

McGovern, Nathan. "A Buddhist Cult of Brahmā: Thick Description and Micro-Histories in the Study of Religion." *History of Religions* 55, no. 3 (Feb. 2016): 329–360.

McGovern, Nathan. *The Snake and the Mongoose: The Emergence of Identity in Early Indian Religion.* New York: Oxford University Press, 2019.

McGovern, Nathan. "The Trīyampawāi-Trīppawāi of Thailand and the Tamil Traditions of Mārkaḻi." *Journal of the Siam Society* 108, no. 2 (2020): 123–148.

McMahan, David L. *The Making of Buddhist Modernism.* New York: Oxford University Press, 2008.

Mitterwallner, Gritli v. "Evolution of the *Liṅga.*" In *Discourses on Śiva: Proceedings of a Symposium on the Nature of Religious Imagery*, edited by Michael W. Meister, 12–31. Philadelphia: University of Pennsylvania Press, 1984.

Moerman, Michael. "Ban Ping's Temple: The Center of a 'Loosely Structured' Society." In *Anthropological Studies in Theravada Buddhism*, edited by Manning Nash, 137–174. New Haven, CT: Southeast Asian Studies, Yale University, 1966.

Ñāṇamoli, Bhikkhu, and Bhikkhu Bodhi, trans. *The Middle Length Discourses of the Buddha: A New Translation of the* Majjhima Nikāya. Boston: Wisdom, 1995.

Nidhi Eoseewong. *Pen and Sail: Literature and History in Early Bangkok.* Edited and translated by Chris Baker et al. Chiang Mai: Silkworm Books, 2005.

Oberhammer, Gerhardt, ed. *Inklusivismus: Eine indische Denkform.* Vienna: Institut für indologie der Universität Wien, 1983.

Olivelle, Patrick, trans. and ed. *The Early Upaniṣads: Annotated Text and Translation.* New York: Oxford University Press, 1998.

Olivelle, Patrick. *Manu's Code of Law: A Critical Edition and Translation of the* Mānava-Dharmaśāstra. New York: Oxford University Press, 2005.

Olivelle, Patrick, trans. *Saṃnyāsa Upaniṣads: Hindu Scriptures on Asceticism and Renunciation.* New York: Oxford University Press, 1992.

Padoux, André. *The Hindu Tantric World: An Overview.* Chicago: University of Chicago Press, 2017.

Pallegoix, Jean-Baptiste. *สัพะ วะจะนะ พาสา ไท Dictionarium Linguae Thai.* Paris: Jussu Imperatoris Impressum, 1854.

Pals, Daniel L. *Nine Theories of Religion*. 3rd ed. New York: Oxford University Press, 2015.
Pargiter, F. Eden, trans. Mārkaṇḍeya Purāṇa: *Sanskrit Text, English Translation, Notes, and Index of Verses*. Edited and revised by K. L. Joshi. 4th ed. Delhi: Parimal, 2019.
Pattana Kitiarsa. "Beyond Syncretism: Hybridization of Popular Religion in Contemporary Thailand." *Journal of Southeast Asian Studies* 36, no. 3 (2005): 461–487.
Peleggi, Maurizio. *Thailand: The Worldly Kingdom*. Singapore: Talisman, 2007.
Penth, Hans. *A Brief History of Lān Nā: Northern Thailand from Past to Present*. Chiang Mai: Silkworm Books, 2014.
Perreira, Todd LeRoy. "Whence Theravāda? The Modern Genealogy of an Ancient Term." In *How Theravāda Is Theravāda? Exploring Buddhist Identities*, edited by Peter Skilling, Jason A. Carbine, Claudio Cicuzza, and Santi Pakdeekham, 443–571. Chiang Mai: Silkworm Books, 2012.
Pitayawat Pittayaporn. "Layers of Chinese Loanwords in Proto-Southwestern Tai as Evidence for the Dating of the Spread of Southwestern Tai." *MANUSYA: Journal of Humanities*, special issue no. 20 (2014): 47–68.
Plato. *Republic: Books 1–5*. Translated by Chris Emlyn-Jones and William Preddy. Loeb Classical Library Plato V. Cambridge, MA: Harvard University Press, 2013.
Pollock, Sheldon. *The Language of the Gods in the World of Men: Sanskrit, Culture, and Power in Premodern India*. Berkeley: University of California Press, 2006.
Porée-Maspero, Eveline. "Krŏṅ Pāli et rites de la maison (Suite)." *Anthropos* 56, nos. 3–4 (1961): 548–628.
Porée-Maspero, Eveline. "Krŏṅ Pāli et rites de la maison (Suite et fin)." *Anthropos* 56, nos. 5–6 (1961): 883–929.
Prapin Manomaivibool. "A Study of Sino-Thai Lexical Correspondences." PhD dissertation, University of Washington, 1975.
Prapod Assavavirulhakarn. *The Ascendancy of Theravāda Buddhism in Southeast Asia*. Chiang Mai: Silkworm Books, 2010.
Priyawat Kuanpoonpol. "Court Brahmans of Thailand and the Celebration of the Brahmanic New Year." *Indo-Iranian Journal* 33, no. 1 (1990): 21–51.
Przyluski, Jean. "Brahma Sahampati." *Journal asiatique* 205 (1924): 155–163.
Ratanapañña Thera. *The Sheaf of Garlands of the Epochs of the Conqueror, Being a Translation of Jinakālamālīpakaraṇaṃ*. Translated by N. A. Jayawickrama. London: Luzac, 1968.
Redfield, Robert. *Peasant Society and Culture: An Anthropological Approach to Civilization*. Chicago: University of Chicago Press, 1956.
Reynolds, Frank E. "Ramayana, Rama Jataka, and Ramakien: A Comparative Study of Hindu and Buddhist Traditions." In *Many Rāmāyaṇas: The Diversity of a Narrative Tradition in South Asia*, edited by Paula Richman, 50–59. Berkeley: University of California Press, 1991.
Reynolds, Frank E., and Mani B. Reynolds, trans. *Three Worlds According to King Ruang: A Thai Buddhist Cosmology*. Berkeley: Group in Buddhist Studies, UC Berkeley, 1982.
Rhys Davids, T. W., and William Stede, eds. *Pali-English Dictionary*. London: Pali Text Society, 1921–1925.
Ribadeneira, Marcelo de. *Historia de las Islas del Archipiélago Filipino y Reinos de la Gran China, Tartaria, Cochinchina, Malaca, Siam, Cambodge y Japón*. Edited by Juan R. de Legísma. Madrid: La Editorial Católica, 1947.
Ricci, Ronit. *Islam Translated: Literature, Conversion, and the Arabic Cosmopolis of South and Southeast Asia*. Chicago: University of Chicago Press, 2011.
Sanderson, Alexis. "Maṇḍala and Āgamic Identity in the Trika of Kashmir." In *Mantras et diagrammes rituels dans l'Hindouisme*, edited by André Padoux, 181–185. Paris: Editions du CNRS, 1986.
Sanderson, Alexis. "The Śaiva Age: The Rise and Dominance of Śaivism during the Early Medieval Period." In *Genesis and Development of Tantrism*, edited by Shingo Einoo, 41–349. Tokyo: Institute of Oriental Culture, University of Tokyo, 2009.

Schopen, Gregory. "Archaeology and Protestant Presuppositions in the Study of Indian Buddhism." *History of Religions* 31 (1991): 1–23.

Schopen, Gregory. "Two Problems in the History of Indian Buddhism: The Layman/Monk Distinction and the Doctrines of the Transference of Merit." *Studien zur Indologie und Iranistik* 10 (1985): 9–47.

Sharf, Robert H. *Coming to Terms with Chinese Buddhism: A Reading of the* Treasure Store Treatise. Honolulu: University of Hawai'i Press, 2002.

Shinohara Koichi. "Changing Roles for Miraculous Images in Medieval Chinese Buddhism: A Study of the Miracle Image Section in Daoxuan's 'Collected Records.'" In *Images, Miracles, and Authority in Asian Religious Traditions*, edited by Richard H. Davis, 141–188. Boulder, CO: Westview, 1998.

Skilling, Peter. "King, *Sangha*, and Brahmans: Ideology, Ritual and Power in Pre-modern Siam." In *Buddhism, Power, and Political Order*, edited by Ian Harris, 182–215. London: Routledge, 2007.

Smith, Brian K. *Reflections on Resemblance, Ritual, and Religion.* Delhi: Motilal Banaarsidass, 1998.

Smith, Jonathan Z. "The Bare Facts of Ritual." In *Imagining Religion: From Babylon to Jonestown*, 53–65. Chicago: University of Chicago Press, 1982.

Smith, Jonathan Z., and William Scott Green, eds. *The Harper Collins Dictionary of Religion.* New York: Harper Collins, 1995.

Smith, Jonathan Z. "The Topography of the Sacred." In *Relating Religion: Essays in the Study of Religion*, 101–116. Chicago: University of Chicago Press, 2004.

Smith, Mark S. *The Early History of God: Yahweh and the Other Deities in Ancient Israel.* 2nd ed. Grand Rapids, MI: William B. Eerdmans, 2002.

Smith, Mark S. *God in Translation: Deities in Cross-Cultural Discourse in the Biblical World.* Grand Rapids, MI: William B. Eerdmans, 2010.

Smith, Mark S. *The Origins of Biblical Monotheism: Israel's Polytheistic Background and the Ugaritic Texts.* New York: Oxford University Press, 2001.

Souneth Phothisane. "The Nidān Khun Borom: Annotated Translation and Analysis." PhD dissertation, University of Queensland, 1996.

Spiro, Melford. *Burmese Supernaturalism.* Englewood Cliffs, NJ: Prentice Hall, 1967.

Streicher, Ruth. "Imperialism, Buddhism and Islam in Siam: Exploring the Buddhist Secular in the Nangsue Sadaeng Kitchanukit, 1867." *Journal of Southeast Asian Studies* 52, no. 1 (Mar. 2021): 7–25.

Styers, Randall. *Making Magic: Religion, Magic, and Science in the Modern World.* New York: Oxford University Press, 2004.

Swearer, Donald K. *Becoming the Buddha: The Ritual of Image Consecration in Thailand.* Princeton, NJ: Princeton University Press, 2004.

Swearer, Donald K. "Buddhism in Southeast Asia." In *Buddhism and Asian History*, edited by Joseph M. Kitagawa and Mark D. Cummings, 107–129. New York: Macmillan, 1989.

Tambiah, Stanley J. *Buddhism and the Spirit Cults of North-East Thailand.* Cambridge Studies in Social Anthropology, no. 2. Edited by J. R. Goody. Cambridge: Cambridge University Press, 1970.

Tambiah, Stanley J. "Famous Buddha Images and the Legitimation of Kings: The Case of the Sinhala Buddha (Phra Sihing) in Thailand." *Res: Anthropology and Aesthetics* 4, no. 1 (1982): 5–19.

Taylor, James. *Buddhism and Postmodern Imaginings in Thailand: The Religiosity of Urban Space.* Surrey: Ashgate, 2008.

Terwiel, B. J. *Monks and Magic: An Analysis of Religious Ceremonies in Central Thailand.* Scandinavian Institute of Asian Studies Monograph Series, no. 24. Lund: Studentlitteratur, 1975.

Terwiel, B. J. "The Origin and Meaning of the Thai 'City Pillar.'" *Journal of the Siam Society* 66, no. 2 (1978): 159–171.

Terwiel, Barend Jan. *The Ram Khamhaeng Inscription: The Fake That Did Not Come True.* Gossenberg: Ostasien Verlag, 2010.

Thite, Ganesh Umakant. *Sacrifice in the Brāhmaṇa-Texts.* Poona: University of Poona Press, 1975.

Tull, Herman W. *The Vedic Origins of Karma: Cosmos as Man in Ancient Indian Myth and Ritual.* Albany, NY: SUNY Press, 1989.

Tweed, Thomas A. "Night-stand Buddhists and Other Creatures: Sympathizers, Adherents, and the Study of Religion." In *American Buddhism: Methods and Findings in Recent Scholarship,* edited by Duncan Ryūken Williams and Christopher S. Queen, 71–90. Richmond, Surrey: Curzon Press, 1999.

Tylor, E. B. *Primitive Culture: Researches into the Development of Mythology, Philosophy, Religion, Language, Art, and Custom.* 2 vols. London: John Murray, 1920.

Van Vliet, Jeremias. *The Short History of the Kings of Siam.* Translated by Leonard Andaya. Edited by David K. Wyatt. Bangkok: Siam Society, 1975.

Veidlinger, Daniel M. *Spreading the Dhamma: Writing, Orality, and Textual Transmission in Buddhist Northern Thailand.* Honolulu: University of Hawai'i Press, 2006.

Vickery, Michael. "Cambodia and Its Neighbors in the 15th Century." Asia Research Centre Working Paper Series, no. 27. Singapore: Asia Research Institute, National University of Singapore, 2004.

Vickery, Michael. "The Constitution of Ayutthaya." http://michaelvickery.org/vickery1996 constitution.pdf. Originally published in *New Light on Thai Legal History,* edited by Andrew Huxley, 133–210. Bangkok: White Orchid Press, 1996.

Vickery, Michael. "The Lion Prince and Related Remarks on Northern History," *Journal of the Siam Society* 64, no. 1 (Jan. 1976): 326–377.

Vickery, Michael. "A New *Taṃnān* about Ayudhya." *Journal of the Siam Society* 67, no. 2 (July 1979): 123–186.

Vickery, Michael. "Piltdown 3: Further Discussion of the Ram Khamhaeng Inscription." *Journal of the Siam Society* 83 (1995): 103–197.

Vickery, Michael. *Society, Economics, and Politics in Pre-Angkor Cambodia: The 7th–8th Centuries.* Tokyo: Centre for East Asian Cultural Studies for Unesco, 1998.

von Stietencron, Heinrich. "Religious Configurations in Pre-Muslim India and the Modern Concept of Hinduism." In *Representing Hinduism: The Construction of Religious Traditions and National Identity,* edited by Vasudha Dalmia and Heinrich von Stietencron, 51–81. New Delhi: Sage, 1995.

Wales, H. G. Quaritch. *Siamese State Ceremonies: Their History and Function.* Richmond, Surrey: Curzon Press, 1992.

Walshe, Maurice, trans. *The Long Discourses of the Buddha: A Translation of the* Dīgha Nikāya. Boston: Wisdom, 1995.

Walters, Jonathan. "Buddhist History: The Sri Lankan Pāli Vaṃsas and Their Community." In *Querying the Medieval: Texts and the History of Practices in South Asia,* by Ronald Inden, Jonathan Walters, and Daud Ali, 99–164. New York: Oxford University Press, 2000.

White, David Gordon. *Daemons Are Forever: Contacts and Exchanges in the Eurasian Pandaemonium.* Chicago: University of Chicago Press, 2021.

White, Erick. "Staging Hinduism in the Bangkok Metropolis: Religious Pluralism in an Urban Thai Buddhist Milieu." In *The Blooming Years: Kyoto Review of Southeast Asia,* edited by Pavin Chachavalpongpun, 280–288. Kyoto: Center for Southeast Asian Studies, Kyoto University, 2017.

Wilaiwan Khanittanan. "Khmero-Thai: The Great Change in the History of the Thai Language of the Chao Phraya Basin." *ภาษาและภาษาศาสตร์* [Journal of Language and Linguistics] 19, no. 2 (2001): 35–50.

Williams, Paul, and Anthony Tribe. *Buddhist Thought.* London: Routledge, 2000.

Witzel, Michael. "The Development of the Vedic Canon and Its Schools: The Social and Political Milieu." In *Inside the Texts, Beyond the Texts,* edited by Michael Witzel, 257–345.

Harvard Oriental Series, Opera Minora, vol. 2. Cambridge, MA: Department of Sanskrit and Indian Studies, Harvard University, 1997.

Witzel, Michael. "Tracing the Vedic Dialects." In *Dialects dans les littératures indo-aryennes: Actes du Colloque International organisé par UA 1058 sous les auspices du C.N.R.S. avec le suotien du College de France, de la Fondation Hugot du College de France, de l'Université de Paris III, du Ministre des Affaires Etrangères, Paris (Fondation Hugot) 16–18 Septembre 1986*, edited by Collette Caillat, 97–264. Paris: College de France, Institut de Civilisation Indienne, 1989.

Wolters, O. W. *The Fall of Śrī Vijaya in Malay History*. Ithaca, NY: Cornell University Press, 1970.

Wolters, O. W. *History, Culture, and Region in Southeast Asian Perspectives*. Revised ed. Ithaca, NY: Southeast Asia Program Publications, 1999.

Wolters, O. W. "Khmer 'Hinduism' in the Seventh Century." In *East South East Asia*, edited by R. B. Smith and W. Watson, 427–443. New York: Oxford University Press, 1979.

Wright, Michael. *Ong-kan Chaeng Nam*. Bangkok: Matichon, 2000.

Wyatt, David. *Studies in Thai History: Collected Articles*. Chiang Mai: Silkworm Books, 1994.

Wyatt, David. *Thailand: A Short History*. 2nd ed. Chiang Mai: Silkworm Books, 2003.

Yü, Ying-Shih. "'O Soul, Come Back!' A Study in the Changing Conceptions of the Soul and Afterlife in Pre-Buddhist China." *Harvard Journal of Asiatic Studies* 47, no. 2 (Dec. 1987): 363–395.

แก้ว สุพรรโณ. *ศาลพระภูมิ: เกร็ดความรู้และแนวปฏิบัติบูชาศาลพระภูมิเพื่อให้เกิดสิริมงคลแก่ทุกคนในครอบครัว* [Shrines to Phra Phūm: Bits of Knowledge and the Method for Worshiping Phra Phūm to Create Auspiciousness for Everyone in the Family]. กรุงเทพฯ: สำนักพิมพ์ไพลิน, 2545 [2002].

คมกฤช อุ่ยเต็กเค่ง. "ผี พราหมณ์ พุทธ: ไสยศาสตร์ หมุดล่องหนและการเมืองไทย" [Spirit Religion, Brahmanism, Buddhism: *Saiyasāt*, a Disappearing Seal, and Thai Politics]. *มติชนสุดสัปดาห์ Matichon Weekly*, May 1, 2560 [2017]). https://www.matichonweekly.com/column/article_33527.

คมกฤช อุ่ยเต็กเค่ง et al. *ผี-พราหมณ์-พุทธ ในศาสนาไทย* [Spirit Religion, Brahmanism, and Buddhism in Thai Religion]. กรุงเทพฯ: นาตาแฮก, 2564 [2021].

จดหมายเหตุการบูรณปฏิสังขรณ์ เทวสถาน สำหรับพระนคร [Record of the Restoration of the Devasthāna for Bangkok]. กรุงเทพ: เทวสถาน สำหรับพระนคร, 2557 [2014].

จินตนา ธรรมสุวรรณ. "ละครแก้บนหลวงพ่อพุทธโสธร" [The Dance for Fulfilling a Vow to Luang Phọ̄ Sōthọ̄n]. Master's thesis, Mahidol University, 2544 [2001].

จุลจอมเกล้าเจ้าอยู่หัว, พระบาทสมเด็จพระ. *พระราชพิธีสิบสองเดือน* [The Royal Ceremonies of the Twelve Months]. กรุงเทพฯ: แสงดาว, 2556 [2013].

ชลดา เรืองรักษ์ลิขิต. *วรรณคดีอยุธยาตอนต้น: ลักษณะร่วมและอิทธิพล The Early Ayudhya Poetry: Characteristics and Influence*. Bangkok: Department of Thai, Fine Arts, Chulalongkorn University, 2544 [2001].

ตำนานพราหมณ์เมืองนครศรีธรรมราช [Record of the Brahmans of Nakhòn Sī Thammarāt]. นครศรีธรรมราช: ศูนย์วัฒนธรรมภาคใต้ วิทยาลัยครูนครศรีธรรมราช, 2525 [1982].

ทวีโรจน์ กล่ำกล่อมจิตต์. พราหมณ์สมอพลือ [The Brahmans of Samọ̄ Phlū̆]. Edited by ล้อม เพ็งแก้ว. เพชรบุรี: เพชรภูมิการพิมพ์, 2556 [2013].

ทศพล จังพานิชย์กุล, ed. *สิ่งศักดิ์สิทธิ์คู่บ้านคู่เมือง: ภาคกลาง* [Holy Things of the Country]. กรุงเทพฯ: คอมม่า, 2549 [2006].

เทวสถาน (โบสถ์พราหมณ์)-เสาชิงช้า [*Devasthāna* (The Brahman Temple)-The Giant Swing]. 2550 [2007].

เทวสถาน: มรดกวัฒนธรรมบนแผ่นดินไทย [*Devasthāna*: Cultural Heritage of Thailand]. กรุงเทพฯ: เทวสถาน สำหรับพระนคร, 2555 [2007].

ปรมัตถ์. *พลังเหนือพลัง* [Power Over Power]. Bangkok: Thonban, 1983.

ประมวลกฎหมาย รัชกาลที่ 1 จุลศักราช 1166 พิมพ์ตามฉะบับหลวงตรา 3 ดวง [Collection of the Laws of the First Reign, *Chula* Era 1166, Printed According to the Royal Copy of the Three Seals]. 3 vols. กรุงเทพฯ: คณะนิติศาสตร์ มหาวิทยาลัยธรรมศาสตร์, 2529[1986].

ประเสริฐ ณ นคร. *โคลงนิราศหริภุญชัย* [*Nirāt* of Haribhuñjaya]. กรุงเทพฯ: สตรีสาร, 2503 [1960].

มานะ ช่วยชู. "ตัวตนและการธำรงความเป็นพราหมณ์นครศรีธรรมราช Self and Maintenance of Nakhon Si Thammarat Brahmins." Master's thesis, Walailak University, 2548 [2005].

ไรท์, ไมเคิล. *ฝรั่งอุษาคเนย์* [Southeast Asian *Farang*]. Edited by สุจิตต์ วงษ์เทศ. กรุงเทพฯ: ศิลปวัฒนธรรม, 2542 [1999].

ฤทัยรัตน์ ศิลธรรม. "อิทธิพลความเชื่อเรื่องสิ่งศักดิ์สิทธิ์ที่มีต่อคนไทยในปัจจุบันศึกษากรณี: ท่านท้าวมหาพรหมเอราวัณ" [The Influence of Beliefs about Holy Things on Thai People Today, a Study of King Mahābrahmā Ērāwan]. Senior undergraduate thesis, College of Religious Studies, Mahidol University, 2547 [2004].

วิราวรรณ นฤปิติ. *การเมืองเรื่องพระพุทธรูป* [The Politics of Buddha Images]. กรุงเทพฯ: มติชน, 2560 [2017].

ศรีศักร วัลลิโภดม. *พุทธศาสนาและความเชื่อในสังคมไทย* [Buddhism and Belief in Thai Society]. กรุงเทพฯ: มูลนิธิเล็ก-ประไพ วิริยะพันธุ์, 2560 [2017].

สุคนธ์ ดวงพัตรา. *ประวัติวรรณคดี* [History of Literature], 2 vols. กรุงเทพฯ: สำนักงานคณะกรรมการศึกษาขั้นพื้นฐาน กระทรวงศึกษาธิการ, 2555 [2012].

สุจิตต์ วงษ์เทศ. "บิดาสุนทรภู่ ไม่อยู่บ้านกร่ำ เมืองแกลง" [The Father of Sunthọ̄n Phū Did Not Live in Village Kram of Klǣng]. *มติชนออนไลน์*. June 10, 2562 [2014]. https://www.matichon.co.th/prachachuen/daily-column/news_1532578.

สุชาดา กิตติตระกูลกาล. "ศาลท่านท้าวมหาพรหมโรงแรมเอราวัณ: การแสดงเชิงพิธีกรรมยุคโลกาภิวัฒน์" [The Shrine of King Mahābrahmā at the Erawan Hotel: Showing the Manner of Ritual in the Age of Globalization]. Master's thesis, Thammasat University, 2540 [1997].

เสฐียรโกเศศ [พระยาอนุมานราชธน]. *เมืองสวรรค์และผีสางเทวดา* [The Heavenly City and *Phī Sāng Devatā*]. N.p.: แพร่พิทยา, 2503 [1960].

โหรอโยธยา. *คู่มือแก้บน อธิษฐานขอพร เสริมมงคง* [Manual for Fulfilling Vows, Asking for Boons, and Increasing Auspiciousness]. หมู่บ้านไอยราเบย์วิว, ชลบุรี: สำนักพิมพ์ยอดมาลา, n.d.

Index

For the benefit of digital users, indexed terms that span two pages (e.g., 52–53) may, on occasion, appear on only one of those pages.

ʿAbbāsid, 61, 62, 213
ʾēl, 32–33, 36, 39–40
Abhidhamma, 42–43, 123, 154–55
adhiṣṭhāna. *See adhiṭṭhāna*
adhiṭṭhāna, 25, 184, 185–86, 187, 191–92, 196, 197–98, 205–7
āgama, 90, 92, 96–97, 98–99, 100–1, 202–3
ākhom. *See āgama*
Angkor, 52, 54, 58–59, 69–70, 72, 73–74, 75–76, 96–97, 125–26
animals, 22–23, 41, 42–43, 49–50, 96, 122–23, 124, 138–39, 140–41, 145, 204–5
animism, 15–16, 18–19, 104, 107, 112–13, 136, 138–39, 140–41, 151, 204, 205
Aniruddha, 150, 216–17, 219
Anuman Rajadhon, 114, 116, 118–19, 131, 132, 134
Aquinas, St. Thomas, 46–47
Arabic, Cosmopolis, 60–61, 63, 66–67, 77
arhat, 184, 186, 191–92, 198
Aristotle, 31, 35, 44–45, 138, 210, 211, 212, 213
Assman, Jan, 30–32
asura, 42–43, 123, 133, 139, 150
athitthān. *See adhiṭṭhāna*
ātman, 37–39
Augustine of Hippo, St., 46, 212
Ayutthayā, 52–53, 70–74, 75, 76, 79, 85–86, 87–88, 95, 96, 111, 122–23, 124–25, 131–32, 142–43, 144–48, 150–51, 152, 176, 181–82, 194, 195, 196, 215–17

Bagan, 68, 72, 74–75
bān, 74, 132, 133–34, 135
bhakti, 64, 65–66, 78, 145–46, 170
Bible, 32–33, 83, 101–2
bon, 9, 10, 11–14, 156–57, 160, 163–65, 181, 192
Brahmā, 1, 8, 14–15, 19, 20–22, 39, 41–42, 43–44, 77, 79, 123, 142–43, 144–45, 156, 163–65, 168–69, 171, 173, 202, 204, 207
brahman, 37–39, 41
Brāhmaṇas, 37–38
Brahmanism, 8, 11–13, 16, 18–19, 55–56, 57, 81–82, 92–93, 94–95, 96, 98–99, 100–1, 102–4, 136, 141, 151, 153–56, 168–69, 170, 175
Brahmans, Thai royal, court, 131–32, 146, 148–50, 153, 154, 155–57, 158–59, 162, 165, 166–68
Brahman Temple, 147–48, 151–52, 166
British, 52–53, 62, 65, 77–78
Bronkhorst, Johannes, 55–56, 57
Buddhadāsa Bhikkhu, 8, 168–69
Buddhist Modernism, 2–4, 21, 29, 47–48, 137, 154–55, 169, 201
Burma, 15–16, 51, 52, 54, 59, 67–68, 70, 74–75, 76, 85–86, 111, 147–48, 181–82, 194, 195, 215–17

Cambodia, 54, 59, 98–99, 133–34, 162–63
cāo, 74–76, 110–11, 113–14, 121, 134–35, 181–82
cāo thī, 114–16, 129, 131–32
Catukhām Rāmathēp, 9–10
cēdī, 162, 178–79, 189, 197–98
Chakri Dynasty, 52, 70, 85, 147–48, 150–51, 182, 193, 216–17
Champa, 56–57, 66–67
Chao Phraya River, 163–65, 194
chéng huáng shén, 116, 134–35
Chiang Mai, 51, 74–75, 76, 111, 181–82
China, 16, 21–22, 34, 61, 72, 74, 108–10, 114–16, 135, 183
Chiu, Angela, 21–22, 182–83, 184
Christianity, 20, 29, 30–31, 34–35, 39–40, 43–44, 45–46, 48, 49–50, 81–82, 99–100, 102, 136–39, 154–55, 167–68, 205, 206, 207, 209, 210, 211–13
Chulalongkorn, King. *See* Rāma V, King
City Pillar. *See lak müang*
Coedès, George, 23, 53–54, 93

Collins, Steven, 53, 67–68
cosmogony, 37–38, 39, 41, 210
cosmology, 21, 22–23, 29, 32, 34–35, 42–45, 48, 79, 81, 88, 108–9, 123, 124–25, 127, 139–41, 142, 143–45, 154–55, 168, 170, 171, 189, 200, 201, 202, 204, 212, 215

daimon, 45–46
Damrong Rajanubhap, Prince, 70, 192–93, 195, 215
Daoism, 11–13, 112–13
Dasaratha Jātaka, 79, 148–50
Davis, Erik, 53, 98–99
DeCaroli, Robert, 17, 49, 139
Delhi Sultanate, 59–60, 62–63, 64–65, 69
devas, 35, 39–40, 41, 42–44, 48–49, 79, 125, 127, 133, 139, 142, 171–72
Dvādaśamāsa, 144–45, 216
Dvāravatī, 54, 69–70, 73, 76

Emerald Buddha, the, 152, 182, 193
Enlightenment, the, 20, 46–47, 137, 138–39, 209
Ērāwan Shrine, 1, 156, 163–65, 171–72, 173
First Plowing, Ceremony, 147–48
France, 51–52, 83–84, 101–2, 216

Gaṇeśa, 1, 79, 163–65, 167, 168, 202
ghosts, 14–15, 41, 42–43, 48–49, 112–13, 116–19, 120, 123, 125, 127–28, 134–35, 137, 139–40, 205
Guangxi Province, 74, 108–9
guǐ, 112–13, 116–18

Haribhuñjaya, 74–75, 178–79, 181–82, 191–92
Hindu enthusiasm, 8, 26, 142–43, 163, 170–71, 173, 207
Holt, John, Clifford, 173, 174–75
holy, 9, 10, 23, 24–26, 82, 84–85, 86–87, 88, 92, 99, 101–3, 171–72, 176, 199, 206–7
hún, 112–13, 114, 119
hybridity, 17, 18

inclusivism, 19, 22–23, 29, 40, 102–3, 144
Indianization, 23–24, 53–54, 67
Indo-European, 30, 34–35, 44, 49–50, 102, 127
Indra, 1, 35, 38, 40, 42–44, 127, 156–57, 163, 168–69, 171, 202
Inscriptions in Thailand Database, 86, 215, 217
Īsān, 51–53, 174–75, 195
Islam, 20, 45–46, 54–55, 59–60, 61, 62, 63–65, 66–67, 78, 81–82, 99–100, 154–55, 209, 212–13

Java, 56–57, 63, 66–67, 152, 217
Jinakālamālīpakaraṇa, 182–83, 194
jinn, 45–46
Jones, John Taylor, 82–83, 84, 101–2
Judaism, 20, 32, 33, 35, 167–68, 203–4, 209, 210, 211–12

kǣbon, 9, 10–13, 14–15, 156–57, 160, 162, 163–65, 181, 192, 193, 195–96
Kailāśa, Mt., 144–45, 162
kānbonbānsānklāo, 10, 11, 15, 19–20, 23, 24, 51, 114, 131, 161–62, 171–72, 173, 176, 177, 178, 180–81, 183, 192–97, 205–7
kāvya, 55–56, 62–63, 68, 77
kham sǭn, 86–88
Khmer (language), 55, 58, 73–76, 133–34, 135, 145
khun, 111, 120
Khun, Chāng Khun Phǣn, 85–86, 131–32, 133–34, 190
khwan, 112–13, 114, 119, 140, 173–74
Kirsch, Thomas, 16, 25–26, 104, 136, 168
Kotmāi Trā Sām Duang. See Three Seals Law
Kṛṣṇa, 144–45, 150

lakhǭn, chātrī, 195–96
lak müang, 116, 118–19, 134–35
Lānnā, 21–22, 51–52, 71, 74–75, 76, 84–85, 127–28, 144–45, 178–79, 181, 184, 215–16
Lān Xāng, 51–52, 84–85, 174
Laos, 51–52, 59, 84–85, 111, 116, 126–27, 132, 134–35, 148–50, 173–75, 195
laukika, 94, 98, 101
Lithai, King, 123, 215
local spirit religion, 8, 25–26, 108, 136, 140–41, 176, 199, 201, 204, 206
lokiya, 100, 202–3
lokottara, 94, 98
lokuttara, 100, 202–3
Luang Phǭ Sōthǭn, 4–8, 9, 15, 19, 21–23, 26, 173, 174, 176, 183–84, 192, 201, 205–6
Luang Prasoet, Chronicle, 71, 75, 215–16
Luang Suwichānphǣt, 156–57, 171

magic, 25, 82–83, 90–91, 99, 103, 136, 153, 170, 199, 206, 207
Mahābhārata, 20–21, 38–39, 79, 143–45, 170, 204
Mahāchāt Kham Luang, 124–25, 181–82, 215–16
Mahāvihāra, 67, 68–69
Mahāyāna, 18–19, 39, 54, 57, 67–68
Malay Peninsula, 52–53, 72, 75, 90–91

Mā Nāk, 14–15, 128
Mangrāi, King, 74–75, 111, 181–82
mantra, 90, 96–97, 99, 185–86, 187, 196
Mass, the, 83, 101
McDaniel, Justin, 18–19, 23, 53
Milindapañha, 184–86, 187, 191–92, 198
mǭ, 89–90, 113–14, 119, 122–23, 140, 166–67
Mon, 54, 67–68, 73, 74–75, 76, 108–9, 135–36, 152, 181–82, 215, 217
Mongkut, King. *See* Rāma IV, King
monism, 35, 38–39
monotheism, 32–33, 39–40, 44–45, 137
müang, 71, 74–76, 87–88, 96, 110–11, 116, 120, 122–23, 126, 132, 134–35, 146–47, 182–83, 195
Mughal Empire, 59–60, 62, 64–65, 66–67

nāga, 49, 123, 139
Nāgasena, 184–86, 191–92, 198
Nakhǭn Sī Thammarāt, 52–53, 54, 75, 146–47, 153, 166–67, 182–83, 194
Nān, 96–97, 120, 143–44
Nāng Nopphamāt, 153–54, 215
Nangsū Sadāng Kitcānukit, 100, 154–55
Nārāi, King, 71, 83–84, 87–88, 132, 145–46, 216
Naresuan, King, 145
Neo-Brahmanism, 56, 57
Neoplatonism, 46, 212, 213
nibbāna, 41, 42–43, 186, 191
Nidhi Eoseewong, 8, 152–54, 175–76, 215
Nirāt Hariphunchai, 176, 178–81, 185, 191–92, 216
Nirāt Müang Phet, 153
nirvāṇa, 2–4, 15, 21–22, 29, 44, 48, 53, 91–92
Nithān Khun Borom, 126–27

Ōngkān, Chāng Nām, 122, 144–45, 215–16

Pakistan, 62, 64–65
Pali Buddhism, 25, 53–54, 69–70, 76, 78–79, 108–9, 126, 143, 144, 202–3
Pali, Canon, 17, 40, 77, 79, 170
Pali *imaginaire,* 24, 53–54, 55, 76–77, 79–80, 81, 97–98, 112–13, 123, 133–34, 142–45, 147, 148–50, 163, 170, 173, 176, 187–88, 189, 196, 197–98, 202–3
Pali Renaissance, 67–68, 77
Parākramabāhu I, King, 68–69
paramarājābhiṣeka. *See* Royal, Consecration, Ceremony
Pattana Kitiarsa, 17–18, 20
Paul, St., 45, 138, 211–12
Payutto, P. A., 8, 168–69
Persianate, Cosmopolis, 54–55, 60–63, 64, 77–78
peta, 42–43, 48–49, 123
Phatthalung, 73–74, 153
Phetburī, 72, 75, 153
phī, 8, 16, 25–26, 89, 108–36, 142–44, 151, 171, 173–74, 175–76, 198, 201, 204–5, 206
Phibūn Songkhrām, 156
Philo of Alexandria, 32, 39–40, 211–12
phī rüan, 134–35, 173
phī süa, 123–24, 134–35
Phitsanulōk, 72–73
Phra Aphaimanī, 88, 89–90, 95, 152–53, 187–89, 217
phrāi, 122–23, 128, 129, 135
Phra Lǭ, 87–88, 89–90, 91, 122–23, 216
Phra Phūm, 14–15, 19, 114–16, 129, 131–32, 133–35, 142–43, 156–57, 162, 171, 173, 174
Phra Śrī Vijaya Jātaka, 87–88
phutthasāt, 24–25, 79–80, 94, 96, 98–99, 101, 102, 143, 155–56, 168, 198–99, 202–3, 204, 206
pisāca, 124–25
Plato, 31–32, 35, 44–45, 138, 209–10, 211, 212, 213–14
pò, 112–13
Pollock, Sheldon, 55–56, 58–61, 67–68, 77
Prajāpati, 37, 38, 39, 41
Prāsāt Thǭng, King, 145
preta, 48–49, 123–24, 125, 127, 139–40, 168–69, 205
Purāṇas, 20–21, 38–39, 79, 133–34, 150, 204
pūyātāyāi, 14–15, 129–32, 134–35, 157, 162, 173

Qín, 109–10
Qur'an, 45–46, 60, 213

rāchāsap, 58, 73–74
Rājādhirāja, 152, 217
Rāma, 79, 88, 89–90, 143–44, 148–50
Rāma I, King, 70, 85, 88, 145–46, 147–52, 153, 166–67, 216–17
Rāma II, King, 88, 90–91, 131–32, 152–53, 217
Rāma III, King, 153–54, 215, 217
Rāma IV, King, 70, 86, 100, 154
Rāma V, King, 70
Rāmakian, 58, 79, 87–88, 89–90, 94, 148–50, 152, 216–17
Rāmarāja, 146–47
Rāmathibodi I, King, 70, 146–47, 215–16
Rāmāthibodi II, King, 145, 147, 168

Rāmāyaṇa, 58, 71, 79, 89–90, 148–50, 216–17
Rāmkhamhãng, King, 70, 119, 122
Reformation, the, 20, 101, 137, 138–39, 207
Revolution of 1932 66–67, 155–56, 165
Ṛg Veda, 35–37, 186
Royal, Consecration, Ceremony, 58, 147–48, 154

Śaiva Age, 54–55, 56–57, 66–67
Śaivism, 20–21, 38–39, 54–55, 58–59, 64, 65, 66–67, 77, 78, 90, 92, 93, 96–97, 98–99, 101, 102–3, 143–44, 148–50, 151, 202–3
saiyasāt, 24–26, 79–80, 82–83, 92–102, 142, 143, 147–48, 152, 154–56, 167–68, 169, 170, 192, 198–99, 202–3, 204, 206, 207
saksit, 1, 9, 10, 11, 15, 18, 22, 79–80, 82, 84–85, 86–92, 99, 101–4, 151, 171–72, 176, 183, 192, 193, 197, 206
śakti, 23, 91–92, 97–99
Sām Kok, 88, 152, 217
saṃsāra, 20, 21–23, 43–44, 48, 79, 81, 94, 98, 144, 191
Samudraghoṣa, 87–88, 216
Sanderson, Alexis, 20–21, 54–55, 56–57
Sang Thọ̄ng, 90–91, 217
sān phiang tā, 131–32, 171, 173
Sanskrit, Cosmopolis, 24, 54–58, 64, 65, 66–68, 69, 76, 81–82, 96–98, 102–3, 133–34, 135, 168
sātsanā, 8, 16, 25, 81–82, 92–93, 99–100, 101, 102, 103, 107, 154–55, 199, 204, 206
Scholastics, 46–47
shén, 112–13, 116–18, 134–35
siddhi, 23, 86–87, 91–92, 94, 97–99
Sīhaḷa lineages, 69, 76
Singkraiphop, 88, 89–90, 91
sing saksit, 1, 4–8, 9, 10, 15, 19, 23, 25, 82, 91, 103, 104, 168–69, 171–72, 173, 180–81, 183, 187, 193, 195–96, 197–98, 199, 201, 206
sitthisak, 86, 92, 95, 97–98, 183
Śiva, 1, 20–21, 38–39, 41, 56–57, 58, 79, 95–96, 142–43, 144–45, 148–50, 151, 162, 163–65, 166–67, 168–69, 170, 202, 204
Śiva-*liṅga*, 150–52
Smith, Mark, 32–34
Somdet Tō, 14–15, 18–19, 128
Southern Asia, 24, 50, 54–57, 58, 59–60, 61, 62–65, 66–67, 69, 77, 81
spirit shrines, 1–4, 11–13, 134, 162
śramaṇas, 20, 38, 56
Sri Lanka, 15–16, 53, 54–55, 67, 68, 173–74
Śrī Vijaya, 72, 87–88
Süa Khō, 87–88
Sukhōthai, 52–53, 58, 70–71, 72–73, 74–75, 91, 96–97, 111, 119, 120, 123, 125–26, 142–43, 153–54, 176, 178–79, 180–81, 185, 187–88, 189, 191, 194, 215–16
Sunthọ̄n Phū, 84–85, 88, 89–90, 152–53, 187–88, 191, 217
Suphanburī, 72–73, 75
syncretism, 1–9, 15, 20, 21–23, 24, 25–26, 29, 30–31, 50, 53–54, 104, 108–9, 140, 142, 201–2, 203–4, 205, 206, 207

Tai-Kadai, 109–10
Tāksin, King, 18–19, 70, 194, 195, 216–17
Tambiah, Stanley, 15–16, 113–14, 136, 166–67, 174
Tāmbraliṅga, 52–53, 54, 75
Tamil, 63, 73, 145–46, 170
Tamnān Phrām Müang Nakhọ̄n Sī Thammarāt, 146–47, 166–67
Tantra, 57, 64, 65–66, 78, 97–99
Taylor, James, 17–18, 161
Terwiel, Jan, 15–16, 118–19, 131–32, 136
Thammayut Nikāi, 154, 193
thǣn, 127
Than Thāo Mahāphrom Ērāwan Foundation, 157–58
Theravāda, 15–16, 18–19, 20, 53–55, 69–70, 88–89, 107, 136, 139, 140–41, 186
Thipphākọrawong, Cāo Phrayā, 100, 154–55
Thonburī, 52, 70, 87–88, 163–65, 216–17
Three Seals Law, 145–46, 216–17
Traibhūmikathā. See Traiphūm Phra Ruang
Traiphūm Phra Ruang, 123, 125, 126, 134–35, 139–40, 144–45, 205, 215
Triple World, 42–43, 123, 133
Trīyampawāi-Trīppawāi, 154, 165, 166
truth, act of, 181, 186–87
tǔdì gōng, 114–16, 129, 133–34
Turks, 60–61, 62–63, 65, 68–69, 78

Umayyads, 61, 64–65, 213
Unnarut, 87–88, 150, 152, 216–17
Upaniṣads, 35, 37–39
Ū Thọ̄ng, King. *See* Rāmāthibodi I, King

Vaiṣṇavism, 20–21, 38–39, 64, 65, 66–67, 78
Vajirañāṇa Digital Library, 86
van Vliet, Jeremias, 146–47
varṇa, 37, 55–57, 77
Veda, 20, 35, 37, 43–44, 56, 76–77, 90, 92, 94–95, 96–97, 99, 100–1, 159, 202–3
Vessantara, 124–25, 181–82, 215–16

Vickery, Michael, 23, 73–74, 111
Vietnam, 66–67, 74, 108–9
Vijayanagara, 64, 66–67, 147
Viṣṇu, 14–15, 20–21, 38–39, 41, 56–57, 58, 79, 96, 132–34, 142–43, 144–45, 146–47, 148–50, 162, 163, 165, 168–69, 170, 202, 204

Wat Sōthọ̄n, 4–7, 11, 178–79, 181, 192, 193–94, 195–96
world religions, 47–48, 65, 77–78, 81–82, 83, 100, 107–8, 136–37, 138–39, 142–43, 154, 155–56, 163, 166–68, 169, 170, 173, 201, 204, 205–6
Wyatt, David, 150–52, 154

Xiān, 71, 73, 75

Yahweh, 32–33, 39–40
yakkha, 49, 123, 124–25, 139
yakṣa, 49, 88, 89, 90–91
Yuan Phāi, 144–45, 215–16
yuè, 74, 109–10